GLOBAL ENVIRONMENTAL POLITICS

POWER, PERSPECTIVES, AND PRACTICE

Ronnie D. Lipschutz

University of California, Santa Cruz

CQ PRESS

A Division of Congressional Quarterly Inc.
Washington, D.C.

F.W. Olin College Library

CQ Press
1255 22nd Street, N.W., Suite 400
Washington, D.C. 20037

202-729-1900; toll-free, 1-866-4CQ-PRESS (1-866-427-7737)

www.cqpress.com

∞ The paper used in this publication exceeds the requirements of the American National Standard for Information Sciences—Permanence of Paper for Printed Library Materials, ANSI Z39.48-1992.

Printed and bound in the United States of America

07   06   05   04   03   5   4   3   2   1

Cover design by Malcolm McGaughy
Composition by Auburn Associates, Inc.

Library of Congress Cataloging-in-Publication Data

Lipschutz, Ronnie D.
    Global environmental politics : power, perspectives, and practice / Ronnie D. Lipschutz.
        p. cm.
Includes bibliographical references and index.
    ISBN 1-56802-749-4 (pbk. : alk. paper)
    1. Environmental policy—International cooperation.   I. Title.
    GE170.L55 2004
    363.7′0526—dc22

                                                                                2003014874

To Mary, Maia, and Eric

The *polis*, properly speaking, is not the city-state in its physical location; it is the organization of the people as it arises out of acting and speaking together, and its true space lies between people living together for this purpose, no matter where they happen to be.

—Hannah Arendt, *The Human Condition*

Contents

Tables and Figure

Preface

My all-time favorite cartoon was published on September 17, 1985. Drawn by Richard Guindon, it shows two startled scientists staring at their computers as a colleague runs into the lab amid a flurry of sheets of paper. "The ecosystem collapsed again! Frogs! We need more frogs!" he shouts. A few years later, in a case of life imitating art, the headline of a *New York Times* article read: "Scientists Confront an Alarming Mystery: The Vanishing Frog." Biologists and ecologists were finding that "amphibians are rapidly disappearing from many ponds, rivers, mountains and rain forests around the world." A professor at the University of California, Berkeley, reminisced that "[m]eadows where frogs were as thick as flies are now silent."* Why were they disappearing in the first place? What did this mean? Who could save them?

The tale of vanishing frogs is by no means unique: in more recent years, similar warnings have been issued about many other species, both animal and vegetable. In virtually all cases, humans seem to be the culpable party, although there is no end of efforts to pin the blame on nature. What's worse, at the same time that many living things seem to be in decline, non-living stuff appears to be taking over. Personal computers, junk cars, paper, toxic wastes, greenhouse gas emissions—all are being generated in ever-increasing quantities and dumped in the fewer and fewer sites willing or able to take them. Indeed, during the 1990s, electronic devices seemed to proliferate beyond all reason, like some alien invader intent on conquering Earth. One can hear the scientists shrieking: "The ecosystem collapsed again! Computers! We need fewer computers!"

If we ask, Who *can* save the frogs? (and, by implication, nature), the answer is not so clear. There are plenty of candidates—governments, scientists, corporations, consumers, control systems, coalitions—and a plethora of books advancing all kinds of propositions and positions. Some, such as Bjørn Lomborg and the late Julian Simon, both economists cited in this book, assure us there is no problem at all. This is the best of all environmen-

---

*Sandra Blakeslee, "Scientists Confront an Alarming Mystery: The Vanishing Frog," *New York Times,* Feb. 20, 1990, C4; for a detailed bibliography of materials on the disappearing frogs, see Kathryn Phillips, "Traking [sic] the Vanishing Frog," online at http://www.hc.keio.ac.jp/~fukuyama/frogs/tvf/tvf-ref.html (6/22/03).

tal worlds, and it can only get better. Air and water are cleaner, ecosystems healthier, and resources cheaper than ever before. But just in case something should go awry, they continue, "economic growth" can save both frogs and nature. After all, rich countries have cleaned up their environments because their inhabitants can afford to and want to. Therefore, the best solution to environmental problems in general is for countries to get wealthier. Even better, depending on economic growth means that no one has to change his or her behavior; all that is necessary is to make more, ship more, buy more, and dump more. But does it not seem a bit odd that, confronted by a growing environmental crisis of global proportions, our "best" response is to do more of exactly that which has brought on the crisis in the first place?

Not everyone thinks that getting the economics right will solve the problem. Like Guindon's scientists, many believe that technology can save us. Fossil fuels are dirty and produce carbon dioxide, but we can't live without energy. In fact we'll always need more, so we must shift, as soon as possible, to alternatives. We know how to manufacture solar cells, clean up coal, harness the wind, and mine uranium. Someday, we might have nuclear fusion. That won't solve all our environmental problems—even nuclear fusion will generate some radioactive wastes—but it will deal with the most pressing ones, such as climate change. Still, if we have these answers, why haven't the necessary policies been put in place? If we know that it's not nice to fool with Mother Nature, surely we have no choice but to stop our fooling? Yet we don't. More research is needed, say some scientists and numerous think tankers, business executives, and politicians, especially those associated with the current Bush administration and U.S. coal and oil companies.

Many who study and practice global environmental politics—scholars, diplomats, policy experts—put their faith in international institutions and interstate cooperation. Air pollution and climate change do not respect boundaries, they say, and must be handled via collaborative international arrangements and law. There is no shortage of such institutions and, by now, they number in the thousands. Nonetheless, the problem-solving ability of such institutions has proved difficult to assess. They take time to organize, and time might be the one thing we don't have. The apparent failure of diplomacy has motivated a search for new methods. If governments cannot save the environment, perhaps the market can! Where have we heard that before?

This book will not reassure you that others are dealing effectively with environmental problems or that international negotiations and bargaining will solve them or that corporations can become good "global citizens" and business can "green the planet." None of those reassurances is more than a faint hope, at best. The paradox in all this is that, in most cases, we *know* how to protect the environment. We could begin tomorrow. The beliefs, practices, and technologies enabling us to use less energy, produce less pollution, catch less fish, log less timber, manufacture fewer cars and computers, and have fewer children are all available now. We don't do these things because the problems we face are *political* and cannot be addressed by economists, scientists, or diplomats devising ever more complex schemes, arcane technologies, and unenforceable agreements. Only enough angry and idealistic people working together politically to change old practices and energize new ones will be able to save the frogs. *Only politics can save the environment.*

That might sound pretty normative, and it is. This book is an incitement to act in the face of what seem to be overwhelming problems, forces, and agents, because social change does not take place by itself. This book demands that *you* practice politics with others of like mind and hope. "Practice" means acquiring consciousness and knowledge about nature as well as becoming actively engaged in the places where we live, love, work, and play. "Politics" does not mean the politics of liberal markets and liberal democracy, which have come to treat everything as a matter of neoclassical economics. Rather, what it means is a *democratic politics,* one that gives to nature as much as we take from it, one that is ethically based and rooted in "right" relationships between humans and nature, one that does not leave all decision making and action to far-away representatives and agencies.

In marking out a path to the practice of politics, therefore, this book offers both an exploration of global environmental politics—framing basic issues and clarifying core problems, such as climate change, biodiversity, and overconsumption—and a critical analysis of conventional approaches to the protection of the global environment. The objective is to provoke both instructors and students to think more skeptically about the litany of environmental solutions offered to date. In order to establish that critique, Chapter 1 begins with an overview of the problem, the tools we will use to probe it, and the philosophical stance that underpins this book. In Chapter 2 I provide an overview of the major competing philosophical perspectives on nature and its protection—cooperation, competition, development, antidomination—and discuss how those perspectives are reflected in both literature and practice. In Chapter 3 I examine and critique the neoclassical economic approach to the environment—pollution as an externality, resources as inputs to production—and the impact of globalization on nature. In Chapter 4 I explore the rationale for political action and some of the ways in which it can be affected. International environmental regimes remain important, of course, in protecting and restoring the environment, and states remain significant actors in global environmental politics. Chapter 5 offers both a description and an analysis of these conventional approaches to understanding the international politics of the environment. Finally, given the normative aim of this book and the argument that reliance only on markets, science, and institutions is likely to make our problems worse, Chapter 6 provides both the rationale for political action and the forms it might take.

International institutions, markets, science, and even green consumerism are, to be sure, all part of the necessary equation, but unless we organize and act collectively, in social movements aimed at revitalizing democracy and politics, we shall save neither the frogs nor the planet nor ourselves. But don't simply accept this book without critical reflection. For those who want to learn more, find this volume too much to digest, or wish to temper the book's strongly normative thrust with more moderate analyses, each chapter includes a substantial list of other books on the same or similar topics. They should be consulted, too.

Acknowledgments

In many ways, this book is the culmination of more than twenty-five years of work on "environmental issues." I was introduced to the environment through brief sojourns at the Union of Concerned Scientists (1978–1979), the Massachusetts Audubon Society (1980), and the Lawrence Berkeley National Laboratory (1981–1983). Graduate studies at the University of California, Berkeley (1982–1987), the founding and operation of the Pacific Institute for Studies in Environment, Development and Security (1987–1990), and thirteen years at the University of California, Santa Cruz, have left me ever more critical (some would say cynical), demanding, and hopeful about the earth's future. That knowledge and those attitudes are all reflected in this book.

No book is ever written by one person, and this book is no exception. I can hardly begin to list those who, along the way, in one fashion or another, made mostly unknowing contributions to what appears here. A short, but hardly complete, list would include Ken Conca, Rick Diamond, Peter Euben, Margaret FitzSimmons, Cathleen Fogel, David Goodman, Lee Grodzins, John Holdren, the late Henry Kendall, Gabriela Kutting, Karen Litfin, Michael Maniates, Judith Mayer, Matt Patterson, and Gene Rochlin. In writing the many papers, articles, and books whose parts have, one way or another, ended up scattered throughout this text, I am indebted to so many other people that I cannot begin to list them. (I, of course, fully indemnify them all of any responsibility for what appears here.) For insightful and thought-provoking reviews of the proposal and manuscript, I thank John A. Agnew, University of California, Los Angeles; Peter Haas, University of Massachusetts, Amherst; Angela C. Halfacre, College of Charleston; Patricia Keilbach, University of Colorado, Colorado Springs; Karen Litfin, University of Washington; Gerald Thomas, the John Howard Society of Canada; and Yael Wolinsky-Nahmias, Northwestern University. For assistance and advice in the research, editing, and work that led to the final product, I am especially grateful to Angela McCracken, Elise Frasier, Charisse Kiino, Joanne S. Ainsworth, and Sally Ryman. Finally, for so many years of patience, tolerance, and love, I thank Mary, Maia, and Eric.

Ronnie D. Lipschutz
Santa Cruz, California
June 2003

1 | What Are "Global Environmental Politics?"

Bananas

Bananas are a pretty common item in the lives of Americans and Europeans. Everyone knows what bananas look like. Everyone knows where bananas come from. Everyone has eaten a banana. And that's all anyone needs to know—or is it?

Bananas are a big business. They are mass produced on plantations in one part of the world and sold, in large quantities, in markets in a different part of the world, which is where we first see them. But between the images of green banana trees swaying in the sun (Hello, Carmen Miranda) and yellow bananas piled high in supermarkets (Hello, Foodworld) there is a void, about which we can ask many questions.

For example: How are bananas grown? Who takes care of them while they are growing? How much are workers paid? What kinds of pesticides and fumigants are used on bananas? What happens to those chemicals? Do they make the workers sick? Can they make consumers sick? How do bananas get to the United States and Europe? What determines their cost? And why should such things matter to you?

A great deal goes on in that void between plantation and plate, and much of what goes on has undesirable environmental consequences. Some of these consequences are relatively local. For example, fertilizer runs off into nearby streams and kills fish; pesticides poison birds; chemicals injure workers. Others are quite global. Greenhouse gases are generated throughout the bananas' *commodity chain,* the production and consumption process, from the ships that transport them to the trucks that carry away the peels. Chemicals applied to the bananas end up in breakfasts, lunches, and snacks eaten all over the world. And all these stages can be linked to the complex social organization of contemporary life, of which you are a part.[1]

Here are some statistics. In 2001 almost 60 million tons of bananas were grown around the world, and 12 million tons were shipped to consuming countries. That made bananas the fifth largest agricultural product traded in world markets, after cereals, sugar, coffee, and cocoa. Most of the world's bananas are exported from Colombia, Costa Rica, Ecuador, Guatemala, and the Philippines, and about two-thirds of those bananas are consumed in the European Union (EU), Japan, and the United States. In the EU, each individual consumes about twenty-two pounds of bananas a year; in the United States, more than twenty-five pounds per year. Annual applications of chemicals— fungicides, insecticides, herbicides, nematicides, fertilizers, and disinfectants— to each acre of Central American banana trees amount to thirty pounds. A lot of those chemicals get shipped to Europe and the United States, along with the bananas.[2]

In Central America, bananas are grown mostly on plantations of 5,000 acres or more; in the Caribbean, they are raised on farms of about 10 acres. This makes a big difference in the cost of production, although it has hardly any effect on the retail price of bananas. More than 75 percent of the international banana trade is controlled by five transnational corporations: United Brands (Chiquita), Dole, Del Monte, Fyffes (based in Ireland), and Noboa (based in Ecuador). In 1995 the first three companies—all American— earned almost $7.5 billion in revenues from bananas. But very little of that money ever reached producing countries, much less farmers and workers. A pound of bananas that sells for a dollar in your local supermarket might be bought for 5 cents a pound or less in the country where it is produced. According to one study, every dollar of retail revenue generated by bananas is distributed as shown in the following list.[3] Similar lists can be made up for other fruits, vegetables, and manufactured goods.

Producer income	$0.05
Export costs	$0.04
International transport	$0.11
Import licenses	$0.09
Ripening process	$0.05

Taxes	$0.15
Distribution and retail	$0.34
Profit	$0.17

Maybe you don't like bananas. "None of that has anything to do with me; I don't buy 'em, I don't eat 'em. Never have, never will!" But you probably like apples. Or pears. Or hamburgers. Or cotton T-shirts. Or gasoline for your car. Or plastic water bottles. Or CDs. Or any one of hundreds of thousands of things produced somewhere else, shipped across oceans, and offered for sale where you live. Bananas, like all these things, are a *commodity*. You buy and consume commodities. And those commodities, when produced, shipped, and consumed, have environmental impacts when they are grown, when they are shipped, and when they are eaten and the skin is thrown away. Even if you detest bananas, you are part of that complicated global system of politics and economics organized around commodities and the environmental degradation associated with them.

You, in other words, are deeply implicated in the condition and fate of the global environment, through the system we call "capitalism." This doesn't mean that you are directly at fault for what has happened to the global environment, but it does mean that you cannot escape some responsibility for what is happening, for global warming, the ozone hole, species extinction, marine pollution, deforestation, pesticide poisoning, and many other problems. You might well ask, How has this situation come to pass? How did it happen? Who consulted me? These are some of the questions addressed in this book. The answers, as will be seen, are not always so evident, and what we might do is not so clear. But, as the saying goes, a long journey begins with a single step.

Thinking about Bananas and Other Such Things

This is a book about the politics of the global environment, the ways in which the global environment is being affected and changed by activities of human beings, and the ways in which people, societies, organizations, movements, groups, corporations, and states are responding to those changes. These days, the term "environment" falls off our lips so casually that we tend to forget what it really means. Broadly speaking, an "environment" is a set of material conditions within which an object exists, although, to be wholly accurate, an environment can also include less tangible social conditions, such as the "home environment." Thus, we can speak of the urban environment, the international environment, the natural environment, and the political environment. What is important here is that those conditions that characterize an environment are of human origin.

The natural environment is no different: ecologists generally agree that there are few, if any, parts of the world that are untouched or unmodified by human activities.[4] We must therefore be careful about imagining that there is, somewhere, a pristine environment, untouched by human hands. Beyond this, our use of the term often seems to imply that we, as human beings, are external to the "environment," that we are "in here," within society, while nature is somewhere "out there." It affects us, we affect it, but little more. Nothing could be less correct. Without nature, humans could not and would not exist; without humans, the natural environment would not exist. There would still be nature, of course, but no natural environment and no conception of Nature.[*]

These remarks might seem like sophistry, but they underline an important point: unless we recognize that humanity and Nature are mutually constitutive of each other—indeed, are virtually one and the same—we cannot meaningfully speak of protecting or sustaining the earth's environment. This is not a position often encountered in the literature on nature and environment. To be sure, nature does not exist to serve humankind, but nature's continued well-being does depend on human actions. Similarly, human beings survive only by co-existing with nature (or, as some might put it, being in nature) and not destroying it or transforming it out of all recognition.

All of this suggests that what is critical to readers of this volume, and to global environmental politics in general, is an understanding of the social meaning of nature and Nature. If one subscribes to the more-or-less conventional economistic and resource-centric view—that nature is comprised of resources that must be used more efficiently if they are to be sustained—it is evident that Nature's meaning lies primarily in nature's ability to supply utility to human society. This conception of Nature has its origins, according to some, with the agricultural revolution some ten thousand years ago, as humans found it possible—indeed necessary—to manipulate and transform the natural world in order to grow food and survive.[5] Others claim it is to be

[*]A note on terminology. I use *nature* (lower case) to refer to the physical and biological world. I use *Nature* (capitalized) to refer to the abstract concept of a philosophical realm of life, thought, and action. The first term is about the natural world as it is; the second as we imagine it or would like it to be.

found in the Judeo-Christian tradition that God created Earth and placed plants and animals on it to serve mankind.[6] Yet others argue that it was not until the Industrial Revolution, which gave birth to both modern capitalism and socialism (as practiced in the former Soviet Union), that a strongly utilitarian view of nature took hold.[7] Whatever the origins of this resource-based perspective, which we can characterize as *strong anthropocentrism,* it is the dominant one throughout the world today. Consequently, much of the debate and activity concerning global environmental issues focus on more efficient use of natural resources and, at the margin, their more equitable distribution.

Against this, we can posit a contrary perspective that seeing humanity as being in nature and for Nature (and neither outside nor superior to it) offers nature rights and standing equal to that offered to people. The language most often associated with such a perspective speaks of "legal standing" or "intrinsic value"; a few even view humankind as an unwelcome addition to the panoply of nature.[8] The natural world, by its very existence, has its meaning in what it is *without* human intervention, modification, or recognition or, indeed, even the presence of people. The goal of action should, therefore, be restoration of nature to something approximating its condition prior to the arrival of human beings on the scene. We can characterize this position as *strong biocentrism,* as placing nature before humans.[9]

Between these two poles, many positions and meanings of nature and Nature can be, and are, on offer. Some of these may, however, represent a more realistic approach to environmental protection and sustenance than others. It seems foolish to believe, on the one hand, that we can return to being hunter-gatherers or, on the other, that we can rely on technological innovation to free us from all material limits. At the same time, we should not dismiss out of hand those proposals that push us beyond the simple reproduction of our current beliefs and practices, and have about them a whiff of utopianism.[10] Our challenge is to explore the feasibility of a union between "what is" and what could be. This is a point to which we will return later in this chapter.

This book is also about the ways in which people are linked into the global environment and, indeed, global political economy, and the role of power and wealth in those links. The global environment is ordinarily conceived of as the large-scale natural systems that are thought essential to the maintenance of life on Earth, but this is a reductive concept that fragments the integral and holistic nature of habitat, both natural and social, localized and world spanning. In contrast to the approaches adopted by most authors and analysts, moreover, I shall take the global environment to be both more and less than is commonly assumed. It is more because many of the causes and consequences of environmental impacts discussed in this book are those not ordinarily thought of as being "global," as the example of bananas suggests. After all, bananas are grown in a specific place and eaten in another. What makes them global are the physical, economic, and cultural linkages that connect those places. But the global environment is also less because, unlike in most books on global environmental politics, it will not be automatically assumed that those environmental impacts that cross borders can be addressed only through cooperative international action or "regimes." [11]

In many books about the environment, political economy is discussed in regard to the environmental impacts of trade or the air and water pollution generated by specific industries or the wastes that result from disposal of worn-out items or the need to incorporate the costs of environmental damage into the price of goods. Political economy, as defined here, encompasses more than just mere economic relations; it is also about the ways in which power shapes the economy and the ways in which the economy, in turn, shapes the application of power. Political economy is at work when a transnational corporation such as Chiquita uses its monetary resources to influence the U.S. position on international trade in bananas to Europe. And it is at work when the energy policy of the United States leans toward fossil fuels and nuclear power rather than renewable energy and conservation.

This does not mean that the methods generally adopted in other texts have been dismissed here; rather, environmental problems of concern are taken to be the outcomes of historically established social processes, especially production and consumption, that have been and continue to be structured by existing political and economic institutions, such as states and capitalism, and the power relations that exist within and among them. At the same time that these processes within the global political economy are taking place across and among countries, however, other processes are under way that are very localized yet are also part of global political economy and social relations. When you drive around town in your car—assuming you own one—you are affecting the local environment and participating in the local economy. Or you might, as discussed in a later chapter, belong to a local environmental organization, concerned about open space or a local stream.

These kinds of activities and organizations appear to be "local" and spatially limited, yet in many ways they are as important as the global ones. There are many more of these kinds of localized institutions and practices than there are global ones. Moreover, as we have seen with bananas, the local is linked to the global. The gasoline you buy down the street might have been refined from oil shipped from halfway around the world. The carbon dioxide coming out of your car's tailpipe could, eventually, play a role in coastal flooding in Egypt and Bangladesh. The environmental organization to which you belong might have chapters or counterparts all over the country or the world.

In other words, in this book the concern is about things going on locally as well as globally, since these are part of the same social matrix that today forms a world-girdling civilization. That civilization is both local and global. The local is tightly tied into the global, and the global is closely bound to the local. Consequently, environmental changes of concern to us are both local and global, and to understand them, their impacts, and how they might be slowed or halted, we need to comprehend better the linkages, both social and natural, that bind the two together. To put the point another way, the notion of a "global environment" is taken as problematic. Questions are asked. What does "environment" mean? What is included in it and what is excluded? Who makes the rules about the environment? Who decides? Who acts? Who will protect us? Who will save the environment? And how might we go about answering these questions? How might we think more clearly about the ways in which we are "in" nature? How might we go about trying to understand how the bananas and other commodities we produce, trade, and consume play a role in the global environment? How can we explain the fact that activities that appear to be restricted to one place can have impacts on other places, far away?

We could, of course, limit ourselves to description, noting where and how such things are produced and consumed and the environmental impacts along the way. This approach would not, however, tell us why these impacts are allowed to happen, or how they came about in the first place. We could focus on the policies that make the global banana trade possible, or the costs of producing, shipping, and selling bananas. But that approach would ignore the environmental impacts. Or, we could focus exclusively on the environmental impacts and how we might get farmers, producers, and consumers to demand organic, fair trade bananas. That would tell us what we might do to change the global system of bananas, but it would not help us to understand why so many environmental impacts are simply ignored in the first place.

What is needed is a framework that brings together all these factors— history, economy, politics, sociology, and culture—and, as a first step, illuminates causes. It would help us to understand why most bananas are grown on massive plantations, cared for by badly paid farmworkers who often suffer from ill health, sprayed with massive amounts of chemicals rather than grown organically, and turned into billions of essentially identical and mundane yellow objects with little flavor, limited nutritional value, and a shot of pesticide. Such a framework would explain how power and wealth have been used to create and sustain this particular system, and why it is so difficult to change it. It would show us why the global banana trade is mostly in the hands of only five corporations, why growers and workers receive so little for their labors, why the use of chemicals helps to increase profits, how the desire for bananas had to be created, and why consumers demand perfect fruit without any brown spots, even though ripe bananas taste better than greenish ones. To this end, three tools will be adopted that are unusual in a text about the global environment. The first is a *historical materialist* perspective, one that takes account not only of ideas about the environment but also human relations with the material world. The second tool is *power*. The third is *ontology*.

Historical Materialism

A historical materialist approach shows how material practices are closely bound up with widespread (and not always correct) ideas about nature, human nature, and the way the world works. For example, you might take it for granted that people are greedy and self-interested by nature, that it is good to be rich, that you can never have enough. There are good reasons to believe that these ideas are not so, but we are socialized, from a very early age, to think they are true. We are constantly bombarded with advertisements for things we probably don't need but which we are told we should buy in order to be stylish or fast or first. Our survival does not depend on being stylish or fast or first, but somehow our society is driven by such notions. From where did they come? Has such need and greed always been with us? Or are these ideas with a history, with an origin?

Historical materialism does not mean that economics determines everything (an idea sometimes called "vulgar" Marxism). Instead, historical materialism offers a way of examining both the social and material arrangements that have led to the exploitation of the environment, the production of goods, and the damages that result. As regards bananas, this would include the history of banana-producing countries, the ways in which they were colonized to generate capital for wealthy investors and powerful countries, the domestic politics that placed production for export over the growth of crops for food, and the creation of markets in rich parts of the world. The historical materialism applied in this book takes history quite seriously, for what was materially constructed in the past—railroads, ports, courts, buildings, orchards, plantations, institutions, corporations, schools, and laws—leaves its imprint on what we deal with today and what we might face in the future, even if those things no longer exist. Slavery was abolished in the United States almost 150 years ago, yet many of its effects remain with us today. The freeways in Los Angeles follow the routes of long-vanished streetcar and electric train lines, which helped to create the urban sprawl and traffic jams that are so problematic now.[*]

In other words, human action in the past has transformed the world and left us that transformed world as the material environment within which we live, work, and play. In this respect, human beings are at some advantage over animals with regard to the world around us. With the appropriate *social institutions*—that is, the values, rules, roles, laws, and practices devised by human societies to ensure our survival—it becomes possible for people to live in, thrive in, and even modify a variety of natural environments and to actively choose how to modify them. Social institutions create and promote the specific conditions required for surviving and thriving under otherwise adverse conditions, although in this such institutions are not always successful. Social institutions, in other words, involve roles, rules, and relationships that, through the manipulation of material and mental worlds, serve as *production* for and *reproduction* by a society. Historical materialism, in turn, tells us how societies developed, through their institutions and manipulation of the material and mental worlds.

Sometimes, of course, those environments modified by humans lose all resemblance to what we think of as nature: the centers of New York City or the clear-cuts of northwestern North America come to mind in this respect. But the natural features of any particular city or place are a result of people's physical transformation of local habitat and their subsequent importation of "foreign" elements of nature not available locally (such as food, plants, and animals). It is not that Manhattan is divorced from nature. Rather, because

---

[*]In the first chapter of *The 18th Brumaire of Louis Bonaparte,* Karl Marx famously observed that "People make their own history but they do not make it just as they please; they do not make it under circumstances chosen by themselves, but under circumstances directly encountered, given and transmitted from the past." Historical materialism is a way of understanding these circumstances.

people's actions have removed large parts of nature from the material city, those parts must be brought back in if humans are to survive and thrive there.* Thus, among the brick and asphalt, we also find parks, gardens, and even clean air.

Consider a relatively simple example: a hunter-gatherer society. The individuals who belong to such a group each occupy a particular role: leader, shaman, hunter (usually male), gatherer (usually female), child, elder, and so on. These social roles exist by virtue of relationships established between individuals, who are often kin to each other, and through rules governing their interactions with each other and with the world around them. Together, people interacting with people and nature make up the social institution traditionally called the tribe or clan. Within such groups, there will be other subordinate institutions, such as family, marriage, celebrations, rites of passage, and so on. (There may also be superordinate institutions, such as alliances between groups cemented through intermarriage and exchange.) In fulfilling specific roles, according to the rules of social interaction, each individual helps to maintain the viability of the group and also to reproduce the relationships, roles, and rules. A failure to do this may mean the group's demise. At the same time, the group requires a material base, or habitat, for its reproduction: the production of food and other essential goods is central to the group's survival and continuity, without which social institutions will disappear. But in this case, production falls within the responsibility of specific roles and those who fill them. Hunters hunt, gatherers gather; these are material roles within the social institution that is the tribe or clan. In producing, group members help to reproduce and legitimize the arrangements that allow them and their descendants to survive.

So far, this sounds rather basic. The element that is missing and that makes these activities meaningful is *culture.* Even societies dependent on hunting and gathering for their survival also have cultures. Cultures provide critical meanings and significance to the roles, rules, and institutions that go beyond just production and reproduction. Some would argue that culture is simply the social matrix within which roles and rules are embedded and legitimated and helps to make those roles and rules more palatable. Others would point out that culture can be seen as those patterned and reproducible interactions that provide groups with their beliefs and worldviews and give

*Sometimes a distinction is made between "first" nature, which is that untouched by humanity, and "second" nature, which is nature as transformed by human action.[12] A few postmodernists also write about "third" nature, which results from the fusion of humans, machines, and nature.[13]

meaning to their members' lives. A funeral, to give one illustration of these two views, serves to send loved ones to the next world as well as to get rid of a potential health hazard.

A more detailed example of these concepts and relationship can be found in the culture and beliefs of the Navajo, and the role of nature in them. Briefly put, the primary relationship in Navajo culture is "mother," as the one who gives and sustains life. But many things can be "mothers": a kinsman, Earth, the sheep herd, corn, even tools. The kinship relationship is foundational to social life and extends beyond biological relations to other members of the nation and to animals, Earth, the sky, the sun, the moon, rain, water, lightning, and thunder. Proper relations with the natural world must always be maintained, and suffering is the result of disorder in such relationships. Everything is permeated by life essence and therefore deserves respect and propitiation. The land relies on human care for its well-being, and ceremonies rejuvenate sacred and special locations. All of this serves to produce and reproduce Navajo society, but also much more, including respect for Nature.[14]

Modern societies such as ours are complex elaborations of the basic hunter-gatherer model. Roles, rules, practices, and relationships proliferate, of course, and the material base is vastly more complex than that faced by hunter-gatherers, even to the extent of moving raw materials, agricultural commodities, manufactured goods, people, and ideas around the world. The number of social institutions in which we participate every day is large; the number existing in the world is astronomical. Nor are they easily separated from one another. We are faced, indeed, with "wheels within wheels," inasmuch as these institutions vary greatly in scope and complexity. Nor do they always mesh very well with each other (many of them are quite evidently dysfunctional and serve to undermine society's ability to reproduce itself).[15] It is this failure to "mesh" that damages habitat and leads to the environmental problematic. That failure may be attributable to roles, rules, relationships, and technologies, or to all four together. Each case of success or failure requires careful examination, with the help of historical materialism, if it is to be explained and addressed.

Power

The second tool used in this book is power. Power is central in politics, and it is an essential component of almost all discussions of global politics. Power is often defined as the ability of one person ("*A*") to get another ("*B*") to do something she does not want to do.[16] *A* can do this in many ways: through force, threats, bribery, or persuasion. In all instances, however, power is defined by *A* doing something to *B*. This is a very narrow and impoverished conceptualization of power. It leaves us to assume that everything else that might affect, encourage, or restrict people's behavior, such as greed, morals, or laws, are something other than power.

The concept of power used in this book will be more nuanced. Power is always about getting the things one wants from other people, but it is a far more complex phenomenon than the use of force or persuasion to get others to act. And power is not simply something possessed by the powerful and exercised against the weak; it is a phenomenon that constitutes our very social existence and makes human society and civilization possible. There are multiple forms of power, and they make it possible for things to happen collectively, in groups. Think, for example, how you might get a group of friends to go for a hike in the woods on a sunny day. You would not threaten them with punishment if they refused, or say, I'm bigger than you so you have to do what I say. Instead, you would argue with and cajole them: We're such close friends, it would strengthen our friendship; there are spring flowers in the woods, and the fresh air is good for you; everyone is going, you don't want to be left out; we're going hunting for mushrooms to put in tonight's pasta sauce. Perhaps you would reassure them: We won't be climbing that steep mountain, but we will go to the lake; when we're together, you don't have to worry about your safety; we're bringing along a lot of food. And you might also describe the less-attractive alternatives: Are you going to sit here, all alone, in your room? Don't you like us anymore? What's more important, schoolwork or friends?

We can also see people doing things even though they are not very eager to do them. For instance, imagine that it is a beautiful, sunny day. Wouldn't you prefer to be outside, rather than in a classroom? What prevents you from skipping class or leaving? College rules? Hardly. Fear of flunking? How much can it hurt to miss one class (as long as it's not an exam day)? Concern that your parents might find out? Unlikely. You remain in the classroom because that is what you do when you are a college student. That's what is expected of you, and you obey.

Or, consider the following scene: It is three in the morning and very dark. A traffic light stands at an intersection. It is red. A motorist approaches the light and stops, even though no other cars are to be seen anywhere. Why does he stop? It might be that he thinks there is a policeman hiding in the bushes nearby. Afraid of being caught, he waits for the light to change. Alternatively, he is a careful driver and always stops at red lights, since that's the law. A third possibility is that stopping at a red light is habit; it's just what people do. We cannot tell why he has stopped unless we ask him, and even then he might not be able to tell us. But the first explanation is based on the notion of direct power, the second on the power of discipline, and the third on the power of normality.[17]

Evidently, power is something more subtle than the conventional definition would lead us to believe. Those who have studied and written about the topic have approached this subtlety in different ways. Some have pointed out that the power to "set an agenda" represents one important modification to the usual understanding. Those who are in a position to decide what is to be addressed through the political process are often able to include all those matters they wish to have considered. Others have noted that the power to "exclude items" from political consideration is equally important, and that such exclusions go beyond simply leaving things off an agenda.[18]

By rendering some matters as being outside the arena of "manners," of social and political acceptability, power can be exercised through what is often called *hegemony*. That is, the very ways in which arguments and worldviews are framed can come to seem natural and, therefore, both unchangeable and unchallengeable. In this case, not only are certain issues kept off the political agenda, they are not even available to be considered.[19] Another conception of power, similar to hegemony, resides in the notion of *discipline*, as developed by Michel Foucault and elaborated by others.[20] The basic notion here is that "normal" behavior depends primarily on individuals limiting their behaviors to those they (and society) regard as legal, moral, or appropriate.

A final form of power can be found in the very foundations of human language and behavior. Language does not create the material world, but it does affect and constrain the way we see and understand material things. Consequently, language also affects how we interact with those things.[21] For example, we act differently toward whales if we conceive of them as a source of fuel and food (as was the case in the past) rather than as fellow beings to be respected and protected regardless of material considerations. How the first understanding of "whale" became transformed into the second understanding of "whale" is a long story, but that transformation involved some of the more subtle uses of power through what is called *discourse*.[22] "Discourse," as Karen Litfin has pointed out, involves the exercise of power, and "the supreme power is the power to delineate the boundaries of thought."[23] Those things that cannot be discussed or are forbidden, that are outside the "boundaries of thought," might, eventually, not even be recognized as being possible.* And discourse includes not only language but also beliefs, practices, and material things.

An example of these various aspects of power can be seen in the discussions and debates over energy policy during the early months of the presidential administration of George W. Bush. Vice President Dick Cheney was charged with the task of formulating a national energy policy. Both he and Bush made it clear that they supported supply-side solutions, such as more drilling for oil, expansion of nuclear energy, and increased consumption of coal. Cheney derided the very idea of energy conservation, calling it the "obsolete" thinking of the 1970s and blaming environmentalists for the electricity supply problems California was experiencing at the time. Although the administration's rhetoric was not allowed to go unchallenged, its very language can be seen as an attempt to cast conservation beyond the pale of policy consideration through ridicule and marginalization (agenda-setting and exclusion). The proposals were assisted by the generally accepted proposition that the United States always needs more, and cheap, energy (hegemony). Finally, many people chose not to disagree with the plan because, presumably, they felt it was "natural" to support whatever the president thinks is appropriate (discipline).

Such examples help us to recognize that the exercise of power is not something that is inherently (im)moral or (un)ethical. That is, power is not inherently good or bad; it is how power is exercised, by what means and to what ends, that must be judged on moral or ethical grounds. Moreover, power is not something exercised only by the powerful against the weak; to follow Michel Foucault's argument, power is everywhere and it circulates everywhere (a point returned to later).[24] The trick is in discovering how to exercise such power—in the "microspaces" of life, as he put it—to accomplish the political ends we might desire.

Ontology

The third tool that is central to this book is ontology. An ontology asks questions: Who are we? Why are we here? What is our purpose and the purpose of

---

*An excellent discussion of this point can be found in the appendix on "Newspeak" in George Orwell's novel *Nineteen Eighty-Four.*

nature and life? Was Earth created by a god, or is it merely the result of chance? Is there such a thing as "human nature?" Do living things have inherent value? In other words, an ontology explains the purposes and principles for our being in the world, and the way we and the societies we live in are; it offers certain a priori assumptions about human nature, about the world, about power, morality, and justice. For example, to say that humans are on Earth to fulfill certain divine purposes is an ontology. To say that humans are on Earth by chance is another ontology. The first ontology might argue that human nature is corrupt; the second that humans are neither good nor evil by nature. The first might enjoin us to observe God's commandments; the second, to make what we can of life.

Environmental ontologies, for example, may picture human beings either as the protectors of nature, put here on Earth to ensure its continuity, or the beneficiaries of nature, put here on Earth to use its resources.[25] Although these two views are not necessarily exclusive, they posit a different purpose for both humans and the world around them and lead to different practices with respect to nature. Human nature is another ontological matter central to our understanding of the environment. To some, human beings are inherently self-interested, violent, fearful of injury and death, and in need of discipline. This is a position sometimes associated with Thomas Hobbes's *Leviathan*. To others, human beings are inherently altruistic, peaceful, cooperative, and self-organizing. This is a position sometimes associated with John Locke's *Two Treatises of Government*.[26]

Explanations of global environmental politics are often centered on one of four basic ontologies (Table 1-1), each based on assumptions of the kind discussed above. The first is based on *competition* and assumes that states and individuals are greedy, selfish, and seek to acquire and control scarce resources for survival. The second is based on *cooperation* and assumes that states and individuals are part of a society and seek to serve their interests and the public good at the same time. The third ontology is based on *development* and assumes states and individuals to be primarily focused on accumulation and wealth. Finally, the fourth is organized around the concept of *domination* and explains environmental problems as a consequence of human exploitation of nature, other humans, and things.

These environmental ontologies comprise the foundations of environmental philosophies, and each of the four ontologies organize and structure a set of philosophies. So, in Table 1-1 we see three philosophies listed under "Competition." Although most books on international relations present

Table 1-1 Ontologies and Philosophies

Organization	Motivation	
	Accumulation of power	*Accumulation of Wealth*
	Competition	*Development*
Individual	Realism	Sustainable growth
	Malthusianism	Sustainable development
	Liberalism	Steady-state economy
		Radical redistribution
	(Anti) Domination	*Cooperation*
Social	Ecomarxism	Neoliberal institutionalism
	Ecosocialism	Ecoanarchism
	Ecofeminism	Social naturalism
	Deep ecology	
	Governmentality	

realism and *liberalism** as two distinct political philosophies, they are actually quite similar because they are both rooted in the same ontology of individualistic competition and threat. Realism focuses on selfish states, and liberalism focuses on selfish individuals. Realism assumes that states wish only to survive; liberalism, that individuals wish only to survive. Hence, when we begin to examine global environmental politics, we will discover that, rather than offering different approaches and answers, realism and liberalism are very much alike.

Ontologies are also important for their relationship to both historical materialism and power. Every society and its social institutions are organized around certain foundational concepts and assumptions that serve to structure human behaviors. A society, such as ours, that holds to the belief that people are competitive, selfish, and greedy by nature, and that the world is harsh and dangerous, is likely to be characterized by institutions and practices based on those beliefs. We see this, for example, in the form of capitalism around which American society has developed, and in the laws, norms, and material structures we deal with every day. For example, our

---

*"Liberalism," as used here, refers to the concept as employed in political philosophy and economics. It has nothing to do with the Right-Left dichotomization of American politics.

transportation system, its laws, and its great reliance on passenger cars carrying single drivers reflect a highly competitive and often deadly form of individualism. This ontology also mirrors and supports power relations within American society. Those of us born and reared in the United States are infused by competitive individualism almost from the day we are born. Only winners count; coming in second is as good as losing.* In education, in sports, in business, we are told and believe that only success is a virtue; failure is an orphan, as the saying goes. Subscribing to and obeying the dictates of a competitive ontology, we produce and reproduce the order of things as though there were no other possibilities. By the time we are adults, we accept this worldview as normal and natural, and anyone who suggests that it is not necessarily so comes to be seen as an idealist (or even a radical) who is sure to be crushed when the going gets tough.

Both history and experience suggest that neither philosophies nor ontologies are any more natural than cars, buildings, or books. Some things are impossible or, at least, very unlikely. As much as you might wish to fly, if you step off a cliff without the appropriate equipment, you will fall under the influence of gravity. You can make the choice freely, of course, but absent something to catch you, the consequences will be largely determined. But we also observe behaviors that, quite clearly, are not competitive or based on greed or selfishness or delusions. People give their wealth to the poor, they dedicate their lives to helping others, they spend their time defending wildlife rather than corporations. A few people will even sacrifice themselves on behalf of their beliefs. Clearly, not all things that we regard as unlikely are impossible, especially where assumptions and beliefs are concerned. At the same time, the material world does impose some limits on what we can do.

These three tools—historical materialism, power, and ontology—will help to guide us through the rest of this book. Although the natural environment is a physical and biological system, one that can be studied in whole and in part and, perhaps, understood in scientific and material terms, the politics that play out around environmental change and degradation are social. Politics is a human activity, organized and structured through a specific material history and based in sets of beliefs about individuals, societies, and the world. Both history and beliefs have the quality of seeming fixed and immutable, and it is this "natural" character that gives them their power and makes them

---

*It was Leo Durocher, manager of the New York Giants baseball team in 1946, who coined the famous phrase "Nice guys finish last."

seem "true." Were everyone to agree on their truth, there would be no politics because there would be no conflict. But, then, the world would be a dreary place indeed.

Thinking Socially

Three additional concepts help to make clear the ways in which humans interact with nature: *social institutions, habitat,* and *agency.* As noted earlier in this chapter, social institutions are practices devised by human societies to produce and reproduce themselves.[27] Habitat usually refers to the conditions under which the living elements of nature reproduce themselves.[28] Habitat is something like a structure, in the sense that, absent human intervention, it changes only slowly and constitutes the fixed conditions under which animals and plants reproduce. Habitat also limits reproduction in that populations are constrained from exceeding limits set by food chains, water supply, and climatic conditions.

Human beings do not face quite the same kinds of limits. Because of our technological capabilities and social relations, we are adaptable and able to live and thrive under a wide range of conditions. Our social institutions facilitate survival under these very different conditions, providing both structure and rules for living. This means that it is not necessary for each new generation to discover anew strategies of production and reproduction. But we cannot survive without habitat, inasmuch as nature provides the material base for food as well as the artifacts we use to grow, harvest, cook, and eat it. Some have argued that humans are now able to survive without any reliance on nature. We can grow food without soil, we can synthesize materials without mining or growing them, we can live in artificial conditions, recycling our own air and water. Perhaps such technologies will materialize in the future, but such arguments beg the question of whether this would detach us entirely from habitat.

Taken together, institutions and habitat represent forms of power as defined earlier in this chapter. They both enable and restrict, they define what is possible and permissible, they punish what is not. They comprise a *social ecology,* a kind of human ecosystem which, if healthy, allows societies to thrive but, if damaged, may gradually or rapidly cause them to become disorganized and to disappear. These social ecologies, too, are both local and global and interconnected in many ways, through economy, culture, politics, and environment. In the short term, damage to part or all of a social ecology can be remedied by moving things around, as when food is sent to the victims of a famine. In the longer term, there are probably limits to such responses; they are more in the nature of treating symptoms than of dealing with causes. There are social limits to what can be done to modify habitat as well as limits to what can be done to change institutions. In the former case, physical laws and structures set the limits; in the latter, social laws and structures do the same.[29]

This raises, in turn, the question of action: if habitat is threatened, what can we do, especially given the constraints imposed by both institutions and nature? Here we must define one more concept: *agency*. In this instance, the term does not mean some organization whose staff arranges things, such as a travel agency or welfare agency. Rather, "agency" refers to an individual's or group's capacity to challenge or change a constrained or limited situation (this is why political scientists often speak of actors). Action seems like a fairly easy and straightforward thing to do, but agency implies more than this.[30] In any given situation, as we saw earlier, not all actions are possible, desirable, or permissible. The key to change is, therefore, to discover what can be done and how to do it.

What does this mean with respect to institutions and habitat? It means that the maintenance or protection of habitat is as essential to social reproduction as is the fulfillment of roles and the observance of rules of a social institution. To protect habitat requires some alteration in roles and rules and some alteration in the relationships between social institutions and nature (and among people) as well as in the meaning of habitat and nature in the context of the social institution. This, to take the point further, means unraveling the power relationships within a society that have established particular meanings and practices and finding ways to change those power relationships.

The Many Roles of Nature

We can synthesize the arguments presented so far by considering the case of temperate forests of the Pacific Northwest coast of North America, including the Alaska panhandle, British Columbia, Oregon, Washington, and Northern California.[31] The logging and timber industries of this region have been part of a larger arrangement of economic and social institutions that have used the forests as a "natural resource" for more than a century.* We shall focus on

---

*As the conventional wisdom puts it, nature becomes a "resource" only when humans are able to exploit it.[32]

housing as an example of the kind of product that results from these institutional arrangements. Historically, houses have been built of all kinds of materials. In North America, wood has come to be preferred to other building materials, because it is relatively light, strong, plentiful, and cheap. Moreover, the American ideal has been a detached, single-family dwelling, which is still widely regarded as the best type of home in which to rear a healthy family (notions of both hegemony and discipline are evident in these normative claims). In this context, forests are seen as a utilitarian means to achieving a particular social ideal, one that serves to perpetuate a particular version of American society. But this set of institutional relationships and practices can remain viable only as long as those forests continue to exist and yield cheap timber—hence, the recurrent struggles over the future of the forests.[33]

At the same time, forests fulfill another central function in American society. To mix metaphors, they can be regarded as "Nature's capital." The primordial forests that covered much of the United States, even as late as the mid-nineteenth century, required no investments to produce. They were there by virtue of whatever natural processes and human interventions (by Native Americans) had brought them into being. But those trees could be cut, milled, sold, and turned into money and profit by individuals and organizations with the economic and organizational ability to do so. For this to happen and succeed, there needed to be a strong demand for the lumber, somewhere. And so there was. As the nineteenth century waned and the twentieth waxed, the single-family suburban household, with a wooden frame and exterior, became a social ideal. Railways, streetcar lines, and roads were built, often through political and economic collusion, to enable and encourage people to move out of the brick and masonry cities. Houses went up, the suburbs boomed, and the owners of forests became even wealthier than they had been before.

Of course, forests do not have meaning only in respect to housing and capital. Another element of social reproduction has to do with the ways in which forests fulfill other desires or practices or even worldviews. Forests are "temples of nature." Or they are dark and scary places inhabited by spirits. Or they represent vanishing wilderness. More to the point, as forests diminish in extent—and, here, we are not thinking of "tree farms" as suitable replacements—those that remain acquire greater value both economically and symbolically. In the former instance, the rising price and dwindling supply of cheap lumber foreshadow a diminishing chance of acquiring a stake in the American Dream. In the latter, the disappearance of the last remnants of the primordial American wilderness looms large in our imaginations and also represents a blow to our identities somehow linked to thousand-year-old trees (in Germany and Britain, few people even think in terms of old-growth forests, since they have not existed there in more than a century).[34]

As the very idea of Nature seems to become more central to our social reproduction, the balance between these two meanings—developmental versus cultural—is slowly tilting from the first to the second, especially since houses can be built of materials other than Northwest timber. What is at stake here, then, is not simply lumber, which can be obtained from tree farms or managed forests; it is more. As the aphorism has it, "A tree farm is not a forest." For some societies, the forest is integral to social reproduction, for material as well as ceremonial and symbolic reasons; for others, it provides a counterpoint to the social ecology of the city.

Imagine there's no forests. It's not so easy.

Institutions for the Earth?

What is the point of this forest exegesis (especially in a book such as this one)? It is here because, as you will discover in the chapters that follow, there are serious reasons to doubt that conventional systems of law or practice will suffice to address pressing environmental problems, both local and global. A serious mismatch exists between those institutions assigned the task of dealing with environmental damage, no matter what the scale, and the sources and nature of those problems. Most of these governmental institutions, whether local, national, or global, originally emerged to serve particular social functions and interests and, less evidently, to maintain existing relationships of power. In place of devising institutional responses appropriate to the nature of contemporary environmental problems, we have resorted to framing the problems in terms of the institutions and practices already in hand. Even those institutions established to deal with specific matters, such as the UN Framework Convention on Climate Change (UNFCCC) and the Kyoto Protocol, of which more will be said throughout this book, are deeply rooted in already-existing institutions and practices that serve more to reinforce the status quo than to address the problem head-on.* On the one hand, they are organized around states and their sovereignty.[35] States resolutely resist

*The Kyoto Protocol is an agreement added to the UNFCCC in 1997 that commits a set of rich countries to reduce their greenhouse gas emissions by a specified percentage over the next ten to fifteen years.

challenges to their authority and power and often refuse to act in ways that could address environmental problems. On the other hand, these institutions increasingly use market-based tools to deal with matters, yet it is the structure of markets that has caused many of the problems in the first place.

To give one example, we are often told that states are the only entities that can address transboundary environmental problems, because they are the highest authoritative political institutions, they maintain the boundaries being transgressed, and they occupy all inhabited space on the earth.[36] As a result, pollution that originates from highly localized activities in one country and has highly localized impacts in a neighboring country can be addressed only internationally, for to do otherwise would be to infringe on the sovereign rights of each state and to demand governmental action where there is no government. A fairly simple *gedankenexperiment* (thought experiment), offering two slightly different scenarios, will illustrate the artificiality of this claim.

> *Scenario 1:* Imagine a rather large river valley with a number of factories running its length. These factories were built over a period of decades, during a time when the entire valley was under the jurisdiction of a single national government. Culturally and linguistically, the inhabitants of the valley are identical and, indeed, are all descended from a few founding families. One day, one of the factories at one end of the valley begins to produce a rather unattractive and mildly toxic plume, which sickens a number of people living at the other end of the valley. The local health department, empowered to act against such polluters, closes down the factory and requires that the owners fix the problem, which they do. While not much has been addressed beyond the immediate pollution problem, at least that has been eliminated.

> *Scenario 2:* Now, consider the following twist. Strategic competition and war have led to a partitioning of the valley between two neighboring countries, one in control of the upper half, the other ruling the lower half. The inhabitants remain the same, as does the geography of the valley and the factories operating in it. One day, one of the factories at one end of the valley begins to produce a rather unattractive and mildly toxic plume, which sickens a number of people at the other end of the valley, *now part of a different country.* The health authorities at the affected end cannot shut down the offending factory, because it is under the jurisdiction of a foreign health authority. Instead, the authorities at the lower end must appeal to their national government to contact the government of the neighboring country,

which rules over the valley's upper end. If the latter is willing, it can order local authorities to shut down the factory. But, of course, since each state is sovereign, the government that exercises jurisdiction over the polluting factory is under no compulsion to shut it down (even though, under the stipulations of the *Trail Smelter* case of 1941 and the Stockholm Declaration on the Human Environment of 1972, international law does forbid the offending state from allowing the pollution to continue).[37]

What differs between the two scenarios clearly has to do with institutional arrangements rather than anything inherent in the valley itself or its geography or its social ecology. Living in a single institutional unit, the residents of the valley are in a position to protect their health; living in two institutional units, they are not. *This remains the case even if the border is fully open and people cross it all the time.* There may, moreover, be many entrenched economic and political interests—factory owners, politicians, municipal authorities, workers—obstructing a resolution to this problem, and they all are implicated in the same institutional conditions. Not to idealize the possibilities, but if the valley were treated as a single habitat or social ecology, with institutions organized in such a way as to take into account the valley's history and political economy, the obstacles preventing a solution in Scenario 2 might not arise.[38] This is the dilemma of the notion of a global environment writ small. States, by virtue of their many and conflicting interests, may find it more difficult to negotiate with each other than would smaller political units, constituted around principles other than national sovereignty and inviolable borders. Yet, to acknowledge such possibilities would be to undermine the principle of national sovereignty, which no national government is eager to do. Consequently, transboundary problems come to be defined in ways that fit existing institutional structures, rather than in other ways that would, among other things, clarify who is responsible for problems, who holds power over whom, and to what ends power is being directed by those who hold it.

For the time being, changes in and among states in this regard are unlikely. It makes some sense, therefore, to conceptualize the global environment in terms of existing institutions, such as states, borders, international organizations, and capital. The lament of the World Commission on Environment and Development (the Brundtland Commission) in *Our Common Future* that "The Earth is one but the world is not" seems to reflect current political reality.[39] This lament is nonetheless an empty one. Were the world actually "one," as the commission envisioned it, who would be in charge? Who would make the decisions? Who would pay the costs? It is not far-fetched to speculate that One World would operate much to the advantage of the wealthier states (and classes) of the planet. The poor would remain poor or perhaps become poorer. One unified world might create many more problems than we now face. Indeed, current approaches to global environmental issues—that is, regarding them as something to be addressed internationally—can, in fact, be considered reductionist. This may seem an odd charge to make. How can a process that treats the whole be reductionist? How could One World be a reductionist concept?

The answer lies more in the nature of the whole than in the whole itself ("the hole in the whole?"). Consider the following story: In 1990 the U.S. Public Broadcasting System ran a program called "After the Warming," a retrospective view of the effects of global warming on human society and nature, as seen from the year 2050. The program's host, James Burke, reassured viewers that the problem had nonetheless been brought under control, through the operations of a centralized management authority—located, of course, in Japan (this at a time when many thought that Japan would be the next superpower). The "Planetary Management Authority," as he called it, would monitor the activities of every country around the world. As necessary, it would issue directives to each to reduce emissions of greenhouse gases. In this way, the world would be saved.

An interesting concept, perhaps, but imagine the power and control that would be required to accomplish such an end!

It is pretty clear that the bane of centralized management is diversity and difference. Managers—especially global ones—prefer predictability and similarity so that a limited number of operating principles and rules cover all possible contingencies—not that all contingencies can ever be anticipated. (Consider how every significant commercial nuclear power plant mishap or accident over the past forty years was unforeseen). Yet, it is also evident that the world is an extremely diverse place and that people are willing to fight in defense of diversity and difference. The problem of reductionism arises, consequently, in trying to conceive of and deal with the world as a single unit, rather than as many, very particularistic places. No single strategy, no single program, no single directive will apply to every person, every place, every society. Moreover, many different types of activities produce the gases that contribute to global warming, but are we to treat all of these sources as equal? Do we count emissions of methane from rice paddies in Asia as somehow the equivalent of emissions from rice paddies in California? Is carbon dioxide from household fires in Africa the ethical equivalent of emissions from long-distance leisure travel in Europe? Is it morally legitimate to rank countries by their aggregate emissions, or do we need to be more aware of what activities are involved? Paradoxically, to be universalistic may be to be reductionist; to be holistic, we may need to be particularistic.

What's in the Rest of This Book?

Chapter 2, "Deconstructing 'Global Environment,' " presents a comparative discussion of the contrasting ontologies and related philosophies for viewing and explaining global environmental problems and politics. As we saw earlier in this chapter, people subscribe to many different foundational assumptions about life, about nature, about humans. Some assumptions are taken for granted, hardly recognized, and rarely questioned; these become the basis for dominant (or "hegemonic") ontologies. Other assumptions are contested, ridiculed, and marginalized; these often comprise what we might think of as "counter-hegemonic" ontologies. Dominant ontologies tend to set the structural conditions under which social problems, such as environmental damage, are addressed; in a capitalist system, the market comes to be regarded as the solution to all difficulties. But there's a catch, as noted above: the practices that have been institutionalized and naturalized under these ontologies are often the cause of the very problems that threaten to undermine social reproduction. If damage to the global environment is due to the particular structures and practices of capitalism, for example, how can capitalism also be the solution? What we do in Chapter 2, therefore, is examine the ways in which ontologies and philosophies understand and explain the very concept of "global environment." This will not make it easier to solve environmental problems, but it will show us how these understandings and explanations may conceal sources and obstruct potential solutions and actions.

In Chapter 3, "Capitalism, Globalization, and the Environment," we examine why the condition of the natural environment has become a global concern.[40] What processes have led to the "transgression" of national borders by air and water pollution, trade in endangered species and genetic resources, and the global dissemination of toxic wastes? What is new about this? Advocates of some philosophies, especially those focused on economic growth, argue that the environment is being damaged because of the absence of certain property rights, low resource prices, and inefficient allocation of funds for protection. To a growing degree, for example, the solution offered for global warming is tradable emission permits—rights to pollute the atmosphere that can be auctioned to the highest bidders. Alternatively, consumers are urged to be "green" and buy only environmentally friendly products carrying the appropriate certifying label. In this book, the questions will be asked whether relying on markets in such ways simply licenses the "right to pollute," and whether such a right should exist.

The specific focus of Chapter 3 is, therefore, on the environmental impacts of industrialism, capitalism, and globalization. To be sure, changes in nature as a result of human action did not begin with either industrialism or capitalism. Still, the scale and scope of contemporary impacts did not reach much beyond regional limits until the extension of markets to all parts of the world and the emergence of industrialism several centuries ago. More to the point, it was not until nature came to be regarded as something that could be exploited for accumulation and profit that the physical and biological world began to be regarded as mere capital, to be bought and sold at will and on a whim.[41]

Globalization, the name for the process of the worldwide intensification of capitalist accumulation, in concert with what is called the "Information Revolution," has only furthered the commodification of nature. In Chapter 3, I argue, in particular, that globalization plays a central role in the contemporary environmental problematic, from three perspectives. First, it fosters the movement of environmentally damaging activities from one location to another, often to another country or another continent. Second, globalization encourages consumption, which leads to increased volumes of wastes, both toxic and otherwise, from extraction, processing, transportation, assembly, packaging, and use. Third, globalization affects social, institutional, and organizational relations. These changes can obstruct solutions to environmental problems while encouraging activities that further damage the environment.

Chapter 4, "Civic Politics and Social Power: Environmental Politics 'On the Ground,' " begins with an aphorism by the late congressional representative Thomas P. "Tip" O'Neill, D-Mass.: "All politics is local." O'Neill, revered and reviled for his staunch liberalism, recognized that he had to respond to the needs of his constituents, who were more concerned about their neighborhoods than the planet. He also saw, however, that it is people who are political, who engage in politics, and who, ultimately, must be persuaded that actions are both good and to their long-term benefit. All environmental politics is, ultimately, about the local: about landscapes, land use, people's beliefs and practices, and insults to the environment that originate in and affect specific places and regions. Some of these matters manifest themselves globally (for example, global warming), although it is specific places and spaces that feel their effects. Others have a much more localized character (for example, soil erosion), originating from specific local sources and behaviors and motivating specific local actions in response.

But who can act to protect the environment? In recent decades, the environmental movement, acting through what can be called social power, has increasingly been able to affect environmental politics and policy all over the world.[42] Social power is, in part, a response to the failure of political authorities to address specific environmental problems and the absence of institutionalized political methods to influence policymakers and corporations in ways that can solve those problems. But social power is also a form of politics operating outside of conventional institutionalized practices, and many of those engaged in social power are seeking to revitalize politics.[43] The environmental movement is not a monolith; it is fragmented between and within countries and between and within groups and organizations themselves.[44] There is a furious debate over the methods used by some environmental groups to lobby policymakers and politicians and over the ethics of corporate sponsorship, a method of fund-raising that has transformed some environmental organizations into corporate mouthpieces.[45] Businesses and corporate associations have become prominent both in debates and in policymaking. This chapter offers a context for understanding social power and an overview of social power as it is deployed both locally and globally.

In Chapter 5, "The National Origins of International Environmental Policies and Practices: 'My Country Is *in* the World,' " we examine states and the environment. Most books on international environmental politics begin with the state. Because nature does not recognize national borders, as we saw earlier, environmental problems cross them. According to some of the philosophies in Table 1-1, if such problems are to be addressed, countries must cooperate to eliminate them. If this does not happen, according to other philosophies, states and people will come into conflict because environmental degradation necessarily implies a growing scarcity of environmental resources. Alternatively, according to yet other philosophies, rich and powerful states will exploit poor ones by exporting environmentally damaging activities to them.

In all of these philosophies, little attention is paid to the way national policies and practices often lead to international problems of concern, even as those policies and practices are also formulated to address those problems.

Although national environmental policies and ministries are of relatively recent provenance, nation-states have had "environmental policies" for well over two centuries. In earlier times, these were motivated mostly by agricultural and industrial development for the purposes of state building. The practices of one country were frequently adopted by others. One result was similar patterns of environmental degradation around the world. Over the past few decades, states have instituted policies and established institutions intended to address insults to the natural environment and their effects on the health of human beings. Each country tends to approach and address such matters differently as a result of differing domestic contexts.[46] At the same time, however, certain practices, such as forestry or water management, become "globalized" and set the standard for the replication of policies around the world. Some policies work in one national setting but not another; conversely, some practices and policies fail in one place but are nonetheless adopted in another, where they fail similarly. Drawing on the burgeoning literature on comparative environmental politics and policy, this chapter offers capsule studies of several environmental issues and the ways in which they have become (inter)nationalized.

As we have seen, human societies are based on social institutions. *International regimes*, a term common in analyses of international politics, are social institutions, most commonly established among states but also in other settings and contexts.[47] *Environmental regimes*, such as the Framework Convention on Climate Change, the International Whaling Commission, and the Basel Convention, are meant to facilitate the production, distribution, consumption, and protection of nature and resources.[48] International regimes are, consequently, nothing new or special; their only unusual feature is that they are agreements among countries, existing in a realm where cooperation is thought to be difficult because of international anarchy. But these are not the only types of institutions or regimes of importance to the global environment. Other types of global regimes are being created, and these involve actors and institutions other than states. For example, the Forest Stewardship Council is an organization attempting to create a private international regime for sustainable forestry. In the future, such regimes, relying on social or corporate power (or both), may be as important to global environmental politics as interstate ones. As we shall see, however, even these regimes cannot succeed without politics.

Chapter 6, "Global Environmental Politics and You: 'The World Is My Country,' " asks where we, both reader and writer, fit into all of this? As consumers of goods and producers of pollution, we are directly implicated in the damage being done to the earth's environment. We can make careful choices about what to buy and how much stuff to use. But, acting alone, we can never make our choices add up to more than those of a single individual. If everyone made the same choice, there would be changes, but experience suggests that such massive changes in preferences are the result of outside influences. To have an important impact, we must act collectively, in concert with others. And, to repeat the theme of Chapter 4, such action involves all kinds of institutions, political and social, ranging from the household to the global.

Finally, even as the book offers a great deal of theoretical food on which to chew, it also follows four distinct issues throughout, as a means of providing concrete examples about abstract arguments:

> *Consumption:* Everyone consumes; it is a necessary part of life. But how much do we each consume, and for what purpose? How do we choose among alternatives, and what motivates our desires? What is necessary, and what is not? And what effects does our consumption have on nature? Some consume much more than others and have a proportionately greater impact on the environment. Others do not possess the wealth to consume very much and must exploit the resources around them. Both types of consumption affect the environment.

> *Biological and genetic diversity:* Living nature consists of millions of plant and animal species, and each species reflects a certain range of genetic combinations in interaction with surrounding ecosystems. Many species are endangered, for the most part by intrusive human activities, and some of these are protected by law. To a growing degree, however, the importance of a particular species is giving way to the value of its genetic constitution and the possibility of using those genes to create products that can be sold for profit. What are the consequences for species of such an approach?

> *Sustainable forestry:* Forests, it is often said, are the lungs of the planet. Whether or not this is the case, they are disappearing rapidly, in both tropical and temperate countries, to meet growing global demand for timber and rangeland. As they go, so do the species that live within them. But recognition of forests' vital role in local and global ecology has not led to a commensurate response to sustain or protect them.

> *Global warming:* In the twenty-first century, global warming has the potential to affect and change the world, its inhabitants, and its species, more than any other environmental phenomenon. Why is it happening? Why do some people argue that it is not happening, or that humans have nothing to do with observed

changes in climate? Who will suffer most from it? Will anyone benefit? Why haven't international negotiations to deal with climate change been successful? What can we do about it? Can anything be done? Will anything be done?

Our Home Is Our Habitat, Our Habitat Is Our Home

Planet Earth is the habitat and home of humanity, plus some 5 million to 30 million other plant and animal species. We are all familiar with the blue-and-white ball as seen from space; it is probable, notwithstanding dreams of Mars and stars, that this is all we have. In one sense, Earth is a single ecosystem, and we really do not know how robust or fragile that system is with regard to the environmental insults initiated by human societies. In another sense, it is thousands, if not millions, of ecosystems and habitats, and some of those are clearly quite fragile even if others are less so. For each of those species, for each member or group of each of those species, the place where they live is their habitat and home. Most, if not all, of those individual habitats are also part of human habitats. And those habitats are being modified, disturbed, or destroyed by human actions, either deliberate or incidental, individual or collective. Most, if not all, of these actions are a consequence of the operation of networks of social institutions that compose the fabric of human existence, practices, and relationships. Again, "wheels within wheels." Where to begin?

The best place to begin is where we are, where we live, and to work "from the ground up." States (countries) are an abstraction. True, we encounter the state every day, through its representatives, money, buildings, roads, rituals, and beliefs. The international system is even more of an abstraction: There is the United Nations building in Manhattan, of course, but what does a building mean? (And why do some people see the UN as "peacekeepers" while others see it as "black helicopters?") The planet is all around us, yet we can never experience more than a very small part of it, the part where we are: Our habitat, if you will. Place is therefore of central importance in determining our identities, defining the meanings of nature, and acting to protect the environment. By caring for the earth's parts, through politics, we can care for the whole.

Lest this sound hopelessly romantic, it is not. This is not an admonition to "tend to one's last," to the exclusion of all others, to pay attention only to our own surroundings and ignore other places. It is essential that we always be aware of the place of our place in the whole, of the relationships, insofar as we can tell, of our part and other parts to the whole. It is essential that we understand the manifestations of international economic forces and international political processes as they appear in the small places that we, ourselves, occupy, individually and collectively. It is essential that we build alliances within places and between them, alliances that are consciously devised to challenge those forces, processes, and practices of power that, in millions of places, degrade or destroy habitat. The "fate of the earth," to use a phrase coined by Jonathan Schell and adapted to many other purposes, does not rest on what we think or believe as isolated individuals but on what we do together through and by politics.[49]

The need for political action, in other words, is the normative thrust of this book. It is an attempt to consider and evaluate alternative frameworks and approaches to environmental problems described as "global." It is an effort to frame these problems in ways that do not hew to the conventional wisdom but recognize that human societies are complex and not amenable to social engineering. It is, finally, a bid to accept and work with human diversity, rather than regarding it as an unwarranted obstacle to business as usual. And if these claims and this book provoke controversy, discussion, and challenges, isn't that what books should do?

For Further Reading

Arnold, David. *The Problem of Nature: Environment, Culture, and European Expansion.* Oxford: Blackwell, 1996.

Carter, Neil. *The Politics of the Environment: Ideas, Activism, Policy.* Cambridge: Cambridge University Press, 2001.

Conca, Ken, Michael Alberty, and Geoffrey D. Dabelko. *Green Planet Blues: Environmental Politics from Stockholm to Kyoto.* 2d ed. Boulder, Colo.: Westview Press, 1998.

Elliott, Lorraine. *The Global Politics of the Environment.* New York: New York University Press, 1998.

Goudie, Andrew. *The Human Impact on the Natural Environment.* Cambridge: MIT Press, 2000.

Hempel, Lamont C. *Environmental Governance: The Global Challenge.* Washington, D.C.: Island Press, 1996.

Hollander, Jack M. *The Real Environmental Crisis: Why Poverty, Not Affluence, Is the Environment's Number One Enemy.* Berkeley: University of California Press, 2003.

Kuehls, Thom. *Beyond Sovereign Territory: The Space of Ecopolitics.* Minneapolis: University of Minnesota Press, 1996.

Laferrière, Eric, and Peter J. Stoett. *International Relations Theory and Ecological Thought: Toward a Synthesis.* London: Routledge, 1999.

Lomborg, Bjørn. *The Skeptical Environmentalist.* Cambridge: Cambridge University Press, 2001.

Maniates, Michael, ed. *Encountering Global Environmental Politics.* Lanham, Md.: Rowman and Littlefield, 2003.

Paterson, Matthew. *Understanding Global Environmental Politics: Domination, Accumulation, Resistance.* Basingstoke, England: Macmillan, 2000.

Porter, Gareth, Janet Welsh Brown, and Pamela S. Chasek. *Global Environmental Politics.* 3d ed. Boulder, Colo.: Westview Press, 2000.

Seager, Joni. *Earth Follies: Coming to Feminist Terms with the Global Environmental Crisis.* London: Routledge, 1993.

Vig, Norman J., and Regina S. Axelrod, eds. *The Global Environment: Institutions, Law, and Policy.* Washington, D.C.: CQ Press, 1999.

2 | Deconstructing "Global Environment"

Thinking Green

What does it mean to *deconstruct* "global environment?" Chapter 1 offered a particular normative perspective on the general issue of global environmental degradation. That perspective included several foundational assumptions regarding the social worlds that humans have organized. For example, in discussing hunter-gatherer groups, we came to recognize that production of the material base and reproduction of the social structure are fundamental to all societies, even as the particular methods of production and reproduction may be very different. In speaking of the Navajo cosmology of life and the world, we saw that meaning is central to the institutional organization and activities of any society. Finally, in describing the George W. Bush administration's approach to energy policy, we were made aware of the ways in which different forms of power are exercised so as to (re)enforce the way things are. But none of these assumptions is fixed or "natural" in any fundamental sense; other cosmologies could explain the world equally well and would play a central role in producing and reproducing their specific societies.

When we speak, then, of *construction,* we are referring to the ways in which basic, taken-for-granted beliefs, meanings, and practices help to organize and discipline a society's culture and life, and to specify rules and roles for the individuals within that society. When we speak of *deconstruction,* we are seeking to unpack and examine those beliefs, meanings, and practices, the better to understand why it is that some forms of social being and activity appear "natural" whereas others do not. To reiterate an example offered in Chapter 1, consider how the two meanings of "whale"—natural resource and endangered species—both construct and are constructed by the beliefs, material base, and exercise of power in the nineteenth and twentieth centuries. When whales were seen primarily as terrifying monsters and a source of oil and food, whole fleets of ships were dedicated to seeking them out and killing them. Any suggestion that they might deserve to be left alone was unimaginable. When whales came to be seen as intelligent mammals and generally friendly, whole fleets of ships were dedicated to seeking them out and watching them. Any suggestion that they might deserve to be killed for food and oil became unimaginable (except in Iceland, Japan, and Norway).

In this chapter, we will examine and deconstruct environmental philosophies as they interpret the global environment and structure practices and policies. Although we have come to take the concept of a "global environment" for granted, using the term as shorthand for the biological and geophysical systems of the planet Earth, the term is much more political and sociological than it is scientific or descriptive. To begin, I will define three concepts in general terms: philosophy, ontology, and epistemology. Using the philosophies and ontological assumptions presented in Table 1-1, we will systematically analyze each, seeing how these conflicting and contrasting frameworks result in very different constructions of why environmental degradation occurs and what can be done about it.

Philosophy, Ontology, Epistemology

The fundamental assumptions and beliefs that go into these contrasting views and practices are both ontological and epistemological in character. The views and practices themselves can be understood as comprising philosophies that are, for the most part, taken for granted and hardly questioned. An ontology, as seen in Chapter 1 and later in this chapter, explains our purpose in the world: Who are we? Why are we here? To fulfill God's commandments? To be happy? To live as one with nature? By random chance? An epistemology explains how we know about our purpose and about the world more generally: Was the earth created by a god or was it merely the result of chance? How do we know? How can we know? God told us. Nature tells us. Science tells us. A philosophy puts such pieces together in a coherent package, so to speak. It provides a plan for how we ought to live our lives and explains why we live as we do.

As an example—one we will have occasion to examine more closely later in this chapter—what is the dominant philosophy in the United States today, and what are its ontological and epistemological foundations? Simplifying and idealizing just a bit, we can describe that philosophy as a form of liberalism that practices representative democracy and seeks to foster free market capitalism. Liberalism extols individual freedom, protects both property rights and individual rights, and tries to minimize state intervention into the private sphere. It also tends to be highly utilitarian, pursuing policies and outcomes that maximize satisfaction and minimize misery. The ontology of liberalism is more difficult to pin down. Its vision of a better, orderly world is rooted in Christianity yet it commits to no specific religion. Liberalism sees humans as fallible yet perfectible, and human nature as centered on self-interest and accumulation. How do we know that these are our purposes and goals? Primarily through deduction and inference. That is, since no one tells us, and we cannot determine our purposive ends through science, we must use our ability to reason. We cannot be here to be miserable and unhappy. We are conscious of our individuality and we do not share consciousness or consciences with each other. We dislike being told "No!" and yearn to be free of restrictions imposed on us by others.

Are these ontological principles true? Is our deductive epistemology correct? Yes and no. To be a liberal and to practice liberalism, one has to treat these principles as true and the epistemological deductions as correct. Through belief and practice by hundreds of millions of people in the United States, both ontology and epistemology come to be taken as natural and for granted—other social philosophies are simply wrongheaded or evil. Because liberalism so evidently accomplishes what its beliefs proclaim, not only is it true, how can there be any other valid philosophy? This last question is a bit disingenuous, of course: if everyone behaves as if a thing is true, how are we to know whether it is true or not? If everyone relentlessly pursues their individual self-interest, how are we to know whether this is human nature or simply masses of people pursuing a practice they believe is true and natural? Ultimately, it comes to seem as if there are no practical alternatives.

Every analytical or philosophical approach to the global environment incorporates such a set of foundational assumptions, based on a certain epistemological method. Often, these assumptions are so embedded that they are not recognized as being just that: assumptions whose "truth" cannot be determined by any means except reasoning or deduction. To take another example: do living things possess what is called "intrinsic value"? That is, do they possess value in and of themselves, without any human judgments? Most of the time, we try to put an economic value on living things: what is a tree worth if turned into lumber? Sometimes, we try to value things in terms of the pleasure, enjoyment, and utility we derive from their existence: a tree is valuable because of its beauty, its shade, its ecological function. If, however, a tree has intrinsic value, we assume that it has a right to life and respect regardless of how humans might value it. That would lead to a philosophical stance that treats living things as ends rather than means. We should simply let the tree *be*. Clearly, a logger or tree farmer might not subscribe to the notion of intrinsic value, since it would lead to a "hands-off" philosophy.

Our deconstruction and contrasting of competing philosophies of "global environment" in this chapter will show us how each leads to different and often conflicting accounts of both environmental damage and political solutions. More to the point, much of what we call "global environmental politics" is the result of conflict over the ways in which philosophies, epistemologies, and ontologies are manifested in people's everyday beliefs and practices when they interact with the natural world. That many of the poor countries of the world believe global capitalism to be a major cause of their environmental problems, while many of the rich countries believe global capitalism to be the solution to those environmental problems, is not merely a matter of contested data or evidence or even values. Rather, it goes to the core of what people believe, how they act on those beliefs, and how their actions inform their beliefs.

Humans and Nature

As we shall see, ontology, epistemology, and philosophy have a great deal to do with understanding various perspectives on the environment and the relationships between humans and nature. In particular, the way in which a problem or issue is defined and understood has a great deal to do with the way in which it is addressed. Indeed, framing an issue in a particular way often points to particular types of solutions, some of which might lead to unintended or even catastrophic outcomes.[1] Some environmental philosophies take humans as the beneficiaries of nature, put here on Earth to use its resources, whereas others regard humans as the stewards of nature, put here on Earth to ensure its continuity.[2] These two views are not necessarily exclusive, but they posit a different purpose for both humans and the environment around them and lead to different practices with respect to nature. Think, again, of the ways in which these two contrasting philosophies affect whales. The first led to their near-extermination during the twentieth century; the second, to their much-beloved status today.

Such a question—whether humans are protectors or exploiters of the environment—gets at one foundational ontological question: is there an inherent *human nature* and what is it? For some political philosophers, human beings are inherently self-interested, violent, fearful of injury and death, and in need of discipline so that civilization is possible. This is a position sometimes associated with Thomas Hobbes's *Leviathan*. Hobbes suggests that the "state of nature" is one in which humans (or, more specifically, men) are without the protection of society and must secure and protect themselves. The world is hostile and chaotic. Each man covets the riches found in nature or possessed by other men. He will defend what he has and fight to acquire what others have. The natural world, in Hobbes's view, is there for the taking. Only the intervention of a sovereign, or state, can eliminate the state of nature among men and the threat they pose to each other, and oversee the division of resources in a peaceful fashion.[3]

To other philosophers, human beings are inherently peaceful and self-organizing but too individualistic to form a society on their own. This is a position sometimes associated with John Locke's *Two Treatises of Government*. Unlike Hobbes, Locke is more concerned with the development of civilization and society than with the origins of government. He, too, assumes that nature exists for the benefit of man, but he believes that it must be exploited in particular ways in order to foster both wealth and the social good. When humans put their own labor into land, they turn it into *property*, which is inherently productive. Ultimately, the development of civilization and society is dependent on the individual accumulation of nature's riches, turned into money, or *capital*. For Locke, the sovereign or state exists to protect individuals' rights to property and riches and to ensure that these rights are not violated.

Both Hobbes and Locke hold a particular view of human nature centered on individualism and self-interest. We were originally created as individuals, and it is only by virtue of a *social contract* that we can fulfill our individual potential and desires. The social contract is an implicit agreement between the individual and the state—it is nowhere actually written down—which grants the former protection and rule by the latter in exchange for loyalty and material support. But Hobbes and Locke differ in their views of the state of nature, Hobbes believing it to have been violent, Locke thinking it peaceful but undeveloped.

By contrast with these two views, others believe that humans are inherently social: they cannot exist as atomized individuals and there never has been a state of nature, as such. The nature of society, however, has something to do with the ways in which both humans and the natural world are treated. Karl Marx and his followers saw all societies as being hierarchical, with some groups dominating others (he called these groups "classes").[4] Such hierarchy was necessary for the society to exist, because the dominant group was too busy organizing and ruling society to work the land and produce the resources needed to reproduce the society. Capitalism was simply another version of this age-old model, although the accumulation of wealth took place much more efficiently than ever before. Marx expected that, eventually, socialism would emerge, in which the working class destroyed or absorbed all other classes, and nature would be exploited for the good of all. Ultimately, however, the domination characteristic of all societies rested on various forms of violence, either direct or threatened. Certainly, violence was characteristic of the societies of the now largely vanished socialist bloc.

Not everyone believed that society need depend on violence; a rather varied lot of anarchists and socialists, such as Prince Kropotkin, saw harmony among humans as foundational and mirroring relations between and among species observed in nature.[5] Society was not simply a gaggle of human beings living together pursuing their individual interests but, rather, a sophisticated organization with a division of labor, and such an organization was impossible without cooperation. Violence among humans and societies was not the result of something inherent in human nature; it came about because of the power of sovereign or state and the structures that allowed the rulers to accumulate more power, in the form of wealth. Left to their own devices, humans could and would form small, cooperative, egalitarian communities, in which power would be unnecessary, domination meaningless, violence nonexistent, and equality natural.

Environmental Ontologies

In order to facilitate our further exploration of environmental philosophies and to see how they are reflected in global environmental politics, we can derive four categories of environmental ontology by combining two foundational assumptions about human nature with two foundational assumptions about human behavior in the "state of nature." The results are *competition, cooperation, development,* and *domination,* as shown in Table 2-1. Each of the philosophies discussed in the remainder of this chapter can be put into one of these four boxes, with one caveat: they are idealized frameworks. "Really-existing" philosophies, as we will see, tend to mix elements of the four categories.

Environmental philosophies based on competition are organized around the proposition that nature's resources are desirable but scarce. Whether the resource is food for people or oil for countries, a shortage will threaten survival. In the absence of an authority that can divide the resources, nature is the object of struggle, and all means of acquiring the resource, including violence, are acceptable if necessary. Furthermore, it is better to acquire or control as much of the resource as possible, so that one will not be left vulnerable in the face of future shortages and struggles.

Philosophies based on development see the problem of scarcity not as one to be solved by struggle but, rather, by producing more of that which is needed, such as food or oil. The material necessities of life remain vital to survival, but they can be provided through appropriate systems of production and exchange. If properly organized, such systems can produce more than enough for everyone's needs, and there will be no reason for conflict or violence.

Philosophies of domination more often take the form of critiques of systems of domination, such as capitalism, patriarchy, and what Johan Galtung has called "structural violence." [6] These philosophies argue for resistance to

Table 2-1   Ontological Foundations of Environmental Philosophies

	Human nature	
State of nature	*More individualistic*	*More social*
Tends toward violence	Competition: Individuals struggle with each other for a share of nature's goods	Domination: Some individuals control others in order to accumulate more than a fair share of nature's goods
Tends toward harmony	Development: Individuals engage in production in order to acquire their share of nature's goods	Cooperation: Individuals work together, and are in harmony with nature, thereby sharing fairly of nature's goods without harming nature

these systems. (No one is interested in legitimizing domination, however common it might be.) Whereas both competition- and development-based perspectives see nature as something to be used to human ends, philosophies of antidomination see nature as a category subject to the same kinds of abuse as are women, minorities, and other groups suffering from discrimination. The real protection of nature requires, therefore, the restructuring or disappearance of the systems and practices that perpetuate domination over all such groups. Resistance is the starting point of such change.

Philosophies based on cooperation propose that political institutions, governed by rules, norms, and laws, can foster collective protection of nature and enable humans to come to consensus. Such ontologies take it for granted that human beings are social by nature and seek to cooperate; na-ture is similarly characterized by symbiosis and organicism. The appropriate social arrangements can, therefore, eliminate struggle, competition, and domination.

Environmental Philosophies

Table 2-2 is a summary of the environmental philosophies to be discussed in this chapter. It is helpful, at this point, to recall that none of these ontologies, or the philosophies they generate, is in any sense objective or descriptive of the "real" world.* They help to *construct* understandings of the world and,

Table 2-2   Environmental Philosophies Discussed in This Chapter

Philosophy	Description
Competitive	
Realism	Resources are scarce; states are fearful and violent; they struggle to control nature; war is the result
Malthusianism	Resources are scarce; population growth places excess demands on nature; conflict and struggle between people and societies are the result
Liberalism	Resources are scarce; competition in the market and privatization foster efficiency and conservation of nature
Cooperative	
Neoliberal institutionalism	States can find mutually agreeable compromises through negotiations in international regimes
Ecoanarchism	Humans can protect nature and live cooperatively through local ecologically sensitive and democratic practices

Table 2-2   continued

Philosophy	Description
Social naturalism	Humans can live in harmony with each other and with nature in small, self-governing communities organically embedded in ecosystems
Development	
Sustainable growth	Resources can be made more plentiful through high rates of growth and market opportunities for the poor
Sustainable development	Both poverty and overconsumption cause environmental degradation; environment and development are intimately related.
Steady-state economy	Too much stuff causes degradation; countries must become self-sufficient and emphasize durability and longevity of goods
Radical redistribution	Production with redistribution can provide resources for everyone and lessen the impact of the rich on the environment
(Anti) Domination	
Ecosocialism and ecomarxism	Capitalists control resources. The dominant position of capitalism in social and ecological hierarchies destroys both people and nature.
Ecofeminism	The dominant position of men in social hierarchies weakens and destroys both women and nature
Ecocentrism (deep ecology)	The dominant position of humans in ecological hierarchy destroys nature; that hierarchy must be eliminated
Environmental governmentality	Power constitutes subjects and social relations; the management of populations, environment, and things for stable ends is central

Note: This table is not comprehensive; there are other philosophies that are not included here, but they tend mostly to be variations on one of these themes.

thereby, to direct our interactions with it. These interactions, in turn, shape and reshape that material world, with material results that affect how we live and understand the world. To put this in more prosaic terms, academics continue to argue at great length over the causes of World War I, and whether

*The debate over "reality" is one that has consumed the energies of many philosophers, intellectuals, and academics. Suffice it to say that the material world exists, but there are enormous disputes over how we describe and understand it and over what constitutes "truth."

certain (mis)interpretations triggered it. No one can deny, however, that the millions killed or the privations inflicted or the chaos generated had no material effect on the world or subsequent generations of people.

To further illustrate this point, and the ontologies given above, let us return to the scenario presented in Chapter 1. In that situation, you will recall, a valley is divided between two countries. The factories at one end of a valley are sending pollution across the international border to the other end. The factories provide benefits, such as wages and goods, to the workers and people living at one end (*A*), but the pollution imposes costs, such as ill health and environmental damage, on the people living at the other end (*B*). The way in which this problem is understood and defined will determine the manner in which it is solved. Each of the four ontologies offer a different perspective on the problem and a likely solution to it.

A philosophy based on a competitive ontology would explain that a clean atmosphere is the crucial resource at issue. The atmosphere, in this case, is contiguous with the land below, half of which is controlled by each state. The pollution from the country upwind (*A*) would be seen as a threat to the well-being of the country downwind (*B*) and a violation of the latter's sovereignty and territorial control. Country *B* could use threats of force to make country *A* cease the offending activity. If *A* failed to do so, country *B* could invade and occupy country *A*'s portion of the valley, shutting down the factories. The complications that could arise from such a "solution" are left as a thought exercise.

From the perspective of a philosophy with a development-based ontology, the problem is one of too little clean atmosphere. But it is difficult to create atmosphere, and the solution is, therefore, to reduce or eliminate the pollution from the factories. Perhaps *A* is too poor to pay the cost or simply refuses to do so. Country *B* should, therefore, find a way of enticing *A*, perhaps by offering to finance pollution control or even through helping to foster economic growth to provide the funds. This approach will be discussed in greater detail when we take up the topic of global climate change.

A philosophy with an antidomination ontology would have some difficulties with this problem. First, the very fact that there are polluting factories, and that people have permitted them to operate, suggests the presence of a powerful class determined to continue accumulating wealth even at the cost of the well-being of nature and society. Of course, the people from both ends of the valley could mobilize and occupy the factories, and install clean technologies, but this might lead to repression as well as conflict among owners, workers, and occupiers. A thorough restructuring of social relations and production systems would be required to ensure that the factories would no longer pollute the atmosphere, and the governments of both countries would probably not look favorably on such a solution.

Finally, a philosophy based on a cooperative ontology would do away with state involvement entirely: the problem lies with states, sovereignty, and power. The people of the valley should dispense with polluting industrialism, establish small-scale, self-sufficient cooperatives, and create a valley-wide federation of villages. Their inhabitants would live lightly on the land, and the factories would be left as abandoned relics of an old order.

Deconstructing Environmental Philosophies

It should be apparent by now that an environmental philosophy comprises a kind of "worldview." It is based on certain ontological assumptions and it provides a framework for how people should behave as well as an explanation for why they behave as they do. But not all philosophies have equal political standing. It is evident, perhaps, that only the first two sets of philosophies, based on competitive and development-oriented ontologies, are widely recognized as the basis for action where nature and environment are concerned. This is because the dominant philosophies in global affairs are forms of liberalism, which put the individual (or the state) above society. The second two sets of philosophies—cooperative and (anti)domination—might be better understood as critiques of liberalism. Although some people try to live by these latter philosophies, it is much easier to subscribe to the dominant ones, as we will see.

Competition

Competitive environmental philosophies are mirrors of traditional international relations theory, focused on struggle and conflict. It is difficult to say that "states" somehow subscribe to environmental philosophies, yet the behaviors of governments do reflect philosophical stances, and global environmental politics has a great deal to do with such behaviors. These competitive philosophies seek to explain human and state behavior as arising from an almost genetic propensity for struggle. Because goods are scarce, there is never enough of anything to satisfy everyone. What is possessed by one will be jealously sought by another. In the state of nature, without government, the result is competition, struggle, and conflict. Within the regulated conditions of the market, the result is competition, struggle, and accumulation. Ontologically, both realism and liberalism regard humans and states as selfish and only minimally inclined to cooperate, unless forced to do so.

Realism: A World of War. Two assumptions ground traditional international relations theory and inform realism. First, states exist in a condition of anarchy, comprising a crude international society called the *state system*.[7] There is no global sovereign or government to rule over states, to command them to do one thing and not another, to punish them if they fail to behave as ordered. As a consequence, each state must look out for its own security and interests, since no one else will; the state system is therefore a *self-help* one. Furthermore, although states can make agreements with each other, there is nothing except fear of punishment by another and, perhaps, reputation to make them keep such agreements. States, according to traditional international relations, cannot really be trusted. As the Romans said, "If you would have peace, prepare for war" (*Si vis pacem, para bellum*). But even if states are in a condition of international anarchy and potential hostility, they are not isolated from one another. They occupy physical space next to each other on the surface of the earth, they watch each other's actions, and they interact and affect one another.

Second, at least in theory, each state is *sovereign* within its own juridically specified territory.[8] This means that the government of each state constitutes the ultimate authority and possesses a monopoly of legitimate violence within that territory (although there are important caveats to this idealization, since many governments do not exercise such a monopoly of violence).[9] Taken together, the state of anarchy and the condition of sovereignty mean that a state cannot be forced to do anything within its own territory that it does not want to do and that no one can keep it from doing within its own territory what it chooses to do.

What, then, does this traditional understanding of the configuration of international relations have to do with the environment? As we saw earlier, one of the general assumptions underlying competitive philosophies is that *all desirable resources are scarce.* That is, whether mineral deposits are limited or supplies are short, the demand for them is always greater than the supply. States and their populations require natural resources to survive. Therefore, competition for access to those resources and goods is seen as a perennial problem.[10] More extreme versions of such realism derive from twentieth-century geopolitical theories about the security implications of strategic raw materials.[11] Scarcity is caused not by absolute supply but by distribution. Minerals are unevenly distributed around the world and are not necessarily found within the borders of the states most in want of them. Therefore, it may become necessary for a state to take by force what it cannot acquire through markets or guile.

The state in possession of a critical resource, the "have" state, can, for any number of reasons, refuse to provide it to the state needing but not possessing the material, the "have-not" state. The "have-not" state can claim, in turn, that the material in question is so essential to national security that its acquisition justifies an attack on the "have" state. This type of dispute formed the backdrop to German expansionism in the 1930s and is one common explanation for the origins of the war in the Pacific between Japan and the United States in World War II as well as the 1991 Gulf War.[12] Some have argued that the same motives apply to the George W. Bush administration's invasion and occupation of Iraq in March 2003.[13]

The same kind of logic has been applied to other natural resources. For example:

> Fresh water is a fundamental resource, integral to all ecological and societal activities, including food and energy production, transportation, waste disposal, industrial development, and human health. Yet fresh water resources are unevenly and irregularly distributed, and some regions of the world are extremely water-short. As we approach the twenty-first century, water and water-supply systems are increasingly likely to be both objectives of military action and instruments of war as human populations grow, as improving standards of living increase the demand for fresh water, and as global climatic changes make water supply and demand more problematic and uncertain.[14]

Arguments of this sort are made frequently and, some claim, form the basis for both analysis and action by states. After all, if states go to war over oil, why shouldn't they do the same over water? And if political leaders believe in such ideas, aren't they likely to initiate war in the event that national water sources appear to be threatened?[15] Water would not be a military objective that one would destroy in order to save, although there have been attempts to use water to destroy those whom some did not want to save. Images of terrorists or saboteurs bombing dams (or threatening to do so as a means of extortion) is a compelling one, but such incidents are as likely to arise from internal political instability and conflict as from the malign intentions of state leaderships bent on attacking neighbors. Water may figure into the strategic calculations of generals and prime ministers, as some writers have suggested, but war is an awfully blunt instrument with which to accomplish objectives having to do with control of this particular resource.[16]

What about renewable resources, such as forests? Here, the scarcity involved is of a somewhat different character, involving the erosion of physical, biological, or life support systems. For example, trees play an important role in the global carbon cycle, absorbing carbon dioxide (CO_2) while emitting oxygen and water. By permitting a forest to be destroyed, the state whose territory encompassed it could be said to be contributing to global-warming conditions that might harm other states. The affected states could argue that the resulting violation of sovereignty justified physical intervention in order to prevent further destruction of the forest.* It would be difficult to sustain such a claim under international law, but in the past, Brazil has exhibited considerable concern that this might happen.[17] But not all problems are so simple or lend themselves to such solutions. The elimination of environmental insults moving across national borders is, for the most part, a circumstance that is not amenable to applied violence, notwithstanding repeated discussions of the subject.[18]

Malthusianism: A World of Deprivation. Realism treats states as autonomous and even autarkic units (that is, they try to be self-sufficient in material resources) that seek security rather than justice. Hence, if the people of a "have-not" state suffer because of a scarcity of a particular resource, that is their misfortune. "Have" states are not obligated to care for "have-nots," even if they possess more of the resource than they need.[19] Such scarcity is relative; the problem is one of distribution, rather than supply. But what if scarcity is absolute, and supply is truly limited?† In that case, the competitive struggle may become a matter of life and death. It is not difficult to imagine the people of a small, poor country exposed to drought and, having ruined the soil, suffering from famine and falling into a brutal "state of nature."[20]

This is called *Malthusianism*, and it links resource scarcity to population size. Thomas Malthus was an eighteenth-century English cleric (and a

---

*The George W. Bush administration has pronounced its "right" to intervene with force in cases where governments are abusing the human rights of their citizens. Why not, then, a similar right with respect to the abuse of nature?
†Economists would argue that absolute scarcity cannot happen; see Chapter 3.

contemporary of Adam Smith, the Scottish economist), concerned to explain the large numbers of destitute people he saw in Britain's cities and towns.[21] Malthus believed that the poor had too many children and were so numerous because English law provided them with a certain amount of subsistence food. Malthus argued that this could not continue forever. Inevitably, population growth would outstrip the country's food production, and this would expose both the poor and the rich to starvation. There would then follow violent struggle over remaining supplies and the destruction of English society. His solution was to let the poor starve now, rather than in the future, in the belief that only hunger would lead them to have fewer children.

Malthus's analysis was flawed in many ways, not the least in that those who are poor tend to have more children so that the household has a better chance of survival.[22] During famines, moreover, food is usually available, but the poor often have no money with which to purchase it.[23] Finally, over the two centuries since Malthus first penned his treatise, changing technology has made it possible to produce ever-growing quantities of food and resources. Malthusianism nonetheless remains a staple of many discussions of global environmental politics. The Club of Rome's *Limits to Growth,* published in 1973, predicted that the world would begin to run out of minerals sometime during the twenty-first century.[24] Paul Erhlich's famous 1968 book *The Population Bomb* argued that "the battle to feed all of humanity is over." [25] Even today, Malthus lives on, with the argument that if there were fewer people in poor countries, struggles for food and resources would not take place. Because there are too many people in such places, war and death are inevitable.

But was Malthus actually wrong? Liberalism seems to argue thus.

Liberalism: A World of Desire. Most accounts of international relations begin with states, realism, and, as Hans Morgenthau put it, "the struggle for power and peace." [26] Liberalism is usually seen as a philosophy that values cooperation. After all, what can be more cooperative and peaceful than the exchange of goods in a market? It might seem odd, then, to argue that liberalism has a great deal in common with realism, and is, in ontological terms, almost identical. Liberalism is a political theory of individuals acting competitively in anarchic markets; realism is a political theory of states acting competitively in anarchic politics. Both theorize action in settings where there appear to be no governing authorities and few, if any, rules. But where Thomas Hobbes imagined a "state of nature" that could be overcome only by a sovereign imposing peace among men, Adam Smith believed that individual self-interest was enough to establish the power of the "invisible hand." [27] The uncoordinated actions of individuals would, through markets, result in an aggregate social benefit. But what would keep people from stealing instead of trucking and bartering? Smith thought that religion and fear of God would provide sufficient moral authority to keep social peace.[28] To put the argument another way, realism can be understood as the projection of a domestic *liberal* system, in which individuals compete in markets for goods and wealth, into an international system, in which states compete for resources and power.[29] Individuals compete with each other to acquire wealth; states compete with each other to acquire power.

A liberal philosophy tends to see people and states as competing for scarce environmental resources, but doing so in a more orderly way than does realism and Malthusianism. This is a form of cooperation, but it takes place at arm's length, so to speak, and the goal is accumulation rather than a fair distribution. Those who cannot participate in such exchange, lacking goods or money to trade, are out of luck. Thus, a liberal philosophy applied to global environmental politics tends to treat states as competitive participants—not unlike corporations—in markets they have established among themselves. This perspective on relations assumes that states possess or control "things" that can be exchanged or traded in a market setting, and the notion is not so difficult to envision in regard to oil, minerals, or agricultural commodities.* But how is it possible to truck and barter in things such as air or forests? To return to the example of our bi-national valley, one can't exchange dirty air for clean, yet both countries want clean air.

If we are to analyze such exchanges between states, we need to clarify three points. First, although one can often point to particular rivers, mountain ranges, plains, or coastlines to explain why a border is here and not there, the particular territorial parameters of any given state are, to a large degree, an accident of history and political economy, rather than a reflection of natural features or geological processes. Hence, as in our Chapter 1 scenario, all kinds of geographical, topographical, and ecological settings may be shared by two or more states, a phenomenon sometimes called *ecological interdependence.*[30] Second, borders do not provide effective protection against the damage that can be done to them by activities taking place *within* other states, a phenomenon that international law regards as a violation of sovereignty. As suggested

---

*Usually, of course, it is corporations who do the trading, not states.

earlier, one solution is to eliminate the problem through war, although this may have the unintended effect of causing greater damage than that resulting from the original activity. Third, international law is weak and there is, as yet, no effective sovereign to enforce it.[31] In the event of environmental damage inflicted upon a state by activities originating from outside its borders, these three points may be further complicated by uncertainty about sources.

For example, although scientists and authorities in Sweden are reasonably sure about the origins of the acid precipitation that wafts into their country from abroad, there is at least some uncertainty as to how much comes from each specific foreign source. Depending on wind direction, moreover, the pollution may blow in from the United Kingdom on one day and from Poland on another. With respect to greenhouse gases such as carbon dioxide, the uncertainties are even greater. These uncertainties are complicated by the fact that such specific insults as might arise will take time to appear and, even then, may not be attributable to specific sources. But even if one country were able to identify the source of an environmental insult originating from the territory of another, what could it do? Under the terms of the Stockholm Declaration of 1972, as noted above, states are forbidden from inflicting environmental damage on each other, because this is a violation of sovereignty. For the very same reason, one state cannot intervene in another—at least in theory, since we know of many examples to the contrary—to eliminate the source of the pollution.

Can nothing be done? As we saw with our valley, in a domestic (or municipal) setting, there are ways to deal with damage inflicted upon one's person or property by another person, agency, or corporation. Laws usually exist, or can be passed, that prohibit such damage or require the payment of fines and costs in the event that injury occurs. Enforcement of the law and collection of damages can be problematic, but the mechanics for addressing the problem are in place. Remember, however, that international law is weak. Alternatively, therefore, a government can try to change the behavior of an offending state by offering inducements, such as money, or by making trades. Again, there is a problem: under the principles of international trade, states (and other agents) engage in exchange of goods and resources, but there is, as yet, no international buying and selling of "bads," that is, damages or negative impacts on the environment.

Indeed, how would it be possible to trade or exchange bads? One does not literally buy and sell pollution; instead, one finds a proxy for the bad, something whose trade or sale will motivate the reduction or elimination of the bad. For example, states can find ways to "internalize" environmental insults. This involves changing the cost structure of the polluting activity so as to make it economically attractive to put a stop to it. The Coase theorem in economics proposes that, if a polluter is unwilling or unable to pay the costs of eliminating pollution ("polluter pays"), it may be economically efficient for those being affected to pay the costs ("polluted pays").[32] Although this may sound unfair to those on the receiving end of the pollution, it has happened that some offended countries have paid offending ones to reduce or eliminate such environmental damage. This point is discussed in further detail in Chapter 3.

A second, more competitive approach to internalizing an environmental insult is to create property rights and markets in the bad. Within a liberal economic framework, one reason that environmental damage is not controlled is that pollution "space" is free. There is no cost to polluting water and air, which means that water and air have no market value. By creating property rights in pollution and putting them up for sale, the true value of pollution space can be determined. Exchange will take place between those who have a surplus of such pollution space and those who need more than they have. This idea may seem more than a little bizarre—after all, who would want to buy pollution? And, yet, this is the basis for control of sulfur dioxide emissions in the United States, under the terms of the Clean Air Act of 1990.[33] This method of control is also likely to be applied to greenhouse gases, as stipulated under the Kyoto Protocol of the UN Framework Convention on Climate Change. In the market envisioned by the protocol's negotiators, states would be able to buy and sell a scarce resource: greenhouse gas emission permits. They might also compete with one another to build projects intended to generate such emission permits, as will be seen in Chapter 3.

The market of classical liberalism is usually considered the exemplar of cooperative action, although it is better seen as an arena of fierce and potentially antagonistic competition among buyers and sellers, modified by rules that set limits to noncivil behavior. But these limits are usually so internalized that we are not even aware of them. Outright violence, for example, is not acceptable behavior in a market setting, although certain forms of coercion often occur. For exchange to take place in a market, we must accept certain constraints. Exchange under duress does not constitute a market; partners enter into a deal with the expectation that things of equal value will be exchanged, with each partner in full possession of relevant information (a condition not always met in practice). Markets also tend to privilege those who have more money and information, which tends to place those who are poorer and less well informed at a decided disadvantage.

Viewing global environmental politics through the lens of competition in the market results in a very narrow view of both means and ends. Everything comes to have a price, and anything whose price does not generate market activity is not worth owning or saving. Those who have the wherewithal to set prices in markets for environmental goods or bads, through either supply or demand, can simply decide the game is not worth playing, and the benefits are not worth the costs. In that case, those without will suffer. We will return to markets and the environment in Chapter 3, and to the contradictions of pricing the environment via markets in subsequent chapters.

Cooperation

From a realist perspective, cooperation appears infrequent and sometimes threatening, but even those who seek power sometimes find it expedient to cooperate, to work together in pursuit of a shared interest. Realism posits a world made orderly through the exercise of power and threats, yet human interactions are, inevitably, governed by rules. Rules are generally based on some notion of exchange: You perform an action, and I won't/will perform another action. You behave and I won't punish you. You behave and I will reward you. In the case of punishment, the rule is a coercive one, based on differentials in power; in the case of reward, the rule is a cooperative one, based on exchange.* Both our interests are served through this trade: I am spared your bad behavior; you get to enjoy my reward.

Cooperation may also result from shared norms and objectives. Both of us believe it is a good idea to share. Not only will it contribute to peace between us, it is unfair that one of us should have more of something than he can possibly need or use. We work together, therefore, in pursuit of our shared goal, even though you or I might end up with less than we would have individually if each simply pursued his self-interest. But is cooperation a part of human nature? Hobbes did not think so, nor do most realists. Expressing the viewpoint of many liberals, Margaret Thatcher, for many years the prime minister of the United Kingdom, once said, "There is no such thing as society!" Whatever cooperation there might be was purely due to competitive self-interest and

---

*To be sure, power is not absent from the second example. Rewards and exchange often incorporate other forms of power, such as those discussed in Chapter 1.

nothing else. Other liberals think differently: exchange requires cooperation and a dense set of rules if it is to be maintained in an orderly fashion. Anarchists believe that cooperation is inherent in human nature, whereas social naturalists think that cooperation exists throughout nature.

Neoliberal Institutionalism: Rules and Rule.[*] From the pure power perspective, cooperation between states seems anomalous. Because cooperation means compromise, giving up valued things and even suffering a loss of power relative to others, no state would willingly cooperate (unless, as Hobbes argued, it is forced to by an international sovereign). But why is cooperation thought to be problematic? This is explained by something called the "collective action problem." [34] For both realists and liberals, this "problem" is rooted in notions of individual self-interest and competition. People (and states) are capable of reason and motivated primarily by self-interest. They will seek to maximize benefits and minimize losses, even at the expense of others. Cooperation usually means less-than-maximum benefits and greater-than-minimum losses, and incentives to cooperate are not always clear. Furthermore, for a group project to be successful, each participant must have an individual stake in the outcome, and each must be prepared to contribute part of the cost—in time, money, or whatever—toward the project's completion.

In large groups (more than fifteen or twenty people), each individual's contribution to the whole is likely to be small and, if one participant fails to contribute, the outcome is unlikely to be affected. In other words, it is possible to get the benefit without contributing to the costs and, because each participant recognizes this "fact," each will be inclined either to "free ride" and get the benefit of the project without paying anything or to "defect" and not be bound to the project at all. Therefore, continues this argument, collective action is difficult to explain because self-interested individuals ought to be loath to cooperate on anything that does not offer clear benefits. In the international realm, moreover, there is no authority to compel states to contribute to the costs of a joint project. Any such action that does succeed must do so because one or a few parties are willing to pay the costs of group action.[35]

Given this rather pessimistic outlook, it comes as something of a surprise to see just how much interstate cooperation actually takes place. Bilateral, multilateral, and international agreements are quite common—by some

[*]It is important to differentiate between "neoliberal" as the term is used here, and "neoliberalism" as it is applied to the global economic system and discussed in Chapter 3 in conjunction with globalization. The two are related but not the same. This point is discussed further below.

counts, in the tens of thousands—and the number of these having something to do with the environment are by now estimated to number more than one thousand.[36] In real life, actors are hardly as antagonistic toward each other as realism would have it. States, corporations, and individuals often share common interests and similar desires and are willing to collaborate on solving joint problems. An important dividing point between competitive and cooperative philosophies of liberalism is to be found in the two notions of "self-interest" and "public good." A competitive liberalism assumes that the desires and preferences of the individual or state have primacy; neoliberalism acknowledges that some interests are shared and that group action is often required to achieve goals that will not be forthcoming otherwise.

How, then, can we explain all the cooperation we see around us? As neoliberal institutionalism explains it, cooperation arises from the combination of two somewhat contrasting incentives. Straight exchange through markets, in pure pursuit of self-interest, can result in clear economic benefits for each of the parties involved. But the parties may have a broader sense of self-interest, one that includes norms, values, principles, and expectations (these being the central elements of a regime), and they may act on a conception of the public good that trades off among these different elements. For many reasons, we cannot know precisely how to behave in order to achieve our goals, and we must be willing to negotiate and bargain in order to find collective ways of getting to them. And we are likely to need quite elaborate rules for negotiations, bargaining, and behavior because complicated problems are not solved in a day. We may have to meet many times, and it is a good idea if we know the rules of the game so that there are neither arguments nor surprises when we do meet. The social arrangements established to deal with such collective issues are often called *international regimes,* and the philosophy that accounts for them is *neoliberal institutionalism.*[37] An international regime is, put simply, an institution whose members are states instead of people (see Chapters 1 and 5). A neoliberal institution is a social arrangement based on the principles of liberalism plus rules. Neoliberal institutionalism recognizes that cooperation is frequently necessary, even if it is sometimes difficult.

A good example of neoliberal institutionalism and its complexities can be seen in the long-standing international negotiations over global climate change, ongoing in one form or another since the mid-1980s.[38] Although the long-term effects and costs of global warming remain highly uncertain, they are likely to be quite unevenly distributed.[39] Rich countries responsible for much of the problem might not feel the effects strongly, and they can afford to adapt to many contingencies. Poor countries are more vulnerable in many respects and do not have the resources to adapt quite so readily. Because of the uncertainty, there are potential benefits from sharing the costs of controlling climate change. But participants might not realize any benefits, paying in more than they receive in return. The United States has concluded that it will be in this latter position and has, consequently, withdrawn from negotiations over the Kyoto Protocol. Despite the uncertainties, there is a general consensus among most of the world's countries that, whatever their individual costs or balance of interests, collective and cooperative action is necessary.

At the same time, however, competition and conflict persist within the negotiations. Conflict is normal, because governments would like to minimize their payments, and each government has different ideas about how to do this. Competition appears because states remain sovereign units, primarily concerned about their individual national interests. For instance, wealthier countries show considerable reluctance to pay costs now if the benefits will be realized in the distant future. Some, such as the United States, worry that large near-term expenditures will affect their economies; others are concerned that competitive advantages might accrue to other rich countries. There is, therefore, continual struggle over the language of the negotiations and the policy documents and actions that come out of them.

Cooperation, as conceived by neoliberal institutionalism, is infused with power considerations, even though these are not wholly acknowledged. In any collective project, not only are some participants likely to be wealthier or more powerful than others, they may also be able to control both knowledge and language. The less powerful can find it in their interest to go along with the demands of the more powerful, if only to get a piece of the action. They may be pressured to agree to terms and to act in ways that they would, in other circumstances, reject. But there is also power in numbers: if enough poor states are willing to support a provision disliked by the rich ones, the latter may find it necessary to compromise or even yield on certain issues. Institutions are designed to "freeze" the rules and to obscure a history of struggles; they become the "normal" way of doing things. As a result, power seems to vanish. Here is where competitive liberalism meets "cooperative" institutionalism, in other words.

Power nonetheless remains present in other, more subtle forms. For example, the discourse of climate change as presented in the Kyoto Protocol is premised on the privatization of the right to pollute, an approach that effectively turns the atmosphere into private property (as discussed in Chapter 3). States will be allowed to sell and trade carbon emission permits in markets in order to meet their commitments to control greenhouse gas emissions. Excluded from the agenda are alternative approaches to climate management, among which is one that would treat the atmosphere as a *global common property resource* (sometimes called the common heritage of mankind), governed under rules severely limiting greenhouse gas emissions by rich countries while permitting higher limits for poor ones. Recourse to privatization and markets signals the power of those states committed to a liberal economic system, even if this, in the long-term, turns out to be ineffective in controlling climate change.

Neoliberal institutionalism is not the end of environmental philosophies of cooperation. It is, nonetheless, the dominant environmental philosophy insofar as it has emerged out of both the diplomatic practices of states and the theoretical frameworks of international relations theory. Diplomacy, as practiced throughout the centuries, has always rested on a combination of coercion and cooperation and, during its heyday in the nineteenth and twentieth centuries, was based on a fairly elaborate set of rules. International relations theory examines the interactions of sovereign states seeking power and wealth and is liberal in its origins. But there are other environmental philosophies of cooperation that do not have this particular history and are not as strongly premised on power.

Anarchism and Ecoanarchism: Can't We All Just Get Along? Both *ecoanarchism* and *social naturalism* (discussed below) are based on cooperation, seeing it as a central and even "natural" element in human social organization. These philosophies envision cooperation within small communities, in which people know each other and the nature around them. Both philosophies are concerned about relationships within society, and between humans and nature. They are opposed to power exercised through the state and markets. But these two philosophies differ in that ecoanarchism is social and argues that humans must not look to nature for lessons in politics. Social naturalism, by contrast, is organic and draws on examples found in nature. Consequently, the two lead to rather different conclusions about how to deal with environmental problems and politics.

Ecoanarchism is a form of leftist anarchism whose best-known advocate is Murray Bookchin.* Anarchists argue that humans are inherently social,

---

*Bookchin calls his philosophy "social ecology," but I use this term later in the chapter to mean something different. I therefore use the term "ecoanarchism."

having evolved in small, interdependent groups (in other words, there never was a Hobbesian "state of nature"). They are, therefore, cooperative. It has been the historical and unjust exercise of power—of men over other men, of men over women, of men over nature—that has created hierarchy, the state, capital, oppression, and war. In an anarchist society, there is no central government—at most, a kind of confederal system of politics in which communities establish loose associations, or what Bookchin calls "municipal libertarianism." [40] Politics takes place through these self-governing, egalitarian, voluntary communes because it is only through the creation of units in which face-to-face interactions are both possible and necessary that the tendencies and practices associated with hierarchy and power can be eliminated.[*]

Bookchin argues that contemporary environmental problems are rooted in an irrational, anti-ecological society and that piecemeal reforms cannot address them. These problems originate in a hierarchical, class-ridden, competitive capitalist system, a system that nourishes a view of the natural world as a mere agglomeration of "resources" for human production and consumption, in which man is bound to dominate nature. Class is linked to the ownership of private property, which permits individuals to treat nature as they wish. Hierarchy is linked to the exercise of power in ways that maintain the position of private property. Finally, capitalism fragments the natural world into units that can be owned and exploited. All these characteristics are antithetical to the protection of nature.

Ecoanarchism is attentive to society as rooted in ecological praxis, or practice, without being a consequence of nature's material conditions (by contrast with social naturalism; see the section "Social Naturalism," below). As a philosophy, ecoanarchism is humanistic and leftist, and Bookchin, in particular, rejects much of the idealism and romanticism often found in anarchist theorizing. Proponents of ecoanarchism tend to view nature in its present form as a product of human action and transformation rather than something to be left alone in some primordial condition. Ecoanarchists believe that the state and "big" capital are inimical to the autonomy of humans and nature. The preservation of nature depends, as noted above, on the reorganization of society into small, relatively self-sufficient units in which altruism and mutual aid are practices of central importance. The impacts of such a political system are twofold. First, small social units will not engage in the

---

[*]This is, of course, a crude description of anarchism, which itself is riven by many different approaches. Bookchin's work provides ample evidence of this.

kind of globalized capitalism that distances production from consumption and externalizes pollution and other forms of environmental degradation.[41] There will be production and trade, but its limited scale will result in a much smaller environmental burden on nature. Second, people will be closer to nature and much more sensitive to the effects of their activities on the world around them. People will transform nature—Bookchin believes this is both necessary and good—but the result will be a rational, technically based culture, refined by spiritual and intellectual insights but not determined by them, and sensitive to and concerned about nonhuman nature.[42]

For some of his critics, Bookchin's ecoanarchism is too humanistic and political and does not give enough importance to the place of humans *in* nature. Its links to both Enlightenment rationality and socialism are evident in his commitment to a science-based understanding of nature and the possibilities of positive transformation of humans and nature together. Bookchin also highlights the struggle to achieve human freedom from state and capital through a form of class struggle, albeit one very different from traditional Marxism. And although he is conscious of the role of power in fostering domination, he seems to treat power as something that will, like Marx's fabled state, wither away in the fullness of time. This seems unlikely.

Social Naturalism: Peace Is in Our Nature. By contrast with ecoanarchism, social naturalism views culture and nature as bound together in a kind of social community. In this community, cooperation among humans and between humans and nature should be organic and harmonious, as it is in nature. Social naturalism's origins are to be found in nineteenth-century romantic views, and its proponents have adopted Prince Kropotkin's notion of mutual aid and cooperation between species as the basis for community. As Kropotkin argued, "It is evident that it would be quite contrary to all that we know of nature if men were an exception to so general a rule: if a creature so defenceless as man was at his beginnings should have found his protection and his way to progress, not in mutual support, like other animals, but in a reckless competition for personal advantages, with no regard to the interests of the species." [43]

But social naturalism goes further than this. John Clark[*] describes it as a philosophy that seeks to relate all phenomena to the larger direction of evolution and emergence in the universe as a whole, and that reaches its apex

---

[*]Clark also uses the term "social ecology," although in a different sense from Bookchin's and my usage below.

in some kind of organic harmony (along the lines of the lion lying down with the lamb). Social naturalism examines the course of "planetary evolution as a movement toward increasing complexity and diversity and the progressive emergence of value and views, and the realization of social and ecological possibilities as a holistic process, rather than merely as a mechanism of adaptation," as Darwin would have it. This evolution can be understood adequately, argues Clark, only by examining the interaction and mutual determination between species and species; between species and ecosystems; among species, ecosystem, and the earth as a whole; and by studying particular communities and ecosystems as complex and developing wholes. Such an examination, writes Clark, reveals that the progressive unfolding of the potentiality for freedom depends on the existence of symbiotic cooperation among beings at all levels.[44]

The goal of social naturalism is, therefore, the creation of a cooperative ecological society found to be rooted in the most basic levels of being. Clark uses the concept of "community" here in a very expansive sense, to include not only people but also animals, plants, ideas, language, history, ecosystems, and other elements of the material and social world. In this respect, social naturalism strongly resembles the worldviews and beliefs of indigenous groups, such as the Navajo (briefly summarized in Chapter 1), who see the world as being of an interconnected piece.[45] No one part of that world can be damaged or destroyed without the rest being affected negatively, but the value of each part to the whole is intrinsic rather than instrumental. More problematically, however, advocates of social naturalism also believe that human practices and institutions must be depoliticized. There can be no harmony so long as there are politics. Clark argues that legislative assemblies "must be purged of the competitive, agonistic, masculinist aspects that have often corrupted them. . . . [T]hey can fulfill their democratic promise only if they are an integral expression of a cooperative community that embodies in its institutions the love of humanity and nature." [46]

In Clark's view, capitalism could still comprise the economic base of such a community, notwithstanding its competitive and individualistic elements: "The dogmatic assertion that in an ecological society only one form of economic organization can exist . . . is incompatible with the affirmation of historical openness and social creativity and imagination that is basic to a social ecology." [47] Clark's vision is, therefore, one of the harmony of Eden before Eve offered Adam the apple, of society unpolluted by conflict, struggle, or politics, of a world in which the corruption of nature by humans has been redressed.

Curiously, perhaps, the roots of social naturalism are also to be found in G. W. F. Hegel's philosophy of the state.[48] In essence, Hegel argued for the organic nature and teleological destiny of the nation-state as an entity that is the "natural" collective community for those who are its members. Hegel believed that the state represented the highest and best form of human social and political organization and that human potential could be realized only through the state. For Clark, the "natural" community replaces the "natural" state, and biological potential replaces human potential. All else is very similar. We might doubt, however, that Clark's teleology is any more likely to come to fruition than has Hegel's.

The synthesis of the two can be found in *bioregionalism,* which posits that the "natural" political community is to be found in ecological units, such as the watershed. Inside these units, it is hoped, there can be a high degree of self-sufficiency, within limits imposed by nature.[49] Presumably, the individual is also organically rooted in and restricted to one's bioregion. Although the inhabitants of bioregions might share normative perspectives on the preservation of nature, it is an open question as to whether the people's staying within their own "natural" borders would breed harmony or distrust.[50]

Development

A third ontological approach to global environment rests on development. Philosophies of development are organized around the idea that economic and social improvements in the condition of people's everyday lives will result in greater public concern for and attention to the environment. To put the argument another way, if people are sufficiently well-off, they will be less exploitative of nature and more willing to pay to protect it. Development-based philosophies also hold that people who are better off will be happier and less likely to commit violence against each other or against nature. Again, we see here that certain assumptions about human nature, as well as about production and reproduction, are embedded in developmental philosophies. A distaste or dismissal of power is often evident in them, too. Whether these assumptions stand up under inspection is not entirely clear, as we shall see, although the frequent failure of developmental projects and practices suggests that they do not.[51]

The four philosophies discussed in this section are largely derived from the cooperative aspects of liberalism. *Sustainable growth* posits a constantly expanding world economy as the savior of the global environment. *Sustainable development* requires major modifications in modes of production and consumption, although it can hardly be said to eschew capitalism as the means through which environment and development can be reconciled. The *steady state economy* proposes that growth is not the same as development, and that we can be better off by consuming less but making things last longer. Finally, *radical redistribution* is hostile to capitalism as it is currently structured and argues that the rich must consume much less and the poor much more if environmental protection is to be achieved. All these philosophies require some degree of political intervention in the growth process so as to direct resources toward both production and the protection of nature. In order to better understand environmental philosophies of development, however, it is helpful to examine more closely the historical background to production and reproduction.[52]

Over the course of human history, the most common form of production and reproduction has been *subsistence.** People and societies produced what they needed to survive and reproduce, and there was little, if anything, left for trade (there was, of course, barter between groups, but not for the purposes of profit). The primary inputs into the subsistence mode were earth, water, air, seeds, animal and human labor, and perhaps some technology. Agriculture was a mode of production that was, for the most part, a closed cycle. Inputs of materials and human and natural energy roughly equaled outputs in food energy, nonedible products, and waste, with the last being returned to the soil. A subsistence mode is, absent a constant increase in inputs, a steady state system (with some seasonal and annual variation). Presumably, subsistence can be maintained over the long term, so long as there are no disasters or inappropriate uses of nature.†

About 7,000 to 10,000 years ago, as agriculture became widespread and centrally organized, the great Middle Eastern, Asian, and Far Eastern civilizations emerged. Social organization became more complex and sophisticated, and divisions of labor began to develop within societies. Many people farmed, some fought in wars, a few ruled. Surpluses beyond the subsistence needs of farmers were produced, and food and other goods could be transported from places of production to the places of consumption, such as cities.

---

*Actually, in terms of duration, the most common form of production during the hundreds of thousands of years of human experience was hunting and gathering; by this metric, agriculture is a relatively recent practice.
†In fact, few subsistence modes have been totally self-sufficient over the longer term. Transactions across societal boundaries were common, and subsistence-based communities sometimes unintentionally destroyed the ecosystems on which they were dependent for their survival.

The rulers of these first cities were able to extract food from surrounding villages and, eventually, to establish large-scale irrigation systems that expanded agricultural productivity far beyond what had been feasible before. Once large food surpluses were able to sustain cities, long-distance trade in valuable commodities began to develop. But these civilizations also began to confront the environmental limits to the engineering of nature, as irrigation of desert soils tended to concentrate salt in them (a common phenomenon, even today). In some cases, the ruination of agriculture by salination may have led to the collapse of these societies. Nonetheless, the environmental effects did not extend beyond the boundaries of the societies in which such agricultural technologies were applied. In global terms, human civilizations remained in the steady state.[53]

Only in the seventeenth and eighteenth centuries, when a second major social transition began in Europe, from agriculture to industrialism, was the steady state breached over a transcivilizational range. The growing reliance on machines and factories to produce goods and the use of coal as a fuel source was united with capitalism and colonialism, leading to the long-distance transport of raw materials, commodities, and finished goods. No longer did human societies return to nature the wastes they were producing, and in some cases the extraction of raw materials, both mineral and biological, left scars on the environment that were irreparable. During the nineteenth century, the profit incentive motivated a further search for those factors of production, such as minerals and commodities, unavailable or very costly in home countries. The result was imperialism, as the more powerful European countries moved overseas to occupy territories that became colonies, offering cheap resources and labor, and to integrate them into their home economies.[54] The growing ability to move materials, labor, technology, and goods around the world easily and cheaply meant that a growing number of societies were no longer wholly reliant on local or regional nature for production and survival. It also meant that resources could be turned into capital, and profits could be extracted systematically from combinations of labor, technology, and materials in new locations far away. Such *accumulation* of capital provided the financial basis for further investment in industrialization and infrastructure and for what later came to be called modernization and development but during the nineteenth century was described as "bringing enlightenment to nonwhite races." [55] Nevertheless, the native inhabitants of colonial lands were often stripped of their access to land and nature, pressed to work for the new regime, and denied the fruits of European civilization.

During the nineteenth century, the conversion of nature into capital focused primarily on those resources that could be exploited for the cost of extraction alone (mostly through labor). Outside of Europe, railroads and ports were built not for transportation but to move raw materials and commodities across the colonies and oceans. Thousand-year-old trees were essentially free for the taking, land being cheap and royalties minimal. They could be turned into lumber by those capitalists who could bring together the skills, tools, and transportation necessary to produce and market the finished product. That lumber was sold at considerable profit and the proceeds were used to pay for further extraction and conversion (as seen in Chapter 1).

Capital was thus accumulated from colonial territories by the industrialized countries, largely in the form of resources, and it was sent back only when there was an opportunity to extract additional returns through investment in infrastructure, plantations, or factories. Most of the people in what are today called developing countries were only weakly linked into the industrialized countries' imperial market systems, possessing neither the cash nor the skills to become full-fledged participants in them.* These individuals found themselves relying for their subsistence on those increasingly marginal resources that had not been appropriated and converted into private or state property.[56] And it is this marginalization that was, and continues to be, the basis for the poverty that afflicts so many billions of people in developing countries around the world.

In this scheme of things, protection of nature and the environment had no value, either monetary or normative—capitalists cut down and moved on, as necessary—and there were no incentives to limit exploitation of or damage to nature. In the longer term, the initial economic "kick" derived from the conversion of low-cost resources to money was, in combination with the factory system, turned into what appeared to be a self-reproducing system. Fewer and fewer people were tied directly to the land and more and more were tied into the market. Most had only their labor to sell, owning nothing else of value. Technology made it possible to produce more food from less land, and synthetic materials and new inventions made nature appear less and less important to production and reproduction. As we shall see, this now appears to be largely an illusion. But capitalist expansion—for this is what we

*The industrialized countries are often called the "North" and the developing countries, the "South." There are about 25 industrialized countries and some 165 developing countries. Some people use the term "Global South" to include not only the developing countries but also the poor in the industrialized countries.

are speaking of—depends on continuous growth and profit, and this requires more resources, expanding markets, and new technologies and products. In other words, keeping capitalism "alive," as it were, demands constant growth, and the products of that growth must be consumed. Consumption produces wastes, which must end up somewhere. That somewhere is the environment. This would seem to point to the necessity of lower levels of production and consumption in the industrialized countries, in particular, but that would undermine economic growth and it might kill the golden goose. What's the answer? Paradoxically, perhaps, some philosophies of development propose further economic growth. How this might be possible and what contradictions are involved will be seen below in the discussion of sustainable growth.

The basic premises of the dominant philosophies of development—that growth is not only necessary but good—are open to serious challenge. However development might be defined, the market by itself cannot generate either growth or sustainability. What is required is some degree of regulation of markets and social policy and, for this to be society- or worldwide, governments and other political actors must become involved.[57] Such intervention may be limited only to the setting of conditions under which growth can be encouraged—through, for example, foreign investment. Or intervention may be as extensive as state management of specific projects and policies, as we would expect to find under eco-Marxism. To be sure, there are alternative conceptions of development that depend less on growth and more on improvements in the quality of life—nutrition, access to clean water, adequate health care, education and rights for women, and other, similar goods—but there has been only limited success in achieving "development without growth." [58] Such improvements require greater commitment to social services by governments and there is only limited support for the direct state provision of such services nowadays.[59]

Sustainable Growth: More Is Better! According to one common argument, the poor, and especially those in the developing countries engaged in subsistence production, are dependent for their survival on access to the natural resources around them. Furthermore, they are in no position to use them carefully.[60] Even though the poor individually consume very small quantities of nature's goods, their aggregate number and demand is so great that the total exceeds supply by far. The result is damage to forests, soil, water, and species. By contrast, if we examine the industrialized countries, we find few people engaged in subsistence production. Most are deeply linked into capitalist markets, where they acquire the things they need to live and want to own. In the industrialized countries, we also find high levels of environmental protection, low rates of population growth, and where technically feasible and economically rational, substitution of capital for natural resources in the form of new materials and technology.

Proponents of sustainable growth therefore propose to reduce pressure on the environment, especially in the developing countries, by making everyone richer. In its simplest form, economic development has to do with growth in incomes, in the utilitarian view that the well off are most able not only to acquire basic needs but also to fulfill their preferences. As an additional benefit, growth in incomes ties people into markets and networks of exchange through which the true price of the environment can be established and nature can be protected. And those who are well-off, it is argued, are more willing to pay to protect nature (we will examine this argument more closely in Chapter 3).

Consequently, if the poor could earn the funds to participate in markets, they could purchase their basic needs from places where environmental impacts are more subject to management and impose less of a burden on the resources around them. For example, households that use locally produced wood or charcoal from over-exploited forests could instead purchase kerosene and burn it in more energy-efficient stoves.[61] Pressure on local wood resources would diminish and so would pollutants from fires. Everyone would benefit. Such changes in resource use would also offer new market opportunities to producers and suppliers. But many people cannot afford to buy either kerosene or the stoves in which to burn it, and importing fuels from countries where it is produced requires often-scarce foreign currency. What are people and countries to do? The answer is to be found in exports.

In order to import, it is necessary to export, and the more that is exported, the more money will be earned.* But what to export? That which can be produced most efficiently for the world market. The global economy is characterized by an international division of labor in which countries, based on their comparative advantage, specialize in the production of certain things. These things—raw materials, manufactured goods, and, in some cases, even technology and information—are exported primarily to industrialized countries, where most of the world's well-off consumers are to be

*Not that this is always the case: If exporting contributes to a global glut of something, the world price is liable to collapse, leading to a decline in foreign earnings. This is what has happened in most raw materials markets since the 1980s.

found. Such exports earn foreign currency. Ideally, the added value from such export and trade accrues to the producer of the goods, who uses the funds to finance further production to the benefit of the country in which the activity takes place.

For example, in the ideal case, a cocoa farmer would be able to use her export earnings to buy more land, plant more trees, and hire more workers. Alternatively, a factory owner could add more machines to the plant, employ more people, and produce larger numbers of shoes or can openers. When people are employed, they earn wages that can be used to buy manufactured goods, including imports. They rely less on local resources and move beyond subsistence. As they become richer, people will pay more attention to the aesthetic quality of their surroundings and be more able and willing to pay the costs of keeping air and water clean.[62] Whether or not such results follow from economic growth is an empirical question—and a rather controversial one, as will be seen in Chapter 3.[63]

At the beginning of the 1990s, Barber Conable, then president of the World Bank, put it thus: "If I were to characterize the past decade, the most remarkable thing was the generation of a global consensus that market forces and economic efficiency were the best way to achieve the kind of growth which is the best antidote to poverty." [64] A decade and a half later, emphasis on economic growth and the market is not only the conventional orthodoxy, it has even colonized less growth-oriented philosophies of development, as seen in the documents issuing from the World Summit on Sustainable Development, held in Johannesburg in September 2002.[65] Nevertheless, Conable's optimism seems less warranted today than ever before, for many reasons. First, notwithstanding the creation of the World Trade Organization in 1995, and the commitment to free trade it is thought to imply, developing countries are finding it increasingly difficult to export many of the products in which they hold a comparative advantage. The industrialized countries have been notably reluctant to open their markets to those goods from developing countries—mostly agricultural products—that would most help the latter toward greater economic growth.[66]

Second, and linked to the first point, even a decade of relatively high economic growth during the 1990s did not lead to the commitment of large amounts of new resources to protect the environment or to major reductions in poverty. Although the overall global level of poverty appears to have been reduced, as a result of growth in China and India, there also are more than 1 billion people living below the UN's poverty line ($1 a day of income; an estimated 3 billion live on less than $2 a day), a larger number than ever before in world history.[67]

Third, even though the industrialized countries are cleaner than they used to be, industrialization is not a clean process. The novels of Charles Dickens provide ample illustration of the dismal state of the English environment during the Industrial Revolution of the nineteenth century, and such conditions existed in many parts of Eastern Europe and Russia well into the 1990s. Those same conditions are being reproduced today in many developing countries, as marketization and industrialization proceed. And funds generated from export are frequently unavailable for social and environmental purposes, often having been earmarked for payment of interest on loans that will never be fully repaid.

Indeed, strategies of externally driven economic development have been notably unsuccessful, and industrialized country governments are less and less willing to loan or grant funds for either development or environmental protection in the developing countries. To a growing degree, corporations are being looked to as a source of finance for both. The notion of *ecological modernization,* which relies on production methods that avoid the creation of pollutants, is touted as one solution to this dilemma (see Chapter 3).[68] If corporations could be induced to finance clean industry in developing countries, not only would employment and wages increase but also nature would be protected. Clean industry looks, however, to be a *positional good,* one demanded only when consumers are sufficiently well-off to have met their other needs. If they are to become richer, countries might have to get much dirtier before they can get cleaner.[69] But this argument ignores the fact that health and welfare are closely tied to a clean environment, as the governments of the emerging welfare states of the nineteenth century well knew when they put public health systems into place.

Fourth, and in line with point three, it is often assumed that developing countries will be able to skip, or leapfrog, over the "dirtier" phases of industrialization, acquiring clean, environmentally friendly technologies either directly or via foreign investment. Taiwan, which has undergone successful capitalist industrialization and modernization, is now considered among the most polluted countries in the world. (To be fair, the regions around Bangkok, Thailand, and the rapidly growing coastal provinces of China are not very clean, either.) Taiwan has embarked on an ambitious effort to clean up its environment, but this is not proving to be an easy or inexpensive task. Moreover, it is not evident that those who hold the patents and property rights to advanced "clean" technologies will be very willing to provide them to those who want them without payment of licenses and royalties. In any case, such technologies are sure to be costly, and developing countries may gain more by relying on dirtier industrial systems, especially if this is a draw to foreign investors who want to reduce their production costs.

Fifth, while it is generally believed that the accumulation of wealth through industrialization and markets will benefit all the people living in a particular country, the neoclassical economist's dictum that "a rising tide lifts all ships" might not hold true for those boats with holes in their hulls. Although some money will trickle down, as factory workers spend their wages in the local economy, many more people will be searching for employment than there are jobs available. This "reserve army of labor" tends to depress wages, and those at the bottom of the pile will, in all likelihood, still remain too poor to move out of the slums or to invest in cleaning up their surroundings.* Added to this is the fact that industrialization and agricultural modernization tend to drive people off the land and into the cities—quite intentionally, it might be added—thereby adding to the pool of unemployed that is so attractive to foreign investment.[70] Again, national economic growth is not an entirely hopeless proposition, as shown by the experiences of various countries in Asia prior to and since 1997, but the same degree of growth has proved difficult to duplicate in other parts of the world. As in the Horatio Alger story, a few individuals will become wealthy, and these will be pointed to as evidence of the benefits of capitalism. Most people, however, will not achieve this degree of success and will remain relatively poor.

Sixth, most of the world's developing countries possess small domestic markets, in which consumers tend not to have a great deal of free cash or savings (liquidity). Thus, successful development usually depends on access to large, open markets elsewhere, into which commodities and manufactures can be exported. To no small degree, growth in China's economy has been dependent on relatively easy access to the American market. But as noted earlier, for many others major restrictions remain on imports into industrialized countries of those goods and commodities in which developing countries have a comparative advantage. Heavy dependence on rich countries for growth carries other risks, too. During the post–World War II period,

---

*If enough new industry is built to employ most of the reserve army of labor, wages will rise in response to a diminished supply. Corporations might then seek to produce in countries where wages are lower, as is currently happening with relocation from some Asian countries into the People's Republic of China.

recession in the United States always meant a drop in demand, a slowdown in growth, and domestic economic difficulties elsewhere in the world. Little has changed. In Asia, this problem has diminished somewhat as domestic markets grow, but in Africa and eastern Europe, where producers hope to export into the European Union, the problem of domestic liquidity and demand remains a serious obstacle to sustained growth.

Have globalization and the "Information Revolution" made a difference? Some pundits argue that an educated workforce can enable countries to tap into new global commodity chains and systems of knowledge production.[71] By providing less-costly information services to industrialized country consumers—in the form of software, data processing, customer service centers— the benefits of development can be obtained without the environmental costs of polluting industries. Some regions in the developing countries, such as that around Bangalore, India, have begun to specialize in information services and export, and India has become a major player in computer programming education and software development. But most of this is oriented toward export markets, and some 800 million Indians remain largely outside of the wonders of cyberspace and the global market. Although the substantial Indian middle class of 200 million is increasingly concerned about both environment and development, in a country as poor as India they are simply too few to provide the tax revenues required for environmental protection.

Finally, wealth may well be a greater problem for nature than is poverty. Rising rates of production and consumption in both rich and poor countries have led to growing quantities of all kinds of wastes, particularly in the European Union and the United States.[72] This phenomenon is especially visible, for example, in the life cycle of personal computers (PCs). PCs are usually assembled in poor countries, shipped to rich ones, where they are used for several years until they become "obsolete," and then shipped back to poor countries for extraction of the valuable metals found in electronic circuits. Each year in the United States, more than 100 million PCs are sold and more than 20 million become obsolete. Nowadays, the average life cycle of a PC is about three years, so more and more will need to be disposed of. Many end up in landfills; a few are resold or sent to users in developing countries; perhaps 10 to 15 percent are recycled.[73] The same can be said of cars, CD players, microwave ovens, and all the other paraphernalia of twenty-first-century life.

In summary, sustainable growth does foster development under some conditions, but the empirical evidence suggests that it is hardly a panacea for poverty or environmental damage. Those who are able to take advantage of opportunities in the market may succeed in becoming richer, although there is no guarantee of this. Those who begin with little or nothing usually find that they end up with little more or nothing. If global environmental protection depends on the poor countries of world becoming much richer than they are today, the prospects for nature are none too promising.

Sustainable Development: More Is Necessary but Not Sufficient. The dilemma of growing quantities of waste, as well as the damage resulting from development in both rich and poor countries, was already of considerable concern during the 1980s. The solution to the shortcomings of economic growth was a new and more environmentally friendly form of capitalism, called "sustainable development." The origins of this concept are to be found in the 1970s, and the term first appeared in print in a 1980 report issued by the International Union for the Conservation of Nature and Natural Resources (IUCN).[74] But sustainable development did not achieve full international recognition until 1987, when *Our Common Future*, the report prepared by the World Commission on Environment and Development (WCED; also known as the Brundtland Commission), was published. The WCED was first convened in 1983, under the auspices of the United Nations, and asked to conduct an inquiry into the condition and prospects of the global environment and the possibilities and constraints of economic development. The commission conducted hearings in many industrialized countries and developing countries (but not the United States, to which it was pointedly not invited). The task was an enormous one and in the finished product were to be found many interesting observations and proposals and not a few intractable contradictions. Such results are not surprising in a report written by a committee.

The fundamental charge to the WCED was to determine whether development and environmental protection involved compatible values and goals and, if not, how the two could be reconciled. The conflict between development and environmental protection had been central to the 1972 Stockholm Conference on the Human Environment and had remained a point of disagreement between industrialized countries and developing countries ever since. If development rested on growth in production and consumption, how could the environment be preserved? Even developing country governments argued that growth must come first, and the environment could be protected later. Northern governments, under some public pressure, thought that the environment must have precedence and that poverty could best be addressed through family planning and fewer people. According to *Our Common*

Future, however, there was no inherent contradiction between environment and development:

> Humanity has the ability to make development sustainable—to ensure that it meets the needs of the present without compromising the ability of future generations to meet their own needs. The concept of sustainable development does imply limits—not absolute limits but limitations imposed by the present state of technology and social organizations on environmental resources, and by the ability of the biosphere to absorb the effects of human activities.[75]

The WCED argued that the "needs" of the world's poor required priority in any effort to devise and implement sustainable development. But to achieve this objective, wrote the commission, growth was essential. By the end of the twenty-first century, it proposed, a five- to ten-fold increase in the size of the world's economy would be necessary to eliminate poverty and preserve the global environment. And only by increasing industrialized country demand for developing countries' goods, reasoned the WCED, would there follow a sufficient transfer of wealth from the former to enable the latter to deal with the problem of poverty and environmental damage. As we saw earlier, the assumption that such economic expansion could occur without serious damage to nature is a heroic one. This "solution" depends on a transition to postindustrial service and information-based economies everywhere, a doubtful proposition given the fact, for example, that even the last requires vast numbers of PCs and other electronic gadgets, all of which must be manufactured and, eventually, disposed of.

For the Brundtland Commission, sustainable development was clearly sustained economic growth, and this does not seem a likely answer to global environmental damage to those who have given thought to the issue. Many who studied the problem concluded that sustainable development was a concept riddled with problems and contradictions and that *Our Common Future* was a badly flawed document.[76] Growth was not sustainable, and no amount of rhetoric would make it so. Today there is little conceptual difference between sustainable development and sustainable growth. Nevertheless, what the concept of sustainable development does do is to provide a platform from which to speak. Insofar as it suggests some sort of international regime or arrangement based on a new global distribution of resources and technology, the concept of sustainability points to some redistribution of wealth from rich to poor (however distasteful this might be to some).

In other words, if developing countries are to embark on this new path of environmental friendliness and economic promise, they are going to require considerable assistance and capital from the developed ones. Much of this help will have to be provided either at no cost or under extremely favorable terms and will have to include access to state-of-the-art design, technology, and manufacturing. Such a prospect is not viewed with great favor by those corporations who would like to maximize the "rents" from their intellectual property rights, or by the industrialized countries who would have to hand over large sums of public revenues that are always in short supply. There is such a transfer mechanism to be found in the Kyoto Protocol, in the so-called Clean Development Mechanism.[77] This mechanism does not quite involve wholesale technology transfers without attached strings, but it goes some way toward this end through the proposed financing of environmentally friendly projects in developing countries via foreign investment by corporations. The expectation is that investors will find many attractive opportunities to deploy low-emission systems, and it is hoped, although not yet certain, that the financiers of such projects will be able to split the resulting greenhouse gas emission credits with host country governments. But these details are still largely to be worked out.

And none of this really defines sustainable development. Is it, as the Brundtland Commission proposed and others hope, environmentally friendly economic growth? Does it require a reduction in consumption in richer countries and an increase in consumption in the poorer ones? Does it mean a steady state economy where growth, as we know it, is tightly controlled or completely abolished? No one, so far, has been able to answer the question inasmuch as no one has actually been able to resolve the conceptual and political contradictions.[78] The result is that, for the most part, sustainable development is merely a mantra; a phrase that bears repeating because it has a calming effect. It seems to imply that, given human ingenuity, we can find our way out of what appears to be an almost intractable dilemma, and we can do so on a global scale.[79]

The Steady State Economy: More Is Death. An alternative to sustainable development is the steady state economy conceptualized by Herman Daly.[80] Daly argues that the fundamental error in our philosophies of development is that we rank flows of materials and money more highly than accumulations, or stocks. That is, we place more value on the number of automobiles and PCs that are manufactured, bought, and discarded each year than on their longevity, a function of how long a car or PC would operate if it were made and maintained to last and not intended to become rapidly obsolete. In a steady state system, the flows of materials in must be approximately equal to the flows out. Therefore, because we wish to minimize the outflows, which are waste, we need to find ways to minimize the inflows, which are raw materials, as well as to slow greatly the rate at which things break down or become obsolete. This means that consumer goods must last a long time, biological and physical resources must be minimally exploited, and organic wastes must be composted. If something is old or doesn't work any more, the materials of which it is made must be recycled.

An economic system based on flows but faced by limited consumer desire, such as the one in which we live, must find a way to increase the rate at which goods are bought and sold. Among other things, advertising and peer pressure are helpful in this regard. Cars could be (and have been) built to last a long time, but styles are constantly being changed. Consumers are urged to base their self-image on being seen driving the latest model and are warned that old cars may subject them to derision and embarrassment. These commercial appeals seem to have an effect: the American automotive market is increasingly dominated by "Urban Assault Vehicles" (also known as suburban utility vehicles, or SUVs) and trucks that consume large quantities of gasoline, seem prone to nasty accidents, and leave large carcasses when they die (they are twice as heavy as most passenger vehicles). The profit margins on SUVs are quite large, however, so automobile companies produce as many as they are able. In a micro-version of realism, in which states arm to protect themselves from other states, many drivers trade in their smaller cars for monstrous SUVs in order to protect their families.

In a steady state economy, by contrast, we would select cars based on fuel efficiency and durability rather than consumer taste or commercial indoctrination. Such a system would remain capitalist but it would be motivated by ends other than the relentless pursuit of profits and growth. For example, if people drove the contemporary equivalent of a 1968 Volvo Sedan or 1970 Volkswagen Beetle, both famously fuel efficient, inexpensive, and sturdy vehicles still seen on U.S. roads today, the effect on oil consumption, air pollution, and disposal would be significant. A fuel-efficient European auto can go more than sixty miles on a gallon of gasoline, and an electric-gasoline hybrid even farther; emissions could be reduced significantly through new drive system technologies; a well-built vehicle could last for thirty years or more if properly maintained; the metal parts and much of the rest of the body and chassis could be recycled, and so on. The flow of resources going into cars would be reduced considerably (a goal that could also be accomplished, albeit less effectively, through closed-cycle recycling, as is being tried in Europe; see Chapter 5).

A focus on durability and longevity would clearly have an effect on an economy as heavily dependent on the automobile as is that of the United States. Many fewer cars would be manufactured each year, the actual number being a function of the extended lifespan of the vehicle. Many fewer people would be employed as auto workers than is even now the case. The demand for auto parts would be reduced. Fewer dealerships would be needed. The economy might grow more slowly. People would have less money with which to buy a new car, which might cost more than those now on the market, but then, they would need to buy a new car less often. American dependence on foreign oil would decrease, which might have salutary effects on world politics.

Even under these circumstances, there would still be major environmental consequences from a steady state economy. Long-lived products would mean less-frequent innovation, and less-energy-efficient items might remain in service and continue to pollute for extended periods. Even were everyone to purchase a long-lived, low-emission hybrid or electric automobile, the environmental costs could still be severe if enough new cars took to the road. To avoid such results, the cost of owning and operating a vehicle through high licensing, fuel taxes, and road use fees would need to be made unattractive by comparison with the cost and ease of using public transportation. That would require major new investments in mass transit and even reconstruction of cities and suburbs to increase accessibility and reduce the need to travel long distances. None of this is impossible—it is done, to some degree, in western Europe—but it is politically unimaginable in those contemporary societies like the United States so dependent on the automobile.

What might a steady state world look like? What would constitute its economic units? In a book co-authored with John Cobb Jr., Daly proposed that the proper unit of "development" in his steady state world would be the nation-state.[81] Each country, according to Daly, ought to be prepared to live within the limits of its own natural endowments. He provides no real explanation for why the state, which is certainly among the most *unnatural* of humanity's social institutions, should be the basis for an attempt to implement a sustainable economy. Daly appears to believe that national self-sufficiency would eliminate conflict over resources and contribute to world peace. His conclusion is questionable; after all, the nationalization of the steady state would do nothing to reduce disparities between well-endowed and poorly endowed countries. Realism might well rear its ugly head even in Daly's world.

Redistribution: A Radical Solution? From the perspective of radical redistributionists, environmental degradation is caused primarily by excessive wealth and the injustices inherent in capitalism and the North-South divide. The rich—most but not all of whom are found in the industrialized countries— comprise some 20 percent of the world's population but consume about 80 percent of its resources, goods, and services. But these statistics hardly begin to illustrate the difference: a typical American consumes 80 to 100 times as much energy as a typical South Asian (see Chapter 3).[82] The waste streams that result spill across borders. They degrade both local and global environments and affect even those whose poverty is so great that they can barely survive and who produce hardly any wastes at all.[83] Despite the general optimism that growth can address this problem, all the consumption in the rich countries hardly seems to make a dent in the condition of the poor. The gap in wealth, between countries and within countries, continues to grow, and the global economic system seems only to exacerbate this difference.[84]

The answer to this dilemma is clear and rests largely on two propositions. First, the rich must cut back on consumption in order to reduce their unfair burden on the earth's resources and environment, and those at the bottom of the 80 percent must be able to consume more. Second, the industrialized countries must transfer massive amounts of capital and technology to the developing countries in order to enable the latter to grow economically, to be less dependent on the industrialized countries, and to skip over the stage of reliance on heavily polluting technologies. There are other elements to this position, but the general sense is that governments must find ways of accomplishing both objectives. Not the least of the problems facing attempts to put such a program in place is the fact that, more and more, capital and technology transfers are in the hands of private corporations rather than public authorities.

How does this position differ from sustainable growth or sustainable development? The key difference is to be found in who makes the rules and decisions. In the contemporary world, the revised golden rule dominates: "She who has the gold makes the rules." And this is apparent in the behavior of international financial institutions as well as international organizations and regimes. The modalities of the Clean Development Mechanism in the Kyoto

Protocol, discussed earlier, have been drawn up almost entirely at the behest of rich countries and corporations. And most developing country governments have found that they must go along to get along: if they do not agree to the rules, they will get none of the riches. As a result, the kinds of projects being proposed under the Clean Development Mechanism are as likely to further impoverish the poor as they are to protect nature.

In other words, nothing short of a world revolution or crisis of capitalism is likely to accomplish radical redistribution. The underpinnings of such change would have to be rooted in an ethical re-evaluation of the injustice of the rich-poor gap. As we have seen, the most common solution offered is to allow the rich to retain their wealth while helping to increase the incomes of the poor. If one has doubts that such an approach is possible, let alone practical, the prospects for both the poor and the global environment are dismal.

Against Domination: Resistance Is Fertile!

Inherent in the three ontological categories we have examined so far is a matter largely downplayed in all of them: power. Not power in the traditional military sense, or even as relative wealth, but structural power, that is, the power embedded in social relations and social institutions, in the ways that they are organized and in the ways that they are reproduced. Power in all its forms normally serves to maintain the status quo or to provide various forms of advantage to some as opposed to others. Therefore, it tends to increase inequities and injustices at the expense of others, who may have little or no ability to resist. The result is domination. Although most people regard power in a negative sense, as a tool of manipulation and self-interest, power can also be regarded in a positive light, as something that makes political action possible.[85]

As we saw in Chapter 1, there are at least four useful conceptions of power. The first is also the most common: the ability and capacity to get people to do something they would not otherwise do, through persuasion, coercion, or force. The second conception rests on authority, that is, the right to define which practices are acceptable and which are not. Those with authority have the right to set agendas in meetings, to limit discussions in public forums, or to forbid certain behaviors. Those lacking authority are expected to behave as the authorities have directed. A third dimension of power is visible in what we can think of as the normalization of practices and beliefs. Thus, the many ways in which men exercise power over women through patriarchy have historically been considered "natural" and have hardly been questioned.

Finally, a fourth conception of power is to be found in Michel Foucault's notions of discipline, governmentality, and biopolitics, in which power is inherent in social institutions, rules, and practices and serves to constitute both individuals and society.

As a way of seeing some of the subtleties of power, consider again the automobile. American society is structured in such a way that car ownership becomes essential not only to economic growth but also to daily life and even individual identity. Through "normal" use, the practices of owning and driving a car are variable only with respect to model and style, with these latter two elements being deployed to encourage people to identify with particular makes. For most people living outside of large city centers, there are few alternatives to owning and using a car. Mass transit is often quite limited; bicycles and scooters are not as safe or comfortable as cars; neighborhoods are not built to facilitate nearby work or shopping and distances are too great for easy walking. Attempts to change these practices and structures, which presently benefit some interests over others, are treated not only as impossible or absurd, because of the embeddedness of power, but also as a threat to social organization and the domination exercised by some over others. Consider how cars became linked to freedom and security after the attacks on New York and Washington, D.C., in September 2001; consider how the American need for oil from the Persian Gulf is based largely on automobiles; consider how war rather than conservation or restructuring becomes the answer to this "need." Even "normal" practices pose dangers, but changing them presents greater dangers.

Indeed, the very structure of language and the way in which it is used can be understood as a form of power, albeit one that can be challenged in productive ways. Reflect on the term "resource," as it has been used in this chapter. A "resource" is something that is deemed to have value for human beings, in that it can be converted from some initial form into a final product. When we speak of "natural resources," we treat all of nature as either having value or being valueless. That which has no value will, consequently, become invisible, like air, and ignored (unless, of course, air pollution begins to threaten our survival). Through this same language of resources, it is only when something can be turned into a marketable product with a price that it does acquire value. Then it is noticed, but by then the resource can also be appropriated and turned into private property (think of oxygen bars in Los Angeles, where one can go to purchase clean air). Hence, a forest that is used as a common property resource by a specific group is regarded under some legal systems as having no "owner." [86] Unless it becomes state land or is privatized, the forest has no market value and is regarded as "wasteland" (see Chapter 5). Denying the legitimacy of common use, especially by the poor, thereby makes the forest vanish and permits authorities to confiscate what is essential to the production and reproduction of the user group. Power and domination, in other words, may be exercised in very subtle ways.

Several environmental philosophies—ecosocialism and eco-Marxism, ecofeminism, ecocentrism (or "deep ecology"), and environmental governmentality—are organized around notions of power and, more specifically, in opposition to domination. Generally speaking, these approaches have their origins in Marxist theory, although they arrive, for the most part, at radically different conclusions. All these philosophies posit relations of inequality between two or more groups of people or beings. They view this inequality not as a simple matter of differences in individual wealth or other attributes but as structural and normalized. In these philosophies, therefore, the exploitation and degradation of nature is understood to occur because those in power legitimate and reproduce both their dominant positions and the social organization that authorizes their rule through normalized and naturalized actions and beliefs. Moreover, these actions and beliefs are broadly accepted as both legitimate and necessary to the survival of the social order. Domination, in this view, cannot be eliminated by more moderate, work-within-the-system means of reform, such as political participation, or even radical redistribution. What is required is wholesale social change. That is a tall order for any political philosophy.

Ecosocialism and Eco-Marxism: Species of the World, Unite! However they are conceived, what sustainable development and even the steady state will not do is to change basic social relations and class structures inherent in a global capitalist economy. The rich will remain rich; the poor, it is to be hoped, will become somewhat richer, but certainly not so much as to pose an effective challenge to the rich. Indeed, according to neo-Marxist analyses, capitalism requires such economic inequality and cannot survive without it. Societies are composed of contending classes—capitalist, worker, bourgeoisie—who struggle for the opportunity to organize modes and relations of production in their particular interests. This is the engine of capitalism.[87]

Essentially, ecosocialists and eco-Marxists argue that the domination of nature by the capitalist class is parallel to its domination of labor. Both forms of domination emerge out of the material base of society or, as David Pepper puts it, "Material production and the exchange of products constitute the basis of all society." [88] Capitalists constantly seek cheaper raw materials and impose wastes onto nature; therefore, capitalism is an inherently anti-ecological and anti-nature system. It encourages greater consumption to maintain profit rates and facilitates the "creative destruction" of old capital and nature.[89] Capitalism also alienates humans from their selves, the things they produce, and nature. It commodifies everything (what is called "commodity fetishism") and drains social meaning from all things. Finally, capitalism creates a "false consciousness" in that things as they are perceived to be is how things must be, now and always. To protect nature, we must exploit it: that is how it has been, and how it will be.*

Classical Marxism—that is, the historical materialism of Karl Marx— saw capitalism as a necessary step on the road to an eventual workers' revolution, under which the fruits of development and technology would be equitably available to all. But although capitalism might disappear, economic growth would not. An ever-expanding industrial product was central to Marxism, albeit not driven by consumer desires but by some conception of the public good. "From each according to his abilities, to each according to his needs." Liberation would come, according to Marx, when each individual's basic needs were provided for. Each person would spend part of the day working, and the rest would be available for culture, study, sports, whatever. Marx and his followers were not very concerned about nature and had few illusions about it: resources were there for the taking and provided necessary inputs into the process of industrialization and production. However else "really existing" socialist countries such as the former Soviet Union failed to hew to Marxist principles, they hardly deviated from Marx's attitude toward nature. Resources were treated as a free input to production, and pollution was seen as inevitable and unavoidable when industrial growth was at stake.[90] †

According to ecosocialism and eco-Marxism, consequently, the way in which production takes place—the *mode of production*—matters for the environment because producing things is one way in which human beings interact with nature. More to the point, in making things, we change the substance of nature into socially useful forms, via the forces of production

---

*This last process is often called "naturalization." Treatment of the market as a "natural" institution is an example of this last phenomenon.
†To be entirely fair, during the early decades of industrial capitalism and well into the twentieth century, smoke-spewing factories were an object of pride and admiration in most industrial towns and cities.

(labor), the instruments of production (technology), and the means of production (raw materials). The social organization through which things are produced—the *relations of production*—are the most critical part of the mode of production. These relations include those political and legal arrangements that sustain social organization, particular forms of social consciousness and specific forms of domination and control. Social change is possible, therefore, only if the material base of society is changed, a process that will lead to the restructuring of its social organization. The protection of nature requires nothing less.

The implications of this analysis for capitalist societies goes rather against the grain of philosophies of both cooperation and development. Whereas the proponents of those two ontologies see the existing global political economy as capable of being reformed—although the specifics of such a program remain somewhat cloudy—ecosocialists and eco-Marxists regard capitalism as fundamentally unredeemable. What, then, is to be done? The ecosocialist program relies heavily on revolutionary action. At the global level, and without a world government, this becomes an awesomely difficult proposition. It is a pretty forbidding one at the national level, too. As David Pepper has put it, "Trying to smash capitalism violently will probably not work while capitalists control the state, so the state must be taken and liberated in some way for the service of all." [91]

Consequently, Pepper tends to favor more localized, less complex and ambitious collective efforts, to wit,

> It follows that the most potentially fruitful kinds of action are those which emphasise people's collective power as producers, which directly involve local communities (particularly urban) and increase democracy, which enlist the labour movement and which are aimed particularly at economic life. . . . But to be more positive and dialectical, perhaps they ["new" approaches to production and social organization] represent part of that order whom the existing economic and social arrangements do not satisfy and which will eventually, by struggle with the existing order, produce a new socialist synthesis. [92]

The contradiction here, as with all Marxist and socialist theories, is that the state, which is part of the problem, also becomes central to the establishment of the new system. Marx believed that the state would, eventually, "wither away"; today's ecosocialists are considerably less sanguine about this prospect. And can small-scale localized changes in production modes generate the transformation in relations of production necessary to give rise to this "new socialist synthesis" and global social change? This is a question to which we will return in Chapter 4.

Ecofeminism: Women and Nature, Resist Oppression and Patriarchy!
There is no single version of ecofeminism; if asked, probably all feminists, whatever their political or philosophical position, would admit to being ecologists.[93] Paradoxically, perhaps, this positioning arises out of the ways in which patriarchy and the common dichotomies inherent in modernism juxtapose those with power against those who are without it. Women are often characterized essentially in terms of their "links" or "likeness" to nature—these having to do with biology, temperament, patterns of thought and reasoning, and so on—with the result that they are treated by men with as little regard as men treat nature. Many ecofeminists eschew Marxism in their analyses, although it is safe to say that almost all are leftist or liberal in their philosophical orientation. Hence, there are those who believe in the possibilities of liberal reform, whereas others call for more radical redistribution of resources to women, in particular, as a means of achieving development and protecting the environment.[94] But the recognition that men treat both women and nature badly points toward a structural problem, rather than one that can be addressed through modification of individual male attitudes and behaviors. For that reason, it is useful to look at the ways in which some ecofeminists, such as Ariel Salleh, apply Marxist reasoning to their analyses.[95]

Whether abuse of women or nature came first is unclear and probably unimportant, but for all ecofeminists the domination of women and nature are inextricably linked. As Salleh puts the point: "Feminine suffering is universal because wrong done to women and its ongoing denial fuel the psychosexual abuse of all Others—races, children, animals, plants, rocks, water, and air." [96] From the structural perspective, the women-nature linkage is not only characteristic of patriarchy and rationalism, which, together, have generated capitalism, it is also central to the maintenance of contemporary social organization in which men and capital hold power. In other words, reform is not enough; as with ecosocialism and eco-Marxism, change must be foundational and must begin with the overturning of patriarchy.

Salleh's version of this structuralist perspective is an intriguing one, although she tends, perhaps, to present women's suffering under patriarchy as identical to the suffering of nature under the same arrangements. Thus, she argues that women's relationship to nature is not an ontological one that claims women to be, somehow, more sensitive to life and nature for biological reasons—which is a position adopted by some ecofeminists. But Salleh nonetheless does argue that "women North and South tend to arrive quite readily at ecofeminist insights as a result of the conditions they live in and the physical work they do." Indeed, according to Salleh, women's labor is designed to protect life, unlike the work of men, and "Women's ecological commitment is fed by an intimate biocentric understanding of how people's survival links to the future of the planet at large." [97] This "intimate biocentric understanding" is not biological, however; it grows out of the very practices of production and reproduction in which women are constantly engaged. Their very experience of oppression, like that of both the working class and nature (were it to have such awareness), provides women with the insights necessary to resist that oppression.

How did such a state of affairs come about? According to Salleh's analysis, the contemporary ecological crisis can be ascribed directly to a "Eurocentric capitalist patriarchal culture built on the domination of nature and the domination of Women 'as nature.' " This grows out of the Enlightenment project of applying rationalism to the management of nature (a theme prefigured in Hobbes's *Leviathan*). "In the West, feminine and other abject bodies are split off and positioned as dirt, Nature, resource, colonised by masculine energies and sublimated through Economics, Science and the Law." Therefore, Salleh continues, "An ecofeminist response to ecological breakdown means finding ways of meeting human needs that do not further the domination of instrumental rationality." For Salleh, ecofeminism offers a comprehensive progressive approach to the ecological crisis: "Ecofeminist politics is a feminism in as much as it offers an uncompromising critique of capitalist patriarchal culture from a womanist perspective; it is a socialism because it honors the wretched of the earth; it is an ecology because it reintegrates humanity with nature; it is a postcolonial discourse because it focuses on deconstructing Eurocentric domination." [98]

Given the overwhelming dominance of and domination by structure in her analysis—manifested most clearly in the omnipresence of patriarchy—what is not entirely clear is how Salleh proposes to attack those structures and destroy them. This is a problem we find with many critiques of domination: they advocate some kind of change in consciousness, hoping that this will lead to collective action (in this, they are not so different from liberal ecologists). Collective action will overwhelm the old structures with its political logic, and the new system can be put in place. But of what kind of action are we speaking? If revolution is not a possibility, and reform has no impact on structure, can small but cumulative changes in the material base eventually result in wholesale structural change? And what are the implications of this analysis for global environmental politics? We will return shortly to these questions.

Ecocentrism: Treat Nature as Thyself. Ecocentrism is often called "deep ecology." Ecocentrists view capitalism (and its industrial aspects) as a system that knows no limits and has no respect for nature. Without nature, humans cannot survive; by exploiting nature as they do, humans may destroy both nature and themselves. Many ecocentrists are also advocates of "wilderness" and "wildness" (Henry David Thoreau: "In wildness is the preservation of the world").[99] These are the only places that are truly natural, and their elimination would result in both biological and spiritual impoverishment. A revolution is, therefore, necessary to alter this order of things, a revolution that establishes harmony between people and the natural world, or even gives nature an advantage over people, one in which humans get no more than their fair share of the world's physical resources and biological product.

Most deep ecologists eschew any philosophical relationship to Marxism. Indeed, many lean toward a Social Darwinian ecologism—a view of "nature red in tooth and claw" related to realism—or Malthusianism, on the one hand, or some kind of theologically based spirituality, on the other. Nonetheless, inherent in their beliefs is the need to overcome the "class difference" between humans and nature. If one were to replace "humans" with "capitalists" and "nature" with "labor" in this schema, it would become evident that deep ecology is not entirely disconnected from certain Marxist propositions. It is interesting, therefore, that leftist tendencies tend to be strongly disavowed by proponents of deep ecology.[100]

Why, then, the similarities? Ecocentrism, like some Marxian philosophies, is also a form of romanticism that idealizes nature and regards it as a source of eternal truth and beauty. Ecocentrists seek to overturn the domination exercised by humans over nature, even as they search for transcendental sources of authority to legitimate such changes. Often, such authority is found in either science or spirituality. In the former case, ecology is called upon not only to describe what might happen should human practices remain the same but also as the basis for imposing order on those changes that take place.[101] In the latter instance, a sort of spiritual essence of Nature plays the same role. In both, ecocentrists claim that what should be done must be done, or humanity will inevitably suffer the consequences.

Humanity and nature might suffer from our actions, or they might not, but what we see here is an attempt to institute one form of domination to counter another: domination by an external authority. The command "Repent or die!" is a powerful one, especially if it comes from a source over which humans have no control. Moreover, there is a certain deterministic quality to such warnings: fail to listen and perish; do as you are told and flourish. The Marxist conception of history has a similar teleological quality to it, as do all Western religions and liberalism. All demand certain kinds of prescribed behaviors as the price of salvation, and all prophesy doom should those prescriptions be violated. In other words, ecocentrism proposes replacing human domination with natural domination (whatever that might mean in practice), in order to overturn the existing class system. In this instance, a class coalition between nature and bourgeois humans can overturn what is, in effect, capitalist domination, replacing it with human-nature harmony in which the full potential of both can be realized.

Governmentality and Biopolitics: Bringing Power Back In? Those environmental philosophies that resist domination are linked to power relations among humans, and between humans and nature. As we saw earlier in this chapter and in Chapter 1, there is more than one dimension of power, which is not something that can be simply accumulated or distributed, as are money or artifacts or weapons. Nevertheless, all of the "antidomination" philosophies discussed so far seek to oppose and resist power in its first dimension—usually the power of capital and the state—in the view that the ideal society is one in which power is evenly and fairly distributed or from which it has been banished. If the unjust exercise of power could be eliminated, goes the implicit argument, not only would intraspecific domination cease (among people), so would interspecific domination (between people and nature).

There is, however, a problem with this argument: it denatures or dismisses politics, so to speak. If politics is fundamentally about power, rather than the distribution of resources, equalizing or eliminating power would have the effect of doing away with politics. In such a society, everyone would have to hold the same beliefs and values, and all decisions would have already been made. It would be either a harmonious society or a totalitarian one. It might be both. It is useful, therefore, to examine one final approach to the problem of power, domination, and the environment, based on the work of

Michel Foucault.[102] Although Foucault said many relevant things about both power and nature separately, he never wrote explicitly about the environment. He did, however, write about power and domination and, in particular, the propensity of some men to manage both other men and things so as to order them. He called this practice "governmentality." [103] Government is not the same as politics; it is better understood as those practices that constitute governing of "a sort of complex of men and things" within a state. As Foucault explained it, "The things with which in this sense government is to be concerned are in fact men, but men in their relations, their links, their imbrication with those other things which are wealth, resources, means of subsistence, the territory with its specific qualities, climate, irrigation, fertility, etc.; lastly, men in their relations to that other kind of things, accidents and misfortunes such as famine, epidemics, death, etc." [104]

In Foucault's analysis, power is not merely something that some men wield over others, it is also something that "induces pleasure, forms knowledge, produces discourse." [105] Power flows between people, it constitutes them, it makes them who they are, and it influences how they behave. This is the case even when power is not visible as influence, coercion, or force. Domination becomes not the exercise of power by some people over others and nature but is the result of people acting as they have been produced by power circulating through what Foucault called the "capillaries" of society.

In effect, governmentality becomes a way of managing those things that are seen to threaten the welfare of that which is governed. This is accomplished through what Foucault called biopolitics. According to Mitchell Dean, a scholar of Foucault and governmentality, biopolitics "is concerned with matters of life and death, with birth and propagation, with health and illness, both physical and mental, and with the processes that sustain or retard the optimization of the life of a population." [106] It is about management of the biological functions and social practices of homogeneous populations. Dean goes on to say:

> Bio-politics must then also concern the social, cultural, environmental, economic and geographic conditions under which humans live, procreate, become ill, maintain health or become healthy, and die. From this perspective bio-politics is concerned with the family, with housing, living and working conditions, with what we call "lifestyle," with public health issues, patterns of migration, levels of economic growth and the standards of living. It is concerned with the bio-sphere in which humans dwell.[107]

To put this another way, all those institutions and practices concerned with exploiting, managing, and protecting the environment, including international environmental regimes and regulated markets, are expressions of biopolitics. They are all concerned with the management of human behavior and populations so as to maintain the material base of life, that is, the global environment.

Unlike the other philosophies discussed in this section, environmental governmentality and biopolitics take power as an essential part of human social structures and relations. Power cannot be eliminated; at best, it can help to produce effects that are less dominating, less oppressive, less manipulative, and more protective of both human welfare and nature. But it does not take much to move from arrangements in which power is productive to those in which power is oppressive: one could easily imagine a system of global environmental governmentality in which nature is protected but each individual's every action is subject to surveillance, discipline, and punishment. That might be too high a price to pay to achieve a cleaner environment.[108]

Thinking Ahead

Governmentality and biopolitics are not simply intellectual phenomena, inasmuch as their discipline is backed by material goods and forces. Those who are dominated usually have some material interest in the structure within which power is being exercised. What this means is that resistance is not enough, consciousness-raising is not enough, and libertarian municipalism is not enough to protect the environment. Most of all, these arguments suggest that "global environmental politics" must be "global" in a way other than how it is commonly understood. The practice of global environmental politics must be centered elsewhere than the state system, international conferences, agencies, bureaucracies, and centers of corporate capital, all of which are part of the processing of governmentality. In the chapters to come, we shall look more closely at certain forms of global environmental governmentality and inquire whether there isn't anything better to protect nature and the global environment. Before doing that, however, let us take a closer look at capitalism and nature, in Chapter 3.

For Further Reading

Bernstein, Steven. *The Compromise of Liberal Environmentalism.* New York: Columbia University Press, 2001.

Clark, Mary E. *Ariadne's Thread: The Search for New Modes of Thinking.* New York: St. Martin's Press, 1989.

Daly, Herman E. *Steady-State Economics.* 2d ed. Washington, D.C.: Island Press, 1991.

Dryzek, John S. *The Politics of the Earth: Environmental Discourses.* Oxford: Oxford University Press, 1997.

Gleditsch, Nils Petter, ed. *Conflict and the Environment.* Dordrecht: Kluwer, 1997.

Harvey, David. *Justice, Nature, and the Geography of Difference.* Oxford: Blackwell, 1996.

Klare, Michael. *Resource Wars: The New Landscape of Global Conflict.* New York: Metropolitan Books, 2001.

Litfin, Karen D., ed. *The Greening of Sovereignty in World Politics.* Cambridge: MIT Press, 1998.

Luke, Timothy W. *Capitalism, Democracy, and Ecology: Departing from Marx.* Urbana: University of Illinois Press, 1999.

Meyer, John. *Political Nature: Environmentalism and the Interpretation of Western Thought.* Cambridge: MIT Press, 2001.

Millbrath, Lester. *Envisioning a Sustainable Society: Learning Our Way Out.* Albany: State University of New York Press, 1989.

Pepper, David. *Eco-socialism: From Deep Ecology to Social Justice.* London: Routledge, 1993.

Redclift, Michael, and Ted Benton, eds. *Social Theory and the Global Environment.* London: Routledge, 1994.

Ross, Eric B. *The Malthus Factor: Poverty, Politics, and Population in Capitalist Development.* London: Zed Books, 1998.

Sachs, Wolfgang, ed. *The Development Dictionary.* London: Zed Books, 1992.

Salleh, Ariel. *Ecofeminism as Politics: Nature, Marx, and the Postmodern.* London: Zed Books, 1997.

Sandilands, Catriona. *The Good-Natured Feminist: Ecofeminism and the Quest for Democracy.* Minneapolis: University of Minnesota Press, 1999.

Sprout, Harold, and Margaret Sprout. *The Ecological Perspective on Human Affairs.* Princeton, N.J.: Princeton University Press, 1965.

World Commission on Environment and Development. *Our Common Future.* Oxford: Oxford University Press, 1987.

3 | Capitalism, Globalization, and the Environment

Effluents and Affluence

In Chapter 2 we examined contrasting, and often conflicting, ontological and philosophical perspectives on global environmental problems and politics. In this chapter we will focus on capitalism and its role in environmental degradation. Free market capitalism is really a mixture of several ontological and philosophical perspectives, combining competitive, cooperative, and developmental elements in a social institution of increasingly global scope. Although capitalism has long been internationalized—perhaps as long ago as the 1500s—it is only over the past couple of decades that it has become manifest in what is often called globalization. As we shall see, the links between globalization and global environmental degradation are sufficiently compelling to suggest that the two are causally related.*

We also look here at the politics and political economy associated with global capitalism. The market system does not exist as a "natural" institution, self-organizing and self-realized, no matter what its most ardent believers claim. It is a thoroughly human creation, with rules, norms, and laws that are by no means neutral in either application or consequence. Environmental damage does not simply happen; it is a result of the ways in which

---

*It is often observed that socialism, as it existed in the old Soviet Union and other communist countries, was much harder on nature and that capitalism does an excellent job of protecting the environment by comparison. This is true but is no reason to treat capitalism as without fault or impact.

production and consumption are organized under capitalism and the ways in which those patterns do or do not take into account the damage being caused. That environmental degradation is not a natural phenomenon but one resulting from these patterns suggests that it might be possible to organize capitalism in ways that are more environmentally friendly.

Yet it is not at all clear that an environmentally friendly capitalism would resemble very much the arrangements that are currently in place. If we recall the tensions inherent in the developmental philosophies discussed in Chapter 2, some forms of capitalism might not be characterized by "free" markets as we understand them today. "Free markets" are, at the extreme, without regulations imposed by governments or other authorities. But all markets are based on some rules, including those guaranteeing property rights. The term "free" is usually used to mean free of rules that impose social costs and taxes. Environmentally friendly markets could be bound up in rules and regulations that were quite restrictive or be based on an ethical system that regarded high rates of consumption as undesirable.

In the first section of this chapter, we examine the relationship between resources and markets in a capitalist system. The primary objective of production in contemporary capitalism is the *accumulation* of capital (or money) that can either be reinvested in the production process or be distributed to its owners (capitalists). The capitalist seeks to minimize the costs of inputs into the process so as to maximize the difference between the cost of production and the price of the good in the market, a difference that is called "profit." According to neoclassical economics, which is free market capitalism's analytical and explanatory framework, environmental problems occur if resource inputs are underpriced and their real value is understated relative to other input costs. The solution to this conundrum is to put a price on everything, including the environment.

In the second section, we turn to the *consumption* side of the equation (which we shall examine again in later chapters). Under a system of free market capitalism, for goods to sell there must be buyers. As we saw in Chapter 2, neoclassical economists generally assume that goods are "scarce," which is to say that they are not so plentiful as to have no price. But what happens if there are more goods than there are buyers willing to consume? Then, both profits and production may collapse, and accumulation will stop. To avoid this dilemma, people are encouraged to consume. But consumption generates waste, and waste hurts the environment. The answer is then to include the costs of environmental damage in the price of the product. But, if that price becomes too high, consumers will stop buying. It is difficult to find a way out of this dilemma.

In the third section of the chapter, we investigate *commodification* and the ways in which all things, it would seem, can be turned into goods that can be sold in markets. In common parlance, a "commodity" is something that is produced in high volume by a large number of producers, that is subject to highly competitive pricing, and that, as a result, generates small profit margins: cars, bananas, computers, shampoo. The trick, then, is to sell many of these identical items. "Commodification" is also applied to things that have not previously been sold in competitive markets—laser eye surgery, trips to Antarctica, pollution permits—but that will generate large profits after their initial introduction. Commodification of "positional goods"—those that convey status and are desired by the well-off—helps to advance accumulation and generate super-profits. Putting a price on things means that they have monetary value and will be treated more carefully than things without a price. But it also means that noneconomic values, such as aesthetics or ethics, don't count for very much unless they can also be monetized. One contemporary example of the commodification of nature involves the valorization of biological and genetic diversity.

In the final section of the chapter, we study the process of *globalization* and its relationship to environmental problems. Globalization involves, in part, the expansion and deepening of transnational capitalism and its extension to things not previously commodified as well as to places and peoples who have not yet been deeply integrated into market relations. Although there is nothing especially new about globalization when defined in these terms, it has taken on new significance because, as more people are pulled into the orbit of markets and their emphasis on consumption, the growing volumes of waste that result have ever-widening environmental consequences. At the same time, globalization might also play a role in a process of "ecological modernization," based upon the technological reconstruction and social reorganization of production and consumption under capitalism. If resources can be used much more efficiently, if wastes can be reduced in volume through engineering and recycling, if society can establish a new ethical relationship to nature, perhaps environmental crisis can be avoided. But there are many "ifs," as we shall see.

Capitalism is central to our understanding of global environmental politics because, at the end of the day, it is the dominant form of economic practice on the planet. Capitalism is deeply enmeshed in the production and reproduction of virtually all societies on Earth, and its smooth functioning is of central concern to virtually all governments on Earth. Growing demands on the planet's resources come, to a major degree, from wealthy human societies, and if the poor do become wealthier, as proponents of sustainable growth hope, they will add their demands and consumption to the world's environmental burden. Whether such a capitalist future is sustainable, let alone survivable, remains very much up in the air.

Money, That's What I Want!

To fully clarify the relationship of free market capitalism to environmental problems, we need to take a brief analytical detour into neoclassical economics. Neoclassical economics is derived, in part, from the premises of liberalism, based on assumptions of individualism, self-interest, scarcity, and the desire to exchange. Markets are composed of individuals who seek to acquire goods that will improve their well-being or status. Such goods are, by definition, scarce—else there would be no need for a market—and individuals either trade some goods for other goods (barter) or bid a price for the goods they want. At a price that reflects a balance between supply and demand, exchange takes place, and buyer and seller are both satisfied. Adam Smith, of course, pointed out how such a system of exchange lacked a central organizer or authority yet was able to greatly increase satisfaction and happiness in society. He called this mechanism the "invisible hand," for it seemed as though self-interested individuals, pursuing their own desires, nonetheless behaved in such a way as to produce socially beneficial outcomes.[1] For Smith and other classical political economists, nature and its resources were given. By itself, nature had no economic value until it was transformed into goods that could be exchanged. Tin, for example, cost something to mine, but it was otherwise free for the taking. Until the ore was smelted, alloyed, and transformed into a pot or kettle, it had no value. Pots could be sold by people who made them to people who needed them. Both would be better off for the exchange. No one cared very much about the despoliation of the landscape, or the pollution emitted in the production process, or what eventually happened to the pot. Those were not things that could be exchanged, anyway.

Neoclassical economics treats resources and nature as inputs into production, whose costs include only what it takes to acquire and process them. Any damage that is caused during acquisition or processing is ignored, unless such damage affects the capitalist's investment.* These inputs, or factors of production—which, classically, also include labor, capital, technology, and knowledge—appear in the manufacturer's cost of producing things, whether those things be raw materials, agricultural commodities, manufactures, or even services and information. What has not conventionally appeared in that cost are things for which the manufacturer does not have to pay: the value of the despoiled landscape or polluted water or final disposal, or any negative impacts on people living near to the production process.

Neoclassical economics, as applied to capitalism, is also based on the assumption not only that markets will clear—supply and demand will match at an appropriate price—but also that producers can make profits in meeting demand. Clearly, producers who lose money on every unit they sell have little incentive to keep supplying that good to consumers. The drive for profit and accumulation is, therefore, the engine of capitalism, and the minimization of the costs of production is central to the process. This means that producers are reluctant to pay for protecting the environment, because that will drive up the costs of production and reduce profits further. And, because resources have, historically, been free for the taking and there has been no cost to polluting, there have been few, if any, incentives to protect the environment.

Creating Property: The Scarcity Factor

But why have nature and resources been presumed to be free for the taking? One of the basic principles of the market is that one must own that which is being exchanged or sold. Otherwise, the transaction is considered illegitimate. Under Western law, ownership is vested through property rights expressed by lawful title. Such title may be a legal document, as in the title to a plot of land, a house, or a car, or it may be a receipt for goods purchased from a seller or previous owner. Title confers legal possession even as it helps to create scarcity, which is why stolen goods are usually much less costly than those being sold by their legal owners. The purchaser of stolen goods is taking a risk that they might be confiscated by the authorities, if found out.

If lawful title to a good cannot be demonstrated, and there is no one who holds such title, the good is presumed to have no owner. In regard to land, the Latin term for this state of affairs is *res nullis*. When Europeans established colonies in other parts of the world, they found that the concept of lawful title

---

*For example, if an impure metal solution were to trigger an explosion in a refinery and destroy it.

did not exist. Property rights were understood in other ways, related to history of use, occupancy, kinship, and community. When the natives of these areas could not produce written proof of ownership, the Europeans declared the resource to have no owner and took possession, issuing written deeds to the state, settlers, and investors at home.[2] Land and its resources—trees, water, minerals—were thus acquired at virtually no cost to the new owner, who could exploit nature and sell resources to the highest bidder. In other words, private ownership of something denies access to others and creates scarcity for those others. They must now pay to gain access to those resources, even if such access was previously free. As a result, the cost of a resource as an input to production has, historically, been limited largely to the expenses of paying for access (sometimes called "rent" or a "royalty"), extraction or removing the resource from its original location, transforming it into usable form, and transporting it to sites of further transformation and production. When rents or royalties have been paid on minerals or oil, they have generally been kept low so as to encourage high levels of extraction and revenues. Paradoxically, perhaps, the creation of scarcity is meant to foster consumption rather than conservation or careful use.

Historically, the actual or potential social costs of exploiting nature were not factored into the cost of either the resource or the final product. Private owners could do with their land as they saw fit, and no one had any incentive to "own" pollution. Other costs, such as damage to the environment or the health of workers, were imposed on society and nature. Pollution and environmental damage would appear as unwanted outputs, dumped in air or water or manifest as soil erosion or toxic wastes or ill health. The marginally greater value of each unit of resource extracted, due to the fact that less remained (called "depletion"), was never included. Finally, the cost of disposal of wastes, both toxic and benign, would appear elsewhere in the economy, or not at all.[*]

According to the neoclassical approach, therefore, the cost of a resource is expressed as follows:

$$A + B + C = D,$$

where

$A =$ costs of capital (technology and other such inputs);
$B =$ costs of labor;

---

[*]The common phrase for this is "privatization of gains and socialization of costs."

C = costs of extraction, processing, royalties, licenses;
D = total cost of production.

If, however, we were to incorporate the environmental and social costs unaccounted for, the equation would be:

$$A + B + C + [S + P + I + H] = D,$$

where

S = scarcity value due to depletion;
P = costs of pollution and disposal generated by the production process;
I = intergenerational costs of environmental damage and depletion;
H = costs to people's health as a result of environmental damage and depletion.

The figures in brackets in the equation are those social costs generally ignored by neoclassical economic accounting. These include negative impacts to the environment, such as air and water pollution, as well as the value of things irreplaceable to the present generation and the costs of the absence of resources to future generations.[3] Thus, for example, the logging of an old-growth forest involves not only damage to ecosystems, soil, water, plants, and animals but also destroys the present value of no longer having those forests and the environmental services they provide (soil retention, food and shelter for other species). Also excluded are the costs, to future generations, of not having those forests as a result of their extinction. All these costs are left out of what the producer pays to acquire, cut down, transport, and process a tree. As long as such factors seem not to affect anyone in direct physical or monetary terms, there are presumed to be no costs associated with them. The absence of these costs then shows up as lower expenditures or, conversely, higher returns on investment (profit). Environmental damage fosters accumulation and makes societies wealthier!

Nor does damage to resources or the environment appear on either side of the equation until such time as a scarcity of "free" inputs, whether as resources, pollution, or waste disposal space, public health, or injury to Nature, becomes visible and begins to have an effect on those whose interests and well-being are harmed. If such inputs begin to become scarce, and all else is equal (as it rarely is), it is assumed that their market price will rise to reflect this scarcity. (As noted in Chapter 2, that's why there are oxygen bars in Los Angeles and Tokyo; clean air has become so scarce that the owners of full tanks of oxygen can make money by "renting" their tanks to those who can pay for bottled air.) Recall, however, that "free" inputs are free because they are not scarce and no one sees reason to acquire title to them. How, then, can "free" inputs acquire a price that will reflect their growing scarcity value?

Under the postulates of neoclassical economics, it is *scarcity of supply relative to demand* that sets prices in the market (to repeat the point: things in apparently unlimited supply, such as air, have no price). People will bid for those things they need or want, and those who can afford to do so will pay more if they cannot buy it at a lower price (consider the way house prices rise in a hot property market). A rising price is generally taken to indicate a shortage of the resource, as buyers compete for a limited supply. But not all "shortages" operate in this fashion; producers can also induce scarcity by intentionally holding goods off the market in order to force prices up. This is what happened during the international oil crisis of 1973 (see discussion below).

When a good becomes excessively costly in a market, and buyers are no longer willing or able to pay the market price, one or more things happen. First, a rising cost may motivate more careful use of the resource, as consumers find they can no longer afford to purchase as much of the good ("conservation"). If, for example gasoline rises from $1.50 to $5.00 per gallon, and your vehicle only gets fifteen miles per gallon, chances are that you and others will drive less.* As consumers use less of a resource, supply will drop back into balance with demand and prices will decline. The market will come back into equilibrium until demand at the lower price begins to outstrip supply again, when the cycle will be repeated.

Second, if supply and demand are more or less unbalanced for a long time, and retail prices remain high, producers will see the opportunity to make money by supplying the unmet demand. The potential returns on investment associated with the higher price of a good will motivate the search for or production of new supplies of the resource. If no new sources can be found at a reasonable cost, alternatives will become attractive and will be provided in the market ("substitution"). Such alternatives could be substitutes for the good in shortage (for example, alternative fuels for vehicles) or technological innovations that use less of the good in shortage (for example, cars that go seventy-five or more miles on a gallon of gasoline).

The story of oil prices over the past few decades provides a good illustration of the supply-demand process, even recognizing that oil markets are

---

*Note that in Europe, gasoline costs between $4 and $5 per gallon, mostly because of high taxes. This limits consumption but to a much smaller degree than one might expect. Cars have become more fuel efficient and, combined with inflation, the relative cost of gasoline has not escalated that much.

hardly like those found in neoclassical theory. At the beginning of the 1970s, the international price of oil was on the order of $1.00 per barrel (a barrel of oil is forty-two gallons; at the time, the price of gasoline in the United States was $0.25 to $0.30 per gallon, roughly equivalent to $1.50 in 2003 dollars). During the 1970s, two major price increases took place as international oil supplies fell below demand. In 1973, oil was held off the market as Arab oil-producing countries imposed a short-term embargo on the United States and the Netherlands in the aftermath of the war brought on by Egypt and Syria against Israel in October. In 1979, international supplies declined during the Islamic Revolution in Iran, as that country's production infrastructure was temporarily shut down.[4] Both times, international oil prices shot up, even though there was no actual decline in the amount of oil that was known to be in the ground.*

The much higher oil prices that resulted made it attractive to exploit more expensive oil deposits as well as to foster development of various alternative energy sources. So-called stripper wells (producing less than ten barrels a day) became lucrative, and oil companies began to explore for new deposits in higher-cost regions, such as the North Sea. There was also considerable interest in and funding for solar technologies, wind energy, and nuclear power. But the search for other energy sources did not last. By the end of the 1970s, markets were more or less back in balance. Higher oil prices had induced conservation as well as economic recession throughout the world, and the global demand for oil declined well below the levels of the early 1970s.

This return to balance was short-lived; now the problem came to be too much oil relative to demand. Not only were consumers using less, many new sources of oil were producing for the international market. As a result, the world price of a barrel of oil collapsed from more than $30 to less than $10, and the shortages of the 1970s turned into the gluts of the 1980s. The excess of cheap oil made new energy sources a much less urgent priority for consumers and governments alike, and alternative energy sources fell out of favor. Solar and wind looked too expensive, and the potential profits disappeared. Governments stopped their funding for new energy sources, corporations halted their development of them, and consumers lost interest in them. In 1985 there was no more oil in the ground than there had been in 1973, but oil was no longer in short supply relative to demand.[5] The social

---

*Indeed, the actual supply of oil might not have even declined. Companies expected that shortages would be coming and stockpiled oil, rather than releasing it into the market.

costs of this up-and-down cycle were huge. Inflation ran rampant; coal consumption began to grow; developing countries incurred massive debts; exploration for new oil deposits led to invasions of ecologically sensitive regions; the U.S. military presence in the Middle East cost $50 billion or more per year. Yet, none of these costs showed up in the price of oil on world markets. American consumers continued to pay the inflation-adjusted equivalent of 1970 prices for gasoline.[6]

A second example of the exclusion of social costs can be seen in the handling of toxic wastes, which requires carefully managed disposal sites. As long as there are plenty of sites, the market cost of dumping such wastes will be low. As public opposition to dumps grows, the number of sites available for new dumps will decline, and there will be greater competition to dispose of toxics at the remaining sites. This will drive dumping costs up because of the "scarcity" of space relative to demand. Producers may look for alternatives, such as shipping the toxics to foreign countries.[7] The social costs will be exported, as well. Alternatively, producers might seek ways to reduce the volume and toxicity of the wastes they produce. Should land dumping and waste export be banned entirely—a move that would imply infinitely high disposal costs—producers are likely to follow the route of "ecological modernization" and find methods of eliminating entirely the production of toxic wastes. In this instance, the social costs of disposal are taken into account, as environmental costs are avoided when there are no wastes requiring disposal.

The logic of the neoclassical perspective on scarcity also suggests one peculiar conclusion: one can never "run out" of anything. When resources grow scarce and their prices rise, either new sources will come into play or substitutes will be developed. And there is considerable evidence to support this claim. As we saw above, when oil became more costly, new deposits were discovered. When cobalt used in magnets became very expensive during the late 1970s as a result of conflict in what was then Zaire (and is, once again, Congo), new magnetic materials were quickly developed. The late Julian Simon, a well-known economist, liked to point out that mineral and commodity prices during the 1990s were lower than they had ever been during the twentieth century.[8] According to Simon, this meant that resources were in greater supply than ever before. There was no need to worry about running out. Nonetheless, at some point in the future, deposits of relatively low cost minerals will have been fully exploited, and prices will be likely to rise, perhaps out of reach of most people.[9] Substitutes, or substitute activities, will have to be found or the world will have to do without. This logic clearly applies to nonrenewable resources (at least, so far), although the availability of many resources is as much a matter of ability to pay as it is of supply. In war-torn countries, where gasoline is often scarce, the rich rarely have to go without. It is the poor who are reduced to walking.

It is less clear that the economic logic of substitutability applies to air, water, or "renewable" resources, such as species and forests.[10] Renewable resources are those that reproduce as part of natural cycles. They are constantly being replenished and appear, in principle, to be limitless. Left alone by humans, the hydrological cycle supplies the water that nature demands, and the natural rate of forest destruction roughly equals the rate of regeneration. But such "balance" holds true only so long as the rate of human extraction does not exceed the rate of natural replenishment. Renewable resources, once destroyed or rendered extinct, are essentially irreplaceable. Furthermore, at some point, the cumulative damage to renewables from the mostly ignored social and environmental impacts, such as pollution or soil erosion or climate change, begins to add up. If climate change makes certain parts of the world inhospitable to plants and species that have long been found there, they might well disappear entirely. The limited capacity of renewable resources to absorb such impacts is being overtaxed, and the eventual effects on human as well as ecosystemic health and welfare are of particular concern.

For the purposes of our neoclassical discussion, the problem is that renewable resources have never been regarded either as scarce or as belonging to anyone. There have been lots of water and trees and animals, and "pollution space" has been more than ample for human needs. Renewable resources have not been bought and sold at prices reflecting their true value, which, in any event, is extremely difficult to assess. Consequently, producers and polluters have had little reason to use these resources more carefully or in lower quantities. Neoclassical economics has an answer to this problem, but it requires what amounts to active intervention into the operation of markets, something that many free-marketeers abhor.

Externalities: Things for Which No One Pays

The use of resources without attention to social and environmental costs leads to what economists call *externalities*. An externality is an impact or effect borne by those who do not benefit from the processes or activities that cause the environmental damage. For example, the sulfur dioxide wafting across the fence of a power plant and falling out on nearby houses constitutes a negative externality for those who live in the houses. The fact that air—that is, pollution space—is free and is not incorporated into the costs of production represents a positive externality for the power plant owners. In this instance, it is commonly said that the market is operating imperfectly. In a "perfect" market, these costs would be included. As we saw in Chapter 2, the Coase theorem provides a theoretical framework and solution to this problem that is claimed to be neutral in regard to who pays for those costs.[11] The goal here is to eliminate the externality, not to be fair or just. Coase argues that the costs of pollution should be incorporated into the cost of production—a process called *internalization*—so that the producer no longer receives a free benefit and the plant's neighbors no longer have to suffer the impacts.

According to neoclassical analysis, there are several ways to internalize such costs. First, working in the public interest, the government, or even a community group, can put pressure on plant operators to reduce emissions. The government is also in a position to set limits on pollution and impose sanctions, fines, or taxes if these are exceeded. Incorporating the cost in this fashion will reduce profits, and the producer will then seek ways to eliminate the pollution and restore former profit levels. Alternatively, if the plant owners claim they cannot afford to reduce emissions, it might fall to the government or community to pay the cost of cleanup. While this would seem to impose unfair costs on those who did not generate the pollution, the Coase theorem argues that such a solution makes sense if the eventual benefits exceed the costs of continued pollution. If the costs of internalization are very high, it might be more efficient to shut the plant down; plant owners sometimes threaten to do so rather than pay the costs, and thereby blackmail the communities in which they operate. Clearly, shutting down the plant could be costly, depriving districts of jobs and tax revenues. Nonetheless, if the benefits of closing the plant exceed the costs of living with the pollution, shutdown may make economic sense. A third possibility is for those who are affected by the pollution to move elsewhere, especially if the aggregate costs of moving are less than those of reducing emissions. The plant owners could pay for the move, or the homeowners could bear the costs themselves. Finally, the plant owner could simply compensate its polluted neighbors, who could use the compensation to move to cleaner climes, or to remain and suffer.

To repeat the point made above, several of these options represent an increased cost to the polluter. She would pollute less but because her costs would increase, her profits would decline. Other options represent a cost to those who are suffering from the pollution. In aggregate, however, the total costs of damage are decreased through internalization. Theoretically, the optimal choice among strategies—all else being equal—depends on which is most cost effective or leaves no one worse off than he or she was before (this state of affairs is called Pareto Optimality). Deciding which strategy will bring the parties closest to this point is not easy. Information about individual preferences is required, but such knowledge is difficult to come by and often costly to obtain. Moreover, one or the other parties may be able to realize a benefit by concealing information from the other.

An alternative to these forms of internalization is to find a means of establishing a cost for the resource that is essentially equal to the marginal cost of controlling the insult to the environment (although even this might not result in the proper pricing of the resource). How could this be done? The neoclassical answer is through private property rights. By privatizing the right to pollute or damage the environment, economic incentives to reduce or eliminate the offending activities can be created—or so proponents of this approach argue. For example, in the case of the polluting power plant, the owners might be required to buy permits, sold in a state-managed market, to emit pollution. Assume that the plant owners can afford to pay only $1.00 per pollution unit; if they pay more, their profits will vanish. The plant's neighbors get together, bid $1.10 per pollution unit, acquire all the available permits, and retire them. The plant will be forced to shut down and the air will, as a result, no longer be polluted. We will return to this notion of pollution permits in our discussion of climate change, below.

Consumers 'R Us

Production is only one side of the equation; consumption is the other.[*] There must be customers for the goods being produced, and the more these customers consume, the more goods are sold.[12] As noted earlier, producers who cannot sell their goods to consumers, be they potato chips or microchips, will end up with costly and useless stockpiles of products and quickly confront bankruptcy. Clearly, consumers are key to contemporary capitalism; without them, the system will crash. Capitalism without growth, or with very slow growth, is conceivable, but the social reorganization required to slow down growth in consumption might have untoward political complications, for several reasons.

[*]Actually, exchange, or trade, is involved, too, and has its environmental impacts, as well.

First, people have been socialized to believe that the accumulation of goods and money is a measure of personal success and that the possession and consumption of more things must be better.[13] If your personal wealth is not increasing, you are doing something wrong; if you are not interested in more, you are seen as somewhat odd, or even a failure. Second, in market-based democracies, there is the implicit promise and widely held belief in progress, that "things always get better." This generally means becoming wealthier and more able to buy the things you covet. "Growing the economy" becomes a political imperative, especially for those holding public office. Finally, because the populations of some market societies (especially the United States) are growing—new consumers are born or are arriving in the country every day—economic growth is the only way to provide income to these people without taking it away from those already consuming. Consequently, constantly growing consumption is essential to capitalism's social and political viability.

The importance of consumption in contemporary capitalist societies can be seen in economic statistics. What is called "personal consumption" accounted for 68 percent of the U.S. economy in 2000. The gross domestic product (GDP) for the fourth quarter of 2000 is shown in the following list in 2003 dollars.[14]

U.S. GDP	$9,394 billion
Personal consumption	$6,373 billion
Durables	$896 billion
Non-durables	$1,887 billion
Services	$3,602 billion

Similar numbers apply to other rich and poor countries. In fact, personal consumption constitutes a greater percentage of national income in poor countries, as can be seen in the following list, because most money there goes to the purchase of basic necessities, such as food:[15]

Germany	58%
Portugal	65%
Mexico	65%
USA	68%
Philippines	73%
Cambodia	87%

The contrast in consumption between rich and poor countries is much more striking, however, when we consider both inputs and wastes. The average American consumes from 10 to 100 times more goods, resources, and energy than the average South Asian. The volume of garbage and pollution that results is comparably larger (perhaps quite a lot more, since there is, on average, much more recycling of used materials in South Asia).[16] Such disparities are clear when we compare consumption on other indicators, for example, gasoline use and paper consumption (Table 3-1). The former is a measure of greenhouse gas emissions; the latter, a measure of landfill wastes. Portugal is not a poor country, but its per capita consumption of gasoline and paper is far lower than that of the United States. Moreover, its economy uses energy much more efficiently. Paradoxically, perhaps, Mexicans, with far lower incomes, consume more fuel per capita than do the Portuguese. Why this is so is not clear—perhaps Mexican cars are less fuel efficient or they are driven greater distances.

One way of assessing the environmental impacts of consumption is through a concept called the "ecological footprint." The ecological footprint is the land area inside a specific country that is required to provide resources consumed by a person living in that country. A second quantity, the "ecological deficit," is the additional area outside the country required to provide imported resources. An individual's total ecological footprint is the sum of these two measures. Thus, a typical American's ecological footprint is 24.0 acres; that of a Bangladeshi is 0.6 acres (Table 3-2). The ecological footprint is a rather crude measure of impact, inasmuch as it relies on quantification of the land area, measured in "global acres," required to supply each person with the resources he or she consumes. But the idea is a useful one in that it provides a basis for comparison of the environmental impacts of rich and poor.

Table 3-1   Per Capita GDP and Consumption in Several Countries

	GDP (2000; dollars)	Gasoline use (1998; liters)	Paper use (1998; kilograms)
United States	34,100	1,688	292.6
Portugal	11,120	263	106.1
Mexico	5,070	303	46.2
China	840	35	29.8
India	450	7	3.7

Source: Data from World Resources Institute, *World Resources 2000–2001* (Washington, D.C.: World Resources Institute, 2001), table ERC.5, online at www.wri. org/wr2000/toc.html (7/17/02); World Bank, *World Development Indicators 2002* (Washington, D.C.: World Bank, 2002), table 1.1, online at http://www.worldbank. org/data/wdi2002/tables/table1–1.pdf (7/22/02).

Table 3-2   Selected National Ecological Footprints, 1998
(in global acres per capita)

Country	Footprint	Ecological deficit	Total ecological footprint
Bangladesh	0.3	0.3	0.6
Philippines	0.6	0.8	1.4
Mexico	1.7	1.0	2.7
Portugal	1.5	3.1	4.6
Germany	1.8	3.4	5.2
Norway	5.9	2.1	8.0
United States	13	11	24

Source: Redefining Progress, *Sustainability Program Ecological Footprint Accounts,* online at www.rprogress.org/programs/sustainability/ef/projects/1998_results.html (7/22/02).

Note: Each unit corresponds to one acre of biologically productive space with "world average productivity."

A more useful metric would also include the following: wastes generated in the production of goods; energy, water, and other resources used in production, transportation, and sale of goods; resources consumed and wastes produced while the goods are being used; and the environmental and health impacts of disposal (including the long-distance transportation of toxic materials). Obviously, such a quantity would be much more difficult to calculate. For example, although it is relatively easy to measure the water content of, say, an imported Polish ham, it would be a good deal more complicated to account for all the water that went into raising, slaughtering, and processing the pig from which the ham originated (including the impacts of growing the food for the pig); manufacturing the container in which the ham is packaged; transporting the ham across the Atlantic to the local market; washing up after the ham is eaten; disposing of the tin and whatever else is left; and apportioning those impacts among the ham's final consumers. The calculation could be done, but it would be a fairly monumental task.

Why are the differences in consumption shown in Tables 3-1 and 3-2 so great? Beyond the acquisition of basic necessities such as food and shelter (which vary among societies), consumption is not automatic. There is no human instinct or gene to acquire things or to "shop until you drop." How do you know, therefore, that you need new shoes? Or that your computer is obsolete? That you want to drive through mud in a four-wheel-drive truck? That you must have the latest CD by Lil' Kim? And what would happen if you didn't acquire these new possessions? Evidently, something motivates such acquisitiveness. It tells you about things you need or want, even if you have never thought about them or wanted those things before. It warns you when something is no longer stylish or useful, so you can get rid of the old and bring in the new. And it admonishes you about what might happen if you do not avail yourself of lots of new stuff. It is difficult to imagine life without all of your possessions. Yet, for thousands of years and for billions around the world, life has gone on without them. What drives consumption?[17]

We can identify three facets of the will to consume: psychological influence through advertising and peer pressure; engineering of "new" products to replace "old" ones (planned obsolescence); and the structural imperatives of capitalist growth. In the first instance, we are constantly being bombarded by messages and blandishments encouraging us to consume—as many as 2,000 each day.[18] Such messages are not merely about the services provided by those things being advertised; they are also about the need for such items if the consumer is to have a complete and fulfilled life and identity. Some products are advertised as "lifestyle" or "identity-oriented" goods; others are touted for their superior performance or particular characteristics. People are not, of course, so gullible as to take at face value the promises made in advertising media. Children might demand something solely on the strength of the claims made in a television ad, but adults have learned that the purpose of such messages is merely to get the listener or watcher to recall the product when a choice is to be made, or to notice the brand of the product when a colleague or acquaintance has bought it. The object is to hook a potential consumer to a specific product or brand and to create loyalty where there was none before.[19]

In the third instance—structural imperatives—consumers are made aware of their importance to the vitality of the economy. To a growing degree, as we saw, personal consumption not only comprises a major fraction of gross domestic product but is also the primary driver behind continual growth of national economies. No longer is heavy industry the primary source of national power and expansion; today, the consumer has a national obligation to consume. Such admonitions were seen and heard in the days and weeks after the September 11, 2001, attacks on New York and Washington, D.C., when it was feared that people's uncertainty about their safety might carry the American economy into serious recession. Ironically, perhaps, many of the goods purchased as a patriotic duty are not even manufactured in the United States but come, rather, from the People's Republic of China, which is sometimes touted as a future American "enemy." [20]

It is the second instance, that of planned obsolescence, that is a particularly powerful driver of consumption. Nowadays, many things become useless or undesirable long before they wear out. This is not entirely accidental: increasing the flow of goods through the economy fosters growth. Left to their own devices, consumers would tend not to replace things until they broke down and could not be fixed. As a result, goods are not made to last a long time, as anyone who has recently purchased a toaster can testify. And given the emphasis on economic value rather than environmental concerns, there seems little point in repairing a two-year-old malfunctioning $150 microwave oven or DVD player when it costs $75 merely to have a repairman open the box. Finally, who has not experienced the frustration of discovering that games are no longer available for a video console or that a computer has insufficient memory to handle new software?

Indeed, personal computers, whether Mac or PC, offer one of the best contemporary examples of planned obsolescence. For $700 to $1,200, it is possible to purchase a computer system whose computational capabilities exceed those that, several decades ago, cost millions of dollars. Today's top-of-the-line computer is, by all measures, at least a hundred times faster and more powerful than those available as recently as 1990. But even this level of performance repeatedly proves to be insufficient. Each incremental improvement in hardware and software is touted as something that no user can do without, and to do without is to be left in the dust. Paradoxically, perhaps, very few owners of personal computers ever avail themselves of the full computing power of their machines (in fact, very few have any idea what that computing power might be or how to use it to its full capacity). For most individuals, a few basic functions, such as word processing and basic computation, are all that are necessary, and a 1990 PC or Mac would be perfectly adequate to such tasks.* It is, however, almost impossible to maintain such a computer except through heroic effort.

As successive generations of Intel- and Mac-based microprocessors render computers ever faster, they also turn older models into prematurely obsolescent antiques for which there is little demand either at home or abroad. Software written for older and slower chips and operating systems disappears from the market, and newer software cannot be run on older systems because of prodigious RAM and hard-drive memory requirements. Indeed, almost as

---

*I recognize that one could not surf the Internet with such a computer, but as one who studied, worked, and wrote for more than thirty years before gaining access to the World Wide Web, I know that it is possible to live a perfectly adequate (and ad-free) life without it.

soon as you purchase a new computer, it is, for all practical purposes, junk—within a couple of years, your $1,000 machine will be worth no more than $100, if that much (old computers are not scarce). To avoid being blindsided by planned obsolescence, you need to buy a new system every two or three years. The result is that, in the United States and Europe, there is a growing computer disposal problem. Some old machines can be "handed down" to children or donated to worthy causes. Others end up stashed away in closets or garages, where they gather dust. Disposal of the growing numbers of discarded computers, laced with toxic metals, is no easy proposition. Landfill operators are reluctant to accept them, and the individual components are worthless. A goodly number of old computers end up in Asia, where valuable metals are extracted while toxic wastes are inhaled, ingested, and dispersed into the surrounding environment.[21] The problem of computer and electronics disposal will be addressed again in later chapters.[*]

Wealth: Is It Good for the Environment?

Recall the discussion of sustainable development, in Chapter 2, and the Brundtland Commission's declaration that "poverty is a major cause of environmental degradation." [22] According to this calculus it is good to consume, and it is even better to consume more, because higher flows of goods and money through the economy lead to a larger pie from which everyone can get a piece. But if the cost of growth in consumption is also a major increase in the production of wastes, wealth can also be seen as a "major cause of environmental degradation." This argument remains somewhat controversial, inasmuch as it is generally taken as given that wealthy societies are more attentive to environmental quality. Repeating a point raised in Chapter 2, according to some analyses, as societies get richer and consumers have more discretionary income, they will become more interested in aesthetics and the quality and attractiveness of their surroundings. The wealthy will demand a cleaner environment and be more willing to spend the money to achieve it. Proponents claim that empirical evidence for this "effect" is seen in the lower levels of air and water pollution found in industrialized countries than in developing ones.[23] The phenomenon is explained by something called the "reverse Kuznets curve," which compares income with environmental quality.

---

[*]Many household appliances have much longer useful lives, of course. Refrigerators tend to stay in service for fifteen to twenty years or more, stoves even longer. But nowadays, such extended lifetimes appear to be exceptions rather than the rule.

The highest levels of pollution are to be found in countries with a per capita annual income of about $5,000.[24] Below this level, industrialization has not proceeded far enough to make pollution a serious problem; above this level, society begins to pay for pollution reduction.

All is not as it seems from this argument—or, at least, not as simple. Historically, much pollution was generated in the production of things, and a good fraction of both production and disposal took place within the country in which those things were used or consumed. But there is now a dynamic in capitalism driving a shift in this pattern and leading to the transfer of pollution and waste to poorer countries, through offshore production and the lengthening of commodity chains (a phenomenon returned to in the final part of this chapter). The relative wealth of a country thus contributes to its ability not only to eliminate pollution but also to displace it to locations abroad. This displacement is evident in the large ecological footprint of the average American (Table 3-2).

Growing incomes and wealth may lead to a demand for a cleaner environment, but they also lead to growing wages, expenditures, and consumption. The material effects of such growth are evident: greater pressure on the environment due to greater extraction from nature in other countries to meet the demand for goods, on the one hand; growing volumes of wastes as products are used and thrown out ever more frequently, on the other. The growing volume of goods produced in developing countries and imported into industrialized ones also encourages consumption by virtue of relatively low prices. Consumers can then buy more goods, even if their incomes increase only very slowly, and feel as though they are better off.

Again, take the example of computers. As observed above, over the past twenty years, the real costs of the personal computers have fallen continuously in regard to both hardware and computing power. The amount of money required to purchase a new, improved machine has decreased as well. Even taking inflation into account, the cost of a new PC is probably half or less of what it was two decades ago. How is this possible? Over that period of time, many of the stages in manufacturing and assembling computers have moved from industrialized countries to developing countries, where labor and other costs are much lower. Goods can thus be produced at low cost in developing countries and sold for a higher price in industrialized ones.

Consider, as another example of this phenomenon, a T-shirt. Including materials and labor, it might cost $5.00 in the United States to produce a

T-shirt that would retail for $10.00. By contrast, it might cost $1.00 to produce the same T-shirt in the Philippines (or only $0.50 in China) and to ship it to the United States, where it would still be sold for $10.00 (some designer T-shirts cost much more). At least half of the markup is profit, which in these examples has increased from $2.50 to $4.50.[25] At the same time, the consumer's purchasing power remains the same because, for him, the cost of the T-shirt has not changed. Now consider the effect of rising wages in the two countries. Assume that the production cost of a U.S.-made T-shirt rises from $5.00 to $6.00. To compensate for this, the retailer increases the price to $11.00. The consumer sees a $1.00 drop in purchasing power because it now takes an extra dollar to buy the same T-shirt. But in the Philippines, wages are likely to remain stable, or rise only slightly, because there is an ample supply of unemployed labor. So there will be no need to raise the retail price. And, insofar as the consumer's income rises during the same period, the T-shirt will actually become less expensive relative to income. When goods decline in cost, people often buy more of them, more often.* (Think about how you respond to a sign advertising "BIG SALE!" You are liable to buy two items in the belief that you are "saving money," even though you only need one item and the cost for two is greater than for one).

Consumption is also encouraged by appealing to consumers' desire for prestige, or positional, goods associated with higher incomes and the upper class. This is evident with automobiles. Of course, the external features on cars are changed every year, even if the mechanical insides remain the same, in order to emphasize the declining status of older ones. But auto manufactures are not above selling two different models with similar mechanical features at different prices. Much of the cost of any automobile is in those parts you don't ordinarily see: the engine, the drive train, the equipment under the hood, and the frame. Yet even though body and interior features, about which so much fuss is made in advertising and which have so much to do with consumer "identity," constitute the smaller fraction of a vehicle's production cost, in the end they determine what can be charged for the car. Therefore, why not replace a plain exterior with a fancy one, install leather seats and an expensive sound system, and claim that the result is an entirely different and "higher-class" vehicle? That is, more or less, the difference between the Lexus and the Toyota Camry, even though the former sells for two to three times as

*This is the same phenomenon as happened with gasoline use. The growing efficiency of cars resulted in a decline in the cost-per-mile of fuel, so people tended to drive more and to travel farther distances.

much as the latter. People buy a Lexus as much for status as transportation. And not only can such consumers afford the more costly vehicle, they can also afford to buy a new one more often.*

The consumer is thus encouraged to consume, to consume more, and to consume more costly goods. Few of these items have long lifetimes. Many can be resold, some can be recycled, but a goodly number end up as waste. Reducing the flow of consumables, by making things more durable and de-emphasizing style, would reduce waste but, in a social order predicated on growing incomes and consumer goods, the political consequences of slow growth and limits to consumption could be quite unsettling. Thus, if poverty is a major source of environmental degradation, as commonly claimed, so is wealth. Poverty, however, does not cast its impacts quite as widely as does wealth. To survive, the poor must generally consume nearby resources, and most of the consequent effects are fairly localized (although it is true that the repercussions of soil erosion can show up thousands of miles away, as can the climatic effects of methane from rice production). The rich, by contrast, can afford to export many of the environmental impacts of consumption, which then become invisible to them. As a result, the poor experience a double burden: the environmental impacts of their subsistence activities plus those resulting from excess consumption by the rich. This is the nub of the problem of environmental justice: the inequitable distribution of damage to both nature and health.[26]

What's Nature Worth?

The central role of consumption in capitalism suggests that everything has its price and everything can be consumed. In many ways, this is not far from the truth, as we shall see. What about those things that cannot be commodified and do not have a price? What, for example, is the value of a forest left standing or a species protected from extinction? How much is the atmosphere worth, especially when it has always been "free?" These are not merely questions of philosophy or ethics (although, perhaps, they should be). In a capitalist system, one must make choices about where to invest and what to buy. By conventional measures, the short-term financial return on a standing, old-growth forest is a good deal less than on the lumber it contains. And over the

---

*And their trade-ins are called "previously owned," which sounds much more prestigious and tasteful than "used."

longer term, income realized from logging the forest can be invested else-where to generate much higher returns than those from leaving the forest alone. But the million dollar questions are: Which is more valuable? Forest or lumber? And how can we know which use is more valuable? Indeed, how can we put a value on ecological necessity and aesthetics?

There are two, quite different answers to these questions. On the one hand, we can establish the market value of the standing timber, impute that value to the forest, and pay the owner or leaseholder that amount to leave the forest intact (in this case, we are internalizing the damage that would arise from logging). There is a considerable body of historical data on which to base such an assessment: the retail price of a board foot of lumber; the num-ber of board feet that come from a tree; the number of trees in a tract of for-est; the cost to log, mill, and transport; the amount of future income that the owner will forgo; and so on. On the other hand, we can try to establish a monetary value for the forest through a method called contingent valua-tion.[27] People are asked how much they would be willing to pay to prevent the old-growth forest from being logged. This amount is then compared with the market value of the timber. If the market value is less than the con-tingent value, protection is in order. Otherwise, down with the trees! The problem with the contingent value approach is that, because no one is actu-ally asked to pony up funds for forest preservation, we are comparing real revenues with imaginary payments. Moreover, it has been found that, when asked to hand over real money, people are only willing to pay a good deal less than their initial offer. Consequently, efforts to establish alternative mone-tary values and forge environmental policy on that basis have been largely stillborn.[28]

For this reason, among others, a sizable and growing portion of the busi-ness of preserving ecologically valuable tracts of land has been taken on by land conservancy and land trust organizations, although the total area of these tracts remains far less extensive than public lands under some form of management for conservation.[29] Such nonprofit organizations raise funds from private and corporate sources, solicit commitments from public agen-cies, and pay something approaching market value for land they wish to pro-tect. Or they try to persuade the owners of environmentally sensitive private property to donate land to the trust. Depending on circumstances, ownership of such lands may then be transferred to public entities, which are expected to turn the property into parks. But not all lands become public; some are traded for other tracts of land and some are sold back into private ownership to generate funds for the purchase of more ecologically valuable properties. Although the protection of such tracts is a salutary goal, their commodification in this form raises several troubling questions.[30]

Perhaps the most serious one is whether nature ought to be valued in such monetary terms at all. For example, by some calculations, the value of the environmental services provided by nature, such as clean air, water, and so on, amounts to $33 trillion per year, a sum roughly equal to the annual global GDP.[31] Yet, putting a price such as this on nature implies that it and capital are substitutes for each other, that capital can always replace nature, and that survival is possible without nature as such. It also suggests that we can actually calculate the "true" economic value of the variety of environmental services provided by nature, such as air, clean water, habitat, and so on, and disregard those values that cannot be monetized. Neither of these two claims stands up under closer inspection, the first on technical, the second on philosophical, grounds. Notwithstanding amazing advances in genetic engineering, there is little reason to think that it will become possible to resurrect extinct species or restore old-growth forests to their original condition. No amount of money can restore that which has disappeared forever. And if an endangered species—say, an amphibian or insect—has no evident "function" in an ecosystem, the implication is that it has no monetizable value. Does this mean it does not deserve preservation? How can we possibly put a value on a nature we have hardly begun to comprehend and which we have no right to judge?

Nevertheless, neither technical nor philosophical difficulties have stood in the way of attempts to commodify things whose economic value is difficult to assess. The most widely used approach in this regard, as we have already seen, involves the creation of property rights in these things, which then permits their sale in markets. In the case of biodiversity, value is attributed not to habitat, species, or individuals, per se, but to the genetic resources within living things, which are appropriated, transformed, patented, and sold.[32] In the case of climate change, as indicated earlier, permits to emit greenhouse gases can be created, apportioned, and traded or sold in a market. In both instances, the creation of property rights permits monetary values to be established, and these become crude proxies for those aspects of nature that cannot be valued in other ways.

The Gene's the Thing to Catch the Conscience. The rapid development of genetic engineering and biotechnological research over the past couple of decades has motivated the emergence of a reductionist but increasingly dominant epistemological approach to biological and medical research. Traditional approaches to biology, ecology, and environmental protection tended to focus on species and ecosystems, regarding the whole as more than the sum of its parts.[33] Biotechnology, by contrast, is based on the search for the causes of biological processes in the smallest parts of the organism, the gene, and its place in the genetic sequence, or "genome." Because the defining characteristics of both species and individual organisms are to be found in the genome, which is a "natural" structure, the implication is that individual deviations from the "norm" in any species have their causes in "errors" in the individual's genome (such as mutations).[*] This perspective is evident from frequent news reports about the "discovery" of genes linked to specific diseases and conditions. The implication of such findings is that "fixing" the "defective" gene could "cure" the medical problem of concern.[35] The potential economic rewards of such genetic research could be enormous. Imagine, for example, that some way was discovered to repair those genes implicated in the development of some chronic or potentially fatal disease, such as leukemia. Imagine further than this repair could be accomplished through the simple ingestion of a pill containing a genetic "repair kit." The company financing such a discovery would be in a position to reap extraordinary profits.

But whether genetic repair and rehabilitation are possible or desirable is less relevant here than the economic and political implications of such research. On the basis of rulings in U.S. courts and international conventions addressing intellectual property rights, any such genetic discoveries—including genetically altered animals—can be patented and turned into private property. This is the case even if public funds were, somehow, involved in the discovery (for example, in the education of the researcher or the building of the laboratories) or if the organism harboring the discovery was "public property." Philosophically, the notion of such private title is legitimized on the basis of John Locke's claim that whoever puts labor into the creation of something is thereby entitled to call it his or her property.[36] We see here how seemingly abstract philosophies and principles come to be embedded in common practice and politics.

Of course, Locke was concerned only with physical labor put into the improvement of land, and he argued that the fruits of that (agricultural) labor, including the land, were the laborer's private property. Under the premise

---

[*]It is interesting to note that human beings do not possess that many more genes than worms and, according to recent research, can be thought of as "mice without tails."[34]

that scientific research, multiplied greatly by capital and technology, constitutes labor, the fruits of such research can now be patented and privatized. The holder of a genetic patent is then entitled to commercialize the discovery and sell or license it to whomever is willing to pay a "fair" market price. (Note, by contrast, that the "discoverer" of a new plant or animal species is not entitled to become its owner, despite the strenuous labor that might have been put into searching for it).[37] What might be the fair market price for such a "product?" Genetic prospecting is not a cheap business; it takes time to gather samples and analyze them in the lab. The research leading to patentable discoveries can be quite expensive—it can cost as much as a billion dollars to bring some pharmaceuticals to market. So the patent holder will want to generate sufficient revenues to cover development costs and provide a tidy profit, which means that most new medicines are quite expensive. This is the case even if their biochemistry is based on genes derived from public resources.

Prospecting costs can be reduced. When searching for potential medical products, it helps to have information about medicinally useful plants. Of particular interest, therefore, to corporate and scientific researchers are the remedies and practices of indigenous peoples. Medicines derived from plants known to possess healing properties may have been part of local common lore for centuries or millennia. These are common property resources, in the sense that they belong to no single individual or corporation, and indigenous users hold no recognized legal title to such plants. As a result, under international and most national law, the plants are assumed to "belong " to the state, which can sell rights to access if it so wishes. Furthermore, under relevant international patent law, such traditional uses have legal standing only if these uses have been documented in scientific journals. Indigenous peoples and peasants rarely have the time to conduct such research and publish scientific papers documenting their findings.[38] Needless to say, they hardly have access at all to the relevant scientific journals. In the absence of such documentation, those who have relied on these substances and materials for their health and well-being may lose rights or title to them. In some instances, traditional users may have to pay patent holders to obtain the products manufactured from the very plants they have used since time immemorial.

What are the implications for plant and animal species of such patent schemes? No longer are such species valued for their contributions to biological diversity and ecosystemic function or their intrinsic value as living things or their roles in indigenous cultures. Instead, they come to be desired for their genetic diversity, their potential as sources of medicines and other commodifiable substances, and the value they add to the corporate bottom line and global economy. For countries—especially developing ones strapped for revenues—the sale of genetic prospecting rights to scientists and corporations offers a source of income that could be used for both environment and development. Furthermore, if something valuable is discovered, the owners of the patent rights to the final product ought to be willing to contribute further monies to the preservation of specific ecosystems.

But several caveats should be heeded in regard to this picture. First, the process of establishing private property rights to genetic resources, and offering them for sale in the market, establishes measurable monetary return as the sole criterion for valuing a species. Those in favor of privatizing biodiversity argue that only under private ownership can resources be protected, because the owners of said property will want to maintain a continual flow of revenues from them and will therefore strive to preserve the resources.[39] * But value in the market today is no guarantee of protection tomorrow. The specific interest behind genetic prospecting and research is not the container but the contents. If the specific genes and properties extracted from a particular species can be analyzed and reproduced in the laboratory, the supply of raw materials—the species—and its preservation no longer matter. With the appropriate chemicals and lab techniques, the same substance can be produced synthetically and manufactured in large quantities with much greater quality control. The species as a source of genetic material is then no longer important to the process. In addition, the life of a patent is limited, typically to a period of ten to fifteen years. Corporations and their scientists are always searching for the next big discovery, one that can be brought to market to generate the revenues needed to pay for all that expensive research. Hence, a species that might have been enormously valuable at one time might become less so as new products are developed. The economic rationale for preservation might simply disappear.

Second, it is sometimes argued that no one knows from where the next great medical or genetic discovery will come and that such uncertainty will induce states and people to protect species. But there are no guarantees. All species are of great potential value—at least until they have been prospected and analyzed. Furthermore, under this accounting scheme, those species that have no special or desirable genetic properties have no value, and they will be protected only if other species in their particular ecosystem do possess such

---

*We return to this argument about "the tragedy of the commons" later in this chapter.

economic value. Inasmuch as the vast majority of species have no evident genetic value, and are unlikely to acquire it in the future, they will not receive direct protection under this scheme. In other words, protection via genetic prospecting and private property rights might seem attractive and politically easy, but it is hardly assured. As experience with once-costly commodities, such as eight-track tape players (and more recently, VCRs) suggests, current monetary value may be more of a hope than a solid basis on which to base environmental protection and species preservation.

The Air, the Air Is Everywhere! Climate change offers a somewhat different, but equally problematic, example of environmental commodification. In this instance, marketization will involve the purchase, sale, and trade of "rights to pollute." The creation of private property rights to unpolluted air is quite a bit trickier than with property rights to genes, especially since it is so difficult to keep others from using the atmosphere as a waste dump. By definition, the atmosphere is generally considered an "open access resource." Everyone uses it but no one owns it. Where there is no owner of a resource, it is often argued, there is no incentive to moderate exploitation.[40] In the absence of strictly enforced regulation or limits, pollution will proceed uncontrolled. As a result, everyone will suffer from bad air even if they gain no benefits from the process generating the pollution. This problem should sound familiar: it is yet another example of an "externality."

The classical term for this situation is "the tragedy of the commons," a concept popularized by the biologist Garrett Hardin in a famous article in *Science*.[41] He told the story of a medieval English common on which the villagers grazed their cattle. The self-interested villager would like to own two cows, but if everyone grazed two cows on the common it would be ruined. Still, because there are already many cows grazing there, the addition of one more would hardly make a difference. So, our mythical villager buys another cow and sends it out to graze (this is a version of the "free rider" phenomenon as part of the collective action problem). The difficulty arises, according to Hardin, because every villager will come to the same conclusion as the first and put a second cow on the commons. The result will be ruination of all, as the pasture is destroyed.

Hardin offered this scenario of devastation in connection with population growth. He claimed that each additional child brought into the world makes only a very small additional contribution to environmental damage, but the tens of millions of additional children being born each year made a significant contribution. Indeed, he argued, if population growth were not limited, the end result would be ruination of the planet. Hardin called for "mutual coercion mutually agreed upon" as the solution, that is, a state that would ruthlessly control fertility and limit childbirth. Because most of the increase in global population was taking place in developing countries (which continues to be the case today), Hardin's analysis was aimed mostly at them.* But his formulation was erroneous in several ways. First, the English commons was not open simply to anyone with a cow or sheep; villagers possessed limited use rights, and violations of the collective restrictions on use would result in the forfeiture of those rights. Second, he presumed that medieval English villagers were selfish individuals who gave no thought to the "public good," an assumption rooted in Hardin's liberal outlook but not necessarily characteristic of the inhabitants of those villages. Finally, although Hardin didn't know it, being a biologist rather than an anthropologist, there are numerous examples, even today, of "common property resources" that are shared without being depleted.[42]

The point of Hardin's argument was that the only way to protect an open access resource is to privatize it. Private owners will restrict the number of cows on their own plots of land and prevent others from putting cows there. To abuse or overexploit the pasture will now cost them directly, instead of the cost being socialized onto others. Consequently, the plots will not be overgrazed and ruined. Thus, along much the same lines as the argument offered about species and the commons, if the atmosphere can be privatized, each of its owners will take much greater care in conserving and protecting it. Although the notion of privatization of the atmosphere might seem a strange one, it is not impossible, since there are ways to privatize the right to pollute, through some version of what are called "tradable pollution units" or "emission permits." [43] Polluters are granted or sold permits to emit a specified number of pollution units per year—usually measured in metric tons—and no more. Should they exceed the permissible limit, they will be fined or might even have their right to future permits rescinded.

How would such a scheme work? First, someone—the government, an international agency, a scientific commission—must make an authoritative decision about what constitutes an acceptable level of pollutants or emissions

*Hardin made this point even more clearly in "Life Boat Ethics," a 1971 article in *Psychology Today* comparing rich countries to people in lifeboats besieged by the world's poor adrift in the water around them. One or two might be brought aboard without significant risk, but the attempt to save everyone would surely result in the death of those in the lifeboats.

in the atmosphere, and what that level equals in total pollution units. This quantity is usually based on a scientific assessment of the potential environmental and health consequences of exposure to that level of pollution as well as on a political judgment about what might constitute an acceptable social cost (for example, in regard to sea-level rise, ill health, total emissions). The total volume of emissions leading to this level of pollutant in the atmosphere—let us say 300 billion pollution units—is then divided by the time period of concern—say, 100 years—to generate the number of pollution units emitted per time period. In this example, the permissible amount would be 3 billion units per year. This quantity would then be divided among the polluters, perhaps as a simple grant, perhaps through public sale (along the lines of an "initial public offering" of shares in a new company). The polluters could keep their units and emit the allowed volume of pollution, or sell them to the highest bidder. The operating logic here is that each polluter can calculate whether it will cost less to reduce emissions or to use up the pollution units.

Thus, some polluters might find they have more emission permits than they require; others might have fewer than they need. Those who have too many can then sell their permits to those who need more at some agreed-upon price based on the need. Alternatively, permit prices in open auction will reflect bidders' costs to clean up their emissions. In both cases, the price reflects producers' calculations of what such a pollution right is worth. Investments in pollution control can then be made where they are most cost effective and offer the highest rate of return. What has been created here, in effect, are property rights to the atmosphere. Each pollution unit gives the holder a right to "use" that volume of air needed to disperse one ton of pollutants. The process is rather like paying an entry fee to dump garbage at a local landfill. A temporary "property right" is purchased from the landfill owner that allows one to enter and get rid of garbage, which "disappears"—in a manner of speaking.

Consider the following example. Let us assume that the cost of pollution reduction by technical retrofitting runs $50 per ton at Plant Victoria and $100 per ton at Plant Albert. Let us assume that the price of a permit on the open market is $75 per ton. It therefore makes more sense for the owner of Victoria to retrofit and the owner of Albert to purchase additional permits. Imagine, further, that each plant has been allocated permits to emit 100 tons of polluting gases per year and that each plant emits 125 tons a year. With an investment of $3,750, Victoria's owner can reduce her plant's emissions by 75 tons a year, leaving 50 tons of permits to be sold for $3,750. In other words, she will break even on the deal. Albert's owner, by contrast, would have to invest $2,500 to reduce his plant's emissions to the 100-ton-per-year level. By purchasing 25 tons of permits for $1,875, the Albert plant can continue to pollute and its owner will "save" $625 in the process.

Marketable permit schemes such as this have been tried on a limited scale in the United States, in particular, with sulfur dioxide emissions from power plants.[44] These schemes have met with some success but have not yet caught on widely. They have not yet been implemented internationally either, although there is already some private carbon emission trading taking place, in anticipation of the eventual emergence of a market in greenhouse gas permits (see later in chapter).[45] But there are at least three problems with such property rights to pollute. The quota approach is based on the assumption that some level of pollution is acceptable (or necessary), even if this level continues to cause environmental damage or health problems. Wealthier parties will always be able to outbid poorer ones in an open market because of their willingness to pay more. As a result, the former may drive the latter out of business. The outcome might be an efficient one, but it is hardly fair, as we shall see. Finally, is it proper or ethical to privatize something that "belongs" to everyone—humans, plants, and animals?

Hot Air for Sale! How might the concept of pollution units be applied to the global environment? Consider the case of the pollution permit system for greenhouse gas emissions that might be established under the Kyoto Protocol. As we saw in earlier chapters, the protocol is an addition to the UN Framework Convention on Climate Change (UNFCCC) and commits industrialized countries to reduce their greenhouse gas emissions over a specified time period. Developing countries are not yet required to make such reductions, although they will probably have to make commitments at some time in the future. The protocol also includes provisions for the creation of mechanisms that will help make reductions possible, including tradable permits.[*]

Let us assume that scientists have determined a permissible level of greenhouse gases in the atmosphere and have calculated how much pollution can be produced over the coming century if damage to people and property is to be limited. Specifying this quantity alone is a major technical and political issue because some countries, such as the United States, might be able to

---

[*]The United States has ratified the UN Framework Convention on Climate Change but has refused to ratify the Kyoto Protocol. Apparently, the Bush administration has decided that, for the United States, adaptation to global warming will be less costly than prevention or mitigation. This also seems to be the growing consensus among other countries.

adapt to the impacts, whereas others, such as low-lying island states, cannot.[46] For the sake of this exercise, assume that a total loading in the atmosphere of 750 billion metric tons of carbon-equivalent (MTCE) gases in the 300 years from 1800 to 2100 will result in tolerable climatic conditions at the end of the twenty-first century.[*] Based on current levels of greenhouse gases in the atmosphere, up to the year 2000, some 400 billion MTCE were emitted during the 200 years since 1800. At the present rate of emissions, moreover, a minimum of 600 billion MTCE will be produced over the coming century.

Given the stipulated limit, this means that, between 2001 and 2100, total emissions can be no more than 350 billion MTCE, or an average of 3.5 billion MTCE per year, as compared with current emissions of about 6 billion MTCE per year. Because it would be difficult and costly to reduce emissions immediately by 50 percent, the permitted annual rate of global emissions would be "front loaded," beginning at current levels and declining to much lower levels by 2100. The total allocation over the coming century might look something like the numbers in Table 3-3. Under this scheme, every country would be allocated a certain quantity of emission permits per year. The specific number might be based on per capita GDP or population, modified in some fashion to reflect both present and historical emission rates. Each government could then decide whether to use its permits to cover its own national emissions, or to reduce national emissions and sell the excess permits. Conversely, a country emitting more than its allocation would have to purchase rights from another, at whatever price the market might demand.

How might such a scheme affect the United States, were it to join the Kyoto Protocol? Currently, the United States emits about 1.5 billion MTCE per year. Assume that for the period from 2000 to 2024, the United States receives only 750 million MTCE per year of emission rights. It must either reduce its greenhouse gas emissions to 750 million MTCE per year, or purchase an additional 750 million MTCE per year of permits from other countries that are not using all of their annual quota. The cost of such a permit would be determined by two factors: the supply of and demand for the permits in some sort of trading setup, and the marginal cost of reducing greenhouse gas emissions through technological and other means. Let us imagine that the U.S. government finds it can eliminate one MTCE of greenhouse gas emissions at a cost of, say, $50, whereas one MTCE permit covering one metric ton

[*]This would result in roughly a doubling of carbon dioxide concentrations in the atmosphere, and the effect could well be quite serious.

Table 3-3 Global Greenhouse Gas Emissions, 2000–2100

Emission period	Average emissions	Emissions per period
2000–2024	5 billion MTCE/year	125 billion MTCE
2025–2049	4 billion MTCE/year	100 billion MTCE
2050–2074	3 billion MTCE/year	75 billion MTCE
2075–2099	2 billion MTCE/year	50 billion MTCE
Total 2000–2100	3.5 billion MTCE/year	350 billion MTCE

Source: Author's projection.

costs $55. All else being equal, the preferred action would be to reduce emissions. But because some reductions might cost more than $55 per metric ton, it would make sense to buy permits for those.

Marketable emission permits could also provide a mechanism for monetary transfers between rich and poor countries. Based on the numbers above, the United States would have to pay other countries some $41.25 billion for one year's worth of emission rights. Nonetheless, the fact that bidding is taking place in an open market could prove disadvantageous for poorer countries. Consider the following illustration. One year, India comes up short and finds that it needs to purchase 10 million metric tons of rights, at a notional cost of $550 million. The United States also badly needs emission permits and offers $75 per MTCE, a price beyond India's means. India is forced to drop out of the market and has to reduce its emissions by closing factories and power plants, restricting vehicle use, and, perhaps, banning some forms of agriculture.* This would result in unemployment, the loss of energy resources, and restricted mobility. U.S. citizens, by contrast, could continue to take vacations in their SUVs and mobile homes. Would that be fair?

Evidently, the question of equitable distribution of these rights does not enter into the market transaction. All that happens is that the right is sold at what is presumed to be its "true" value, that is, whatever bidders are willing to pay for it. In particular, if demand for permits exceeds supply, the price will rise and those who cannot afford the new price will not be able to buy. That is how markets operate. But there are several ways to address the distribution problem. We could imagine two separate markets, one offering rights at a controlled price, another at an unregulated price. India could purchase its requirements at a low fixed price while the United States bought permits at a

---

*A considerable quantity of India's greenhouse gas emissions comes as methane, from agriculture and cattle.

much higher cost. Alternatively, the purchase of permits by poor countries could be subsidized by a tax on all permits bought and sold by rich countries. These kinds of questions remain one focus of debate in the climate change negotiations and have yet to be resolved.[47]

Another major objection to marketable emission permits has to do with monitoring and enforcement. Measurement of national emissions is more of an art than a science, and the UNFCCC secretariat in Bonn, Germany, relies on annual country reports in order to monitor compliance. For many countries, imports and exports of energy are well documented and their reports can be audited. For others, especially those with substantial domestic or subsistence energy production and agriculture, verification of national reports is much more difficult. And some countries refuse to even consider outside audits of their emissions or reports, claiming that it would amount to a violation of national sovereignty. Furthermore, because there is no world government or international institutions with coercive authority, there are no easy means for enforcing contracts. A country could quite easily violate the terms of a permit-based agreement and suffer few, if any, consequences. Short of sanctions imposed by major trading partners or the international community, a violator could not be forced to adhere to the terms of such an agreement.

Finally, countries don't emit the bulk of greenhouse gases. Individuals and corporations do. How will permits be distributed to them? And how will they be bought and sold? Each emitter will have a different marginal cost of reducing greenhouse gas pollution. Some may prefer to reduce emissions, others to purchase additional permits beyond those they already possess. We cannot say with certainty what might happen, although it seems likely that producers, rather than consumers, will receive most of the permits, perhaps on the basis of a life-cycle calculation, and will then be allowed to internalize the cost of the permits in the price of the products they make. For example, we can imagine an auto manufacturer having to purchase the requisite number of pollution units for each car it sells. This would include emissions resulting not only from building a vehicle but also from processing the raw materials and forming them into metal, tires, windows, and so on; shipping the car to the salesroom; driving the car during its lifetime; and disposing of or recycling the carcass when it is junked. The cost of a car might well increase by several thousand dollars.

At the end of the day, the conundrum posed by commodification of the atmosphere is much like that involved with genetic resources. In this instance, however, marketization is based on the idea that there is a viable tradeoff between the economic cost of environmental degradation and the cost of prevention. Beyond a certain point, it is almost impossible to calculate the impacts of global warming, especially if related costs are stretched out over decades. By contrast, the expenses of addressing climate change must be paid in current funds, and such expenditures are easily computed. There is a great reluctance to pay these costs, especially in the United States. Ultimately, the hope is that market exchange of pollution permits will generate the resources and technological transfers necessary to moderate the emission of greenhouse gases into the atmosphere. This, unfortunately, is no stronger a reed than that relied on to protect biodiversity.

Globalization and the Environment

What is "globalization"? These days, the term is used so freely and frequently that it has no clear meaning, although it is generally associated with the intensification of capitalist production and growing global communication linkages.[48] This new industrial revolution entails more, however, than just changes in modes and patterns of production.[49] The global economy has expanded from less than $5 trillion in 1950 to more than $35 trillion today.[*] World exports have grown from about $300 billion in 1950 to about $6 trillion today, this even as the global population has increased by only about 250 percent, from 2.5 billion to 6 billion.[50] And by some estimates, daily transactions in international currency and capital markets may total as much as $1.5 trillion.[51] The movement of such volumes of capital is not merely electronic; ultimately, it can have significant physical effects through foreign investments in dams and factories and unemployment that follows currency crises as happened in Asia in 1997 and 1998.

But globalization is more than just the movement of capital. It is simultaneously material, ideological, and organizational. Globalization is material in that it involves the movement of capital, technology, goods, and, to a limited degree, labor to areas with high returns on investment. This movement takes place without regard to the social or political effects on either the communities and people it relocates or on those left behind at old production sites. Globalization is ideological in that such displacement is rationalized in the name of "efficiency, competition, and profit." Growth is "good" and so, therefore, is globalization. Finally, globalization is organizational in that it

[*]All dollar figures in this paragraph are 1990 U.S. dollars.

fosters social innovation, reorganization, and change in existing institutions, composed of real, live people and with little regard for the consequences.

In some ways, there is nothing new about globalization. Human ideas and practices have been "globalized" for millennia; societies and civilizations have always learned from one another. The spread of agriculture was an ancient case of globalization; the incorporation of non-European lands into international capitalism was another. In historical terms, therefore, the present phase of globalization is only the latest in a process of international economic extension, expansion, and integration that, by some accounts, began about 1500 and perhaps even earlier.[52] What is new is the scale and volume of capitalist expansion and the commodification of things never before exchanged in markets, such as genes, air pollution, and whale watching.

Chains, Chains, Chains!

The enormous growth in transnational flows of money and capital, enumerated above, has also fostered growing investment in "emerging economies"—developing countries favored by investors—as well as industrialized ones. Increasingly freer trade, combined with high labor and social costs in industrialized countries, has facilitated movement of production offshore, along with its attendant major environmental impacts. The production and commodification of knowledge and a shift from the mass production of identical products to differentiated production involving goods manufactured to individual tastes have made production patterns increasingly complex.[53] Raw materials, commodities, semiprocessed materials, parts, and finished goods are moved among locales and corporations in different countries before arriving at retail outlets, primarily in industrialized countries. The spatialization of production across many countries has also had the effect of diffusing environmental impacts, and growth in global free trade has made it easier to "export" environmental bads, such as toxic wastes and pesticides banned in industrialized countries, to countries less able to afford and less willing to impose strict regulations.

Globalization not only involves more complex forms of production, trade, and consumption of material and intellectual goods, it is also very information intensive. It is information intensive in regard to the complexity of production processes, in regard to the commodification of knowledge, and in regard to our understanding of its effects on both social and natural environments. In particular, the rearrangement of patterns of production, trade, and consumption results in a whole range of environmental externalities that are of three basic types. First, as production is moved around and reorganized, environmental impacts are also relocated, with concomitant effects on health and nature in new locales. Second, changing forms of commodification and growing levels of consumption increase the volume, diversity, and, perhaps, toxicity of the resulting waste stream. Finally, the drive to increase the efficiency of investment and production results in organizational externalities. As traditional or familiar forms of social relations and relations of production are altered or destroyed, people may find it necessary to overexploit their local resources or to move to urban areas with inadequate housing and infrastructure.

What is not altogether evident from these organizational changes, either theoretically or empirically, is how the resulting environmental impacts are distributed. It has long been argued that producers will seek to build factories in countries where environmental and other social standards are lowest, since this will reduce their costs of doing business. Whether this really is the case remains in dispute.[54] Nonetheless, there is only limited consistency in environmental regulation, monitoring, and enforcement among countries, and there has been a general worsening of environmental quality in those countries where production for export has been a driving force behind rapid economic growth (as in Southeast Asia and the People's Republic of China).[55]

The reorganization of production under globalization has led, in particular, to the creation of extended "commodity chains" that spread environmental impacts over many countries. A global commodity chain has three dimensions. First, there is what is called the "input-output structure," consisting of a set of products and services linked together in a sequence of value-adding economic activities, including final consumption. Second, there is a sequence of "territoriality," which includes a spatialized pattern of production and distribution networks made up of enterprises of different sizes and types. Finally, there is a "governance structure," which involves authority and power relationships that determine how financial, material, and human resources are allocated and flow within a chain.[56] But there is a fourth dimension that is not ordinarily considered in discussions of commodity chains: the generation of wastes at each step of the process.

Figure 3-1 shows a schematic diagram of a generic commodity chain. The final product could be a car, a T-shirt, a VCR, or even a banana. Step A usually takes place in locations with high levels of intellectual knowledge, where people possess specialized design and analytical skills and work with

Figure 3-1   Commodity Chains and Waste Chains

Country	Production Process	Production Steps	Wastes
A	Design	Concept Market study Schematics Inputs	Office wastes Air pollution Energy Land use Greenhouse gases
B	Primary commodity production	Mining Growing	Land change Chemicals Tailings Air and water pollution Greenhouse gases
C	Primary and secondary processing	Smelting Casting Milling Weaving	Tailings Biomass wastes Air and water pollution Toxics Greenhouse gases
D	Sub- and final assembly	Parts manufacture Cutting and sewing Finishing	Excess materials Energy Air and water pollution Packaging Toxics Greenhouse gases
E	Consumption	Driving Watching Eating Wearing	Air and water pollution Sewage and toxics Energy Greenhouse gases

F	Disposal	Burning or burying
		Recycling and reusing
		Extraction and
		   discarding of
		   metals, plastics
			Air & water pollution
			Excess materials
			Toxics
			Greenhouse gases

computers at desks in offices. Even the conceptual design of a product generates various kinds of wastes, as shown in the figure. If we are dealing with a product that requires raw material inputs, the second step (B) of the chain involves mining, refining, or growing. Here, we find land being transformed, with concomitant soil erosion. Mining leaves behinds piles of spoils (tailings), and the processing of minerals may require not only crushing but also separation with chemicals. What is left after the desired mineral is extracted is of little use and is often simply piled on the ground or dumped into evaporation ponds. Agriculture can also be chemical intensive, polluting land and water and poisoning both workers and other species.

In step C, the raw materials are further processed. Minerals may be smelted and cast into more tractable forms, such as bars and ingots. Grain may be milled, and fibers woven. Left behind are more unusable tailings, plant wastes, chemical pollutants, dust, and greenhouse gas emissions. Only in step D does the product begin to acquire a finished form. Here, in a process that may take place in more than one factory or country, bars, ingots, fabrics, and other chunks of material are turned into parts for final assembly. Again, all kinds of waste products are left behind, to be thrown out the door, shipped into the country, or sent to landfills or for recycling. Some of these wastes may be of value to the poor, but some may also be quite toxic.

Between steps D and E comes shipping. Goods are sent from the host country to the home country, by truck, ship, or plane. Transportation requires energy, and energy generates greenhouse gases and other pollutants. From the port or airport the goods go to warehouses and then to retailers. More energy is used. The consumer travels to a store to buy the product. More energy is used. The activity associated with the product (step E) may produce wastes and use more energy. Finally, at the end of its useful life, the product is thrown out (step F). Some parts may be recycled, but not all are either desirable or safe. Others might be burned or buried. Everything has to go somewhere.[57]

One example of the complexity of the environmental effects of commodity chains can be found in the forest industries of the Pacific Coast. Although Canada is counted among the industrialized countries, the economies of its western provinces remain heavily resource oriented. For many years, lumber from British Columbia was produced below cost with government subsidies and shipped in volume to Japan, where it commanded premium prices. Notwithstanding rigorous environmental regulations in British Columbia, deforestation proceeded rapidly. When the Japanese economy went into decline in the early 1990s, Canadian exports to Japan dropped significantly and instead shifted southward to the United States. In the wake of the 1993 North American Free Trade Agreement (NAFTA), U.S. timber companies feared an ever-growing flood of cheaper Canadian wood and pressured the administration of President Bill Clinton to impose limits. The consequent Softwood Lumber Agreement between Canada and the United States blocked timber exports from British Columbia. But because the U.S. demand for lumber boomed during the 1990s, the result of the agreement was to shift deforestation southward and unemployment northward. Canadian forests did not escape the ax, either. The agreement did not cover all woods or all provinces. Exports increased from Canada's eastern provinces to the United States, and government subsidies provided incentives to keep up the logging.[58]

Another area in which globalization is having major environmental impacts is in food production. With technological changes in farming, refrigeration, and shipping, it is now possible to cool and quickly move fruits, vegetables, and flowers around the world.[59] Over the past fifty years, this trend, along with the expansion of international markets in grains, has led to a massive shift from subsistence farming to cash cropping in developing countries. Indeed, cash crops have become a favored generator of hard currency. Specialization in food production has also been fostered by industrialized country trade barriers to certain types of agricultural imports. For example, it is easier to trade in vegetables than grains, because the latter are heavily subsidized by industrialized country governments. As a result, during the Northern winter, it is possible to purchase virtually all kinds of foods, imported from the Southern hemisphere, that were simply not available twenty years ago.

What are the consequences of these changing patterns of agricultural production and trade? Most export crops are capital, rather than labor, intensive. Farming for export relies on chemicals for uniformity, machinery for volume, and high-quality land for productivity. These requirements tend to favor richer farmers (mostly male) and corporations, who own more land and are considered more creditworthy than those with less land and money, for such agriculture almost always requires the taking out of loans. Cash cropping often uses more technology and requires less labor than subsistence agriculture; thus, poor farmers are essentially forced off their small plots and onto lower-quality, often hilly land, and the landless have to migrate to cities. In the former instance, serious land degradation may follow from agriculture on steep slopes; in the latter, growing numbers of impoverished migrants may outstrip the capacity of the urban infrastructure, more often than not already in poor condition, to handle the increased burdens that result.[60]

What Do You Know, and When Did You Know It?

In recent years, much economic growth has come through expansion of what can be called the "information and intellectual capital industries." Growing wealth, especially in the "Triad" of North America, Europe, and Japan, has fostered a growing demand for goods and services, the copying of American cultural and consumption norms, and the expansion of education and travel. This sector of "production" includes all those activities associated with finance and speculative capital. Such changes are generally assumed to have minimal environmental impacts as part of what is sometimes called the "dematerialization" of the economy, yet they are all associated with higher levels of consumption and waste production, as we have seen earlier in this chapter.[61] The transformations of society and individual identity associated with informational and intellectual capital are integral to commodity chains, as consumption of information and goods is required to effect those changes. That is, inasmuch as individual identity is "produced" by appearance, clothing, cars, houses, travel, and so on, an individual's consumption becomes a central part of the production commodity chain of those goods. Environmental impacts follow.

First, as drivers of the economic prosperity of the 1990s, these industries fostered the growth of an increasingly richer middle and upper class, one of whose most conspicuous features was (and remains) visible and conspicuous consumption. Second, the worldwide dissemination of cultural norms and practices sets examples for consumers in other societies, who want to emulate many of them. Third, growing levels of education—primary, secondary, higher—are all associated with increased incomes and cultural awareness, again a facilitator of higher levels of consumption. Finally, the globalization of television and consumers' growing use of the Internet, both of which are advertisement-saturated media, not only foster consumer temptation but also help to "spread the wealth" through diversified forms of information processing and production. Rapid global communication systems make it possible to undertake all kinds of information-based activities "at a distance." Software is written in Bangalore, India, and transmitted to Silicon Valley or Seattle, Washington. Catalog orders by consumers in Texas are taken by operators in South Africa and filled by workers in Iowa. Airplane ticket receipts are compiled by computer workers in the Philippines and returned to Atlanta, Georgia. Incomes grow and so do wastes.

The environmental impacts of the service, information, and intellectual industries are difficult to quantify, but there is no gainsaying the longer-term environmental consequences of intensified consumer capitalism. Poverty remains endemic, and it is important to remember that some 20 percent of the world's population uses about 80 percent of the world's resources and that the income of the richest 50 million people in the world is the same as that of the 2.7 billion poorest. Moreover, during the 1990s, all the gains in the world's income went to the richest 20 percent of the world's population, even as the income of the bottom half declined.[62] And, as we saw in Tables 3-1 and 3-2, the production of wastes by the average American is many times that of the average Indian. By the year 2050, the earth's population will be about 10 billion. Even as few as an additional 200 million "very rich" beneficiaries of globalization will impose an intolerable burden on the earth's environment. Under those circumstances, it seems that it will be extremely difficult to make capitalism "sustainable."

Can Capitalism Be Saved?

Does this mean there is no hope for our current way of life unless we see through radical changes in our economic system? Perhaps not. *Ecological modernization* might provide a means of "saving" capitalism from destroying its material base. Ecological modernization involves, in essence, reducing flows of inputs into the production and consumption process and eliminating, as much as possible, the wastes flowing out of them. Subject to limits imposed by the laws of physics, it is possible, in principle, to extract and process raw materials in much more efficient ways, to develop new production processes that use less toxic or nontoxic chemicals under conditions of constant recycling, and to manufacture goods for high levels of recycling. Some industries, such as pulp and paper manufacturing, have found that ecological modernization reduces not only pollution problems but also production costs.[63] And, as we shall see in Chapter 5, recycling programs in Europe are quite far advanced, requiring that even cars and computers be made in such a way as to make them easy to disassemble and separate into their constituent materials. These materials can then be used to reduce inputs of virgin materials into the production process and, in many cases, to save energy as well.[64]

There are limits to what can be accomplished through technological improvements, however, so ecological modernization must include more than simply new technologies if it is to succeed. As we have seen, externalities are a consequence not only of physical processes but also of social motivations and institutional organization. There is little point in developing ever more fuel-efficient automobiles, for example, if the result is an ever greater number of cars driving ever-increasing distances. In this instance, changes in transportation systems, patterns of living and working, systems for distributing goods, indeed, in the very conception of the "good life," would all be essential to effective ecological modernization. Not only would the mechanisms of the global capitalist economy need to be changed, so would the very purpose of that economy, that is, the endless generation of wealth. As is often the case in situations such as this, the real challenges are social and political, not technological or economic.[65]

Want Not, Waste Not?

Ken Conca argues that between the enormous wealth and staggering poverty characterizing the world there is a "'sustaining middle'—the large but fragile segment of the planet's population that lives, works, and consumes in ways that most closely approximate genuine sustainability." [66] This group, numbering several billion, is not in the position of the very poor, relying heavily on local resources for survival. Nor are its members prodigious consumers, disposing of goods almost as soon as they are acquired. But the sustaining middle is being squeezed, warns Conca, by globalization and ever-expanding capitalism, which entice them to consume more but, often, make it more and more difficult for them to maintain their sustainable lives and practices.

Capitalism, as it exists today, is dependent on continual growth. Notwithstanding the machinations of Adam Smith's "invisible hand," there appears to be nothing, except crisis, that can push the global economic system toward an environmentally sustainable direction. But until that crisis happens, most of those with an interest in the market system as it exists today will argue that it is off in the future and can be dealt with then. Once the crisis arrives, it may be too late to do anything. Capitalism, in any event, does not deal well with far-off times; in fact, they hardly matter at all.

Can capitalism be made environmentally friendly? In principal, there is no reason why not. Environmental and social costs could be internalized into the prices of goods; production systems could be devised that produce much less waste, or none at all; products could be made to last much longer than they do now and they could be recycled at the end of their useful lives. The preservation and conservation of land, water, forests, species, and ecosystems could all become central organizing principles of a sustainable economy. The lives of the poor could be improved through education—especially for women—access to health care services, greater participation in both politics and the economy, and so on.[67] But such a system might be hardly recognizable as the "capitalism" we know today. For the well-off, there would be fewer choices in the marketplace, less opportunity to travel, greater regulation for the public good, higher taxes to pay for necessary public services, in short, many of those things that contemporary governments are so afraid to contemplate, much less legislate. And none of these objectives can be accomplished simply through the market; not only do they require political intervention into markets in order to internalize social costs, they also require political mobilization to generate public support and motivate directed action. In other words, the decision to modify our current economic practices must fall into the provenance of politics. And it is to politics that we turn in the next chapter of this book.

For Further Reading

Clapp, Jennifer. *Toxic Exports: The Transfer of Hazardous Wastes from Rich to Poor Countries*. Ithaca: Cornell University Press, 2001.

Davidson, Eric A. *You Can't Eat GNP: Economics as if Ecology Mattered*. Cambridge, Mass.: Perseus, 2000.

de-Shalit, Avner. *Why Posterity Matters: Environmental Policies and Future Generations*. London: Routledge, 1995.

Gilpin, Alan. *Environmental Economics: A Critical Overview*. Chichester, West Sussex: Wiley and Sons, 2000.

Grove, Richard H. *Green Imperialism: Colonial Expansion, Tropical Island Edens, and the Origins of Environmentalism, 1600–1860*. Cambridge: Cambridge University Press, 1995.

Hays, Samuel P. *Conservation and the Gospel of Efficiency: The Progressive Conservation Movement, 1890–1920*. New York: Atheneum, 1980.

Heilbroner, Robert L. *An Inquiry into the Human Prospect: Looked at Again for the 1990s*. 3d ed. New York: Norton, 1991.

Howitt, Richard. *Rethinking Resource Management: Justice, Sustainability, and Indigenous Peoples*. London: Routledge, 2001.

Milani, Brian. *Designing the Green Economy*. Lanham, Md.: Rowman and Littlefield, 2000.

Ophuls, William, and A. Stephen Boyan. *Ecology and the Politics of Scarcity Revisited: The Unraveling of the American Dream*. New York: Freeman, 1992.

Pearce, David W., and R. Kerry Turner. *Economics of Natural Resources and the Environment*. Baltimore: Johns Hopkins University Press, 1990.

Princen, Thomas, Michael Maniates, and Ken Conca. *Confronting Consumption*. Cambridge: MIT Press, 2002.

Roodman, David Malin. *The Natural Wealth of Nations: Harnessing the Market for the Environment.* New York: Norton, 1998.

Schumacher, E. F. *Small Is Beautiful: Economics as if People Mattered.* New York: Harper and Row, 1973.

Shiva, Vandana. *Tomorrow's Biodiversity.* New York: Thames and Hudson, 2000.

Soderbaum, Peter. *Ecological Economics: A Political Economics Approach to Environment and Development.* London: Earthscan, 2000.

Stevis, Dimitris, and Valerie J. Assetto, eds. *The International Political Economy of the Environment.* Boulder, Colo.: Lynne Rienner, 2001.

4 | Civic Politics and Social Power: Environmental Politics "On the Ground"

All Environmental Politics Are Local

In Chapter 3 we saw that markets, although offered as the "solution" to all environmental problems, can only modify those practices and institutions that do the damage. We never ask whether there are other ways to achieve the ends we seek, ways that might avoid those nagging environmental problems in the first place. A search for alternative means of environmental protection takes us into the realm of politics, for we may find that much greater changes in our beliefs, practices, and institutions are necessary than can be achieved through market-based methods. Such changes will require us to consider how power is used or is present and to decide how it ought to be deployed in order to accomplish our goals. We should expect a considerable amount of debate, conflict, and resistance in the process. After all, societies are organized for consistency and stability, not for change.

How would such an environmental politics appear? It could not be simply a politics of reason or economic calculation. It is not that people are unable to reason or calculate their own interests, but they are strongly and emotionally committed to customs, habits, and expectations. An environmental politics could not be one purely of emotion and impulsiveness, either, for people would soon discover themselves worse off than before. It could not be a politics of global change, for there is too much difference and diversity in the world for a single program to address. And it could not be a politics of individual change, for politics happens only through collective and concerted action. The environmental politics we seek must be one of appropriate scale, with opportunities for productive contact, conflict, and collaboration. And that, it would seem, requires some manner of face-to-face politics.

If "all politics is local," as Tip O'Neill put it, then all environmental problems and environmental politics must be local, too. This chapter is about such local environmental politics, or what we called "social power" in Chapter 1.[1] In the first section, we explore the claim that "all environmental problems and politics are local." They are "local" in the sense that we experience them directly in our own locale. To be sure, it is possible to travel to other places in the world and to see firsthand both problems and politics, but it is the rare individual who is "at home" in multiple locations. Nor does this mean that problems in those other places are irrelevant to us; rather, to have broader impact, politics must be exercised locally.

In the second section, we examine the appearance of environmental politics and social activism in recent decades. Neither is, strictly speaking, a new phenomenon: concerns about the transformation of nature and responses to those changes can be traced back hundreds of years.[2] But most historians of environmentalism agree that the 1960s marked some kind of watershed in the perception and treatment of the environment, one growing as much out of that decade's tumultuous politics as from the evident damage to nature. Of the many social movements that emerged at that time, environmentalism has become most institutionalized and bureaucratized, the most normalized and mainstreamed, the most connected with "business as usual." Indeed, this absorption into the body politic has become something of an obstacle to the practice of environmental politics.

In the third part of the chapter, we take a look at several forms of civic politics and social power that engage with the environment. These include watershed groups, political parties, market activism, and corporate responsibility. These forms are not the entire universe of such activities, but they serve to illustrate some important strategic and tactical distinctions between approaches, as well as some shortcomings from which several of them suffer. In particular, it may be found that those activities that use mainstream methods to accomplish their goals have done little to change the institutions and practices that are the cause of environmental problems in the first place.

The chapter concludes with a brief discussion of social power as a specifically political strategy. This argument is developed in greater detail in Chapter 6, but it is based on the proposition that social change requires deep political engagement with the conditions and arrangements that are the source of environmental degradation. It is not enough to make reasoned arguments that such activities and the damages they cause run contrary to the interests of the offenders and the affected, in the hope that the former will see the light. Environmental politics must involve praxis. *Praxis* is a Greek word meaning "action," but it is action guided by purpose, values, science and, most of all, ethics applied in a political context.

Why All Environmental Politics Are Local

"Social power" is the practice of local politics and as used in this book refers to the political activity and activism of people in civil society, outside of the institutionalized politics of representative democracies. Civil society comprises those groups and associations that are neither part of the state nor part of the market.[3] Some of these—for example, bowling leagues—have no political content at all; some, such as civic improvement associations, have major economic objectives.[4] Others may be part of movements, local reflections of politically mobilized collectives all over the country or world. Many groups see no farther than their neighborhood or city, whereas some are informed by ideas, practices, and contacts that link them to other similar organizations and movements around the world. It is these locally active but globally connected groups that are the practitioners of social power as it most concerns us here.

In the environmental arena, social power of this type spans a broad range of activities and behaviors, including lobbying of municipal authorities, efforts to affect and pass local legislation, social activism and movements, nongovernmental organizations (NGOs) with a local focus, and even so-called NIMBY (not in my back yard) and wise use groups. Those engaged in these activities have local concerns and objectives but are informed and inflamed by ideas and practices they have learned about, or know of, in other places.[5] This does not mean that local action cannot have broader consequences but, rather, that political engagement among people in the places where they live, love, work, and play is at the root of civic politics and social power.

The argument that all environmental politics are local proceeds, therefore, from two premises, a materialist one based in political economy, and a social one growing out of collective practices, habits, and customs.[6] The first premise is rooted in the historical development of local and regional political economies, which stand as background structures to environmental change.

These relatively fixed arrangements, which are visible in human impacts on landscapes, are nonetheless being constantly transformed through actions and processes linked to the global political economy. Think, for example, of the ways in which the disposition of roads and the distribution of traffic is linked to the production of petroleum half a world away or to the building of factory zones throughout Asia to supply parts for the cars that fill those roads.

The second premise has to do with the ways in which we imagine the places in which we live, work, and play, and the ways in which these images become the models for the changes we impose on nature. As Karl Marx put it in *Capital,* "what distinguishes the worst architect from the best of bees is this, that the architect raises his structure in imagination before he erects it in reality. At the end of every labour-process, we get a result that already existed in the imagination of the labourer at its commencement." [7]

In other words, we confront human habitats, or *landscapes,* structured by dynamic and ever-changing social ecologies. Those landscapes reflect decades or centuries of patterned and organized human activity and provide the "tracks," as it were, over which we move today.[8] But those landscapes can be changed, either deliberately or accidentally, and we make those changes with some imagined goals in mind. Our goals might be romantic, practical, self-interested, or even destructive, but we envision them before we execute them. Together, these two factors—what is given and what has been imagined—comprise the material and conceptual localities in which the consequences of environmental change and damage are most clearly evident.

A developer might decide, on her own, to build a housing tract and thereby change the landscape. Although she would need to receive all kinds of planning permission to proceed, and might even solicit "public input" into the design, the idea and project would be hers alone. By contrast, social power rests on the very idea of environmental praxis—of directed, ethical action—and involves an approach to politics that depends on bringing like-minded people together to discuss, debate, and design a specific environmental project, and then to develop it themselves. This is the essence of both civic politics and social power.

History, Political Economy, and Place

In *The 18th Brumaire of Louis Napoleon,* Marx wrote that, "Men make their own history, but they do not make it as they please; they do not make it under self-selected circumstances, but under circumstances existing already, given and transmitted from the past. The tradition of all dead generations weighs like an Alp on the brains of the living." [9] To this, we might add, as well, the material artifacts of that history. Human activities are, to a large extent, patterned and habitual. Not only do we fall into rather fixed schedules in our everyday lives, we also tend to repeat behaviors and duplicate practices that appear to result in the ends we desire. For more than a century, for example, railroads were the most efficient way of accessing continental interiors and moving around people, armies, and goods. They were often quite profitable for those who financed and built them. Railroads transformed landscapes through their construction, and they have provided the instrumentalities of transformation ever since. They affected the success or failure of agriculture; they contributed to the growth and shrinking of cities; they moved mountains of raw materials and commodities over thousands of miles. For the most part, those railroads are still today in the places they were originally laid down. [10]

But during the 160-year history of railroads, other forms of transportation were imagined and developed. The development of the internal combustion engine ultimately led to the production of hundreds of millions of automobiles and trucks and to the construction of vast road networks. And these were laid down, sometimes on top of already-existing rails, sometimes parallel to them, sometimes with no consideration of those tracks at all. New transformations, new patterns, new landscapes followed. The old landscapes did not, however, vanish, nor did their continuing impacts on human consciousness and practice. As on a palimpsest, whose earlier writings have been overwritten but not entirely obliterated, landscapes overwritten by later human practices never vanish completely.

In other words, the environments that people confront in their daily lives are not easily changed, abandoned, or erased. Those environments are understood best not as a collection of resources or a hierarchy of ecosystems but, rather, as landscapes created over time through complex interactions between patterned human practices and nature. The history of those practices is etched, so to speak, in political economy, in both institutions and artifacts. From this perspective, nature is never "pristine" or untouched by human action, and may even be the result of millennia of human intervention and modification. [11] The landscapes we transform are already part of "second nature." [12] *

---

*Recall that "second nature" is nature as transformed by human action, for example, apparently primeval forests managed by indigenous peoples through controlled use of fire, or the nature we find in New York's Central Park.

Imagine, for example, the human transformation of San Francisco Bay. Before the arrival of European explorers, the Native Americans living around the bay hardly made a mark on its shape and topography, leaving along its shores not much more than shell mounds.[13] With the California Gold Rush, the bay came to be used not only for shipping, for which docks had been built, but also as a sewer, a place to dump wastes, and a source of new living space on landfill. Cities grew up, marshes and wildlife disappeared, concrete and asphalt were laid down. By 1950 perhaps a third of the pre-European bay had disappeared. During the second half of the twentieth century, "unfilling" began, as growing numbers of development restrictions were imposed, wetlands were restored, and certain activities restricted.[14] Thus, on the one hand, the bay as a land and waterscape was transformed by more than a century's municipal growth and industrialization. Some of its original features were obliterated, but those that remained established the parameters influencing subsequent action. In the Marina District of San Francisco, housing was built on old landfill. No one imagines destroying that housing—earthquakes notwithstanding—and moving the fill; that part of the bay is gone. On the other hand, efforts to protect or restore the bay have been informed and motivated (and limited) both by changes in global political economy—for example, in shipping patterns and technologies—and by the growing influence of environmentalism and its projects.

But landscapes are constructed and transformed not only through human methods of production, which is how we often think of environmental change and degradation, but also as a consequence of social reproduction, a process we rarely consider. To understand more fully how imagination is turned into material reality, however, we need to examine how and where such visions originate. What are the sources of "imagined landscapes"? How do these visions mirror the inner life of human societies, beliefs, and behaviors? Why are some transformations accomplished and others not? The antediluvian biological and geophysical world ("first nature") offers opportunities for and imposes constraints on what changes can be made to it—mountains are difficult to move. The same is true of second nature, altered and molded as it is by people in ways that meet human needs and desires. In other words, the transformation of nature involves not only the physical process of modification (and degradation) but also cognitive processes of imagination and design. These visions of nature transformed are implemented locally, no matter how far away the visionaries, architects, and financiers might live. The politics of those visions are local, not global.

There are at least three important types of vision and action involved in such "reconstructions" of nature. First, people arriving in a new place tend to reproduce what is familiar and customary, recreating old abodes and material practices in their new homes. That is why parts of the American Midwest often appear similar to landscapes in northern and central Europe. But such efforts sometimes fail. Nature does not permit all changes, and people already living in such places—whether indigenous or not—often resist new arrivals and their grand ideas. Still, traces of "the old country" can be found in landscapes everywhere.[15]

Second, people's perceptions of the physical environment are mobilized as cognitive elements in the transformation of nature. That is, some might see a wetland as a "wasted space" while others regard it as a marine "nursery." Those who want to "develop" the wetland must convince a host of people that it is useless or inefficient as it is and will be more benign if converted into commodities and capital (as in turning it into housing with canals instead of driveways). If the developers succeed in their project, the conversion of one landscape into another will generate capital, foster accumulation, and enable people to seek out other opportunities for further transformation of nature and accumulation of capital.[16] The altered landscapes can be returned to their former condition only at great economic and political cost, and efforts to protect what remains unexploited often encounter stiff resistance from those who benefit—or think they do—from continuing transformation and modification.

A final form of transformation arises from what we could call "environmental idealism," the effort to restore altered or degraded landscapes to some approximation of a previous condition, a historical nature as it might once have been.[17] Nature, in these schemes, becomes not only something to be manipulated in the pursuit of material ends but also a reflection of who people are or whom they would like to become. Restored wetlands and wildernesses are the material realization of such environmental "idealism," expressions of notions of humans as stewards or guardians of nature.[18]

Such transformative processes are central to the claim that all environmental politics are local. It is not that the causal chains of damage necessarily arise locally or that the effects of our local activities do not extend beyond our locale. Rather, it is that the greatest impacts of both environmental insult and praxis are primarily local, and these patterns or forms are reproduced elsewhere. A stream or river that might be dying or dead because of the pollution dumped by factories along its banks is there for all to see. National or state law might mandate cleanup and compel factory owners to reduce or eliminate pollution, but this may require legal or even police intervention. People are likely to resent outside interference in municipal affairs and to resist it. Politics must focus, therefore, not only on changing the material conditions whereby environmental degradation takes place but also on the social (imagined, ideological, and cognitive) conditions that rationalize and support the continuation of that degradation. These are conditions that, if not local in origin, must be changed through local action. We will return to this point later in this chapter.

The Structures of Contemporary Political Economy

In Chapter 3 we saw how much contemporary production and consumption has been organized in the form of long-distance, transnational "commodity chains." Just as goods are produced in places far away from where they are consumed, environmental problems tend to be treated as originating in other places and thereby requiring action far away. Thus, it is not uncommon to read that population growth and poverty in developing countries are the "real threats" to the global environment, and, therefore, that is where policies must be put into place.[19] Yet, as decades of failed development have shown, it is not so easy to manage people at a distance.[20]

The commodity chain model illuminates two aspects of the difficulties associated with "management at a distance." First, the impacts of production and consumption happen, for the most part, in specific places. Second, the arrival of things from "far away" leads to mystification of that process as well as the establishing of linkages between global and local economies and environments. An entire production and consumption chain may be spread over many different locations or countries (see Figure 3-1), but each step of the process occurs in a specific place or country. Raw materials and commodities are extracted from the environment, and parts are shipped to the production, processing, and consumption sites. Various types of wastes and pollution are emitted at each stage, too. Thus, while greenhouse gas emissions from the production and use of an automobile are rapidly discharged into the "global" atmosphere, they originate from very specific and localized sources. Their complex organization means that centralized coordination of behaviors throughout such chains is virtually impossible.

Mystification is rather more complicated, for we are encouraged "not to know" about where things come from, how they were produced, or the kinds of social and environmental problems with which they are associated.* A conventional perspective on the distinction between local and global relies solely on the spatial character of the resource in question. For example, soil erosion is normally treated as a local matter, even though it is a problem found all over the world. It is usually attributed to the specific practices of farmers, loggers, land developers, and others who modify the landscape in ways that degrade soil retention mechanisms and permit water to carry soil away.[21] Why they engage in such destructive practices, even when they "know better," is rarely considered. Structural factors, such as economic pressures and legal incentives to increase agricultural production, to build on undeveloped land, and to cut down forests are recognized as important in motivating these behaviors, but they are not given much attention. They are regarded as part of the social background and "business as usual." Responsibility for soil loss is therefore attributed to the individual or group; these individuals or groups must be "educated" and "trained" in less harmful practices and, if they fail to learn the lessons, criticized.

Within the global political economy, this distinction between individual practices and structural effects arises from the liberal ontology and legal principles that infuse capitalism. Under contemporary legal systems, most of which are based on either Anglo-American or European law, liability for actions is attributed to a specific actor, be it an individual, a corporation, or a state; structural conditions never enter the debate. This point has been made forcefully by Johan Galtung in a discussion of the relationship between Western legal systems and structural violence.† He argues that the legal organization of industrialized, capitalist societies rests on the principles of actor culpability and liability. At the same time, Western law renders invisible the role of structures, such as the organization of and incentives in markets, in engendering material impacts and violations of norms, ethics, and laws.[22] To put this another way, no one has ever been indicted, convicted, and fined or imprisoned for engaging in "business as usual," even though it is the cause of most environmental damage.

A structural analysis of environmental impacts in a commodity chain reveals a sequence of processes that concentrate culpable actions at specific

*Indeed, with a few exceptions, the rules of international trade prohibit discrimination against imported goods based on how they are produced, so long as they are "essential equivalents"— more or less identical in form and function—of goods already for sale in the importing country.
†Structural violence involves injuries, such as hunger and ill health due to endemic poverty and injustice, that arise not from individual action but, rather, structural conditions, such as the operation of markets.

points, even as the logic operating throughout the chain is one over which individual actors have little control. The factory owner is compelled to dump wastes illegally because he is a subcontractor operating under strict contractual conditions laid down by the foreign corporation. The owner could act otherwise, but the result would be higher costs, loss of business, and, perhaps, plant closure. This emphasis on specific actor liability serves to mystify the causes of environmental degradation and to displace environmental (and other) politics from one arena of action to another. Thus, we can see soil erosion in specific places as a consequence of an individual's necessary response to compelling factors inherent in market organization and relations. The individual must respond to these compulsions (cost cutting) or suffer the consequences (hunger or bankruptcy). The displacement of responsibility onto the individual obscures the role of power in the political decisions about market rules and organization made and enforced in other places, by other people.

Or we can see the international treatment of climate change as a way to shift responsibility for high levels of greenhouse gas emissions out of the arena of production and consumption within societies and onto other parties. This transfers the problem from the realm of local and national politics into the arena of interstate market relations, where politics are muted, if not entirely absent. The result is to displace the focus of climate change policies from structural arrangements and practices that encourage continued and growing emissions to questions of how much each individual state should be permitted to emit now and in the future. What is never addressed politically are the ethics of maintaining greenhouse gas emission rates, linked to production and consumption, at such disparate levels among countries or people. Again, the role of power in the structuring of these market relations is partially, if not wholly, obscured.

To put this another way, the claim that all environmental politics are "local" is based on what has been called the "agent-structure problem," which can be understood, in this case, as a disconnect between the individualist orientation of capitalism as a social order and the structural features of capitalist political economy.[23] We make our choices in the market, and in our everyday lives, on an individual basis, often with little thought to how they might affect or be linked to other individuals nearby and far away. Such choices, as we saw in the discussions of advertising in Chapter 3, are not simply the product of our individual desires or needs. They are connected to structures, and those structures affect the environment and have global reach. The structures are not particularly amenable to change through action by individual agents; acting alone, each of us can hardly have an impact. Collective political action is required to modify or transform such structures, and it may best be initiated where agents are offered the greatest opportunity to act, in localized settings where praxis is possible and practical, rather than in national or international ones where no one is interested in structural change.

The Power of Social Power

We are often told that local efforts to engage in structural change make sense only if all other localities act similarly. After all, why should people in your town deliberately and with intent drive fewer miles if no one else is doing it? The difference in national or global emissions would be minuscule, and it would be foolish to suffer the economic losses that would surely accompany such a project. This argument is valid, however, only if we accept individualist market logic as providing the definition of what is rational. It is the inverse of the old question often posed by parents to their children in debates about peer pressure: "So, no? If everyone else jumped off a cliff, you would, too?"

It would be equally rational to define a political ethic whereby each locality would recognize, resist, and reorganize the invisible incentives imposed by structures of production and consumption. Such an ethic would not regard the local as one, self-interested individualist point among many, bound to lose in an eternal competitive race if it were to give up even one step. Instead, it would see the local as the people who live and work there, a group with collective principles and goals that give due consideration to others, whether human or not. Moreover, those who implement such an ethic through their praxis would recognize both the power of their collective action and the ways in which it would inform similar groups in other places. Civic action and social power are, potentially, expressions of such praxis.

Is Collective Action a Problem?

But what about the parent's question to the child about peer pressure and competition? Is it so easily dismissed? The frequent displacement of politics to higher levels of collective behavior is often justified by a popular ontological argument that problematizes political action outside certain limited settings. As discussed in Chapter 3, this is called the "collective action problem." [24] The collective action problem is a contemporary version of both the Hobbesian "state of nature" (discussed in the subsection "Realism: A World of War" in Chapter 2) and the parable of the stag hunt as related by Jean

Jacques Rousseau, the eighteenth-century French political philosopher. Both are arguments about the individual temptation to defect from collective action and the necessity for some authority to prevent defection.

In Rousseau's story, a group of hunters is pursuing a deer, which will be killed only if everyone in the group cooperates in the hunt.[25] If the deer is captured, everyone will eat; if it escapes, everyone will go hungry. One hunter spies a rabbit. He realizes that the group might fail in its pursuit of the deer. He will have no trouble snaring the rabbit on his own and satisfying his hunger. What should he do? Men are selfish and self-interested, according to Hobbes, Rousseau, and the theorists of the collective action problem.[26] Our selfish hunter chases the rabbit, catches it, and eats. The deer escapes, however, and everyone else goes hungry. Self-interest mandates defection. Knowing this, how can a hunt even take place to begin with?

Although Rousseau was interested in the origins of government, his parable presents a purely economistic picture of human motivations. It implies that only through some sort of coercion—custom, law, pressure, threat of loss, or ostracism—will people forgo their individually harmful acts and work together for the social good. Adam Smith subsequently introduced the "invisible hand" into this calculus in order to explain how, in markets, individual action can serve the collective good and is, therefore, not a problem.[27] But Smith, as we have already noted, also believed that a shared morality, rooted in religious belief and practice, would moderate individual appetite and prevent purely selfish injurious behavior.[28]

Rousseau's argument, as well as Hobbes's, is much the same as that made by Garrett Hardin in "The Tragedy of the Commons," discussed in Chapter 3. As we saw there, Hardin was concerned about high rates of population growth and the effects of too many people on both food supplies and the environment. He could not imagine a group of herders cooperating to maintain a field owned in common, thinking that each would seek to maximize his individual take, with the consequence that the field would be destroyed. Hardin did not think that a local politics of pasture could exist in a world of self-interested men. He believed that either privatization or police power (that is, a sovereign) would be necessary to keep the pasture from ruin.[29] Hardin's arguments have had an enormous impact on environmental politics and environmentalism, for they seem logical within their own terms (liberalism and individual self-interest) and frightening in their implications. In fact, Hardin appears to have been wrong in both his parable and his fears for the future.[30] There are many documented cases of cooperation in the protection of commons without the element of overt coercion.[31] To be sure, in most of these instances, the users of a resource held in common realize material benefits from it and pay costs to sustain it. But the users are disciplined in their use of the resource not by a sovereign but by bonds of trust and obligation, mutual reliance, and some sense of a common good. Free riding or defection may result in a violator's expulsion from the user group and loss of livelihood and sustenance. Awareness of this ultimate sanction keeps users from engaging in wholly self-interested and, ultimately, destructive behavior.

The collective action problem is not without an inherent politics of its own, which is obscured by its compelling economistic logic. Not only is our experience in a capitalist society one of constant and never-satiated needs, but our socialization has conferred on us the foundational assumptions of material envy and self-interested behavior.[32] "Wanting more" is naturalized through belief and practice. If everyone else does it, we would be foolish not to do it, too. And how can it be otherwise? In effect, by making the claim that collective action is rational only when each individual realizes a clearly defined benefit, the reasoning behind the collective action problem makes other forms of collective action appear foolish and even inexplicable. Consequently, social activists who engage in politics outside established institutions, and who appear to realize small or nonexistent benefits from their activities, are made to seem both irrational and even dangerous to business as usual.[33] Indeed, if too many people were to act in such a fashion, business as usual might well be threatened.

This is evident, once again, in the American position on global climate change. The costs will be concentrated over a small group (rich countries) while the benefits will be dispersed over many people or groups (both rich and poor countries). Why not spend that money protecting ourselves, and continue to benefit from our environmentally harmful practices? And, in the long run, others cannot be trusted to adhere to the Kyoto Protocol, so why should we? That we might all hang together as a result of climate change does not seem to have much effect on either practice or consciousness.

Collective Action Is Not a Problem

Does widespread adherence to the collective action problem mean that collective praxis is impossible? Not at all! We see people acting together all the time, apparently in defiance of the logic of the collective action problem. But why does this happen? Are people irrational or do they know something? Indeed, we can construct counterarguments to the collective action problem that invoke collective interests as well as ethical principles, and it is these arguments that help to illuminate both social power and civic politics. The first argument involves intergenerational concerns, that is, the interests of future generations who are not in a position to make decisions today.[34] The second is based on intragenerational equity and justice and the fact that many of those most affected by environmental degradation have little or no power over the processes that cause it.[35] These are not the only counterarguments available, but they may be the most important ones.

The intergenerational argument rests on the assumption that we would wish to leave our descendants a world that is, at a minimum, not in worse environmental condition than the one in which we live today. This would mean, for example, avoiding drastic climate modification or a world laced with toxic wastes. In such a world, some are likely to be better off, some will be no better or worse off than we are today, and many others are likely to be worse off. But we do not know who these different groups of people will be and whether they will be kin or not, co-nationals or not. Such uncertainty ought to make us cautious, and for the benefit of everyone in the future, we should act so as to minimize the harms that we do to the environment today, even if the costs are high for the present generation. This is sometimes called the "precautionary principle."[36] In essence, if we have doubts about the potential for the negative effects of an action, we should avoid that action.

The intragenerational argument rests on the claim that environmental impacts resulting from highly distorted and unequal patterns of consumption cannot be justified under any set of ethical principles that recognizes all humans as deserving of equal consideration. This is especially the case if the actions leading to those impacts serve to improve the condition of the better-off while worsening that of the poor. Inasmuch as simple reliance on markets and economic growth to address these concerns appears unlikely to alter greatly the existing distribution of impacts, we must act in a way that does change that distribution.[37] Therefore, on the principle that we should try to minimize such suffering as we might impose on others, we are ethically bound to moderate and modify our current desires as well as the practices causing the environmental degradation. While we will experience material costs from such changes—and they may be quite substantial—the benefits to those who are worse off will compensate us not only through the ethical satisfaction we realize from our changed behavior but also through reductions in the environmental impacts of both wealth and poverty.*

---

*This is a utilitarian argument, but it also arises from the principle that humans (and nature) deserve respect and should be treated as ends and not means.

The logic of the critique of the collective action problem implicit in these two arguments, while more difficult to articulate, is nonetheless compelling. Ultimately, as conscious beings we do not act only on the basis of self-interest ("interests" that are, as often as not, associated with the interests of capital). There are norms that we follow in pursuit of a common good, even if not always in a consistent fashion. Norms are principles that express a society's sense of what is proper and good, and they can be the subject of political debate and action.[38] Much of the collective action we observe does take place on the basis of such norms. For example, the preservation of an old-growth forest, for both ecological and aesthetic reasons, might mean forgoing its conversion into lumber, capital, collective enrichment for a few and "affordable" housing for others.[39] But even if trees can be replanted and forests grown, as is often argued, a world without old-growth forests is one impoverished in many nonmonetary ways. Those who suffer from such actions can be compensated for their losses; forests cannot defend themselves.[40] There are good reasons not to cut off your nose, even if everyone else is doing it. But such changed awareness and practice does not come easily, especially if we rely on individuals acting by themselves. People may act as individuals, but they do so on the basis of social beliefs and habits. And societies do not, as a rule, easily or quickly change their foundational norms and principles. Except during periods of crisis, arguments in favor of change are regarded as odd, irrational, or even subversive. Moreover, people tend not only to resist such arguments but to insist that the ends of those claims cannot be achieved and would be too costly, if not suicidal.

This is the essence of realism as both philosophy and practice: we must deal with the world as it is, and not as we might wish it, with the "is" and not the "ought." Were that really the case, social and political change would never take place. That such change does, sometimes, occur indicates why "realism" is given that name and generally deployed to protect those interests and structures that benefit the powerful. Under these circumstances, realism is no more than the ideology of those dominant in society.[41]

Social Power: Against "Realism"

Civic politics and social activism are responses to the ideology of realism. Institutionalized political practices—voting, lobbying, representation—are mechanisms for reproducing a society's foundational principles and relations in a stable and predictable fashion, without the appearance of coercion or constraint.[42] At best, however, such practices can generate only small variations in the status quo, in response either to the moods of the electorate or the wishes of elites. Social power is a means of countering the conservative tendencies inherent in all democratic political systems.

In order to understand better the concept of social power and the practices associated with it, we need to delve a bit into liberal political theory. Most readers of this book are likely to be living in politically liberal, market-based countries. Although the details will differ from one to the next—as between the United States, Germany, and Japan, for example—the social world in which individuals find themselves is composed of two arenas of institutions and action: the public and the private. The public sphere is generally associated with the state and comprises what we conventionally understand as "politics." The private sphere is generally associated with everyday life and is composed of family, civic associations, businesses, and markets.[43] * This distinction between public and private is not entirely straightforward, but in market democracies it is a means of differentiating between "legitimate" political activities that do not challenge the social order and those activities that support the social order on a daily basis but appear to play no overt role in its political organization, institutions, and relations of power.[44] To put this another way, the private sphere remains central to the maintenance of power exercised through established political institutions because the social order, or "civil society," defined as nonpolitical, is the basis for this power. Because of this separation, "normal" action within the private sphere is structurally unable to challenge or change the organization and institutions of the public sphere. The privileging of the autonomy of the individual and his or her self-interests characteristic of market-based democracies reifies individual action and further obscures the possibilities for social change.[45] A little reflection on the public-private distinction illuminates more clearly its function in the containment of non-institutionalized political activity.

The family is conventionally regarded as central to the private sphere and an arena from which the state should be excluded.[46] Yet, the state is routinely involved in regulating both forms of and behaviors within the family. Both conservatives and liberals complain about such regulation—for different reasons—but the intrusion of the state illustrates just how artificial the public-private divide really is. In the United States, the campaign to outlaw

---

*Sometimes, a distinction is made between the private (family), the state, and the market. As we shall see, the private-public distinction is most germane here.

non-heterosexual marriage, to alter the tax code to favor nuclear families, to encourage sexual abstinence among teenagers, even the requirement that the name of a child's father and mother both appear on a birth certificate, all represent the extension of the public hand into the private sphere. Conversely, media exposure of the sexual peccadilloes of public figures and the illegal activities of their children, as well as efforts to legislate morality, among other things, show us how the private lies at the heart of the public.

All human life involves politics. Setting boundaries between public and private disciplines the private even as it serves to depoliticize many so-called private issues that are political and public at heart. This notional separation of public and private becomes a means of stabilizing, reproducing, and naturalizing certain hegemonic social relations, such as the "nuclear family." Challenges to these relations and their inherent politics, such as those arising from civic politics and social power, are thereby rendered highly controversial and threatening. There are no officially approved political channels for contesting such naturalized arrangements and the politics they carry in everyday life.

Social power, which includes both civic politics and social activism, originates in the private realm but is aimed at the public sphere. The dividing line between public and private is rather vague in the case of civic politics, which involves the activities of professional and bureaucratic associations that deal largely in the formulation, implementation, and modification of public policies. Civic politics is also practiced by both NGOs and corporations, which rely on lobbying, influence, and expertise to accomplish their objectives. Some of these groups have their origins in movements of social activism but have become somewhat institutionalized as they have become well established, with trained, salaried staffs. Strictly speaking, such aggregations of social power violate the tenets of representative democracy, which is organized primarily around the individual expression of preferences through the vote and secondarily on the basis of individual efforts to communicate preferences to duly elected representatives.

Social activism is, by contrast, less attentive to the separation between public and private. The exercise of social power involves provocations and resistance to the public order and takes place outside of the constraints of institutionalized politics.[47] Action occurs when social movements, composed of a broad range of individuals and organizations, sometimes organized into coalitions, seek to extend the private into the public, thereby pressuring governments and institutions to change their policies or even reject them. At times, these movements are able to mount major challenges to established power, and come to be treated as threats to the institutionalized public sphere.[48]

Taken together, civic politics and social power constitute the arena of civil society. Some political philosophers and theorists characterize civil society as a realm of private, selfish, bourgeois activity; others argue that it is central to the constitution of public politics and the state.[49] This point of dispute is relevant, however, only in liberal democratic societies, in which political action outside of approved channels is regarded as inappropriate, illegitimate, or even threatening to the social order (as expressed, for example, in the application of the term "environmental extremism" to relatively benign activities).[50] The so-called public-private distinctions, and disputes over them, also apply to what has been called "global civil society." [51]

The Origins of Contemporary Social Power

Why is there so much organizational and movement activity today focused on the environment? Fifty years ago, there was no global environmental movement, as such, and very few environmental organizations. Today, it is virtually impossible to count all these organizations, and they appear and disappear almost at will. Environmental movements—there is more than one—include many players and have become major influences on both law and practice in many different forums. Most social movement theorists invoke some form of self-interest to explain the motivations behind social power. They argue that financial, informational, and human resources must be available to support activism and that the "opportunity" to act must present itself to activists. But to what degree these instrumental elements are required for the activation of social power is a subject of considerable debate among those who study the phenomenon.[52]

Why do such arguments matter? A group or movement that is driven by self-interest, mobilizes resources, and seeks opportunities to act is not much different from the traditional interest or lobbying group: it is an element of social power but not a challenge to political structures. In the United States, at least, we have come to regard such organizations as part of the institutionalized political system, even if some people regard them as pernicious interlopers into the mechanisms of representative democracy. By contrast, movements of social activism are motivated by emotion, justice, and altruism and, as we saw earlier, are frequently regarded as acting (illegitimately) outside accepted political practices. From the perspective of those within the institutionalized political system, social movements can be difficult if not impossible to manage and domesticate. Yet, the conditions that give rise to social power and, especially, social activism, must arise from changes within society that somehow trigger popular mobilization and engender high levels of commitment to issues and problems. Because we are interested specifically in the environment, these conditions must be related to the arguments about local environmental politics made earlier in this chapter. Generally speaking, we can identify four mobilizing conditions:

- Material change: Changes to the local political economy are a central element in the mobilization of social actors seeking to protect the environment, for they shape the material base that people see and experience around them. Changes in this material base—as in a shift from heavy industry to services—are tied to changes in perceptions and experiences, as well as to alterations in class structures and relations. Impacts on health and well-being are part of such changes in the material base, too, and they alter the ways in which people are linked to their localities and perceive their relations to others. An example of this might be the construction of a road through a local forest or wetland, which results in greater traffic and housing densities, with concomitant effects on air and water quality.
- Challenges to shared meanings of nature: People living in a particular place tend to hold similar perceptions of nature in that place (even when they are at odds ideologically). Certain biological (forests, wetlands) and physical (rivers, mountains) features are marked as signifiers and symbols of place, and their presence acts as a kind of local "glue." When, however, these signifiers are threatened physically by "normal" activities undertaken through the local political economy, a growing collective consciousness can develop in opposition. For example, city leaders might urge further development of nearby "underutilized" agricultural lands in order to foster economic growth, generating concern among those who would rather see preservation of open space.
- Common epistemological framing: A shared understanding of environment, and how it ought to be treated, is also important to social power (and here is where ideological differences become critical). As the material base changes—for example, from direct exploitation via industrial production to indirect exploitation through recreation and

ecotourism—the epistemological relationship between nature and people is reframed.[53] Such reframings are motivated by processes both external and internal to locality. Conflict can develop, for example, between those who seek to use the environment for further private accumulation and profit and those who seek to "use" the environment for its role in both aesthetic and health concerns.

- Normative shifts: Finally, changes in the way people value their relationships to nature—a consequence of material shifts around them and epistemological shifts in their understanding of the physical world—play a central role in the mobilization of social power. Ultimately, it is the sense of what "ought" to be, rather than what is, that motivates many people to act. Like Marx's architect, they imagine that "ought" and seek to turn it into an "is," and they do so in concert with others of like mind and capacities.[54]

What we see here is a process whereby material and cognitive (social) elements prompt and inform each other, encouraging people to recognize material change, comprehend its material impacts, formulate an understanding of its significance, and mobilize around alternatives, with the objective of opposing or redressing that change. But theorists of social power disagree on the mechanisms whereby social and political change are ultimately effected. How does action within the private realm of liberal societies lead to political impacts and outcomes? How might change happen? Four approaches are discussed below: consciousness-raising, resource mobilization, party organization, and "praxis," that is, active engagement with structures.

Consciousness-raising

There is general agreement that, as a political and social phenomenon, contemporary environmentalism is not much more than forty years old, and the publication of Rachel Carson's *Silent Spring* in 1962 is often regarded as the starting point, if not the trigger, of the movement.[55] But it is often difficult to separate out environmentalism from the other forms of political and social activism that, in many parts of the world, characterized the 1960s.[56] What all social movements and activism of that decade did share was a growing skepticism for the authority of political, economic, social, and scientific institutions. In particular, throughout much of the period following the end of World War II, from 1945 to 1960, science was regarded as possessed of awesome powers of explanation, prediction, and control. Although it had produced the atomic bomb and the threat of a nuclear World War III, science also promised a glossy future, absent of the demons of hunger, illness, and poverty that had plagued humanity for so long.[57] *Silent Spring* was only one of several critiques of this optimistic view that appeared during the 1950s and 1960s.[58] Carson's arguments about the effects of DDT on birds were strongly resisted, and even attacked as subversive, by both industry and government.[59] Nonetheless, her critique resonated strongly with that segment of the American public becoming disillusioned with both science and the state (a disillusionment that also contributed to the rise of opposition to the Vietnam War).

Whatever the trigger of social activism might have been, there is no denying that the 1960s saw a considerable expression of social power around the world, certainly more than there had been for several decades.[60] The antiwar, civil rights, anti–nuclear weapons, and free speech movements in the United States had their parallels in other countries. The events of 1968—in Czechoslovakia, France, Mexico, the United States, and elsewhere—marked it as a watershed year for political and social protest and resistance, which left their imprint on many Western countries.[61] Authority has never fully recovered.[62]

Environmentalism can be seen as an outgrowth of these other movements and the skeptical tendencies that gave rise to them. In the United States, the environmental movement encompassed, in particular, a segment of American society—young, white, and well off—many of whose members had not been deeply engaged by other, more obviously political issues. In subsequent decades, environmental activism spread throughout the world, expanding to include people and groups left out at the creation, such as racial minorities, indigenous peoples, and even nationalist movements.[63] Environmental groups also built transnational coalitions with other movements focused on issues such as human rights.[64] The emotions and actions associated with the movements of the 1960s fed into what were later called "post-material" values.[65] Some people became less concerned with livelihood and more concerned about the norms and values under which they lived. This change was also driven by an ongoing economic shift from heavy "metal-smashing" and highly polluting industries to services and knowledge-based production.[66]

Among other things, "post-material" values include a growing aesthetic appreciation of nature and concern about individual health, both of which require more attention to pollution and other forms of environmental damage. In other words, while material factors were central to this change, the key element, some argue, was a shift in individual consciousness, a process that has come to be called "consciousness-raising." Because people find meaning in their lives on the basis of their ideas about life and living, a change in ideas can result in a change in meanings and consequent action. If enough people alter their ideas and practices, they will effect social change.

But consciousness-raising has its limits, as can be seen in the example of "green consumerism." [67] A growing number of commercially available products are certified, in one form or another, as environmentally friendly (although the consumer often has to take such guarantees on faith; see the discussion of certification later in this chapter). If enough people shop with an environmental consciousness, goes the argument, producers will see the growing demand as a profit opportunity and will supply appropriate goods. Eventually, the preponderance of products will be environmentally friendly, a result brought about wholly through directed changes in consumer preferences.[68]

Certainly, demand for such goods has been growing, even though they tend to be more expensive than their nongreen counterparts, and more and more companies are producing them.[69] Organic farming has grown by leaps and bounds over the past decade, largely as a result of consumers' desire for foods free of agricultural chemicals.[70] Yet, the act of buying a particular product, based on preferences, arises almost entirely out of individual choice and not collective decision making or activism. Individual action of this type cannot be the basis for social power. Markets, moreover, are not the best institution on which to rely for political objectives. Consumer preferences change, often under an onslaught of advertising or peer pressure or economic change. Manufacturers change their product lines, especially if profit margins drop. If politics is about collective action, green consumerism and consciousness-raising are not politics.

Resource Mobilization

Although there are competing explanations for what are called the "new social movements" and disputes over whether they are really "new," resource mobilization theories are generally based on three elements. First, people are frustrated by certain conditions that are not addressed through institutionalized political processes. Second, some people possess the resources—skills, knowledge, and money—to underwrite collective action that agitates for something to be done. Finally, movement leaders espy certain kinds of political opportunities that enable them not only to organize frustrated people but also to demonstrate that frustration publicly. If enough people join together to act, their "contentious politics" may pressure political authorities to respond and change those conditions.[71]

One example of resource mobilization is visible in the series of demonstrations and protests held in recent years during various international economic and trade meetings (in Geneva; Genoa; Göteborg, Sweden; Seattle; Washington, D.C.; and other cities). This is often called the "global justice movement." According to the framework of the new social movements, growing numbers of people are angry about the negative social and environmental effects that result from globalization (see also Chapter 3). They are seeking outlets for their anger and ideals and want to pressure governments and institutions to reform. These repeated demonstrations have sensitized political and economic elites to growing dissatisfaction with the world economic system, but they have also made governments rely much more on police power to limit such activities.[72] More broadly, numerous local, national, and transnational organizations—in the tens of thousands or more—are dedicated to a variety of post-material issues, including environmental protection, enforcement of health and labor regulations, sustainable development, fair trade, human rights, indigenous peoples, and many others (Table 4-1).[73] These groups have their own projects, sources of funding, and supporters, and they are always concerned about bringing more attention to their particular issue area. As we have seen in earlier chapters, there are links between globalization and many of these problems, and it is a relatively straightforward matter to highlight these linkages. There are not, however, many opportunities to bring these connections to public attention or into the political arena. In most countries, governments are committed to neoliberalism and globalization either by choice or necessity, and institutionalized political channels for expressing opposition and resistance are limited.[74] Moreover, when confronted by activists' demands, individual governments and officials respond that the necessities of remaining internationally competitive do not permit them to change their policies so as to address the concerns of the protesters. To do so would be to cave in to anarchy and the street. Besides, such policies are the result of "market forces," argue governments, over which no one really has any control.[75]

Through this structural sleight of hand, the locus of responsibility for the problems raised by the global justice movement is shifted out of the national sphere and into the international one. There, the Group of Eight, the World Bank, the International Monetary Fund (IMF), and the World Trade Organization (WTO) symbolize, even if they do not actually run, the global

Table 4-1   Transnational Examples of Social Power

Issue area	Sample of activist regulatory campaigns
Women's rights	Amnesty International Campaign for Women's Human Rights
Climate	Climate Action Network
Forestry	Forest Stewardship Council; Forest Products Certification
Species diversity	TRAFFIC; Conservation International
Anti–big dams	International Rivers Network; World Commission on Large Dams
Toxics	WWF Global Toxics Initiative; Center for Ethics and Toxics
Anti-GMO	Campaign to Ban Genetically Engineered Foods; Genetic-ID
Organic food	Organic Consumers Organization; IFOAM; Pure Food Campaign
Labor	Campaign for Labor Rights; Maquiladora Health and Safety Network
Tobacco	International Tobacco Control Network; Tobacco-Free Initiative
Indigenous rights	Survival International; Int'l Indian Treaty Council
Child soldiers	Coalition to Stop the Use of Child Soldiers
Small arms trade	International Action Network on Small Arms
Land mines	International Campaign to Ban Land Mines
Trade monitoring	Global Trade Watch; Ethical Trading Initiative
Diamonds	Fatal Transactions International Diamond Campaign
Corporate accountability	As You Sow; Business for Social Responsibility
AIDS/HIV	Global Strategies for HIV Prevention

Source: Author.

Note: WWF = World Wildlife Fund/Worldwide Fund for Nature; GMO = genetically modified organisms; IFOAM = International Foundation for Organic Agriculture Movements.

economic system.* These institutions become the target of social power and street demonstrations. (Note that private financial institutions and private capital are not often targeted, even though they account for the bulk of international loans and investments.)[76]

Given these many projects, campaigns, alliances, networks, and coalitions, in combination with rapid communication and relatively cheap international

*The "Group of Eight" (G-8) consists of Canada, France, Germany, Italy, Japan, Russia, the United Kingdom, and the United States.

travel, it is a fairly straightforward task to mobilize people, "create" a move-ment, and encourage those people to show up wherever meetings are taking place (authoritarian governments, such as that of Qatar, can deny visas to protesters and keep them far away; democratic ones, such as Canada and Italy, have more difficulty but try nonetheless). International economic con-claves are high profile but relatively boring, and so the opportunity for media attention and publicity is quite high. The resources are mobilized and the op-portunities are seized.

The trouble, as is apparent in the case of the global justice movement, is that these international institutions (or regimes) are not quite so autonomous or powerful as they might seem at first appearance (see Chapter 5).[77] Although they are classical bureaucracies, and sometimes act independently of the wishes of individual governments, they are nonetheless very much constrained by their member states, especially the powerful ones. The U.S. Treasury continues to exercise an inordinate amount of influence over both the World Bank and the IMF, not surprising given that the headquarters of both organizations are located in Washington, D.C., close to the White House and the U.S. Congress.

Is Party Politics the Answer?

These constraints on mass demonstrations suggest, perhaps, that social power ought to be aimed at national politics.[78] Why not transfer the energy of social movements into political parties and greater engagement with exist-ing political institutions and processes? Might this not bring about the kinds of changes demanded by social movements? If a party can find sufficient popular support, it could end up in the national legislature, or even a gov-erning coalition. There, it would be able not only to pressure the authorities to implement environmentally friendly policies and programs, it could even be involved in their formulation. An instructive, and sobering, case to con-sider here is that of the German Green Party (Bündnis 90/Die Grünen, an al-liance of Greens from East and West Germany established just before the first post-unification election in 1990). At this writing, the Green Party is a junior partner in the German government, in coalition with the German Social Democrats (SPD). The German Greens currently hold several ministerial po-sitions, including Foreign Affairs.*

The German Greens have not always been a political party, nor were they the world's first Green Party; that honor belongs to the Values Party in New

*In the elections of September 2002, the German Greens won almost 9 percent of the national vote, giving them about 55 seats in the 600-member German Parliament.

Zealand.[79] The German Greens were, however, one of the first such parties to see members elected to local, state, and national legislatures. Established in the late 1970s as a leftist environmental and peace movement, the Greens began to gain large numbers of supporters during the Euromissile debates of the early 1980s.[80] Getting involved in institutionalized politics was not a simple matter. Even when putting candidates up for office, the German Greens were not a political party in any conventional sense of the word. Its members held diverse views, ranging from Marxist to liberal and even, in a few cases, conservative. Some members already belonged to established political parties (and later dropped out of the Greens). But, as an extra-parliamentary movement, the German Greens were able to organize, educate, mobilize, and demonstrate and to find growing numbers of supporters who eventually voted for them in elections.

Difficulties arose, however, when the party finally did manage to win seats in the German Bundestag (parliament) and split into two factions, each with a different idea of how the party should operate. The *fundis,* or "fundamentalists," felt that it was imperative to maintain the Greens' radical social and political positions. They did not want to fall into line with conventional parliamentary practices and behavior (in fact, the *fundis* had serious doubts about being in parliament at all). The *realos,* or "realists," believed that, in order to establish the party's legitimacy, its members of parliament (MPs) had not only to look and act like those members from older parties but also to cooperate and collaborate with those parties, especially the SPD. Initially, party members agreed that, to prevent the Greens from becoming too bureaucratized, its MPs would hold their seats for only one year and then pass them on to colleagues. The rule remained operative for a very short time, as it became apparent that one year was insufficient time to learn the ropes. Today, members of the German Greens elected to the Bundestag and other positions in governments hold their seats for a full term. It was this decision not to rotate positions that finally split the party and drove the *fundis* out. They returned to their social movement activities.[81]

As a result, the German Green Party today is a largely middle-class one, stripped of much of its early radicalism. Following the national elections of 1998, the party was asked to join a governing coalition. After sixteen years in power, the Christian Democrats, headed by Helmut Kohl, were outpolled by the SPD, which offered the Greens a junior role in the new government.* This

---

*In parliamentary systems, governments are formed by whichever party or parties command a majority of the vote in the legislature. They select the prime minister, who holds executive power.

was quite an achievement. But the party's members also found themselves having to compromise and go along with many SPD decisions that they once would have opposed, such as NATO's bombing of Serbia in 1999. Remaining in power requires party discipline. If the Greens refused to support the coalition on critical issues, new elections could be called and they might find themselves back in the opposition. In other words, political participation is not cost-free and it can undermine much of the rationale for the original social movement.[82]

In countries like Germany, with systems of proportional representation, it is possible for social movement parties to gain access to political institutions. By 2002, Green parties held more than 150 national legislative seats in nineteen European countries (out of the fifty or so counted as "European") and more than 30 seats in the European Parliament from eight member countries of the European Union.[83] They also had ministers in six European governments. In places with "first past the post" systems, however, reaching public office is much more daunting.* There is a national Green Party in the United States as well as state and local chapters and, in 2003, some 169 Greens held elected offices in twenty-three states.[84] But no Green candidate, with one short-lived exception in California, has been elected to a higher office. The same is largely the case in the United Kingdom. This does not mean that Green issues and concerns are not represented in the institutionalized politics of these countries or of others with similar electoral systems. Rather, they are present as additions or modifications to business as usual, articulated and presented by members of existing conventional parties. The results are not always edifying.

As we saw earlier in this chapter, a complex system of civic politics has developed around environmental issues, just as is the case for other types of issues. Such activities tend to focus on distributive questions—that is, how much funding will go to environmental protection—rather than more fundamental structural ones. In other words, they reproduce and legitimate those political, economic, and social arrangements that are the sources of environmental degradation in the first place. The German Greens have had major impacts on the country's environmental policies, but they have managed to effect few, if any, real structural changes in the economy. Is this all there is, or are there alternatives to reformism?

---

*In such a system, the candidate winning a plurality of the vote is elected to office. The United States and the United Kingdom both employ this arrangement.

Praxis: Agents Coming to Grips with Structure

Praxis as a form of social power presents a rather more complicated picture than the activities offered above. Praxis draws on both consciousness-raising and resource mobilization, to be sure, but it also recognizes that *agency-structure* relations are important to action.[85] What this means is that individual and group behavior are strongly constrained and limited both by material conditions and by social factors, the latter including laws, norms, customs, perceptions, beliefs, and values. Nevertheless, structural elements do not fully determine outcomes or eliminate the potential for praxis and the possibility of change.[86] Of course, social movements represent the coalescence of frustration with political and economic systems, and fulfillment of their goals requires changes in the way people see and understand the world around them. At the same time, however, history and materialism—linked to local political economy, as discussed earlier—play an important role in the specific form that movements take, as well as their success, failure, or co-optation by existing institutions and parties. The argument presented here, which draws on various strands of Marxist and neo-Marxist thought (including that of Antonio Gramsci), is as follows.[87]

First, as we saw earlier, most institutionalized political systems in liberal states are also individualized ones in that they rely on the aggregated choice of individual voters. They limit the degree to which any particular individual can become involved, however, beyond such ritual practices as town meetings, petitioning, periodic voting, communicating with representatives, and lobbying. Election results are presented as the articulation of some kind of "general will," even though they are mostly the additive consequence of individual preferences. Other political activities—which can, of course, be defined so broadly as to include everything that involves more than one person—are outlawed, frowned upon, or marginalized. Limits on non-institutionalized activities come not only in the form of explicit laws, but also as norms ("no decent person would do that"), perceptions ("you're a traitor if you don't support the president"), beliefs ("this is the best of all possible countries, and if you don't like it here, go somewhere else"), and values ("God made us great!"). And don't forget money ("it's a free country; anyone can buy the opportunity to express his or her beliefs"). These limits are structural, not because they forbid actions but because they restrict what will be construed as legitimate.[88]

Second, no human institution, including well-established political systems, is without flaws and inconsistencies. That is, there is no reason to expect material conditions and belief systems to be fully in concordance with each other or, for that matter, internally coherent (such incoherences are called "contradictions"). Despite considerable evidence to the contrary, it is an abiding principle of neoliberalism that capitalist markets will make everyone richer ("a rising tide lifts all boats"). In point of fact, although economic growth does increase aggregate societal income, that income is differentially distributed. Some people get wealthier while others become poorer, either in relative or absolute terms.[89] But another central principle of contemporary neoliberalism is utilitarianism, which implies that it is not only good but also just that people be better off (and happy). Therefore, the gradual impoverishment of some people and groups exposes a contradiction between the material conditions and the beliefs of neoliberal politics and economics. This contradiction can be exploited for political and social purposes.

Let us return to the example of the global justice movement to illustrate these points. The supporters of global neoliberalism, and all that it includes, are numerous. They occupy elite positions in government, social institutions, and the media and are defenders of the "conventional wisdom" regarding what constitutes "proper" social arrangements. They include political leaders and legislators, public intellectuals, news reporters and pundits, academics, businessmen, corporate executives, and the staff of various think tanks and public associations. Their primary concern is to ensure that the material and ideational arrangements supporting neoliberal globalization remain largely intact and, if possible, unchallenged.[90] To accomplish this end, these elites need only engage in business as usual and justify it as necessary and natural. If the consequences of business as usual are negative for some, it is not the fault of the social arrangements. Rather, these consequences occur because certain people, such as the poor and unemployed, are not behaving in the manner required to produce positive outcomes for themselves. Or intervention in markets by corrupt government officials is to blame. Or more time is required for the benefits to work their way through society. In each case, there is no need for structural change because specific individuals or groups are to blame for their own misfortunes.

Those who are involved in laying the groundwork for the case against this type of globalization—arguments with a long intellectual history—point out that the contemporary neoliberal economic regime generates unfair outcomes for many people, especially those in developing countries.[91] Those who have jobs must work long hours, in dangerous and unhealthful conditions, for low wages. Others suffer from the environmental damage resulting from export-oriented exploitation of natural resources. Global trade, conducted under rules negotiated among countries and embedded in the WTO, is based on comparative advantage and measured primarily in monetary terms. Trade rules take little or no account of these externalities.[92]

In other words, the outcomes promised by neoliberalism's advocates are not being, and cannot be, delivered under existing structural arrangements.[93] If enough people can be convinced that this is the case, and mobilized to demand structural change, the underlying belief systems that support globalization will be exposed and undermined. They will forfeit their legitimacy. One result could be a reconfiguration of the economic system and its politics so as to restore this lost legitimacy. The precise form of such change is not determined and cannot be predicted. We might imagine reforms in the operating rules of the WTO, international financial institutions, and private funders that would incorporate both social and environmental considerations. The World Bank has made extensive efforts to do this over the past ten years, but with limited success.[94] Organizations change radically only in the face of crisis.

Alternatively, we might imagine new international organizations, dedicated to social and environmental regulation, with authority and power commensurate with that of the WTO. Organizations that oversee these two issue areas do exist, in the International Labour Organization and the UN Environment Programme, but they do not have much in the way of international authority or financial resources. A more powerful organization would represent mostly costs to countries, corporations, and citizens, as against the benefits of free trade accruing largely to capital. Such an organization would not find it easy to contend with the WTO and its unequivocal supporters.

A third possibility is that social movements and organizations might be able to pressure national governments to enforce both international and domestic laws applicable to social and environmental matters. If they were to do so, some states might find themselves at a competitive disadvantage with respect to others. This is not, therefore, a step to be taken lightly. The likelihood of each of these outcomes would be a function of the effectiveness of political alliances and coalitions assembled by different parties to the conflict as well as a compelling presentation of the real costs of business as usual. As Margaret Keck and Kathryn Sikkink have pointed out, governments and international organizations can be influenced in many different ways, some of which might, at first glance, appear quite improbable.[95] A good example of such politics, and coalition building, can be seen in the fate of the Multilateral Agreement on Investment (MAI).

The MAI was originally negotiated by the twenty-five-odd industrialized and developing countries belonging to the Paris-based Organization for Economic Cooperation and Development (OECD). It was meant to establish uniform rules governing both domestic and foreign investment in the OECD's industrialized countries, as well as in its two developing ones. The members intended to formulate the agreement, sign and ratify it, and then open it to nonmembers, which are mostly developing countries. These states would have to join or miss out on investment from signatory countries. But the MAI was derailed just as it was about to be finalized. A coalition of NGOs and social movements was able to raise doubts about the MAI in strategic places. Both the French and Canadian governments came to agree with the NGOs and social movement groups: the MAI would be disadvantageous and unfair to developing countries, the vast majority of which had no say in its terms. As a result of the ability of activists to influence key states, the agreement was withdrawn from consideration.[96]

Certainly, although the collapse of the MAI constituted a defeat for international capital, it did not do much to alter the structure of the global economic system. New versions of the MAI are being planned, and there are other channels through which countries can be pressured to adhere to rich countries' desires concerning foreign investment. What the collapse of the MAI did demonstrate, however, was that social power, especially in coalition with doubtful governments, can have an impact on the form and operation of global economic structure. At a minimum, those who favor business as usual must take into account the growing resistance to globalization and the inequities it fosters. Those elites may respond peacefully and agree to the creation of new institutions and rules. Or they may decide that repression is called for, as was the case when Italian police clashed with demonstrators in Genoa in August 2001.[97] Outcomes are not determined.

Social Power in Action

These largely theoretical explanations of civic politics and social power—consciousness-raising, resource mobilization, party politics, and agency-structure praxis—are embodied in a broad range of activities and actions relevant to global environmental politics. But what does social power look like in action? By focusing on "real life" examples, we can begin to see how history, political economy, and local action fit together as essential parts of environmental praxis. Recall that it is the history of a place that accounts for the shape of the landscape and its social organization and that establishes many of the patterns of interaction among people. It is political economy that accounts for the ways in which the local environment has been and is being used and abused as well as for the roles of individuals, groups, and business in that process. Finally, it is in the face-to-face encounters of people that debate and action—politics—takes place. This is not to say that all environmental praxis is or must be limited solely to place; it is to argue that a global environmental politics must be rooted in the politics and practices of specific times and places.

Three examples of social power in action are given here: watershed restoration, environmental justice, and market-based activism. Each of these has a somewhat different character and politics. Watershed restoration groups come in a variety of forms, but many practice social activism outside of the frameworks of institutionalized politics. It is difficult to maintain this separation because, inevitably, such groups come into contact and conflict with political authorities, bureaucrats, and property owners. Environmental justice groups find it necessary to engage in institutionalized politics, practicing a mix of social activism and civic politics, because the problem of improper toxic waste disposal arises as a result of inadequate public regulation of private activities. Finally, organizations involved in market-based activism, either through efforts to influence consumer choice or change corporate behavior, use many of the tools of institutionalized politics in an effort to implement the environmental regulation and protection that the institutionalized political system cannot or will not provide.

Watershed Groups: The Mattole Restoration Council

Over the past couple of decades, watershed protection groups have become ubiquitous throughout the world. Along with local activism, there have emerged government projects as well as transnational coordinating organizations focused on watershed stewardship and protection.[98] These projects seek to improve water quality, prevent stream bank erosion, protect fish-spawning areas, limit damaging activities such as logging and cattle grazing, and encourage streamside property owners to treat the watershed as something of a public good. Watershed protection is not a political act in the conventional understanding of the term, but it becomes political when it challenges established economic and social institutions and artifacts.

Such groups—the *National Directory of River and Watershed Conservation Groups* lists 3,600 in the United States alone—exemplify both social power and civic politics in action, at a local scale, but with global implications.[99] Thus, for example, although there are rivers and creeks all over the world, and groups dedicated to their protection and restoration, we do not find activists dedicating themselves to some universal conception of river or creek. Instead, it is the specific river or creek that runs through their community and the meaning of that waterway to place that are important. That meaning may have economic content, but it is also as likely to involve some notion of community identity. In other words, it is rooted in the history and political economy of that place.[100] At the same time, there are rivers and creeks in other places, in other countries, and groups in those locations seek to protect and restore their waterways, which have specific meanings for their communities. All watersheds are similar in some respects, and they all channel water, which is essential to life. So, there are also meanings, as well as actions, that are shared globally.[101]

The Mattole Restoration Council, based in a 304-square-mile river valley in Northern California, is one such watershed group.[102] Most of the land in the watershed is privately owned, although some 12 percent is within the Bureau of Land Management's 52,000-acre King Range Conservation Area. Historically, the economy of the area was dependent on logging, fishing, and ranching, the ranches having been established late in the nineteenth century. Beginning in the 1960s the area experienced an influx of "new people," with an especially large number arriving during the late 1970s.[103] The cash flowing into the region from marijuana cultivation, a cultural renaissance, and individuals engaged in craft-based and other types of work created something of an economic boom.[104] *

The decline of the salmon run in the Mattole River was the trigger for the creation of the local watershed group; in 1978 a group of new arrivals in the region established the Mattole Watershed Salmon Support Group, whose goal was the restoration of the chinook salmon runs. The group went about its work systematically. It surveyed salmon populations, spawning grounds, and nests. It looked for existing and potential causes of fishery decline. The group did whatever possible to maintain or restore salmon habitat in the river, including establishment of homemade hatching and rearing facilities. In the course of the group's work, it became clear that one of the major

---

*According to some calculations, marijuana cultivation is one of the largest agricultural crops in California, although there is no way to be sure of this. In any event, a major part of the California marijuana crop comes from the "Emerald Triangle" of Mendocino, Humboldt, and Trinity counties.

sources of damage to the fishery was erosion and the deposition of sediment into the river, via landslides, from road maintenance and activities associated with ranching. Consequently, in 1983 some of the local activists established the Mattole Restoration Council, which emphasized improvement of fish habitat and passage, reduction of sedimentation, and restoration of vegetation, where possible. Inevitably, perhaps, the council's analyses and pinpointing of the private causes of degradation, and the necessary responses, brought it into conflict with local landowners. These individuals saw the council not only as a hotbed of environmental radicalism but also as a threat to their property rights.

In January 1991 a regional meeting was arranged, at the behest of the council, to discuss how erosion into and sedimentation in the Mattole River was affecting the salmon fishery. Subsequently, an Agenda Committee was set up, which included council members as well as six local ranchers but no government representatives (although representatives from the U.S. Department of the Interior's Bureau of Land Management, a landholder in the watershed, later joined the committee). Another public meeting, attended by 250 people, was then held at the Mattole Grange in April 1991, at which the salmon problem proved to be the issue around which the very divergent interests of ranchers, environmentalists, and others could converge. During that meeting, the Mattole Watershed Alliance (MWA), representing activists, timber companies, ranchers, and other residents, was established. MWA members concluded that salmon restoration would require restrictions in the fishing season, and communicated this point to California Fish and Game, the responsible state agency. Consequently, the agency agreed to close the Mattole to all recreational fishing and, later, to restrict commercial fishing off the river's mouth. In another instance, the MWA persuaded the Mendocino County Public Works Department to cease pushing debris cleared from a road into the river. The MWA was able to get state funding reinstated for its "backyard wild hatchery program" by the state committee responsible for such matters. Finally, it was also able to negotiate an agreement with salmon trollers to close the commercial fishery at the mouth of the Mattole just during the time that the wild fish are gathering for their spawning run upstream. But the MWA did not last; its members eventually stopped meeting because of disagreements over property rights.[105]

The Mattole Restoration Council and the Mattole Salmon Group continue to exist, however, and they have spawned several other watershed groups in the same area.[106] These groups have also established links up and down the Pacific Coast as well as in other parts of the United States and the world. Although they work with government agencies and seek to collaborate with local landowners and government agencies, they have no official standing in the region. Indeed, some consider them to be threats to legitimate property rights and political processes. The social power of these groups derives from members' ability to decide on projects and activities, to get other residents of the watershed to collaborate, and to transform their visions into reality. Environmental praxis cannot take place without recognition of the history and political economy of the Mattole River Valley, but it does not happen in the absence of determined collective action.

Environmental Justice: Citizens Clearinghouse for Hazardous Wastes

Not all examples of social power take place in rural areas; many are found in cities. An example of such localized social power can be found in the community organizations of the environmental justice movement. For some time, observers of urban politics have noticed what seems to be a preponderance of toxic waste sites and air pollution problems in poor, minority, and immigrant-dominated urban neighborhoods.[107] Although this claim continues to be strongly contested by some, who challenge the validity of the empirical evidence, there are good reasons nevertheless to believe that such environmental discrimination does take place.[108] First, affected neighborhoods are disproportionately located in or near present and former industrial zones. Which came first, industry or neighborhood? In many cases, working-class neighborhoods grew up around factories and, in subsequent decades, offered affordable housing for the poor and disadvantaged. Subsequently, many brownfield sites—those where industrial activities took place in the past—have been used for further disposal, precisely because land is cheap and the neighboring communities have little power with which to oppose the practice.

Second, poor, minority, and immigrant neighborhoods tend to be found in or near the centers of urban areas, where traffic is heavy and much remaining industrial activity is still located. Air pollution from traffic and toxic emissions from factories are concentrated in these locations, so those who live nearby suffer a double insult: both the land on which they live and play and the air they breathe are heavily polluted. Some observers object to the imputation that such disproportionate exposure to toxics and pollution is the result of societal discrimination. After all, if factories were there before the poor, and land is cheap, both history and economics militate for using such areas for waste disposal. One can hardly blame society for the logic of either history or economics. In any event, people are free to move elsewhere if they believe they are being poisoned—or so it is sometimes argued.[109] Those who live in these heavily polluted areas think otherwise.

The origins of the environmental justice movement are to be found, however, not in poor, minority, and immigrant communities, but in a largely white, middle-class neighborhood built over New York's infamous Love Canal disposal site, near Niagara Falls. In the early part of the twentieth century, the Hooker Chemical Company dumped toxic wastes in the canal, an unfinished and abandoned navigation channel. In the 1950s, Hooker sold the contaminated property to the local board of education. Schools and homes were built on the land. No one suspected anything amiss. Two decades later, however, heavy rains caused the buried chemicals to seep to the surface, on the school grounds and in people's yards. Some residents began to suffer from impaired health and became concerned. Soil and water tests in the area revealed the presence of eighty-eight chemicals, more than a dozen of which were confirmed health hazards. Surveys of the area indicated higher than normal rates of cancer and birth defects among residents. Homeowners found themselves trapped at Love Canal. After all, who would want to buy a house built on a toxic waste dump?[110]

Such hazards were not confined to Love Canal; the indiscriminate dumping of toxic wastes was standard industrial practice during the nineteenth century and much of the twentieth. As people became aware of this, and more discovered their proximity to abandoned or active dumps, a national movement emerged. Much of the impetus for this movement originated from the organizing efforts of the residents of the Love Canal neighborhood. Lois Gibbs, head of the Love Canal Homeowners Association, found she was answering so many phone calls from other communities seeking information and help that she and her colleagues established the Citizens Clearinghouse for Hazardous Wastes. Similar organizations and groups were subsequently established around the United States, national campaigns were set up, information services were created, and scientific bulletins were published. Environmental justice groups began to appear in poor, minority, and immigrant neighborhoods as well, and the environmental justice movement grew to become much more politically powerful than the sum of its individual participants and organizations.[111]

Responding to growing concern, in 1994 President Clinton issued an "Executive Order on Federal Actions to Address Environmental Justice in

Minority Populations and Low-Income Populations." The order required federal agencies to take toxic waste and pollution problems into account in their programs and policies, especially when they affected poor and minority neighborhoods. Clinton's executive order has not become the law of the land, and there remains significant opposition to the environmental justice movement and its objectives (it has hardly been supported by the second Bush administration). Nonetheless, the movement continues to grow and has become an international one.[112]

The toxic waste problem is unlikely to go away. It might be addressed through ecological modernization, which focuses on technological changes in production processes, rather than "end of pipe" disposal.[113] But reengineering older plants is not cheap, and disposal costs within the industrialized countries are quite high. Both eat into corporate profits and have provided incentives for producers to find other ways of getting rid of the wastes. Some of these methods are patently illegal and take unfair advantage of the poor, the weak, and the unrepresented (who are often the same people). If the "squeaky wheel gets the grease," only activism will make sufficient noise to be heard. Social power must remain central to protecting people from these, and other, hazards.

Consumer vs. Corporation: "Doing It" in the Market

In recent years, social power has been supplemented or supplanted by what might be called *market activism* which, in turn, has led to the *corporate social responsibility* movement.[114] The first denotes efforts by social activists to use market mechanisms as a means of protecting the environment; the second represents the defensive response by capital to these activist regulatory arrangements. Both rely to a significant extent on consumer consciousness-raising. Market activism and corporate responsibility take place in relation to capital investment, on the one hand, and consumer preferences, on the other. Hence, they are not "local" in the same way as watershed protection or neighborhood environmental activism. Nonetheless, because both production and purchasing take place in specific locations, and the target of action is the individual consumer, market activism and corporate responsibility can both be seen as "local" manifestations of social power.

What, exactly, is market activism? As we saw in Chapter 2 and the first section of this chapter, the growing complexity of commodity chains and associated consumption have relocated environmental and social externalities to the widely separated sites where production and consumption take place. The ability and willingness of local authorities to regulate these externalities is highly variable: some countries have much stronger laws and enforcement than others, and the costs associated with production are, therefore, higher in some places than others.[115] All else being equal, capital will seek to invest and produce in places with lower levels of regulatory attainment. Even though such countries may have strong laws on the books, weak enforcement permits capital to reduce the cost of doing business and increase profit margins. Although it is not clear how large this effect actually is, it appears that some regulatory arbitrage does take place between developing and industrialized countries.[116] It has been known to take place within industrialized countries, as well.[117]

In an effort to combat egregious violations of laws and norms, a growing number of social activists and transnational coalitions have launched campaigns directed toward the behaviors of specific corporations and industrial sectors. Using publicity, education, and the threat of consumer boycotts, activists try to pressure companies to change their practices within the confines of their specific commodity chains in ways that are both environmentally friendly and more supportive of labor. By engaging in these actions, activists try to garner greater public and corporate attention to the environment. All else being equal, however, corporations prefer to set their own terms for social and environmental regulation. The corporate responsibility "movement" has, subsequently, emerged as capital's response to market activism. In the belief that it is better, for reasons of both cost and public relations, to observe the law willingly than to be forced to do so, individual companies have begun to adopt codes of conduct and performance standards.[118] Codes and standards are intended to pre-empt external pressures for responsible behavior even as they often tend to be less rigorous than those mandated by local law or desired by market activists. In addition, national and international business associations and corporate groups are developing environmental management standards for various production practices.[119] The United Nations has promulgated something called the "Global Compact," which commits signatory corporations to "good global citizenship." [120] Some of the standards in these codes are very general; others quite specific.

One of the more egregious examples of the two trends toward "offshore production" and a "regulatory race to the bottom" takes place in the *maquila* zone along the border between the United States and Mexico. Under the terms of U.S. customs law, manufacturers can bring parts into the zone, have them assembled, and re-export the finished goods into the United States. Tariffs and taxes are paid only on the difference in value between the parts and the finished product. That added value is primarily the cost of labor. Over the years, the zone has become an area of significant employment and industrialization, and in recent years has been extended into areas deeper within Mexico.[121]

Wages in Mexico are considerably lower than those in the United States, and enforcement of labor and environmental laws is very weak in the former.[122] The same is true in the *maquila* zones. Companies operating plants in the zone are required to dispose of their wastes properly and safely, under the terms of both NAFTA and Mexican law, but this can be a costly proposition.[123] Consequently, many wastes are illegally dumped, and many *maquila* workers labor in manifestly unhealthy conditions.[124] Logically and ideally, the state and federal governments of Mexico would allocate both resources and personnel for monitoring and punishing violators of its laws but, even with NAFTA, neither is available in that revenue-strapped country. Recall that, under the premises of the Coase theorem, if Mexico cannot afford the costs of cleaning up pollution affecting the United States, the latter ought to pay to have the wastes properly handled. This happens to some degree, but hardly to an adequate one. For the most part, therefore, pollutants continue to be dumped locally. And Coase says nothing about dealing with those effluents that do not affect either American territory or residents but have serious impacts in Mexico.

What can be done? What is being done? Under one approach, market activists target specific companies for their violations. They put advertisements in U.S. media urging consumers to boycott specific products. They protest outside corporate headquarters, trying to inform and influence shareholders attending annual meetings. And they demonstrate outside the factories themselves, hoping to generate local opposition to corporate activities. Company executives, fearful of a decline in profits and mindful of their ethical responsibilities, will, it is hoped, respond accordingly. In their own defense, corporations under such pressure will draft and adopt codes of conduct and best practices, requiring that they be followed within subcontractors' plants as well as their own, wherever they might be located.[125]

Codes of conduct are sets of rules established within factories or company facilities. They are intended to address minimum wages, working hours, health and safety conditions, grievance procedures, environmental quality, and so on.[126] Companies agree to post the codes in visible places, to inform workers of their existence and significance, and to ensure that management obeys them. Workers, in turn, are expected to perform the duties assigned to them and to accept directions issued by their supervisors. These codes have no legal standing in local courts, however, and there is no obligation on the part of local authorities to see that they are enforced. Thus, although some plants in some places handle their wastes carefully, others are not subject to such pressures. Under these circumstances, it is difficult not to continue a regulatory race to the bottom.[127]

Best practices are somewhat different. They involve the systems that companies use to produce goods and to reduce the pollutants associated with those goods. As we saw earlier, it is possible to control the environmental impacts of production in two ways: end-of-pipe reduction and ecological modernization. The first entails the capture of pollutants from smokestacks, wastewater pipes, and other outlets. The second focuses on changes in manufacturing processes and technology so that less waste is produced. In other words, ecological modernization generates fewer pollutants requiring disposal. Producers will, we can assume, select among alternatives so as to minimize their costs of retooling (recall the discussion of greenhouse gas permits in Chapter 3). In some instances, the more efficient use of inputs provides enough savings to more than compensate for the greater cost of implementing ecological modernization. Again, however, the commitment by a corporation to best practices has no legal status, and there are generally no political or legal mechanisms to compel good behavior.*

In all these examples, companies are engaged in *self-regulation*. That is, corporate executives have voluntarily agreed to alter company practices, sometimes with the understanding that, in exchange for socially responsible practices, activists will cease their negative campaigns. The problem with this approach is evident: if there is no legally binding requirement that the company change its practices, how will anyone know for certain that it is observing its commitments to do so? Under regulatory systems created and supported by governments, violations of the law should be detected and violators punished. The threat of punishment acts as a deterrent—if the threat is a real one—and individuals and companies alike obey the rules. Under self-regulation, however, there is no system of monitoring for violations, there is

---

*The U.S. Clean Air Act includes a provision for "new source review" that requires large plants to improve pollution controls during expansion or modification. The Bush administration, however, has proposed some exemptions from this rule, which will probably lead to increased air pollution in parts of the United States.[128]

no threat of punishment, there is no incentive actually to observe the commitments made. There is only good faith and the possibility of exposure by activists. Experience often shows this to be a weak reed.

One solution to the enforcement problem is called certification or "eco-labeling." Once again, this relies on the modification of consumer choice or preferences. An eco-label is a claim placed on a product having to do with its production or performance. The label is intended to enhance the item's social or market value by conveying its environmentally advantageous features, making the product more attractive to the environmentally conscious consumer. Three categories of eco-labels are widely recognized.[129] First party certification is the most common and simplistic approach. It entails producer claims about a product, for instance, that it is "recyclable," "ozone-friendly," "non-toxic" or "biodegradable." But these are claims made without external or disinterested verification. Therefore, the only guarantee to the purchaser that the product performs according to those claims is the producer's reputation and brand name.

Second party certification is conducted by industry-related entities, such as trade associations. These groups establish guidelines or criteria that must be met if producers are to make environmental claims about their products. The group offering the label may or may not actually monitor and verify the producer's adherence to the guidelines and criteria. Once the standards are met or the guidelines followed, an industry-approved label is placed on the product stating or verifying the product's environmentally friendly qualities. In this instance, the certifying organization will seek to ensure the label's value and to mandate its use, so that no single producer will gain an advantage over any other. An example of second-party labeling can be found in ISO 14000, sponsored by the International Organization for Standardization (ISO). The ISO is an association of national standards groups, some of which are private and others public.[130] ISO 14000 comprises a set of management standards that companies apply within their plants and to other operations. Each individual company is responsible for certifying that it has followed the standards and, if it has, it is permitted to put the ISO logo on its products.

Third-party, or independent, certification is performed by government agencies, nonprofit groups, for-profit companies, or organizations representing some combination of these three. As with second-party labels, third-party eco-labeling programs set guidelines that products must meet in order to use the label. Sponsoring organizations also generally conduct audits in order to ensure producer compliance with the guidelines. As the name implies, third-party certifiers are not affiliated with the products they label. An example of third-party labeling can be found in the programs of the Forest Stewardship Council (FSC).[131] The FSC has developed and adopted a set of global guidelines called Principles and Criteria for Forest Management and it accredits certifying organizations that agree to abide by these principles, criteria, and standards. The certifying groups, in turn, inspect and monitor timber operations seeking the FSC's stamp of approval. The final product appears on the retailers' shelves with the FSC logo affixed.

First-party certification is not considered very reliable, inasmuch as a company's claims are restricted only to the extent that relevant law limits them. Second-party labeling rests on corporate assurances to the relevant trade association that it has fulfilled the minimum standards required for certification; there is frequently no mechanism to verify such claims. Only third-party certification, which relies on outside inspection and monitoring, appears to provide a means of checking a company's claims of environmentally friendly behavior. But even approval by third-party organizations is fraught with problems. Who certifies the certifiers? Who has vetted the procedures whereby certifiers conduct their inspections? What, besides consumer disapproval, motivates a company to rectify violations detected by certifiers? What prevents a company from shopping around for the most friendly certifying organization? And to what extent do consumers actually choose their purchases on the basis of certification, especially if such goods are more costly than uncertified ones? All these questions remain largely unanswered, and viable empirical data that might help to answer them remain sparse.[132]

At the end of the day, the value of certification is very much like brand reputation. Many consumers have a preference for food labeled "organic." But, whereas brands are the private property of specific companies, certification is not. In the absence of effective regulation and enforcement, anyone could call their food products "organic." This is why certifying organizations are established. For organic foods, farmers and producers have created associations and formulated rules defining how to obtain organic certification. There now exists an international association for this purpose as well as local, state, and national groups and laws.[133] But as the market for organic foods has expanded, so have opportunities for both profit and fraud. After all, confronted with multiple certifiers, how is the consumer to know which ones are legitimate? In the United States, consequently, the Department of Agriculture has formulated regulations specifying requirements for organic labeling.

Although these did not, initially, gain the wholehearted support of organic farmers, they are now generally regarded in a positive light.[134] Now, the force of law stands behind various systems of self-regulation, in effect, "certifying the certifiers." International organic certification is also developing to cover foods being shipped across national borders, as a search on the World Wide Web quickly demonstrates. In some instances, certifiers use U.S. standards as the basis for their assessments, but other bodies and countries, such as the European Union, the International Organisation for Standardization, and Australia, have their own sets of standards.

One final question must be asked: At the end of the day, what are the political impacts of market activism and corporate responsibility? This question brings us back to a problem encountered in Chapter 3 regarding the use of market mechanisms to control pollution. What remains unchanged in the arrangements described there is the fundamental structure of the pollution process. The use of markets as the means of allocating rights to pollute relies on economic tools to achieve political ends. Whether it is right to pollute is never asked. Even the "precautionary principle," which advises erring on the side of safety when undertaking potentially damaging actions, does not inquire about the ethics of the action itself.* A similar criticism can be applied to market activism, corporate responsibility, and consumer consciousness. Campaigners argue that companies ought to reduce their polluting activities because it is the right thing to do, and they use the threat of a reduction in market share to goad companies into implementing best environmental practices. But, at best, changes take place only in those factories and facilities where their goods are produced. Other enterprises remain unaffected and no change in national law or enforcement results. Responsible corporate executives—recognizing that there might be some commercial advantage in advertising their company's good behavior—try to ensure that these practices are being followed by plant managers and others.[136] But none of this has much impact on more general political conditions or regulatory arrangements within countries. That sweatshops continue to exist throughout the United States, even though they are illegal, simply illustrates the real and potential shortcomings of self-regulation through market mechanisms.[137]

The result is that the actual impacts on matters of concern are patchy, at best. This can be seen in the case of the *maquila* zone as well as elsewhere.

*The precautionary principle states, in essence, that if there is doubt about the safety of a practice or product, it is better to avoid it, rather than to take the risk and have to ameliorate the effects.[135]

Under the terms of NAFTA, environmental issues along the U.S.–Mexican border are supposed to be addressed through a binational commission. This commission has the authority to hear complaints and issue orders against environmental violators. But it has no enforcement powers of its own and relies on the good will and commitment of the appropriate agencies within each country.[138] If enforcement and sanctioning are not forthcoming, polluters will have few incentives to change their behavior and behave "responsibly," even if their codes are posted on factory walls. None of these criticisms means that market activism and corporate responsibility are worthless; they can have positive impacts in specific instances. But the broader society-wide "spillover" that results is likely to be quite limited. Absent active engagement with politics, and changes in the structural conditions of production, consumption, and pollution, more of the same is likely to lead to more of the same.

Local Politics, Global Politics

The transnationalization of civic politics and social power, through networks, coalitions, and activism, is made feasible by the physical infrastructure of global communication and transportation, and it is this transnationalization that has captured so much attention in recent years.[139] But whether global or local, in order to accomplish the kinds of social changes discussed in this chapter, activists must still affect the beliefs and behaviors of real human beings, whose social relations are, for the most part, highly localized. Ideas do not fall from heaven or appear as light bulbs; they must resonate with conditions as experienced and understood by those real human beings, in the places that they live, work, and play.[140] Moreover, it is in those local places that politics, activism, and social power are most intense and engage people most strongly. How such environmental praxis articulates with the national and international will be the focus of Chapter 6. In order to arrive at that point, however, we must first examine national and international environment politics more closely. This we will do in Chapter 5.

For Further Reading

Bomberg, Elizabeth. *Green Parties and Politics in the European Union*. London: Routledge, 1998.

Cable, Sherry, and Charles Cable. *Environmental Problems, Grassroots Solutions*. New York: St. Martin's Press, 1995.

Foreman, Christopher H. *The Promise and Peril of Environmental Justice.* Washington, D.C.: Brookings Institution Press, 1998.

Glazer, Penina M., and Myron P. Glazer. *The Environmental Crusaders: Confronting Disaster and Mobilizing Community.* University Park: Pennsylvania State University Press, 1998.

Lipschutz, Ronnie D., and Ken Conca, eds. *The State and Social Power in Global Environmental Politics.* New York: Columbia University Press, 1993.

Lipschutz, Ronnie D., with Judith Mayer. *Global Civil Society and Global Environmental Governance.* Albany: State University of New York Press, 1996.

Magnusson, Warren, and Karena Shaw, eds. *A Political Space: Reading the Global through Clayoquot Sound.* Minneapolis: University of Minnesota Press, 2003.

Rubin, Charles. *The Green Crusade: Rethinking the Roots of Environmentalism.* New York: Free Press, 1994.

Szasz, Andrew. *Ecopopulism: Toxic Waste and the Movement for Environmental Justice.* Minneapolis: University of Minnesota Press, 1994.

Tarrow, Sidney. *Power in Movement: Social Movements and Contentious Politics.* 2d ed. Cambridge: Cambridge University Press, 1998.

Walton, John. *Western Times and Water Wars.* Berkeley: University of California Press, 1992.

Wapner, Paul. *Environmental Activism and World Civic Politics.* Albany: State University of New York Press, 1996.

5 | The National Origins of International Environmental Policies and Practices: "My Country Is *in* the World"

The State and the Environment

As we have seen throughout this book, the standard account of global environmental politics begins with the borders between countries: Because many environmental phenomena, such as air pollution, cross national borders with alacrity, they escape the jurisdictional control of individual governments. Because no state is permitted to violate the sovereignty of another—at least in theory and international law—such problems can be addressed only through negotiation and joint action among governments. Through application of scientific knowledge to the give and take of bargaining among countries, agreements can be developed that deal with such transboundary issues and serve the interests of all concerned signatories. Although there may be some degree of residual unfairness in such *international environmental regimes* (IERs), their objectives serve the common global good.[1]

But is this really the whole story? From where do these agreements and regimes emerge? Are they the product of uninterested technicians of diplomacy, who seek to ensure that the resulting "balance" of duties and responsibilities is equitable and fair? Do these regimes accurately represent the interests of all states, especially those that are most severely affected by the problem? And who decides what principles, tools, and practices are to be applied to the problem? Where, exactly, do those principles, tools, and practices originate? There are very few (if any) international institutions that do not have their sources (or origins) in the principles, tools, and practices of particular states, especially the wealthier and more powerful ones.[2]

The story offered in this chapter is somewhat different from the conventional one about global environmental politics. The difficulty with the standard account is not that cooperation or conflict do not occur (the "neoliberal institutionalist" view) or that international agreements and regimes are mere epiphenomena of state power (the "realist" view). Rather, it is that an approach that puts states and the borders between them at its center is bound to ignore history, political economy, and, most importantly, social forces, many of which also "cross borders." Indeed, as we saw in Chapter 1, those very borders are a product of history, political economy, and social forces. Their locations have been constituted historically and socially, in response to both natural conditions and human activity and as a result of specific exercises of power. What might appear straightforward, therefore, is not at all simple.

We begin this chapter with a brief review of the concept of an international environmental regime. A "regime," according to the now-standard definition, is an international institution established by states to deal with shared or common problems.[3] We then turn to the national origins of these IERs, or what may be stylized as "environmental (inter)nationalism." The parentheses around the prefix "inter" are intentional and are meant to connote the extension of particular forms of nationalism and national practice into the international realm. Those states with greater resources and power have, both historically and today, managed to impose their own ways of "doing things" on others. (This is not the same as the "transnationalism" discussed in Chapter 4, associated with social power operating across national borders.) Thus, as we shall see, international projects for sustainable forestry management depend heavily on approaches developed within specific countries. The resort to market mechanisms in the Kyoto Protocol is a direct result of American preferences and domestic practices. And so on.

Consequently, the point of origin of international environmental practice is to be found in the historical relationship between the sovereign state and nature. The environmental policies and practices of specific countries cannot be explained without understanding the way in which national development requires "natural development." A second point is also largely national in origin but global in objective. As we have seen throughout this book, nature has been commodified and turned into a good to be exchanged and consumed within the global economy, rather than standing as a focus of ethical concern requiring political attention. The result—which is common to all international endeavors—is a constant tension between the national and the global, between expressions of sovereignty and alterations to that sovereignty, between what states might wish to do and what they find themselves compelled to do. These tensions and constraints will be illustrated through several of the case studies that have run through this book. We will examine forestry and water policies in historical terms, as a set of practices originating largely in one country but diffused to others. We will then turn to the contemporary version of this diffusion process, evident in the commodification of goods, in the form of genes, and bads, in the form of wastes.

Finally, we shall conclude with a brief inquiry into the implications of this tension for the roles and practices of international environmental regimes. Inasmuch as IERs constitute the focus of much work on global environmental politics, they can hardly be ignored.[4] But analyses that argue that IERs are, on the one hand, simply the handmaidens of powerful states or, on the other hand, the product of complex bargaining among states, miss their historical and normative content, reflected in the current trend toward market-based approaches to environmental governance and management.

International Environmental Regimes: The Standard Account and Some Caveats

An international regime is an interstate solution to the transboundary scenario described in Chapter 1 and the collective action problem discussed in Chapter 3. Recall our discussion in Chapter 2 of the realist and liberal perspectives on relations among states. Both realists and liberals view states as operating in a Hobbesian "state of nature," lacking any social institutions and governed by only one rule: save thyself. This particular injunction can be read to mean that, even if your activities harm another, when those activities are central to survival, they are not only justified but necessary (liberals call this "rational egoism").[5] It follows, therefore, that cooperation among states is similar to a herd of cats: neither exists. Unlike cats, however, the leaders of states can be persuaded, by power, wealth, and knowledge, that their interests may be better served through collective action. Some animals find safety and survival in herds. Are states more like cats or caribou?

An international regime is the answer: it facilitates collective action among states without sacrificing rational egoism. According to the now widely accepted terminology, a regime is a set of "principles, norms, rules, and decision-making procedures around which actor expectations converge in a given issue area." [6] This unusually opaque definition masks what is, in fact, a

common activity: patterned relationships and interactions among individuals, in which behaviors and actions are governed by rules and whose results are intended to be fairly predictable (see Chapter 1). We all participate in
such practices, or institutions, every day of our lives, even though we think of
ourselves as cats rather than caribou (think of the deprecatory implication of
the phrase "running with the herd"). In other words, regimes are no more
than institutions, except that the actors are states rather than people.

Why, then, are regimes not called "interstate institutions" and thereby
recognized as a common form of human relationship, albeit among political
communities? Aside from the many ways in which we use the term "institution"—an organization, a building, a research center, a long-established custom or practice—the term "regime" serves two particular functions. First, it
suggests an apparent uniqueness of international relations: states, the term
seems to imply, really are different. Second, it obscures the extent to which interstate institutions are actually quite common and nothing new. Even war, as
uncontrolled as it may be, is hedged about by all kinds of written agreements,
implied understandings, and customary practices.[7]

An international environmental regime is no more than an institution
intended to facilitate specified patterns of behavior with respect to some contested or shared resource or problem. The "transboundary" concept acknowledges that, within states, there are usually many institutions to address
such matters, whereas, among states, there are many fewer. And such interstate institutions often need to be created from scratch, as it were, especially if
a new issue or problem has been identified as being of shared concern. At the
same time, no regime simply emerges from a social vacuum: "principles,
rules, norms, and decisionmaking procedures" emerge out of very specific
social and historical contexts. More often than not, these contexts are associated with particular countries and periods of time.

We might usefully compare two different IERs to see how context affects
form. The International Whaling Commission (IWC) is one of the older IERs
in existence, established in 1949 when the very survival of virtually all species
of whales was in doubt.[8] Although IWC membership was generally composed of countries with whaling fleets, this was not a requirement to join.
Every year, the IWC met to set whaling quotas, which specified how many
of each type of whale could be taken and which allocated shares among
countries. The quotas were set, more or less, according to the concept of the
"maximum sustainable yield" (MSY) that would maintain the number of
each species at a relatively constant level.[9] MSY was also applied to various

bilateral and multilateral fishery regimes, although it did not, in the end, prevent serious depletion of many fish stocks around the world.*

The point here is that the very concept of a quota involves rationing of access to the resource. Rationing is a *political* function requiring centralized decision making, for it presumes that someone knows how much of a particular good is available, and how much should be kept in reserve for emergencies at a later time. Having this number in hand, a duly appointed authority can then decide how much to allocate to each individual or participant. It is not surprising that the IWC was based on what is, essentially, a form of rationing. During World War II, all the combatants found it necessary to ration civilian access to food, fuel, and other goods, and some countries, such as Great Britain, continued rationing into the 1950s. Although rationing is usually criticized as costly and inefficient, the presumption is that it is fair. But it also means that some people will gain access to less than they want, whereas those who are willing to pay more than the going rate can usually satisfy their desires through the black market. The IWC has not altered its basic approach to the regulation of whaling—although it has put in place a moratorium on whaling that is now strongly contested by several countries. Other fisheries have found, however, that the quota system is not only subject to cheating but has not, as noted, prevented decline and collapse in many parts of the world. The solution that has been settled on is to create regimes that commodify access to fisheries, that is, to let the market "decide" who will be able to fish.[10]

Many of the world's fisheries are overcapitalized. That is, there are too many boats with too much fish-capturing capacity. The straightforward answer would be for governments to pay fishers to stop fishing and destroy their equipment. This, however, raises all kinds of technical problems: who should be paid, what will they do if they cannot fish, where will the resources come from to fund such a project? An alternative is to have the fishers pay for the *right* to fish. If such permits are issued in limited numbers (similar to greenhouse gas emission permits) and are sold by auction, the marginal cost of a permit will rise to the level of the marginal benefits expected from fishing. Only wealthier fishers will be able to afford such permits, and everyone else will have to find something else to do. Pressure on the fishery will decrease and stocks can grow back to sustainable levels.

---

*There are problems with the notion of maximum sustainable yield, not the least of which is getting accurate counts, which, among some fish species, can vary drastically from one year to the next. The idea has since been replaced by other concepts and practices.

This, at any rate, is the theory. Permits are not, however, the same as quotas, and it might not make economic sense for individual fishers to continue to operate their boats independently. What has been happening is that corporations have bought up permits from individual fishers, hiring them to operate and crew the boats for a fixed salary. But now, in order to cover the costs of the permits and other things, capture efficiency must be increased. As a result, fewer boats operate in fisheries where such a system has been put in place, but they catch more fish and stocks continue to decline. Quotas, as we saw in earlier chapters, are an essential element in any marketable permit scheme.

The quota method is touted as being more "efficient" as well as "effective," but it marks a major shift in the operating principles of IERs, a shift that can be ascribed directly to discursive changes—the shift from the welfare state to a neoliberal one—in the United States and Great Britain during the 1980s and 1990s.[11] Quotas and rationing are difficult for governments to implement and enforce, and cheating is always a problem, but these approaches are motivated by some sense of equity and the common sharing of burdens. People may not get as much as they want under rationing, but they do receive a fair share of what is available. Marketable permitting systems are complicated to set up but, once in operation, are relatively easy to monitor. They generate up-front revenues for the authority that creates the system, and operating costs can be recovered through a small tax on transactions. But access is directly related to the individual's ability to pay for the permit. This approach is philosophically linked to the American and British shift to neoliberalism* and a greater reliance on markets, rather than politics, as allocational mechanisms.[13]

To put this point another way, IERs whose procedures are rooted in market-based transactions provide structural advantages to rich countries. There is nothing inevitable about such a result; the negotiations and bargaining that are the staple of all IERs are meant to address such structural inequities. Poor countries may be granted certain exemptions or provided with access to special funds or technologies or allocated a certain number of permits at concessional prices. All these mechanisms are intended to "level the playing field," to some degree. Yet, they do not alter the basic structure of the IER or the philosophical imprint put on it by dominant countries, such as the

---

*Here, neoliberalism refers to a more market-based approach to resource allocation, and includes reduced state welfare spending and privatization of public services.[12]

United States. This pattern—that is, the national origins of international environmental practices—is apparent in other IERs, as well.

The Historical National Origins of Environmental Internationalism

These philosophical imprints on the structural reorganization of IERs cannot be explained simply by recourse to the changing short-term interests of states or corporations. If we apply the analytical approach laid out in Chapter 1, it is clear that we need to look more deeply into history and political economy, and so we shall. For our purposes, the significant starting point of this discussion occurs about the beginning of the nineteenth century, a period during which two related trends, capitalist industrialization and nationalism, were joined together in order to exploit nature. This union—and some argue that the two processes were of a piece and never separate—was mediated by cultural, economic, and social forces that differed among individual countries.[14] The ways in which forestry was practiced in Germany differed from that in Great Britain, although, over time, the two influenced each others' practices.[15]

Most studies of nationalism focus on one of two of its aspects. The first involves the rhetorical articulation of the nationalist vision and the mass mobilization that is presumed to be required.[16] The second addresses the "protection" of a society's cultural attributes from intrusions by others through various defensive or offensive measures.[17] This second aspect is often identified with the industrial requirements necessary to the accumulation and application of military power.[18] But what is often ignored in studies of nationalism are the ways in which the general concept overlooks the great differences among individual countries' specific institutions and practices. There is no single way, for instance, of organizing industrial production or educating people or growing food. Yet, development of these institutions and practices is central to the nationalist project, for they provide the material goods and socialization that underpin both public support for the nation-state and its ability to secure itself relative to other nation-states.

Nature fits into this scheme because it is one of the two raw materials—the other is people—out of which the nation-state is constructed. The "taming" of nature involves the transformation of an "undeveloped" environment through the application of capitalist and industrial methods in order to increase the production of commodities and goods, especially military ones.

Dams are constructed and rivers channeled in order to control floods and expand arable land; canals and railroads are laid out to facilitate the movement of minerals, grains, animals, and armies; water supply systems are built to irrigate farms and provision cities; and so on. Landscapes are transformed.[19] These projects not only bring many of nature's hazards under human control, they also facilitate extraction of material inputs and wealth for state building.

Of course, nature was exploited long before nationalism emerged as a pan-European phenomenon during the nineteenth century. Until then, the exploitation of nature was driven by the sovereign's desire to accumulate wealth and power, but in the results we can begin to see the stirrings of what later became nationalism. As the historian E. L. Jones put it,

> Cultural homogeneity seemed desirable because it confirmed loyalty to the crown, simplified administration, taxation and trade. . . . Policies successful in one province might more easily be extended to all corners if the state were unified. . . . A motive [for internal expansion] . . . was to secure internal supplies of raw materials. Scientific ventures of the day . . . were often just as much resource appraisals as science. . . . A further motive, distinct from the aims of earlier periods, was to keep faith with a sense of cultural and political nationalism, and unify and develop state and market. . . . Motives and processes were therefore mixed . . . but they all drove towards the settled, occupied and unified nation-state.[20]

In England, the rapidly growing use of coal as an energy source and the appearance of factories for the manufacture of goods began, during the 1700s, to transform landscape, economy, and nation. But it was not until the following century that industrialization was put fully into the service of state power. As a result of the Napoleonic Wars, in particular, nationalism appeared as a mass social phenomenon, spreading from one country to another.[21] Geographically, Europe was too compact a land mass for the practices and experiences of one country to be ignored by others. Indeed, one state's failure to pay attention could result in occupation and conquest by another.

It became clear to elites that the security of state and sovereign was now intimately tied to national industrialization. To resist future invasions and maintain balances of power among them, states had to maximize their military capabilities through the mobilization of both industry and labor. And, even though few countries actually followed the French example of mass mobilization until much later in the nineteenth century, the state meant to muster its citizens for both work and war.[22] In other words, the project of state building launched by intellectuals and engineered by economic elites had as its goals not only the creation of a national consciousness but also a state that could hold its own against the other existing or emerging nation-states within Europe.

Under the new regime of nationalism, nature came to fill a double role. First, the construction of a nation-state and its "civil religion" demanded a historical account of the attachment between people and land, a link that, in some places and in later decades, might be further legitimated through archeological exploration and discovery (although, as many have noted, these histories were often pure fiction).[23] Second, as we saw above, nature and people came to constitute the raw materials out of which the nation-state was to be built. As the control and "improvement" of nature came to be one of the primary responsibilities of the newly bureaucratizing, nationalist state, techniques of nature management became the focus of scientists, and practices of nature management became the focus of administrators. One could say that, around the world, lessons were learned from England, France, and what would, eventually, become Germany (Prussia). The strategies and programs of one country were carefully studied and reproduced by the scientists and administrators of others, although not always with complete success.[24] What worked well in one part of the world might be an utter failure elsewhere. Whole ecologies could be destroyed, as they were in any number of places.[25] We shall see, later in this chapter, how these processes affected the control and supply of water and the management of forests.

The Contemporary National Origins of Environmental (Inter)nationalism

Nationalism has not vanished with the arrival of the twenty-first century, and the transformation of nature remains central to the nation-state. Today, however, the state has become less an agent for its own national projects than a facilitator of a global project of economic growth.[26] * In place of the nation-state as the object of popular veneration, globalization and liberalism encourage individuals to seek their own goals through consumption. In

---

*This remains the case, notwithstanding the apparent revival of the "war-making" state.

Chapter 2, we read about sustainable development, and in Chapter 3 we saw how it is being transformed into a rather different practice, sustainable growth. Here, we revisit these two concepts to see how, as forms of "environmental (inter)nationalism," they have their origins in what are, for the most part, the national beliefs and practices of the United States.

As argued above, the global shift toward market-based approaches to addressing environmental problems has its roots in ideological shifts in the United States and the United Kingdom during the 1980s. Because "free-market capitalism" came to be regarded as the solution to the economic stagnation and inflation of the 1970s, state regulation came under increasing attack.[27] The turn to the market for environmental protection was, if not inevitable, strongly determined by this discursive change, and the trend toward commodification of both nature and environmental externalities, initiated in the United States, diffused into the international realm.[28] Recall the discussion of externalities in Chapter 3. There, we saw that an externality is a cost or benefit arising from an economic activity for which the producer does not pay. Such costs can be addressed through direct regulatory means, either by imposing performance requirements on the offending activity—for example, setting emission limits on pollutants from power plants—or by taxing the activity and altering the polluter's balance of costs and benefits. Alternatively, some aspect of the offending activity can be turned into a commodity, to be bought and sold in a market setting, as in the case of marketable permits to pollute. In effect, both taxes and privatization are meant to raise the marginal cost of an activity to the point where it equals the marginal benefit. But the distributional effects are quite different.

A pollution tax applies equally to all offending activities above a certain set level, regardless of the economic condition of the polluter. Both the poor polluter and the rich one are subject to the same penalty, regardless of ability to pay. The rich polluter will, however, be in a better position to pay the costs of pollution reduction; the poor polluter may go broke. Privatization, as we saw in the case of marketable emission permits, discussed in Chapter 3, responds to the polluter's ability to pay and helps to direct economic resources where they can be used with greatest effect. In this instance, the rich polluter can outbid the poor polluter, or buy the latter's permits. This time, the poor polluter will not necessarily go broke, but she will most certainly have to go out of business. The outcome will be efficient, if not necessarily fair.

Why, then, has privatization become so popular? First, a market-based approach to protection and internalization "lets the market decide" about winners and losers. This may offer a means of avoiding difficult political struggles, some of which might threaten powerful states and their interests. By arguing that the market is an impartial institution in which decisions are based only on willingness to buy and sell, and ability to pay, the problem of distributive justice and unexpected outcomes are largely avoided.[29] Second, markets do require rules to function, and those rules are usually ones favored by and favorable to the wealthy and powerful.* The poor and weak often find it difficult to participate both in rulemaking and in exchange, as a result, and are excluded and further disadvantaged.[31] Finally, some might choose not to participate at all in such markets (or institutions), regarding them as unfair or disruptive. A lack of interest, or even hostility, to privatization may be regarded as a threat, and those states who take such a position are likely to find themselves labeled "rogues" or "defectors," cut off from access to other international institutions (consider the attitude of European countries to the American defection from the Kyoto Protocol).

This marketization trend also takes a leaf from the standard narrative of the U.S. experience. The relative stability of the American political system is often attributed to the expansiveness of its economy. Many political scientists are wont to repeat Harold Lasswell's claim that "politics is about who gets what, when, how." [32] Because financial and other resources are never unlimited—by the strict economic definition, they are "scarce"—difficult and contentious decisions must be made about how they will be distributed. In this view, the primary purpose of politics in a democratic system such as that of the United States is the distribution of resources, an activity subject to a great deal of pushing and pulling, lobbying and logrolling. An economy that grows too slowly or not at all, combined with the redistribution of resources toward the middle classes that is typical of democratic systems, may intensify struggles over shares of the pie, triggering class conflict and the instability so feared by political and economic elites as a threat to their interests, status, and position.[33] There is virtue, therefore, in ensuring a constantly growing "pie" or pool of resources, for, even if relative shares of the pie remain the same, absolute shares will increase and people will have a sense that their situation is getting better.[34]

The need and demand for environmental protection may threaten this formula, for several reasons. Such programs can insert a new competitor into

---

*The French philosopher Anatole France once noted that "The law, in its majestic equality, forbids the rich as well as the poor to sleep under bridges, to beg in the streets, and to steal bread."[30]

the struggle over the division of resources. Intensive environmental protection might require "limits to growth" in some or all sectors of the economy, which could reduce the flow of goods and money through the economy and cause the pie to stagnate or even shrink.[35] Moreover, the demand for high environmental quality has long been seen as a middle-class desire, on the proposition that the poor have more pressing matters about which to worry. Well-off neighborhoods may become cleaner while poorer ones get the garbage.[36] Serendipitously, perhaps, a rapidly growing economy appears to address these difficulties, providing both the growing pie and the resources necessary to protect the environment. Indeed, proponents of the "green economy" go so far as to claim that environmental protection is entirely consonant with high rates of economic growth, if that growth comes primarily in environmentally friendly sectors (note, however, that this is not the same as the argument about the "reverse Kuznets curve" discussed in Chapter 3).[37] This is nothing other than an argument for sustainable growth! During the past decade, this principle has been exported by the United States into the international arena and offered as the way to pay for global environmental protection as well as an alternative to the more problematic concept of sustainable development (see Chapters 2 and 3). But, wait! There is more!

Growing the global pie requires appropriate forms of investment and development in places and sectors where it will produce the greatest economic returns. In line with "letting the market do it," governments are not considered to be competent to make such decisions, especially given the dismal record of development programs over the past fifty years.[38] The international debt in developing countries exceeds $1 trillion, and international financial institutions are increasingly loath to loan new funds to them without assurances that debt service will be prioritized over social needs, such as environmental quality. What is to be done?

Tales of Privatization

From where will investments come? The answer appears to be greater corporate involvement, that is, more privatization, a strategy evident at the Johannesburg World Summit on Sustainable Development in August 2002.[39] Even as governments have deliberately and consciously supported the shift of various aspects of environmental regulatory authority out of the national domain and into the international arena, business has come to be viewed as a potential protector of nature. This is another trend that has been tracked throughout this book. Only corporations have sufficient capital to finance "green" industry and, so long as it generates adequate profits, only they have the incentive to make such investments. As discussed in other chapters (see, especially, Chapter 4), there are good reasons to doubt that corporations can "save" the environment. This will not prevent them from trying, especially with encouragement from the World Bank, the U.S. government, and the European Union, and particularly if they can make a nice profit from the effort, as we shall see from the stories below.

Making Scarce Water Even Scarcer

Urban water supply is one sector in which large-scale privatization is taking place. Water is essential to life. Water is, by many accounts, also growing scarce.[40] More than 1.2 billion people lack access to clean drinking water, and more than 2 billion lack access to proper sanitation.[41] Many urban distribution systems around the world are in a state of chronic disrepair, and massive quantities of water are lost through old, cracked pipes. Building new supply systems and fixing old ones is an expensive proposition that governments are unable to afford in these days of scarce public resources. By one estimate, it could cost $325 billion over the next twenty years simply to repair existing water systems in the United States alone.[42] But where public authorities see nothing but problems, private entrepreneurs see nothing but opportunity. By charging a higher price for water, they can generate the revenues necessary for repairs and earn a tidy profit! The private water supply business—not counting bottled water—earns revenues of $300 billion per year serving a few hundred million people in more than 130 countries.[43] Since everyone needs to drink water, the revenue potential appears almost limitless.

Should water therefore be treated as a commodity, to be bought and sold according to one's ability to pay for it? So long as water seemed plentiful, it was virtually free for the taking; now that farmers, industrialists, and consumers are demanding more water than is available in many places, some means must be found to allocate it. Allocation through markets is one means of doing so. This, at least, is the logic that is being propagated globally, to a growing degree, by those individuals and institutions who pay for and play a role in financing and building water delivery systems.[44] But there is something of a paradox here: the growing scarcity of water is, in many ways, a direct consequence of the national development of large-scale water projects. Dams and reservoirs made agricultural, industrial, and urban growth possible. In the early days of these projects, water supply far exceeded demand, so consumption was encouraged and subsidies were paid by governments to ensure that the water would be so cheap as to make it seem free.[45] This discouraged its judicious use and made the deserts bloom. Supply created demand, and then demand outran supply. How could this have happened?

Dam History. The earliest hydraulic projects were constructed in the Middle East and Asia for irrigation of agricultural lands during dry seasons. We might speculate that the first such projects were quite small and crude and were washed away every year by seasonal flooding. With the rise of city-states, kingdoms, and empires and the emergence of divisions of labor between leaders, workers, and peasants, irrigation systems became essential to ensuring an adequate and reliable food supply. Thus, the early systems were extended in scope and came under more centralized control. They also began to have serious and widespread environmental impacts, most notably salinization and water-logging of soils. Some have argued that these problems led to the declines in agricultural productivity that played a major role in the collapse of the civilizations that built those irrigation systems.[46]

Storage and irrigation projects covering tens or hundreds of square miles did not appear again until a little more than a century ago. The dams of the nineteenth and twentieth centuries were built to control floods and generate electricity as well as to irrigate farmland. Although the first dams were rather small and sometimes privately built, later ones were constructed by governments, at increasingly larger scales and with consequent environmental effects over greater areas. Ultimately, only states were able to mobilize the capital, expertise, labor, and land to build big dams, and only states had the power to force people to move out of the dams' way.[47] In virtually every instance, the goal of hydraulic projects was not only to "manage" the resource but also to transform the landscape and people. The rivers of Africa, the American West, Brazil, China, Europe, India, Israel, the Soviet Union, Turkey, and elsewhere were tamed. All big dams followed a few large-scale variations of a standard hydraulic technology. When completed, these projects were regarded as great national accomplishments. And those who worked on these projects and on the land were lionized as the heroes of the nation. The future seemed bright. It was not.

The gradual failure of large-scale hydraulic technology became apparent only over time. On the one hand, dams and irrigation systems were a great success in their specific objectives: vast areas were transformed into productive farmland, cities appeared where none had been possible before. On the other hand, those same dams often displaced millions of people, gradually led to the ruination of lands and ecosystems in some places, and slowly filled up with silt to become almost useless in others.[48] Large-scale water storage and irrigation systems constructed in dry and near-desert areas have created much the same problems with water-logging and salinization that plagued the early civilizations of the Middle East. Large dams still have their defenders, for they remain central to the development strategies of countries such as Brazil, China, and India. But global environmental activism, and the enormous cost of such structures, have virtually halted the construction of all but a very few new ones.[49] Indeed, there is a growing view, emerging from the United States, that floods cannot and should not be controlled, but that people should, insofar as is possible, move out of riverine flood plains.[50] Few states look any longer to large-scale hydraulic projects as a means of developing the nation.

At the same time, however, irrigation is more essential than ever. New types of genetically engineered crops require reliable supplies of water, as do the burgeoning populations of the world's cities. What to do? It appears that the growing need for water will have to be achieved through demand rather than supply strategies: water will have to be used more efficiently, and many people may have to make do with less. Conservation does not make much of a contribution to "state-building" in the traditional sense, so other methods must be found. The solution, it would appear, lies in the new international "ideology" of free-market economics.

Selling the Springs of Life. The water supply problem is, therefore, twofold. First, as we saw above, in many parts of the world the infrastructure of water storage and delivery is unable to meet the demands of growing populations, especially in cities. Second, agriculture, industry, and cities are all competitors for the same limited water supplies. Because of the enormous cost of making more water available through new capture, storage, and distribution facilities, it makes economic sense to reduce demand. It usually costs less to save water through reducing demand than to capture new water.[51] But demand management appears to come in only two forms: rationing or higher prices. Rationing is fairer, but lends itself to all kinds of problems, including theft, corruption, and black markets (an excellent illustration of this can be seen in the film *Chinatown*). Higher prices will persuade people to value water and use it more carefully. We know that this approach will reduce demand because the very poor, who often must buy their water from water sellers offering their product at extortionate prices, use very little water. And, unlike rationing, no complex allocation system is required: people will respond directly to the price signal.

How is this to be accomplished? It would seem fairly simple to raise water prices, but often it is not. For one thing, many water systems are publicly owned and governments are loath to offend voters. It is easier to raise funds by selling municipal bonds to pay the costs of repairs. For another thing, water is still not metered in many places throughout the world; public companies have no way of measuring anything but aggregate consumption. A private company, by contrast, will value the resource for its profit potential and will find ways to squeeze the greatest return out of its investment. This means repairing existing systems to reduce water loss, improving water quality, and carefully measuring what consumers use. All these tasks cost money, and the new owners have little choice but to raise prices. When that happens, people will use less water, making the remainder available for "more productive" uses.

It is an interesting exercise to imagine how much water might have to cost in order for demand management to work. In the United States, water typically costs a few dollars per thousand gallons. A gallon bottle of distilled water runs between $0.50 and $1.00. Twenty-four liters of bottled drinking water can be purchased for $10.00 to $15.00, whereas a single small bottle might run as high as $3.00 a bottle or, roughly, $10.00 per gallon. The typical American family of four uses between 300 and 1,000 gallons of water per day, so an average monthly water bill runs anywhere from $10.00 to $30.00. It is unlikely that a doubling, or even a tripling, of this sum would have very much effect on demand. But at $300.00 per month—a roughly ten to thirtyfold increase in price—many people would begin to conserve, cutting back on watering their lawns and washing their cars. It is difficult, however, to imagine a water supply company being allowed to raise rates so precipitously: the public outcry would cow any public utilities commission that authorized such an increase.

At any rate, water privatization has taken the world by storm. International financial institutions, such as the World Bank and International Monetary Fund, actively encourage privatization of water systems. Governments are eager to sell off public water systems in order to generate one-time revenues to reduce budget deficits and to avoid future expenditures on infrastructure. Private water companies see the opportunities for significant profits, so long as the price of water is set sufficiently high.[52] Even NGOs, such as Environmental Defense (formerly the Environmental Defense Fund) in the United States, have jumped on the bandwagon, arguing that free markets in water are a means of conserving a valuable resource.[53] In some settings, especially where wasteful users are well off or producing high-value products, there is some sense in raising the price of water to that which the market will bear. In others, however, it may be nothing short of a social disaster.

A Bolivian Tale. The story of the water system in Cochabamba, Bolivia, is an instructive one. Under pressure from the World Bank, Bolivia has privatized numerous public corporations, such as the national airline, the train system, and the electric utility. In September 1999, the Bolivian government gave a forty-year concession to Aguas del Tunari to operate the water and sanitation systems of the city of Cochabamba. The owners of Aguas are based not only in Bolivia but also in the United States, Italy, and Spain.[54] (The giant U.S. engineering contractor Bechtel is one of Aguas's owners.) The logic of the deal was fairly straightforward. With financing provided by international lenders, Aguas paid the Bolivian government for the existing utilities. The company was slated to build new water storage and distribution lines and to rehabilitate the municipal delivery system. In return, it would be permitted to raise water tariffs to a level that would provide a nice profit to the company and its shareholders. But there was a catch.

The catch was that the financing could not go forward without the water rates being raised first, to ensure that repayment of loans would begin immediately. And the rates were raised—more than 200 percent, by some accounts.[55] One resident reported that his water bill went from $12 in December 1999 to $30 in January 2000; this in a town where many families earn only about $100 a month.[56] A municipal uprising followed, along with a four-day general strike, marches, and, eventually, violent confrontations with police. Almost two hundred people were injured. The Bolivian president, Hugo Banzer, declared a state of siege in the entire country, which led to more violence. At least one person, and perhaps more, were killed.[57] At that point, the government revoked the concession to Aguas and returned the water system to the municipality. Water rates were reduced. Today, the situation remains largely unchanged from its pre-Aguas state, although Aguas is suing the Bolivian government for $25 million in profits lost as a result of the concession's termination.[58]

Not all privatizations fall victim to these kinds of problems, to be sure, but the basic argument continues to be repeated and implemented. The commodification of water and the attendant higher prices are judged to be necessary in order to reduce "waste." Why is water being "wasted?" Not because people are inherently wastrels. Rather, in order to encourage economic growth and development, water has been heavily subsidized. And where there was water, people would come, build, and work. It might appear as though households constitute the bulk of global water use, but this is not true. The world over, about 80 percent of stored water is dedicated to irrigation; the rest is left for industry and people.[59] Why, then, does it seem as though households bear the brunt of water privatization?

In wealthy countries, with many water-thirsty appliances, consumers pay relatively low water rates but can afford relatively large price increases. In poor countries, there are many fewer such appliances, and household water use is relatively limited. But households are not the main source of economic growth; farmers and industries are. If farmers have to pay market rates for their water, they might go out of business—in California, farmers have been enormously resistant to higher water costs. Agricultural conservation technologies are expensive, too, and make sense only for crops whose water requirements are fairly limited. Industries make similar claims about their water needs and, as the source of much economic growth, governments are loath to impose high rates on them. Only household consumers are left to squeeze. Making them conserve will save water, but it will have an impact on less than one-fifth of the total demand in most places around the world.

Not Seeing the Forest for the Trees

A similar logic of privatization is being applied to forests, although here the methods differ considerably. Forests, too, are growing "scarce," less for the timber they provide than for their ecological importance. Forests serve a broad range of ecosystem functions that are not often incorporated into their economic value. Aside from the intrinsic value of the various species of trees themselves, they provide habitat for other plant and animal species, environmental services such as water purification, soil retention, local climate moderation, and reservoirs of genetic diversity. With the inclusion in the Kyoto Protocol of provisions allowing for the protection and planting of trees as a means of carbon storage, more attention than ever is being paid to the "fate of the forest(s)."[60] The exploitation, preservation, and restoration of forests, tropical, temperate, and boreal, are therefore of growing international concern. Wherever there are trees, however, trade in timber competes with preservation and other uses of forest resources. Many countries and companies earn significant revenues from lumber production, and they do not wish to see restrictions imposed on logging.[61] As a result, some forests are being replaced by plantations, and others are being left in ruins. This is not necessary, yet timber companies show considerable reluctance to log in a sustainable fashion which, many believe, is more costly.[62]

Each country has its own regulations governing the protection and exploitation of forests, but those that export are driven by competitive pressures to log heavily. There is not yet any significant international regulation of forest practices. Most of the efforts that have been made to craft an international forestry convention have failed, usually because of resistance by governments, who fear intrusion on their sovereign prerogatives, and by corporations, who fear having to pay greater costs for access to timber. In lieu of an effective international system, a large number of competing private, market-oriented regulatory initiatives have sprung up, seeking to foster some form of "sustainable forestry" and to become the (inter)national standard for the future.[63] To understand how these have come about, however, we need to begin with a brief history of national forest practices.

The Forests of Nations. Virtually all contemporary forest management systems the world over appear to have been derived from principles and practices first developed in Prussia and Saxony in the eighteenth century as a response by state authorities to a growing shortage of wood.[64] These systems were later revised or altered in various ways, adopted by Britain, France, the United States, and other countries, and subsequently diffused throughout European colonial territories.[65] In all instances, national practices were implemented as the "best available approach" to forest management (although, in retrospect, it is not always clear that this was the case). "Scientific forestry" was based on the precise measurement of the distribution and volume of wood in a given parcel, the systematic felling of trees, and their replacement by standard, carefully aligned rows of monocultural plantations that could be harvested at scheduled times.[66] As James Scott points out, this approach succeeded beyond expectations during the first growing cycle of eighty years or so.[67] It began to fall short, however, during the second cycle as a result of unanticipated ecosystemic damage and destruction. No matter. By then, the model had been adopted around the world and the principles and practices had become the law of many lands.

What is noteworthy about scientific management is that its goal was not preservation of forests, or even "sustainable development," in the sense that those are understood today. Rather, as Scott has observed, the objective was entirely economic: increasing the wealth of seventeenth- and eighteenth-century kings and queens.

> The early modern European state, even before the development of scientific forestry, viewed its forests primarily through the fiscal lens of revenue needs. To be sure, other concerns—such as timber for shipping, state construction, and fuel for the economic security of its subjects—were not entirely absent from official management. These concerns also had heavy implications for state revenue and security. Exaggerating only slightly, one might say that the crown's interest in forests was resolved through its fiscal lens into a single number: the revenue yield of the timber that might be extracted annually.[68]

Little changed during the following centuries. Forest management was overseen by state agencies, intent on maximizing production in the national "interest" and for national objectives. That forests might be used by others who were less interested in timber was hardly relevant. Exclusion of peasants from forest commons was one more means of forcing them off the land.

Actual practices differed from one country to the next, of course. Even though most forest land in the United States and Canada was and is privately owned, for example, a considerable amount is held by the state as a "public good." In the interest of revenue generation, portions of these national forests are systematically leased to private timber producers, who do not always harvest carefully.[69] In India the British Imperial government took ownership of virtually all forests, declaring them to be "wasteland" and, therefore, no one's property (see later in this chapter).[70] Again, one result was less-than-careful logging combined with denial of access to villagers, who relied on these commons for wood and other basic needs. In Indonesia, forests are legally state-owned but in practice are treated as private property. In Brazil, a lack of national government capacity almost literally renders Amazonia's forests open-access commons, available to anyone with an ax.

In all cases, these public forests are viewed as a national resource, that is, the sovereign property of the state. In this role, the conservation of forests is tightly linked to the production of timber and other commodities that generate both capital and jobs. The economies of large regions have come to be almost wholly dependent on natural resource production from those public forests, and they suffer greatly when the trees begin to run out or cutting is restricted.[71] In the domestic scheme of things, timber producers are quite politically influential, both for the jobs they offer and for the campaign and other funds they can sometimes divert to policymakers. The timber industry often gets its way when it comes to legislation governing public forests and is able to find ways of getting around many restrictions that might be imposed. Although industries in some countries often argue that they plant more trees than they cut, the results are rarely the equivalents of the forests that have been destroyed.[72] Production generally trumps conservation.

A Tale of India. The way these processes play out can be seen in India's forest policy, which is especially complex as a result of its history, geography, and demography. The British bestowed on India a system of government whose task it was to control a large, fragmented territory of high ethnic and cultural diversity. While the Raj (the colonial British government) tended toward a form of "divide and rule," leaving many administrative tasks to local leaders and villages, after 1948 the government of India pursued strategies intended to unite the disparate parts into a whole. The consequent tension between localism and union has never been wholly resolved and can be seen with particular clarity in ongoing struggles over the environment.

The first postindependence government of Jawaharlal Nehru pursued a program of state planning, industrial centralism, import substitution, protectionism, and urbanization. At the same time, India's growing population required land and food, at any cost. Together, these two demands resulted in the exploitation of the country's natural resources, as they became critical inputs into the development process, in general disregard for the protection of nature.[73] Perhaps of greater importance was (and continues to be) the fact that there is almost no "primeval" nature within India. The region has been inhabited for so many millennia, located at the crossroads of so many civilizations and migratory flows, that most of the land has been worked and transformed many times.[74] Without romanticizing the carefulness and capabilities of rural villagers, we might say nonetheless that, for the most part, the inhabitants of the subcontinent were able to maximize their usage of resources while also managing to sustain them. This is not to imply that there was any equity in access to nature, of course, since the actual structure of village life is a good deal more complex than suggested here, and class and caste differences have always complicated the use of resources and their maintenance.[75]

Nevertheless, what "balance" there was, was upset, first, by the Raj and, to a much larger degree, by postindependence governments. As N. Patrick Peritore puts it:

> The environment is in the hands of complex and elephantine bureaucracies, which apply contradictory policies, and of local elites connected to national parties, contractors, and mafias. Outmoded colonial laws treat villagers as strangers in their own land and criminalize actions creating autonomy. Government permission, requiring years of legal battles and large bribes, is required for villagers to reforest their own catchment watershed or commons or to build small dams and modify village water tanks.[76]

The effects of these legal regimes are evident in India's forestry policy. During the Raj, timber was considered essential to British interests and was largely exploited for export. To this end, the British sought to conserve forest commons usually shared by neighboring villages, declaring that they were not owned by anyone and were, therefore, state property. An 1878 law defined three classes of forests: restricted and closed to the public; protected and open to the public within certain limits; and village forests open to all. The 1927 Indian Forestry Act gave complete control of all forests, except those within the princely states, to the Raj.[77] Imperial foresters took it as their mandate to prevent villagers from gaining access to these now-public lands. Following independence, the Union government of India pursued the same policy, first in order to give state and private corporations access to timber and, later, to conserve dwindling forests. The Indian Forest Conservation Act of 1980, designed with this purpose in mind, further centralized control of forests. It required the permission of the central government for all changes in uses of forest lands by anyone, including government agencies.[78]

As a result, locals continued to be excluded from access to essential forest products, whereas logging went on, sometimes under state sanction, sometimes illegally. Poverty continued to increase and forests continued to disappear. These circumstances gave rise to movements such as Chipko Andolan ("Hug the Trees Movement") which, during the 1970s and 1980s, became well known for its efforts to halt logging in the Himalayan foothills.[79] Chipko has since largely vanished, but similar movements have taken its place.[80] These have achieved some successes. India's Forest Department has concluded joint management agreements with tens of thousands of village councils, establishing committees that care for lands formerly under the strict control of the state. But even this innovation has not completely freed village forests from the development plans and programs of the government.[81] And these same patterns of state control are found the world over. So long as timber remains a valuable commodity and there are forests to be exploited, governments and lumber companies will seek ways to exploit them. Trees, it would seem, are too valuable to be left to the people.

Forests for Sale? Although the many forest functions enumerated earlier are extremely important to the local and global environments, as we have seen, none is as central to the economies of many countries as timber production. Moreover, the secondary benefits provided by forests, especially ecological ones, have much less to do with sovereignty and much more to do with the global good. These might be thought of as positive externalities for which no one pays but from which everyone benefits. In political terms, however, the concentrated interests in and maintenance of national control over forests far outweigh the diffuse and scattered stake that the world appears to have in these secondary benefits. This is evident in the recent history of efforts to craft international forestry law.[82]

In 1992, representatives of 180 of the world's nations met at the UN Conference on Environment and Development (UNCED), the "Earth Summit," in Rio de Janeiro to consider, among other things, the adoption of an agreement on forestry principles. The document bore the unwieldy title "Non-legally Binding Authoritative Statement of Principles for a Global Consensus on the Management, Conservation and Sustainable Development of All Types of Forests." That statement was the result of several years of sustained, intensive negotiation and controversy, a product of growing concern during the 1980s and early 1990s about the future of the world's remaining tropical forests. That this meeting was taking place in Brazil was especially apposite for two reasons. On the one hand, the burning forests of Amazonia had, during the late 1980s, served to focus global attention on their survival as well as their role in the global environment. On the other hand, the Brazilian government had expressed strong opposition to any hint of internationalization of its sovereign resources and territory.[83] At the time, national governments were leery of being bound to a single set of rules, and many environmental NGOs believed that an agreement would only foster increased international trade in timber and even higher rates of deforestation than had been taking place.

Unwilling to lose the momentum generated by the Earth Summit's Forest Principles, however, in a joint initiative in 1993, the Canadian and Malaysian governments created the Intergovernmental Working Group on Global Forests (IWGF; the word "global" was later dropped). In April 1994 the IWGF held a meeting of experts and officials from fifteen key forest countries and several NGOs to facilitate dialogue and consolidation of approaches to the management, conservation, and sustainable development of the world's forests. By the second meeting, in October 1994, participation had expanded to include technical and policy experts from thirty-two countries, including Brazil, Finland, Gabon, Indonesia, Japan, the Russian Federation, Sweden, the United States, five intergovernmental organizations, and eleven NGOs.[84] At the end of 1994, the final report of the IWGF was presented to the UN Commission on Sustainable Development, which, at its third meeting in 1995, proposed to establish an ad hoc Intergovernmental Panel on Forests (IPF) to further examine issues and develop proposals and recommendations. The IPF held four subsequent meetings through 1997, when its final report was submitted to the commission.[85] As a follow-up to the work of the IPF, in 1997 the UN Economic and Social Council established the Intergovernmental Forum on Forests, which pursued the work of the IPF and developed additional action proposals. Ultimately, the IPF and the Intergovernmental Forum on Forests together issued 270 proposals for action.[86] And, finally, in 2000 the UN's Economic and Social Council established a permanent entity, the UN Forum on Forests, to build on the work of its predecessors.[87] None of these initiatives led, however, to a global forestry agreement, and therein lies a tale.

Initially, the United States was a strong supporter of such an agreement, in the view that tropical deforestation represented a major contributor to global warming. Although the United States preferred to see other countries, especially developing ones, reduce their emissions by emphasizing forest protection, the Forest Principles were the most to which the developing countries would agree. After UNCED, however, many governments, including European and Canadian and those of developing countries, came to favor a global agreement. By 1996, however, the U.S. position had changed completely, as industry opposition grew because of the inclusion of boreal and temperate forests in the agendas of the various panels and forums addressing deforestation. Environmental organizations, too, were opposed to a global forest agreement and wished, instead, to see forest conservation addressed through the Convention on Biological Diversity.[88] The nail in the coffin, as it were, occurred when the Kyoto Protocol became the locus of global forestry regulation, under the rubric of "LULUCF," or "Land Use, Land Use Change, and Forestry." In effect, the United States and several other countries began to see in forests the potential for sequestering carbon and avoiding the need to reduce greenhouse gas emissions in other sectors, such as transportation and industry. Through various projects and mechanisms, carbon emissions in the form of standing trees would be traded, and sustainable forestry would then become something quite different from what was originally envisioned.[89] Although a few countries, such as Canada, continue to call for an international agreement, for the moment, global forestry regulation appears quite unlikely. It is not altogether surprising, then, that what has emerged is a growing effort to regulate national logging through international markets, specifically, consumer markets in industrialized countries. There are as many as fifty such schemes in existence around the world, but two have emerged as dominant: the Forest Stewardship Council (FSC) and the International Organisation for Standardization (ISO). Both of these are discussed below.

With international government processes in apparent stalemate, the FSC has been seen by many as the "magic bullet," a market-driven mechanism able to fill a critical niche in the effort toward achieving sustainable forest management where governments cannot. The FSC was launched in 1993 in Washington, D.C., by environmental groups, the timber industry, foresters, indigenous peoples, and community groups from twenty-five countries, with initial funding provided primarily by the Worldwide Fund for Nature/World Wildlife Fund (WWF). An interim board was elected, a mission statement adopted, and a draft of the guideline "Principles and Criteria for Forest Management" formulated soon thereafter. The FSC was originally based in Oaxaca, Mexico, but has recently moved its central office to Bonn, Germany, where it will be better positioned to compete with other standards-setting organizations. It is a membership organization composed of three equally weighted chambers—environmental, social, and economic—and membership within each chamber is also equally weighted between North and South. As the FSC's Web site puts it:

The Environmental Chamber includes non-profit, non-governmental organizations, as well as research, academic, technical institutions and individuals that have an active interest in environmentally viable forest stewardship;

The Social Chamber includes non-profit, non-governmental organizations, as well as research, academic, technical institutions and individuals that have a demonstrated commitment to socially beneficial forestry.

The Economic Chamber includes organizations and individuals with a commercial interest. Examples are employees, certification bodies, industry and trade associations (whether profit or non-profit), wholesalers, retailers, traders, consumer associations, and consulting companies.[90]

Each chamber represents 33 percent of the vote at annual meetings, and the board of directors has rotating members reflecting these interests. By 2001 the FSC was an internationally recognized organization with members in fifty-six countries, 221 in the economic chamber, 86 in the social chamber, and 174 in the environmental chamber.[91]

According to its mission statement,

1. The Forest Stewardship Council A.C. (FSC) shall promote environmentally appropriate, socially beneficial, and economically viable management of the world's forests.
2. Environmentally appropriate forest management ensures that the harvest of timber and non-timber products maintains the forest's biodiversity, productivity, and ecological processes.
3. Socially beneficial forest management helps both local people and society at large to long term benefits and also provides strong incentives to local people to sustain the forest resources and adhere to long-term management plans.
4. Economically viable forest management means that forest operations are structured and managed so as to be sufficiently profitable, without generating financial profit at the expense of the forest resource, the ecosystem, or affected communities. The tension between the need to generate adequate financial returns and the principles of responsible forest operations can be reduced through efforts to market forest products for their best value.[92]

As part of its program, the FSC has developed and adopted guidelines for forest management, and it accredits certifying organizations that agree to abide by them. Purportedly, the FSC also monitors the operations and portfolios of such certifying groups on an annual basis. In cooperation with lumber retailers, the FSC has created "Buyers Groups" in consuming countries. Members of these groups are committed to selling only verified "sustainably produced" timber in their stores.[93] As of January 2003, the FSC had granted 466 "forest management certificates" in fifty-six countries, covering almost 77 million acres, and 2,801 "chain of custody" certificates in sixty-seven countries.[94] The actual ecological and social outcomes triggered by the FSC system are not yet clear, however, and have not yet been well studied.[95] Some indications are that in some locations, the system is not leading to ecological or social outcomes that exceed those already required by existing government policies. In other instances, FSC standards may not actually be implemented by producers, because of the weak institutional base of the FSC. Funding and personnel to monitor implementation are scarce, and penalties for failing to observe the rules are few.[96]

An additional challenge to the FSC's success may be the broader trend toward green labeling that it has inspired. Its forest product certification program has triggered numerous corporate and government responses, and considerable alarm. The large financial stakes involved have led forest products companies to become actively involved in standard setting and implementation activities in other countries, such as Indonesia, Malaysia, and Sweden. A growing number of business organizations, including the American Forest Products Association and the Canadian Pulp and Paper Association in conjunction with the International Organization for Standardization, have developed certification programs.[97] And there is, under way, a program to establish what is called "mutual recognition" among different national standards programs in order to pre-empt both the FSC's growing domination and the possibility of regulation by national governments.

The International Organisation for Standardization is one of the transnational competitors in the forestry arena, although it is far behind the FSC in regard to getting its standards out and accepted. The ISO, based in Geneva, is a quasi-governmental body with member organizations in 119 countries. It is the official standards-setting and labeling body recognized by the World Trade Organization and other international agencies. Founded in 1946, " 'ISO's mission is to promote standardisation and related activities in the world with a view to facilitating the international exchange of goods and services and to developing cooperation in the spheres of intellectual, scientific, technological and economic activity' by developing worldwide technical agreements which are published as international standards." [98]

With an annual operating budget of $125 million provided by governments and corporate members, the ISO is far larger than the FSC and other comparable certifying organizations. Around the world, it hosts as many as

ten standards-setting meetings each day.[99] Unlike the FSC, the ISO is frequently the recipient of praise and support by governments and most of the
forest products industry. The organization provides only the context within
which standards can be negotiated and promulgated; it does not engage in
policing corporate behavior, enforcing standards, or penalizing violators. In
fact, individual corporations generally devise their own internal performance
programs, which are vetted and certified by an authorized company or organization. In other words, a producer whose program receives certification
from an ISO-approved auditor is, for the most part, self-regulating and responsible for seeing that it meets the terms of its programs.

Historically, the ISO has neither worked on nor developed competency
in either environmental or forestry issues. Until the early 1980s, it limited itself to purely technical standards, such as the size of nuts and bolts. The demand for environmental standards grew out of a concern that these might be
imposed "from above" as a result of interstate agreements and conventions.
Growing public agitation over the absence of any environmental considerations in the General Agreement on Tariffs and Trade (GATT) and, later, the
WTO also contributed to the ISO's entry into the environmental standards
business.[100] In 1993, therefore, the ISO initiated a process of developing a
new "ISO 14000 series" of Environmental Management Systems standards.
This was intended to build on the success of the ISO 9000 Quality Management Systems, which are de facto requirements for companies engaging in
most sectors of international trade.[101] Those standards are driven by the
market and based entirely on self-regulation.[102]

The ISO adheres to the "Environmental Management Systems" approach. This approach differs from the FSC's guidelines for forest management in that Environmental Management Systems only prescribe *internal*
management systems for companies that wish to continuously improve
upon an environmental performance level that they themselves define. Adherence to externally agreed-upon standards (ostensibly set by all interested
stakeholders) is not required (as it is in the FSC). Furthermore, the ISO has
no adequate mechanism either to ensure corporations' compliance with or
the effectiveness of their individual action plans or to control the use (or
misuse) of logos and certification marks. In other words, self-regulation
based on the ISO 14000 series involves only "first-party" certification (see
Chapter 4). As a result, there is, according to one observer, a "potential for
confusion. . . . [T]his situation is worse in the case of forest management
certification, where some economic interests are seeking to use the ISO

framework to develop a forestry-specific application of the Environmental Management System . . . approach in order to counter an existing and operational environmental labeling scheme—that of the Forest Stewardship Council." [103]

Although the ISO has well-developed procedures on consensus and participation, these have not been well followed in creating the ISO 14000 series. Environmental organizations have not been allowed to attend standards-setting meetings, ostensibly to avoid "politics." [104] Instead, corporate forest product industry efforts seem to be aimed at imbuing the ISO with an aura of scientific, technical, and social legitimacy, all the while maintaining a near-perfect level of control. Nevertheless, forest industry members and supporters of the ISO 14000 series are using the discourse developed by the FSC and environmental groups to describe their system's approach in terms very similar to those adopted by the FSC. For example, a 1997 press release issued by the Canadian Sustainable Forestry Certification Coalition (an industry group), promoting ISO forest certification, claimed that "we have identified the background information that forestry organizations will find useful as they implement and progressively improve upon their environmental management system. This major step forward in relating the key elements of the ISO standard in the context of a range of international forest management measures will further the UN Agenda 21 goal of promoting sustainable development." [105]

Some ISO members continue as well to actively push forward the development of international ISO forest management system standards. Some, concerned that certification might obstruct free trade, are active in the WTO Environment Committee to limit the definition and mutual recognition of eco-labels by GATT country signatories. Consequently, although timber products may carry ISO certification, what lies behind the label is not so clear.

Who Will Regulate the Regulators? Does privatized forestry regulation work? The answer is not evident. Both the FSC and the ISO rely on consumer preferences to validate their programs, an approach discussed in Chapter 4 and fraught with problems. Can action through the market provide the incentives for the maintenance and enforcement of this kind of private self-regulation? Producers will be attracted to such approaches only if environmentally conscious consumers choose their environmentally friendly certified products. A few retailers have begun to sell certified timber, hopeful that they can grab a larger chunk of the estimated $500 billion per year lumber indus-try. It is assumed that consumers will pay more for certified lumber—for the time being, demand appears to exceed supply—but how much more? It is one thing to tack a 10 percent green surcharge on a piece of furniture that may cost between $100 and $1,000; it is quite another to charge an extra 10 percent on a $20,000 remodeling job or a $300,000 house.

It is also quite difficult, however, to find hard data on the effects and the effectiveness of such certification on the health of those forests that have been certified by the various programs. The vast majority of certified forests are in industrialized countries, and it appears that most of those forests were al-ready being managed close to certifier standards. Furthermore, the long-term consequences of certification, especially for natural forests (whether old-growth or new-growth), cannot be assessed until a significant fraction of a harvesting cycle has passed. Consequently, for the time being there appears to be no way to determine whether certification, as a policy instrument, offers a viable long-term means of protecting the environment.[106]

Is forestry regulation through the market an adequate substitute for an international convention or national law? For the moment, as seen above, there is no such agreement stipulating standards for sustainable forestry that could be the basis for policies in many different countries. Although a few governments would prefer to have such regulations in place, timber produc-ers and associations have made clear their preference for "self-regulation." Under ideal conditions, private regulation might be a "second-best" solution to the problem, but the proliferation of certification schemes and, especially, fragmentation among national standards, suggests that we are far from even a consensus on private standard.[107] It would be unreasonable, of course, to expect completely effective certification and sustainable forestry even under a global convention, but there would, at least, be a single framework from which to develop the required policy tools.

There is, moreover, an unrecognized trap hiding in the market-based approach to regulation of sustainable forestry, and that is, as we have seen, that markets are particularly weak arenas in which to seek political goals. Politics is, by definition, a public, collective endeavor, whereas markets involve private exchange between individuals. Politics is based on the visible aggregation of power, which markets eschew. Politics through market-based methods, which is what private certification amounts to, rests primarily on attempts to alter the preferences of large numbers of consumers in order to put pressure on producers. Because consumer preferences are not political and are strongly influenced, if not determined, by the very system of production and consumption that motivates the social disruption and externalities of concern, there is a certain tautological process at work here. If capital is able to acquire political power, it is more a form of displacement than an alternative: the "corporate citizen" becomes, in a sense, a franchisee able to cast a vote using its dollars. The relevant question here, then, is not about "best" or "second-best" solutions to what appears to be a largely technical problem about maintaining best practices in forestry or any other environmental sector. If sustainable forestry is as critical to the sustenance of biological diversity and the environment as is often claimed, institutions that emerge from and through the market are unlikely to provide the necessary normative and legal structures that will last through much more than a few harvesting cycles, at most.

Genes and Markets

Not all natural resources have a long history of state manipulation and management combined with a more recent transformation into commodities. The very concept of genetic resources is, as we have seen, a relatively recent one that has emerged as a result of innovations in biotechnology and gene manipulation. Historically, it has been left to governments to devise restrictions on hazardous materials, such as radioactive substances, toxic chemicals, and explosives, and to facilitate the marketing of drugs and the certification of the purity of food additives. Genes, however, present a rather special case. Every living thing on Earth, including all the foods we ingest, contains genetic materials. Sometimes, genes "go bad" and mutate. Some mutations are harmless whereas others have disastrous effects on the organism harboring them. And some genetic combinations can be deadly to other organisms: snake venom is possible only by virtue of certain genetic combinations, and hemlock is deadly by virtue of others.* But, so far as we know, the genes themselves are not toxic to living things.

More than that, humans have been engaged in manipulating and trading genes for thousands of years. Domesticated animals are a product of selective breeding for favored characteristics, which depend on particular combinations of genes. Almost all of our foods originate from cultivars that were the result of the crossing of related plants in order to increase productivity and change

---

*The recent appearance of SARS, or "severe acute respiratory syndrome," a coronavirus that appears to be related to the common cold, suggests just how deadly genetic mutations might be.

appearance. And the mass production of specially bred seed stocks, such as high-yield rice and corn, means that new genetic combinations are shipped to all four corners of the world. Of course, for every successful hybrid, there are many failures: no offspring, weak offspring, or undesirable characteristics in offspring. Yet, there seem to be no instances in which such hybridization has proved to be directly dangerous or fatal to other living things. Nonetheless, the issue of genetically modified organisms (GMOs) has become an especially contentious one in international politics, and it is here that we see a clash between public and private regulation, and between the stand of the United States and that of the European Union. Indeed, the long-term global economic prospects for GMO-based foodstuffs may well rest on who wins this clash.

What, exactly, is the problem? Throughout Europe, there appears to be widespread public discomfort with the idea of GM foods or, as some have called them, "Frankenfoods." The European attitude seems to have its origins, in part, in the outbreak of "Mad Cow" and foot-and-mouth disease in Britain, and their subsequent appearance on the Continent as a result of British beef imports (no matter that there is no connection between these diseases and GMOs).[108] People have begun to pay much more attention to the contents of what they eat and, where guarantees of food purity are concerned, the European public seems quite distrustful of government reassurances. Despite considerable American and European research and scientific data that show no untoward effects from GM foods—data that continue to be strongly disputed by environmental and health organizations—public skepticism remains strong.[109] According to a Eurobarometer Survey published in 2001, almost 95 percent of Europeans "want to have the right to choose when it comes to genetically-modified foodstuffs."[110] There also remains some uncertainty about potential environmental impacts of GMOs, although it is the case that GMOs have been found widely in crops that were thought to be GMO-free.[111] This has further exacerbated opposition in Europe.

In the United States, by contrast, there appears to be a much lower level of public concern. A survey sponsored by the International Food Information Council in early 2001 found that "only 2% of the consumers polled named 'altered/engineered food' as something they were concerned about." Only 2 percent responded that they would like to see "genetically altered" included on food labels, although 58 percent agreed with critics who attacked the policy of the U.S. Food and Drug Administration (FDA) that such labeling was not needed on any GM foods whose essential qualities were unchanged from nonmodified foods.[112] Another poll conducted at the same time for the Pew Initiative on Food and Biotechnology concluded that "Americans know relatively little about genetically modified foods and biotechnology." This poll found that 58 percent of consumers "oppose the introduction of genetically modified foods into the food supply," although they are uncertain about the safety of such foods. Finally, 75 percent "say it is important to them to know whether a product contains genetically modified ingredients." [113]

At the root of the transatlantic conflict are differing approaches to ensuring food safety as well as contrasting levels of trust in sources of information. In the United States, the FDA views GM foods as "essential equivalents" to other products already on the market, and it takes no action to control or restrict them in the absence of scientific evidence showing that they are harmful.[114] Only foods that are potential allergens or whose nutritional composition has been changed as a result of genetic modification must be labeled. By contrast, the EU operates on the precautionary principle with respect to food safety. There, GM products are regarded as being different from traditional hybrids, and they must be tested for safety before being sold on the open market.

In 1998, responding to public pressure, six EU members were able to bring about a Union-wide moratorium on new GMOs in Europe (this occurred in conjunction with a ban on imports of certain types of American beef). The United States called both moves protectionist.[115] According to WTO rules, restrictions on the imports of food and other products are permitted only for health and safety reasons and not on the basis of production method. If an imported good is otherwise identical to the domestic good, it must be allowed in. Any country violating this rule can be brought before a WTO tribunal for a hearing and, in effect, can be forced to accept imports of the good in question. Eager to avoid yet another transatlantic "trade war" or a test of the moratorium at the WTO, in 2001, the EU established the "European Food Safety Authority" (EFSA) to provide independent scientific assessment of risks related to production and consumption of food. The EFSA is not a regulatory body like the FDA but operates more along the lines of the U.S. National Academy of Sciences. That is, it collects such scientific data and other information as are available about food safety and assesses and disseminates it to the appropriate regulatory authorities and the public.[116] In mid-2002, the European Parliament proposed labeling GM foods and their contents as a compromise position.[117] In November 2002, EU agriculture ministers agreed to implement this proposal, despite continued strong opposition from environmental organizations. Soon after, the United States warned that it might haul the EU before the WTO, and finally did so in May 2003.[118]

What's so bad about labeling? After all, there is already a considerable amount of information on food content required in both the United States and the EU. Labeling is, however, strongly opposed by the United States, for several reasons. First, because of cross-contamination in American crops, it would be difficult to be sure that many food products—especially those made from grains—are GM-free. Second, American producers fear that European (and American) consumers will shy away from GM-labeled foods. And, third, because both the United States and the EU are eager to export processed foods and grains to other parts of the world, there is concern that American products might be put at a competitive disadvantage by labeling and consequent consumer fears. The resolution of this conflict will, in all likelihood, have a major impact on the commercial prospects for GM foods.

It is, of course, the case that the UN-affiliated, Rome-based organization Codex Alimentarius ("Code for Food") is tasked with the responsibility of setting international food standards for national governments.[119] Within those limits, however, national governments have considerable leeway, and the final approaches adopted by the United States and the EU will probably become models for other countries. In other words, if the EU labeling decision sticks, other countries are likely to adopt the same approach. If such labeling does have an impact on consumption of GM foods, their future may be quite limited, even in countries that seek to increase food production and imports. Alternatively, if the United States does, eventually, manage to get the EU to drop the labeling decision, the market for GM foods will expand enormously, and they are likely to become quite common.

The implications of these two contrasting approaches are quite illuminating for our discussion of the marketization of the environment. GM foods promise significant profits for those corporations—primarily American—involved in research, development, application, and agricultural production. By treating such goods as "essential equivalents," the United States is giving primacy to the market over health and environmental concerns, which can be construed as political. The European Union, which is less invested in GM foods (but not entirely so), is opting for a certain degree of caution, if only by letting consumers know what they are buying. In this instance, politics has been given primacy over markets. Foods are the quintessential commodity in rich countries, but that does not necessarily mean that food safety matters should be left to markets to decide.

Other aspects of nature are subject to similar processes of marketization, both in historical terms and today. Seen as inputs to national industry and economic growth, even where economies were substantially private, resources and environment came to be treated instrumentally and with little view to the long run. If supplies of particular resources began to run short, new ones were found abroad or substitutes were developed. And, where new "resources" emerged, such as genetic diversity, little time was wasted on their incorporation into the national development scheme. Globalization has altered the terms of nature's exploitation to some degree, although not in any substantive fashion. National development is now equated wholly with annual rates of economic growth. Restrictions on damage to the environment are subject to concerns about limits that might be imposed on such growth. This ideological emphasis on capitalism and markets is not unique to the United States, but the United States, as the world's dominant power, has been a leader in shifting the policies and practices of environmental internationalism toward growing reliance on both markets and economic growth as solutions to environmental damage.

This observation raises questions about both the sources and effectiveness of international environmental regimes. As we shall see later in this chapter, certain assumptions are made in the literature about how such regimes are created and how they function. Although it is widely recognized that power (and wealth) do matter when international issues are at stake, many students of international relations nevertheless assume that negotiation and bargaining can redress some of these inequalities. After all, in markets, we often find individuals with enormously disparate financial endowments engaging in peaceful and cooperative bargaining and exchange. But no one would argue that the Jaguar salesperson is, somehow, the equal of the multimillionaire interested in purchasing a car. The former does have the power to deny the latter her purchase, but at what cost? A similar logic applies to bargaining among states.

How International Are International Environmental Regimes?

So far in this chapter, we have seen that the environmental practices of particular states have, historically, been observed and copied by other states, albeit with various national modifications. Just as the political systems of some countries—mostly former colonies—are modeled on the British parliamentary system, others have adopted forms and practices similar to the United States executive-legislative arrangement, and a very few retain the centrally directed party governments that originated with the Soviet Union. There are always national and cultural differences in the ways these institutional patterns are implemented, to be sure, but the basic features of state organization remain visible and similar.[120] Such "social learning" among groups is the norm for human beings and has probably been the case since quite early in the history of the species.

What has become increasingly common during the past two centuries is that specifically national practices have become the basis for international institutions. When the British Empire ruled the seas, national and colonial economies were run along the lines favored by London. When countries tried to defy the British Empire (for example, by repudiating their debts), gunboat diplomacy was born, ensuring that the rules would be followed.[121] Since 1945 the United States has played this central role in shaping and directing international politics and economics (the Soviet counterhegemony notwithstanding), one that has only become more prominent during the years following 1991.[122] To be sure, other countries and entities, such as Japan and the European Union, are major players in shaping the global political economy and IERs. It is difficult, nonetheless, to construct and maintain multilateral and international initiatives without the participation of the United States (the second Bush administration's proclivity for defecting from international treaties will put this hypothesis to the test over the coming years). And the United States has made it clear that, if multilateral and international initiatives are not organized and pursued in a way that is acceptable to Washington, the United States will not participate.

The fate and future of the Kyoto Protocol to the UN Framework Convention on Climate Change sheds some light on this general point. The United States has stood fast on its refusal to sign the protocol, the U.S. Senate has made it clear that ratification will not happen without commitments by developing countries, and the Bush administration is determined to stick to voluntary reductions in greenhouse gas emissions.[123] With the unanimous support of the other Annex I countries (that is, industrialized and former socialist bloc states), the parties to the protocol can (and probably will) provide enough ratifications for Kyoto to come into force without the participation of the United States. Among other things, the United States would be then barred from taking part in future negotiations concerning the protocol.

Failure to ratify might also expose the United States to various kinds of trade and other sanctions, intended to pressure it into ratifying the agreement. There is a catch, however, and it poses a serious threat to the entire effort to address global climate change: no country is likely to impose such punishments, knowing full well that the United States could retaliate and, in all likelihood, inflict much greater pain on the sanctioning states. In this case, the defector from the agreement is both the hegemon and the largest individual contributor to the international problem of concern; a failure to bend to American demands might well turn the protocol into a faint hope rather than a guide to action. Under such circumstances, a few countries, and perhaps even the EU, will adhere to the protocol, but many might well defect.

The example of the Kyoto Protocol suggests some important insights into both the anatomy and autonomy of international environmental regimes. Most IERs are of relatively recent provenance, having been established sometime during the past three decades (although a few date back to the beginning of the twentieth century).[124] Prior to 1970 there were a few of what we would now call international environmental agreements—for example, the International Whaling Commission—but these were not then recognized as IERs.[125] In any event, as discussed at the beginning of this chapter, such agreements were intended to manage the exploitation of resources, such as whales, seals, and birds through quotas, rather than to protect or preserve them. Many of the "next generation" of IERs (if we can use that term), were heavily influenced by the presence and participation of the United States. An excellent example of this influence (and another case of hegemonic defection) can be seen in the negotiations over the Third UN Convention on the Law of the Sea (UNCLOS), a process that began in the early 1970s and ended in 1981.[126]

UNCLOS was intended to replace earlier conventions and to address many new issues. The United States was deeply involved in these discussions, and the final document addressed its major objectives. These included concern about several countries' unilateral extension of territorial jurisdiction over offshore areas beyond the traditional three-mile limit, military access to certain national waterways, and an institutional mechanism for exploitation of mineral nodules, containing nickel, manganese, and chromium, found on the deep ocean floor.[127] But in 1982, just when American ratification was expected, the United States backed away from UNCLOS. It was opposed, in particular, to the provisions governing nodule mining, seeing them as tantamount to "international socialism," something anathema to the free market

Reagan administration. (According to other reports, the nickel industry feared a glut and price crash if the seabed nodules were brought to the surface and refined.) The White House announced that it would neither sign nor ratify UNCLOS, and over the intervening years the United States has not done so, even though the treaty finally became international law in 1994. Between 1982 and 1994, UNCLOS came to be regarded as customary international law, and even the United States observed those provisions deemed relevant to its maritime interests. No one has yet found it profitable to mine the seabed for mineral nodules, and therefore that specific portion of the treaty deemed so offensive by the Reagan administration is, for the time being, moot.

The point here is that the U.S. imprint on the IER looms quite large, *even though the United States is not a signatory.* No IER can afford to forgo the interests and desires of the United States, whether it ratifies or not, and such American influence extends to virtually all other IERs. This forces us to ask how autonomous of states are IERs? To what degree do they reflect some sort of collective international, multilateral, or global interest? Can international organizations, such as the UN Environment Programme, act independently of the wishes and preferences of the major powers involved in their establishment and operation? Can the members of an IER decide to act in opposition to the interests of a hegemonic member? Are IERs (and, by extension, other international regimes) simply superstructure to material bases of power and wealth? Most realists, such as Stephen Krasner, and a few political economists, such as the late Susan Strange, have argued something close to the last point.[128] Regimes are mere reflections of the distribution of power in the international system. IERs are able to function, they argue, only with the forbearance of its dominant member(s), and they become dysfunctional if those states refuse to participate. Liberal analysts are more likely to see the possibilities of autonomous action by IERs and associated international organizations. After all, the latter are ordinary bureaucracies, composed of individuals with different degrees of power and authority as well as access to resources. International organizations can play central roles in agenda setting, in managing the negotiating process, and in overseeing implementation.[129]

But the very discourse of regimes, which presents them as forms of liberal international cooperation, tends to obscure relations of power and domination internal to those institutions. What appears to be cooperation is normally a constrained form of the same. As we saw in Chapter 2, power is not always displayed in visible form; sometimes it is embedded in institutions, language, and practice in ways that are rather subtle. Many of the institutions with which we are familiar (although not all of them) serve our ends and interests, even if unequal power is inherent in their structure and functioning. Such institutions have historical and customary legitimacy, as well. Most IERs, however, are of relatively recent provenance and have been created within a relatively underdeveloped social context. Neither history nor custom serves to buffer their hard edges or the fact that they exist primarily to serve the interests of the dominant members. What this means is that the autonomy of IERs is limited not only by the overt exercise of power by these states but also by their very structure. At best, relatively minor matters are left to IERs, such as conference oversight, information collection, and, perhaps, harmless inspections. Major issues that directly affect the interests of the dominant members are kept off the organization's agenda or shifted into the purview of another regime in which power can be exercised with less trouble.

An example of this can be seen, once again, in the trials and tribulations of the UNFCCC and the Kyoto Protocol. Both agreements are intended to address anthropogenic emission of all greenhouse gases. Carbon dioxide constitutes a major fraction of these emissions, most carbon dioxide emissions come from the burning of fossil fuels, and a substantial portion of those fossil fuels are combusted in vehicle engines. We might expect, therefore, that an effective agreement would address directly the energy problem and seek to moderate consumption of fossil fuels in the transportation sector. Yet, neither the UNFCCC nor the Kyoto Protocol include provisions along these lines, such as a direct carbon tax on fossil fuels. Indeed, such a tax has been adamantly opposed by that group of industrialized countries ("JUSCANZ"— Japan, the United States, Canada, Australia, New Zealand) and oil-producing ones (OPEC) that would be best able to absorb it. Instead, tradable emission permits are being touted as the solution. As we have seen throughout this book, however, trade in emission permits allows rich countries to purchase rights to pollute from poor ones and to continue their high energy-consumption lifestyles. Reductions in energy use, according to this logic, will come about if the implicit cost of carbon emissions rises and if such cost increases are incorporated into the price of fossil fuels and carbon-intensive products. But in this case, the embedded "tax" accrues not to public coffers, where it might be used to buffer the impacts of higher fuel prices on the poor. Rather, it is the private possessors of the permits who will reap the rewards. This is "efficiency" at work.

In many ways, the issues raised here point to the precise opposite of the collective action problem. In regard to the Kyoto Protocol, a logic contrary to the collective action problem seems to be operating. If the members are able to act collectively then, even minus the participation of the United States, they may be able to ratify and implement the protocol. The United States will reap benefits from not participating, whereas some of the members will have to pay costs that are likely to exceed the benefits they would realize individually from free riding or defecting. Moreover, given a relatively high discount rate, there is little chance that most signatories will realize any commensurate return, inasmuch as benefits will not be evident for some decades to come. (Recognizing this, at least one South Pacific island nation, Tuvalu, has contracted with New Zealand to accept its entire population as immigrants if and when they are forced to evacuate by sea-level rise).[130] For the time being, the European Union has taken on the role of hegemon in the protocol, but it is a problematic role in the absence of the United States, as discussed earlier.

Are all international regimes subject to such logic? One could argue that the World Trade Organization has acquired significant autonomy and is able to operate without undue interference from its dominant members. The Trade-related Intellectual Property Rights Agreement (TRIPS), an element of the WTO, incorporates monitoring, sanctioning, and enforcement powers not yet found in other international regimes.[131] These powers can be used even against the United States and its corporations. Surely that constitutes autonomy! But even this claim is somewhat disingenuous, given the recent history of international intellectual property rights (IPRs), such as those covering genetically modified organisms and seeds. IPRs were originally addressed under the provisions of the World Intellectual Property Organization (WIPO), which succeeded several earlier international agreements concluded toward the end of the nineteenth century. WIPO dealt only with the mutual recognition of national copyrights and patents by its member states. Signatories agreed to accept copyrights and patents granted in other member countries as binding. Any country that was not a member of WIPO could, with relative impunity, violate IPRs granted in others.[132] Because there was no way to enforce such rules except within the national courts of member states, violations and piracy were not uncommon. Not only could this result in major economic losses to the IPR holder, the pirated version of the IPR could leak into international markets, leading to additional losses (a fairly common problem these days with trademarked products, recordings, and software).

In an effort to remedy this problem, and under pressure from pharmaceutical and biotechnology corporations, the United States led a move to "forum shift" IPRs from WIPO to a new regime within the WTO. The latter incorporates many enforcement and sanctioning mechanisms not available to most other international regimes. These include the right to bring trade disputes for adjudication before special panels as well as the imposition of damages on a country whose laws or behavior are found to be in violation of WTO trade rules.[133] TRIPS incorporates even more stringent remedies. For example, a TRIPS dispute resolution panel can order national judicial authorities to search for and seize evidence of IPR violations. The panel can then use such discoveries to make judgments about whether violations have occurred and what kinds of sanctions should be imposed. Such authority largely benefits corporations in rich countries—especially the United States and Europe—that want to halt the pirating of IPRs in poor ones, but these mechanisms can also be used by rich countries against each other, should the occasion arise. But because transnational corporations operate throughout the industrialized world and have an interest in mutual protection of IPRs, they are less likely egregiously to violate each others' patents.

An explicit example of the ways in which TRIPS is biased toward transnational corporations and rich countries is the controversy over the sale of AIDS drugs in poor countries (especially Africa). TRIPs permits developing countries to produce generic versions of patented pharmaceuticals in situations of dire need for domestic use only. The export of such generics is expressly forbidden, on the principle that this would undermine international law and deprive companies of legitimate profits.[134] In the case of the AIDS drugs, transnational pharmaceutical companies not only opposed domestic production in South Africa, they also charged high prices for the drugs they did sell there. As a result, access to the drugs was quite limited. The South African government then announced its intention to begin production of generic versions of the drugs (even though it did not possess the capability to do so) and was hauled into court by a group of companies intent on protecting their patents. These companies were less concerned about generics being produced in South Africa than the chance they might be imported from India. In that case, the companies would have demanded the convening of a dispute resolution panel, whose decision would likely have favored them, but not without a great deal of bad press. Eventually, public and other pressures led to a settlement of the suit, and an agreement to lower the cost of the drugs (which still remains too high for most people in South Africa). The companies won their battle, but garnered a great deal of unfavorable publicity in the process.[135]

The particular structure of both TRIPS and the WTO is strongly biased toward the American position on trade matters. As we have seen, this reflects a higher value put on trade than on environmental protection as well as the abiding belief that free trade enriches countries and leads them to be more concerned about nature. But the structural bias built into the WTO does not mean that it will always respond to specific American preferences, if those deviate from the norm. At the Seattle ministerial WTO meetings in 1999, for example, President Clinton proposed that the organization's members consider the inclusion of labor and environmental provisions in its next negotiating round. He was roundly opposed by leaders of developing countries, who saw this as a ploy to establish new trade barriers against the entry of certain of their goods into rich country markets. As a result, the meeting collapsed. The George W. Bush administration shows almost no interest in making free trade more environmentally sensitive and, indeed, seems bent on moving in the opposite direction.

The obstacles to environmental internationalism are further increased by the contradictory effects of global neoliberalism. As we saw in Chapters 2 and 3, even as developing countries are being urged through IERs to protect and restore their environments, they are also being pressured to reduce their domestic expenditures on social and environmental problems in order to provide more attractive settings for foreign investment. Unless new, ecologically modernized industries or enterprises replace older, polluting ones, however, levels of environmental damage will increase.[136] Any additional revenues that accrue from foreign investment are more likely to be directed toward payment of interest on debts than environmental improvement. And the movement of people into the cities, drawn by the promises of jobs, will increase the stress on urban infrastructures and environments. The contradictions will continue. Both people and the environment will suffer.

A Successful Case of Environmental Internationalism

The European Union offers a special case of environmental internationalism. Its policies and practices are, in part, a product of those of the fifteen member states (soon to expand to twenty-five) and the several hundreds of millions of members of their civil societies. These policies and practices are also the creations of the one legislative and two executive branches of the EU. These are the European Council, which is composed of member states with weighted voting; the European Commission, composed of expert directorates (bureaucracies); and the European Parliament, whose members are elected from individual states but who tend to organize into party-aligned groups and caucuses.[137] The EU's environmental agenda is generated with a heavier dose of technical expertise than is the norm for purely national politics. This is possible because the commission is a technocratic system of departments, insulated to some degree from both national and EU politics and holding considerable authority to override the wishes of the other EU institutions and member states.[138] At the same time, however, weighted voting in the council, and the political structures and preferences of individual members and their jurisdictional subunits, affect commission directives and the extent to which they are implemented. All this is further complicated by the fact that NGOs are able to influence legislation through both the commission and the parliament, sometimes in opposition to the wishes of member states and the council.[139] The EU's environmental legislation is also the basis for the environmental laws of its ten prospective members (for example, Cyprus, Hungary, Poland, Turkey). The member states are required to integrate commission directives into their national laws as a prerequisite for admission. If twenty-five countries, comprising the world's largest economic bloc, all adopt comparable environmental laws, they could well become de facto international standards. How might this work, given disparate power relations? A good example can be seen in the recycling of nontoxic wastes.

Both individual member states and the EU have had waste management and recycling laws on the books since the 1970s. As more laws were passed, and became more rigorous and extensive, they sometimes acted as barriers to trade between member states. For those producers operating in smaller national markets, recycling requirements might provide a competitive advantage, since it is expensive for bottlers in other states, seeking to sell goods throughout the EU, to retrieve their containers. In 1981, for example, Denmark passed a law requiring that beer and soda be bottled in recyclable containers and mandating that Danish retailers take back all the containers. In order to facilitate recycling and limit costs to retailers, the government restricted the number of acceptable containers to about thirty types. Many of the containers produced in other member states did not meet these stipulations, and the government prohibited the sale of such "foreign containers" within Denmark.[140] Bottlers in other member states then complained to the European Commission that the Danish law made it too costly for them to sell their beverages in Denmark.

The commission agreed that the Danish standards constituted a restriction on trade and were, therefore, in violation of European Community law.

The Danish government amended the rules, but these changes were deemed unacceptable, too. At that point, the commission filed a complaint with the European Court of Justice, charging, in essence, that the Danish regulations constituted an illegal form of "environmental protectionism." The details of the case are rather complicated and need not concern us here.[141] The court, however, found the Danish law legal, with one exception: there could be no restrictions on container types, so long as all containers were recyclable. This meant that non-Danish bottlers had to find ways to collect their bottles and bring them back home. Nevertheless, the law stuck and set the stage for EU law and a growing recognition that waste disposal was a problem throughout the Union.

In 1991 the German government began to implement a much more rigorous recycling law. This one was designed to reduce wastes destined for both landfills, whose capacity was limited, and incineration, which contributed to air pollution. The German law required producers to take back and recycle all packaging, eventually including even candy and butter wrappers. In order to comply with the regulations, three thousand companies created an enterprise to handle recovery and recycling, the Duales System Deutschland. In return for participating in this system, producers could put a "Green Dot" on their products, certifying that the packaging was recyclable. Needless to say, a torrent of complaints followed from companies based outside of Germany.[142] They charged that this law, too, represented an illegal barrier to trade and was too costly to implement. Moreover, the plan's very success created another problem: more wastes were being collected than could be recycled within Germany. In some instances, recycled materials were sorted by consumers, collected by municipalities, and then dumped in landfills.[143] The surplus was exported to other EU countries, where prices for recycled materials and domestic recycling programs both collapsed. This was hardly a viable solution to the municipal waste problem.

Recalling the Danish container case, and not wishing to appear anti-environmental, the European Commission was reluctant to challenge the German law. Consequently, in 1994, the commission approved a packaging directive for the entire Union. It was much less stringent than the German law but, on average, more so than existed in most member states. Several countries, including Germany, now opposed the EU directive, claiming it to be too weak, but to no avail.[144] The directive stood. In 1996 Germany trumped the commission and passed the "Closed Loop Economy Law." This encouraged producers to use fewer materials, create less waste, and avoid hazardous materials in the manufacture of goods. (In the chemical industry, for example, petroleum in plastics has been replaced by sugar and starch, so that the resulting products are biodegradable.) Although the German law and the general trend toward closed-loop recycling has been strongly opposed by manufacturers—especially American ones, who regard it as yet another trade barrier—the European Parliament and some commission directorates are seeking to expand the process further. In 2000, for example, the parliament passed a directive placing complete responsibility for the environmental impacts of junked automobiles onto automakers, who are expected to ensure that virtually all auto parts are recyclable and appropriately marked as to content. Consumers will pay a portion of the recycling costs, but the manufacturers must put in place a system for accepting old cars for recycling.[145] The Directorate for the Environment is committed to extending this principle to other sectors, too, such as electrical and electronic equipment. Finally, the EU also intends to develop policies to prevent waste generation through new technological and packaging methods.[146]

What this example of recycling illustrates is a tension between the environmental policies and practices of member states and the "international" EU, as well as the ways in which there is, nonetheless, a process of exchange between the two levels. Individual states have their own preferences, often determined through a history of conflict and compromise among environmentalists, state, and capital (a phenomenon common in the United States, as well). But different standards can act as barriers to trade between members and one of the charges to the EU is to facilitate such trade. Eliminating these barriers requires some degree of regulatory harmonization among member states. Generally speaking, one might expect a "race to the bottom," as the weakest set of rules becomes the group standard. This has not happened in the EU, for several reasons. First, the environment is one of the issue areas in which the European Commission has acquired a considerable degree of authority and autonomy, and its Environmental Directorate is, therefore, able to formulate directives that may have more basis in "science" than politics, thereby overriding national standards and preferences.

Second, there is considerable pro-environment sentiment among the citizens of many of the larger EU members. NGOs and movements sometimes go to the EU to put pressure on member governments, as was the case with more recent recycling directives.[147] The political organization of the EU opens up numerous opportunities for lobbying and logrolling, for coalition building and blocking, and these are used frequently. Finally, within the EU, market access is of central importance to producers, and it is in this context that garbage becomes something like a commodity. It is not, however, the garbage itself that is at issue but the packaging and goods that must, eventually, be recycled. The cost of disposal is internalized into the cost of the product. This sets up a competitive dynamic in which manufacturers strive to minimize that additional cost in order to make their products more attractive to consumers. Here, the market is being used to environmental ends, but it is the interplay of politics within and among member states that creates and structures that market.

But are EU environmental "regimes" really an example of environmental internationalism? Or are they more akin to an emergent environmental "nationalism," along the lines we find in the United States and other large countries? If the former is the case, what we are seeing is a type of regulatory harmonization, in which individual regime members are being pressured to adhere to higher standards than they might prefer, in the interest of intra-Union integration. Because the EU's institutions have been granted certain forms of conditional power over the individual members, such pressure can protect the environment. In the longer run, this form of international authority could work to create truly autonomous IERs and provide a model for broader environmental internationalism. If the latter is the case, however, the EU will, gradually, find that it has certain Union-wide interests that conflict with other large and powerful states. The stories presented in this chapter, on GM foods and recycling, are not conclusive. The jury remains out.

Are There International Environmental Politics?

In this chapter, as throughout this book, we have seen that "global environmental politics" includes much more than what is offered by the standard formulas of international relations. Moreover, the social relations of environmentalism and environmental politics do not divide themselves neatly into standardized categories or levels of analysis. In the long run, and depending on the degree and severity of environmental phenomena themselves, IERs could acquire a good deal more power and authority than they possess today, and environmental internationalism might flourish.

It would probably take a crisis of global proportions to generate such change. A sudden rise in sea levels from the collapse of the Ross Ice Shelf in Antarctica, which would quickly raise sea levels by fifteen feet, could do it.[148] Alternatively, a massive die-off of people as a result of rising temperatures and climatic changing conditions might compel the states of the world to agree to what would, in effect, be something akin to a world government. Inasmuch as the timing of such catastrophes is difficult to predict in advance, even if we are certain they will happen at some point in the future, it is not so clear how states might be pressured to become more environmentally sensitive and committed to true environmental internationalism. What, then, are we to do? This is the question we take up in the final chapter of this book.

For Further Reading

Bryant, Raymond, and Sinéad Bailey. *Third World Political Ecology*. London: Routledge, 1997.

Clapp, Jennifer. *Toxic Exports: The Transfer of Hazardous Wastes from Rich to Poor Countries*. Ithaca, N.Y.: Cornell University Press, 2001.

Drahos, Peter, with John Braithwaite, *Information Feudalism—Who Owns the Knowledge Economy?* New York: The New Press, 2003.

Garcia-Johnson, Ronie. *Exporting Environmentalism: U.S. Multinational Chemical Corporations in Brazil and Mexico*. Cambridge: MIT Press, 2000.

Guha, Ramachandra. *The Unquiet Woods: Ecological Change and Peasant Resistance in the Himalaya*. Expanded ed. Berkeley: University of California Press, 2000.

Haas, Peter, Robert Keohane, and Mark Levy, eds. *Institutions for the Earth: Sources of Effective International Environmental Protection*. Cambridge: MIT Press, 1993.

Hirsch, Fred. *Social Limits to Growth*. Cambridge: Harvard University Press, 1976.

Karliner, Joshua. *The Corporate Planet: Ecology and Politics in the Age of Globalization*. San Francisco: Sierra Club Books, 1997.

Keohane, Robert, and Mark Levy, eds. *Institutions for Environmental Aid: Pitfalls and Promise*. Cambridge: MIT Press, 1996.

McCormick, John. *Environmental Policy in the European Union*. Basingstoke, England: Palgrave, 2001.

Vogel, David. *Trading Up: Consumer and Environmental Regulation in a Global Economy*. Cambridge: Harvard University Press, 1995.

Young, Oran R. *International Governance: Protecting the Environment in a Stateless Society*. Ithaca, N.Y.: Cornell University Press, 1994.

6 | Global Environmental Politics and You: "The World Is My Country"

Into the Streets!

On March 26, 2000, a rather peculiar demonstration took place in Boston, Massachusetts. As 7,000 scientists and others attended "Bio2000," a five-day conference to discuss the latest advances in biotechnology, 1,500 people rallied outside the meeting venue in Copley Square to assert their opposition to the production of genetically modified organisms, especially in food. Police and authorities feared another "Battle of Seattle," but they didn't get it. The protest remained nonviolent. A reporter for the *New York Times* wrote:

> [T]he demonstration was not wild but wildly creative. Street theater abounded; several protesters ran around dressed as white-coated fanatical scientists wielding giant syringes and several others fluttered about as butterflies to symbolize the monarchs that a study has shown were harmed by genetically altered corn. A man in a Frankenstein costume pushed a shopping cart bearing genetically engineered "Frankenflakes," and another wore a papier-mâché killer tomato on his head.[1]

In anticipation of the protest, some 2,000 scientists signed a "Declaration in Support of Agricultural Biotechnology." According to the organizer of the declaration, Dr. C. S. Prakash of Tuskegee University in Alabama, "biotech crops allow farmers to grow more food on less land with less synthetic pesticides and herbicides."[2] Food fights, no less! But what was at stake?

For biotech proponents, it was feeding the hungry and malnourished; for biotech opponents, it was nothing less than the future of life on Earth. According to the advocates of biotechnology, GMOs promise a new Green Revolution that will provide bounteous food supplies to the world and prevent global famine; its detractors worry that engineered genes, let loose into the food supply and environment, might wreak havoc on the health of both people and nature and contaminate them beyond repair. Meanwhile, as we saw in Chapter 5, many Americans seem largely indifferent to the presence of GMOs in their food, whereas in Europe, distaste for genetically engineered goods has become so great that cultivation and sale of such foods has been stopped almost completely. Observers are puzzled. What, exactly, do these demonstrators want, ask media pundits? Don't they know that there are poor and hungry people out there in the world? How can these protestors say they are for justice, especially when so many are white and middle class? Better they should go back to their studies and jobs and let the experts and economists take care of business. Anyway, these problems are "global," and not amenable to action on the ground.

Such demonstrations are hardly new and, with the rise of what is called the anti-globalization (or "global justice") movement in recent years, they have become the staple of front page news, activist hopes, Internet strategizing, and editorial page dissing.[3] Many observers give the demonstrators little credence, for they do not seem to have either a "strategy" or a "program." Few, if any, newspapers or other media report on the much more numerous local movements and groups, such as those opposing the construction of big dams, working to restore local watersheds, opposing disposal of toxic wastes, or fighting to preserve critical habitats. Yet, it is these latter activists, rarely remunerated for their efforts, who are the bedrock of global environmentalism and who do have both strategies and programs. There is nothing particularly earth-shaking about projects to clean and protect creeks, streams, and rivers, but it is such efforts that, in the long run, foretell growing political awareness about what we must do to protect the environment.

In this final chapter, therefore, we turn to two questions. First, "Where do you, dear reader, fit into all of this? What can *you* do?" As consumers of goods and producers of pollution, we are all directly implicated in the damage being done to the earth's environment. We can make careful choices about what to buy and how much of it to use, with the hope that we might influence producers. But even if others make similar selections and decisions, the choices you or I make, acting by ourselves, will never add up to more than the preferences of a single individual (there's that collective action problem again!). Second, as asked in Chapter 5, "What are we to do?" Can we find ways to make governments and states more environmentally sensitive? Or, if the burden is on us, how can we protect the environment?

The thrust of this book is that environmental problems are, first and foremost, political and, therefore, about power. They have been caused through the exercise of various forms of power and, if they are to be dealt with, it will have to be through the exercise of other forms of power. To exercise such power, we must act collectively, in concert with others. Our actions must be political and have a political purpose. We need to understand what politics is missing from our governing systems and restore those missing elements through a new environmental ethics and praxis.[4] Finally, we must undertake these actions within all kinds of institutions, ranging from the household to the global. The environment will not be protected unless we do so.

In this chapter, we examine the form and content of such an environmental ethic and what it implies in terms of politics and praxis. We begin with a discussion of the impoverishment of politics in a world dominated by economistic approaches to social problems, such as environmental quality and human health. The "capture" of environmental discourse and practices by neoclassical economic theory has transformed environmental politics from a matter of ethics to a problem of economics. Consequently, we no longer inquire into the deployment of power for environmental ends or the politics behind that power; rather, we ask "How much is it worth to protect the environment?" If the ratio of benefits to costs looks good, we do it. If we find the "correct" price for a good, we can achieve our desires without making any greater efforts than shopping as usual. If the price is too high, we can do good by not buying.

But what, exactly, is this "good" we accomplish through such a practice? Consider the case of the last redwood on Earth. Being the last of its kind, its notional market value would be immense, although, paradoxically, it would have little, if any, ecological value. Still, some people might be willing to pay exorbitant sums for a piece of the last redwood on Earth. For many, it would not be a "good" move to cut down the tree, but a few might decide it would be better to have a relic than to let the tree die a natural death and decompose into its constituent elements. More to the point, according to the principles of the market, what people would be willing to pay would be the "correct" price for the last redwood and it would be of economic benefit to log it.* Surely, this would not be our intention.

That is why an environmental ethic is so critical to global environmental politics, to which we turn in the second section of the chapter. An ethic is generally understood as a set of principles of right conduct. Defining "right conduct" is, quite obviously, no easy task. We could define it in terms of survival—certainly a critical issue—or utilitarianism—whatever makes people happiest. Or, we could decide that what is most important to right conduct is recognition, respect, and empathy for people and for nature.[5] Whatever our conception, it will be strongly contested and a focus of considerable conflict, and it can be realized only through politics and praxis.

So what *are* we to do? Demonstrations, such as those that took place in Boston and so many other places in recent years, are only a small part of the answer. They are essential to wider awareness of a broad range of environmental and social problems and deserve to be treated as a legitimate form of political action. But the question of strategy and praxis is one that needs to be addressed, albeit not quite in the way it is generally understood. The problem here is that we generally focus on somehow affecting environmental policy, on the assumption that public opinion as well as scientific and other forms of knowledge are tools of persuasion and change. But, as Deborah Stone has pointed out, "public policy" is not about politics, per se, but about accomplishing particular ends in a rational (read "market-oriented") manner. That is, for policymakers, social goals are already known, and all that matters is how to achieve them most efficiently and with least resistance.[6] That is not politics. Stone looks to Plutarch to make the distinction: "They are wrong who think that politics is like an ocean voyage or a military campaign, something to be done with some end in view, or something which levels off as soon as that end is reached. It is not a public chore, to be got over with; it is a way of life." [7] Politics, as we shall see, is about engagement with the principles and conditions of life and about the explicit processes whereby people make decisions collectively and act on them. Strategy and praxis must, therefore, be related to politics in this elemental sense.

The propositions offered in the final section of this chapter as alternatives to politics as usual are, as much out of prudence as a recognition of the difficulties in strategizing and praxis, more in the realm of possibilities than

---

*In practice, of course, the last redwood on Earth would probably be protected by legislation and, perhaps, a strong fence and armed guards.

certainties. Not all strategies are "global" ones with grand objectives; indeed, it is such grand approaches that, often as not, produce unintended consequences and failure. It is less important to think big than to act, to decide with others of like mind (or those who can be persuaded) on praxis, to become political as a way of life rather than to treat politics as a chore and bore. Such praxis can be as simple as working toward a greener community or as complex as coordinating watershed groups around the world. The important step is to recognize that power can be a productive force and to act on that insight.

Markets Are Not Politics

The growing reliance on economic principles and practices to "protect" the global environment raises troubling questions, as we have seen throughout this book. Most problematic, perhaps, is the eclipse of politics. Recall Harold Lasswell's classic definition of politics, cited in Chapter 5: "who gets what, when, how." [8] Inasmuch as this conception of politics is simply about distribution and its justification, and the market has come to be seen as the preferred mechanism for accomplishing such distribution, why not apply it to ostensibly noneconomic matters, such as environmental protection? After all, is not pollution control merely an issue of how to distribute the costs and benefits of a limited supply of clean air? What better means, then, to reduce damage to the environment than through the market?

Is Everything for Sale?

As we saw in Chapters 3 and 5, the tendency to commodify nature in order to deal with human insults to the environment has two important implications: first, it reinforces the very status quo that is causing the problem, and second, it ranks efficiency and returns on investment above fairness, justice, and the well-being of humans and nature. Reliance on existing institutions to solve pressing social problems tends to reify and reinforce the practices of those institutions as "the answer," even if those approaches are at the core of the problems being addressed and serve to exacerbate them. New institutions rarely offer major innovations on the principles and practices of old ones; at times, they even close down spaces of opportunity offered by others that already exist. The more efficient use of financial and other resources is premised on the goal of "more bang for the buck," that is, saving money by maximizing reductions in environmental damage rather than protecting those who suffer the greatest exposure. This makes economic sense in a world of finite budgets, but it has no effect at all on the power relations or institutions responsible for the insults. To put this point another way, the substitution of market-based mechanisms for politics serves a larger purpose: maintenance of systemic stability, even in the face of potential catastrophe. Although "free" markets are inherently risky to investors, producers, and consumers, reliance on market-based mechanisms for adaptation to challenging conditions serves to reinforce the very structural framework that is the source of the problem (an externality) in the first place. Markets alone cannot repair the flaws generated by markets.

Moreover, in applying market mechanisms to environmental problems, we come face-to-face with what can only be described as sleight of hand. Under more traditional regulatory schemes, offenders were fined, taxed, or required to retrofit their industry, the costs of which were, perhaps, passed on to their customers. In return, a benefit accrued to the general public in the area affected by the pollutant. To be sure, the improvement might have been small and diffuse, but the benefit was understood to be greater for those who were unduly burdened because of their proximity to the source. That seemed only fair. The move to market-based mechanisms, however, dispenses with this logic. It turns offending acts into commodities from which polluters may profit (or, at least, reduce their losses). To be sure, polluters must choose whether to pay for equipment to reduce the polluting activities or for permits to continue them. But a permit-based arrangement may well diffuse or privatize the benefits such that those most affected see no local improvement in air quality at all. This short-circuiting of a vaguely political process not only turns citizens into consumers of environmental quality, it also cuts many people entirely out of the decision-making loop. What little power they may have possessed is stripped from them.

This problematic is seen most clearly in regard to environmental justice in urban areas, particularly under the so-called bubble system of air quality. The bubble system treats an entire air basin, or "airshed," as a single physical unit (in effect, the Kyoto Protocol's permit-trading scheme treats the entire atmosphere as a "bubble"). The logic behind this political chemistry is that, although much air pollution originates from point sources, such as power plants and factories, and may disproportionately affect those near to or downwind from the emissions source, all pollutants tend to mix and mingle across airsheds. (There is also considerable pollution from diffuse sources, such as cars and furnaces, but these should to be controlled at the factory, so to speak, through development of less-polluting devices.) Atmospheric mixing is especially evident in places such as the Los Angeles basin, where circulation is restricted by the surrounding mountain ranges. By treating the airshed as a single unit, regulators assume that the precise location of emission reductions, or the benefits of reduced emissions near the point source, do not matter. Instead, it is the aggregate reduction across the airshed that counts.* Hence, so long as the total volume of emissions is reduced, it does not matter which facility does the reduction or where it is located. Those plants able to reduce emissions to less than some stipulated level can sell their "unused" emission rights to those for whom the cost of reductions would be greater than the benefits. The end result, it is argued, is that everyone in the airshed enjoys lower pollution levels than would be the case under a "command-and-control" regulatory system.

A little reflection on this "solution," however, highlights some ethical difficulties and consequent injustices. Residents of Beverly Hills or the Santa Monica Mountains, both of which are within the Los Angeles airshed, already enjoy cleaner air. Living far from and high above the offending emission sources, they can avoid some of the worst effects (except when they have to drive to Hollywood or UCLA). What they receive as a result of the bubble system is a better view. Residents of South Central, Southgate, or the City of Industry, having both lower incomes and elevations, live in closer proximity to emission sources and freeways and are, hence, exposed to higher concentrations of pollutants. These people have very little political voice with respect to any regulatory processes and they possess no wealth that will allow them to move away from the pollution. Even under the bubble system, emission levels will remain highest near the pollution sources, and those nearby will suffer. But they should be able to see the mountains on a clear day.

There is a rather tricky philosophical aspect to the bubble system that is also worth considering. If we regard the local atmosphere around a pollution source as an open-access commons, similar to that written about by Garrett Hardin (even if incorrectly), a "tragedy" arises not because of crowding by those living near the facility—their contribution is minimal—but because the plant's owners have chosen to treat the commons as their own private property (which is rather like one individual owning a hundred cows but blaming those who each own only one for ruining the commons).[9] In effect,

---

*This process replicates the distributive consequences of economic growth in liberal economies: it is aggregate growth that counts, and not the distribution of increased income.

bubbles and emission permits formalize this situation by making legally private that which was previously treated as informally private.

So what? one might ask. After all, is not emissions reduction a form of investment, and are not corporations entitled to receive returns on their investments? If they invest in the most efficient means of pollution reduction, they will see the greatest returns, and that is only fair. This, however, is not the appropriate response. For centuries, polluters have been pouring toxic and unhealthy wastes into what are, after all, public commons, resources owned by no one but vital to everyone (and that is a true "tragedy of the commons"). Pollution represents the private appropriation of the resource—enclosure of the commons, if you will—without compensation to people (or other species) who have relied on the atmosphere since life began.* This ethical lapse is hardly something that can be addressed through markets.

Indeed, the question of whether it is right or ethical to pollute the environment at all is usually dismissed out of hand. Some degree of damage must be accepted, we are told, if polluters are not to go out of business and suffer economic harm that will also impose costs on others. Because all human activities affect the environment, it is assumed that acceptance of such environmental impacts is merely a question of utility. But this assumption is at heart an ethical one, and therefore political, for it denies recognition to those who suffer from the impacts. More to the point, it also treats the environment as a means to human happiness and well-being, rather than an end deserving consideration in itself. We shall return to this point later in this chapter.

The Deal We Can't Refuse?

It is in this context that the capture of environmental discourse by economics becomes so troubling: when everything must be turned into a monetary value, even those things that are priceless have no value at all. This will to enumerate monetarily is a particular commodity fetish of liberalism.[10] It contributes, moreover, to an obsession with "values," and pays little attention to ethics. Throughout much of the world, and especially in the United States, there is incessant chatter about all kinds of values: family values, national values, democratic values, moral values, environmental values, good value,

---

*It is, perhaps, true that the public benefits from the products that come along with the pollution. Whether this is adequate compensation for the resulting health and environmental impacts is not at all clear. See the discussion in the next section of this chapter.

comparative values, relative values, efficiency as a value, and so on. This discourse of values is hardly an accident or coincidence, although it would be a functionalist error to argue that it is the result of intentional decision making with respect to marketization.

No, this economization of everyday life arises from certain foundational principles inherent in liberalism as a philosophy, embedded in liberal belief and practice as they have developed over the centuries, and diffused throughout the world as a result of neoliberal globalization.[11] In so-called traditional societies, people undoubtedly have what we would consider both values and preferences, but these are strongly moderated or even suppressed by hierarchies of power, bonds of obligation, and relatively fixed social roles. As peasants, we might think it important to have the food, family, and shelter available from our lord, but those hardly constitute "values" as we understand the term today. In any event, as peasants, we would not have much choice about "values."

Liberalism, by contrast, relies on the myth, if not the fact, of social mobility and consumer freedom. We need not be bound by the circumstances of our birth, our status, or our income; opportunities to improve our lives abound, and making the right choice can change our situations radically. And this is key: *liberalism is about the freedom to choose,* as Milton Friedman argues, but it is *only* that freedom.[12] It is not about the freedom or equality or justice of consequences and outcomes, or about the circumstances under which choices are offered and choices are made. In order to make a choice, however, we must have some way to compare alternatives, and that is where values come in. If we are socialized into a particularly rigid set of moral perspectives, such as damnation following from a failure to be devout, the freedom to choose hardly matters. And, if we are socialized into choosing the less expensive of two items—the one that gives "better value"—the freedom to choose is only notional. But what happens if we must choose between two quite different possibilities, say, between going to medical school and running off to the circus? Or protecting a stand of old-growth redwoods as opposed to turning them into decking for a house in the suburbs? Which provides greater value? Which do we value more? Which should society choose?

As we saw earlier in this book, the "father" of classical liberal political economy, Adam Smith, believed that individual appetite would be constrained by "moral sentiments," that is, religious beliefs and strictures.[13] He hardly reckoned that almost every selection an individual made would be measured by markets and prices alone. He thought that there were choices that could not be measured in the market, and that a common morality, based in Christianity, would see to such noneconomic choices while restraining economic ones. Industrial societies are no longer so constrained, notwithstanding the rise of conservative religions around the world. And, so, choices generally come down to the bottom line: "Which deal can I not refuse?" This monetization of everything has been extended to consideration of the environment no less than other things. Here, as we have seen, the application of market-based values includes even those matters that, in some instances, involve life or death (what *is* a human life worth?).

Thus, even if global warming poses an unprecedented threat to human civilization and the environment, there is no monetary value to be realized in concerted action at this time, and the problem can be addressed only by commodifying the very actions that are the source of the threat. Rather than restricting or even banning the offending practices, we look for ways to make a buck on the deal. In a somewhat Swiftian fashion, this is rather as if criminals had to bid for scarce permits in order to commit first-degree murder, under the theory that high prices would reduce the incidence of homicide. Certainly, it could be argued that such an approach would be much more efficient than present arrangements: Death Row could become self-financing, the state could generate funds to pay for more policing, there would be fewer appeals and fewer convicts awaiting execution. Much would be saved in insurance and other payouts on the decedents, too. But it is hard to imagine that this form of legalized murder would generate much public support outside, perhaps, of a few libertarian think tanks.

The point here is that market-based solutions to market-generated problems do not eliminate the problem, they only shift the costs elsewhere, usually onto those who have less power and wealth. But the solution is not necessarily to get rid of markets, as such; rather, it is to foster structural change by reasserting the primacy of politics over markets. And this must happen in two respects. First, we must recognize the importance of an ethical stance, rather than an economistic one, in respect to the environment and other social problems. Second, we must revive the practice of politics in ways that transcend voting, lobbying, and the occasional letter to representatives. It is to these arguments that I turn in the final two parts of this chapter.

Toward an Environmental Ethic

The various ontologies and philosophies described in Chapter 2 all reflect particular ethical perspectives on Nature and, especially, on the relationship between human beings and the environment. In a broad sense, these approaches can be separated into those that are anthropocentric, or humanist, and those that are biocentric, or nature-centered.[14] The former tend to place a higher value on human beings and social systems, the latter on the equality of species and ecosystems. As John Meyer and others have noted, these distinctions reflect a relentless search for an authority that can replace the religion so important to Adam Smith's political economy and so lacking in ours today.[15] The search for transcendent "laws of nature" emerges from the desire for a biocentric ethic.* The discovery, and affirmation, of physical and biological rules and limits on human behavior would, some seem to hope and believe, bring rationality to the human world and restore Order and Harmony to Nature. If we can be made to see the consequences of our excesses—injury and death to both nature and humans—surely we will find it in our interest to regulate our activities, either voluntarily or through coercion. (This, it should be noted, is precisely Garrett Hardin's conclusion regarding the "tragedy" of unlimited breeding as well as Thomas Hobbes's about the State of Nature.)[16]

By contrast, the humanist search, at its extreme, seems to suggest that Order is immanent and whatever human beings decide it ought to be.[17] That is, it is up to us to decide on those limits, even if nature's laws alert us to the possibility of disaster. We should, of course, be prudent, but there is no one and nothing to force us to behave in a particular way. Again, if we are sensible and rational, we will see that it is in our interest to impose limits on what we do—*but we can make a choice about whether we want to or not.* The very idea that such unauthorized choices might be possible is extremely disturbing to some biocentrists, who believe that it would permit license do to anything and everything to nature. As a result, they find themselves positioned in a rather curious stance, not so far from the conservative one that would prefer a transcendent source of law.[18]

In a world of more than 6 billion people (rising to 10 billion by 2050), thousands of distinctive cultures, and 190-odd countries, we might doubt that any kind of environmental ethic, whether transcendent or immanent, will find universal appeal on the basis of either logic or passion alone. There is, as well, little interest in, let alone possibility of, imposing such an ethic through some form of direct coercion. The anthropocentric-biocentric

---

*The term "laws of nature" does not mean the same thing as "natural law," which, as one of the bases for human and other rights, is a social construction.

debate (we ignore here the fact that we are all anthropocentric, but not in an environmental sense) thus becomes a rather empty one: both are *oughts*, confronted by a deeply embedded *is*.

Some have attempted to finesse this problem by adopting familiar discourses and anthropomorphizing the environment, as if to say, "If we cannot become a part of nature, then let nature become a part of us." The results are, again, rather odd and contrary. Christopher Stone asks, "Should trees have standing?" and argues that nature should have legal rights or, at least, an ombudsperson.[19] Ulrich Beck proposes that nature has, in effect, been absorbed by a technical-regulatory "subpolitics" whose object is management in the interest of something like a vast world-spanning machine.[20] Donna Haraway suggests that we have so transformed nature through technology that we and our civilization have become "cyborgs" and we should not struggle against that.[21] The central argument of this book is that the environmental problematic is not, strictly speaking, about *either* humans or nature. (Nor, for that matter, is it about Nature.) Rather, the environmental problematic is an effect of the contemporary relationship between politics and economics, between the public and the private, between power and public policy, and it is particularly manifest in industrialized market democracies. The same processes that generate environmental damage also generate a host of other externalities, including poverty, hunger, refugees, human rights violations, and even violence.[22] That these are, for the most part, treated separately from damage to the environment has mostly to do with the reductionism characteristic of a liberal ontology, which treats causes as independent phenomena leading to independent consequences.[*]

But what does this mean, exactly? In *The Great Transformation,* Karl Polanyi argued that the two world wars were a direct result of this "disembedding" of economics from social life, and that attempts to make these two spheres completely distinct could only have resulted in what he called a "stark utopia," which "would have physically destroyed man and transformed his surroundings into a wilderness." [23] Marxists point out that capitalism is a social system unlike any other in human history, in that it requires the separation of politics and economics.[24] States, as the grantors and guarantors of private property rights, give the owners of property what is, in effect, a private

---

[*]Whether such a problematic would arise in a similar form or in such magnitude under other socioeconomic systems is largely an academic matter (note that the centrally planned economies of really existing socialism, present and past, do not constitute a "different" system in the sense meant here).

grant of political authority within limited domains. In theory, owners of such property are empowered to do whatever they wish with it, including destroying it, even if such destruction affects things vital to life and well-being. The state is enjoined from intervening in those privatized domains, having given up its prerogative to impose rules there. Of course, states find it necessary or desirable to constrain individuals in what they can do, but this is frequently decried as "political intervention in markets." Hence, benefits to private parties are counterposed to costs to others and, because the former are concentrated and the latter usually diffuse, private interests frequently trump the public good.

Eco-Marxists argue that only the abolition of capitalism and its replacement by socialism can address this contradiction; eco-economists believe that correct prices will do the trick. Neither solution appears terribly plausible. In the near term, at least, socialism's prospects are dim, and the prices required to fully internalize social externalities could never stand the test of public acceptability (consider that in March 2003, the average price of a gallon of gasoline exceeded $2.00 in California, a level considered confiscatory by many drivers, even though it was half or less of what European drivers pay). Both of these solutions view such problems in distributive terms, which can be addressed through the appropriate economic tools. Neither is particularly interested in the extent to which politics has been displaced by markets or, indeed, how this state of affairs has come about.

The argument I made here is about *politics*. What we regard as politics, contrary to the definition found in most texts on the global environment and other social matters, is not about distribution or who gets what share of the pie. Politics is, instead, about *constitution*, about how, and to what ends, power is to be used. As we saw in Chapter 1, power has multiple facets; not only can it be used to persuade or coerce, it can also be used to construct and produce. In practicing politics, we seek to do more than bribe or reward others for their support for our project; we also try to persuade others that our project will include them in all its stages, that it will recognize their needs and status, and that it will generate productive outcomes that are just and beneficial for both people and nature.

At the end of the day, people are concerned most about fairness and justice. Most people, knowingly or not, believe that, if politics as we now practice it does produce fair and just outcomes, there is no reason to fix the system. But liberalism and capitalism address opportunities, rather than means or ends. Accordingly, the environmental problematic, and all the other externalities listed above, can be addressed only through an ethic that considers means as well as ends—one that pays more attention to the justice and fairness of both means and ends. To put this another way, there is no ontology, philosophy, or ethic specific to the environment and nature. If we can be fair and just, it is a good bet we can also protect the environment. An ethic of justice and fairness will, of necessity, consider relations among people as well as relations between people and nature. Rather than springing, like mythical mushrooms on a rainy day, from the soil of a suddenly dysfunctional ontology, such an ethic must emerge slowly and painfully out of what is, for the moment, rather unfertile ground. To push the metaphor just a bit further, what an environmental ethic requires is appropriate compost, and compost is created through action, through praxis.

Toward an Environmental Praxis

What is this "praxis?" How might we enrich the metaphorical soil and coax from it an environmental ethic? Praxis is politics, in a fundamental sense. It involves learning about power and how to use it productively. According to Paulo Freire, "Human activity consists of action and reflection; it is *praxis;* it is a transformation of the world. And as praxis, it requires theory to illuminate it. Human action is theory and practice; it is reflection and action. It cannot be reduced to either verbalism or activism." [25]

Michel Foucault argued that power is constitutive of contemporary social relations. The (post)modern subject—each of us—is a product of power, power that is diffused in "capillary" fashion throughout human civilizations and societies. In a sense, power is about management, but about people managing and disciplining themselves in concert with institutions of governance, or what Foucault called "governmentality" and "biopolitics" (see Chapters 1 and 2). Rules, laws, norms, practices, and customs are the articulation of this scheme of self-management from which there appears to be no escape. We participate actively in weaving the web in which we are ensnared.

Neoliberalism is a discourse that constitutes a particular type of governmentality, both ideologically and materially. It proposes to people how they ought to behave and disciplines and punishes them if they do otherwise. "Discourse" has several different definitions. Most commonly it is understood as the utterance of language: a speech. Often, it is used to describe a form of authority rooted in language: the right to name things, actions, and processes. A third understanding of discourse is as a structure of language, actions, and things that constitute specific, power-based ways of living in the world: a way of life, in other words. The power of discourse, framed as the "right" way of life, helps to make us who we are: worker, student, teacher. We can resist or oppose that power, but for the most part the result is either reincorporation or marginalization. We can change our identities, our jobs, our goals, but if we carry such change to an extreme, we might well find ourselves treated as an "odd case" or even ostracized. Acting against power in this fashion is much like tilting against windmills: it looks brave, but it hardly makes a difference.

Fortunately, Foucault also pointed out that power is productive, and not only a mode of oppression or a tool of consensus. As he famously wrote,

> If power were never anything but repressive, if it never did anything but say no, do you really think one would be brought to obey it? What makes power hold good, what makes it accepted, is simply the fact that it doesn't only weigh on us as a force that says no, but that it traverses and produces things, it induces pleasure, forms knowledge, produces discourse. It needs to be considered as a productive network that runs through the whole social body, much more than as a negative instance whose function is repression.[26]

Although Foucault was nowhere very explicit about how power, in his understanding, could be directed against the "productive network"—indeed, some read him as arguing that "resistance is futile" and condemn him for it—we might recognize that power can "traverse and produce things" in more than one fashion, through praxis, even if we are captives in the biopolitical webs of neoliberal governmentality.[27]

This does not involve rearranging that web so as to create a different organization of governmentality, or destroying it so as to create a chaos out of which a new system might be spun. Rather, it is about generating, through politics, new or different productive networks. To put this another way, on the one hand, power "produces" the subject, in the sense described above; on the other hand, power can also produce discursive ruptures in the web of governmentality, small discontinuities that are hardly noticeable at first. A spider's web can tolerate many such small ruptures, and these are of no real concern to the spider until the web falls apart. Then, the spider simply spins a new one. What happens as such ruptures accumulate within the system of governmentality is much less clear. This metaphor of a web is a very crude one, but it begins to suggest something about politics, power, and praxis.

Power must be applied, and praxis exercised, within the micropolitical spaces of contemporary life, in the realm that, in Hannah Arendt's words, "rises directly out of acting together." [28]

Although Arendt is hardly a logical complement to Foucault in this discussion, she had much to say about politics, power, and action that is germane here. Writing about "Action" in *The Human Condition*, Arendt noted that "What first undermines and then kills political communities is loss of power and final impotence; and power cannot be stored up and kept in reserve for emergencies, like the instruments of violence, but exists only in its actualization." And, she continued, "Power is actualized only where word and deed are not parted company, where words are not empty and deeds not brutal, where words are not used to veil intentions but to disclose realities, and deeds are not used to violate and destroy but to establish relations and create new realities." [29] Where can such politics take place? In the "space of appearance," according to Arendt, which "comes into being wherever men are together in the manner of speech and action, and therefore predates and precedes all formal constitution of the public realm and the various forms of government, that is, the various forms in which the public realm can be organized." [30]

For Arendt, politics could take place only through the *polis*, as it had been constituted in ancient Greece and, especially, Athens. Here, however, she points out that "[t]he *polis*, properly speaking, is not the city-state in its physical location; *it is the organization of the people as it arises out of acting and speaking together*, and its true space lies between people living together for this purpose, no matter where they happen to be. . . . [A]ction and speech create a space between the participants which can find its proper location almost any time and anywhere." [31] This particular conception of the *polis* is an interesting one, for it suggests that place is not an essential concomitant to politics, action, and praxis. We shall return to this point later, but first we have to consider how politics, in the space of appearance, can create an alternative to governmentality that does not serve to reproduce the relations of power that constitute both it and the political subject.

Within such a "space," democracy becomes possible in a form that is radically different from that which we normally take it to be, in its diluted representational form. And engaging in such action is, perhaps, the most important step in challenging governmentality and recognizing just how limited our representative democracies really are. After all, how can we know what democratic politics is if we have never participated in it? How can we comprehend what is missing from our "democratic" systems if we have not experienced democratic politics? And how can we challenge the marketization of politics if our only concern is about the monetary cost of decision making rather than the disposition of power in politics?

This is why environmental ethics and praxis are not to be found in an ever-greater proliferation of international NGOs. Using the American model of institutional politics, increasingly based on the deployment of money and lobbyists, many NGOs have adopted a neocorporate approach to organization and practice. When the media reports on national or international environmental matters, it is these NGOs that are usually consulted. When governments feel the need to include environmentalists in delegations and on commissions, it is from these NGOs that individuals are seconded. And when legislatures formulate and debate laws intended to address environmental problems, it is these NGOs who provide the legal expertise and testimony in support of or in opposition to the legislation under debate. Their participation in "global environmental politics" has become routine and bureaucratic. They seek to participate in policymaking as full-fledged "stakeholders." They search for operating revenues through various types of projects supported by a broad range of funders, including both government agencies and private corporations. They differ from those they criticize only in regard to "what is to be done," and rarely in regard to "what must not be done any longer." These NGOs have become part of the very structure of neoliberal governmentality that is the source of the problem.

To where, then, can we look for answers?

Global Environmental Politics from the Ground Up

In her 1990 book, *Justice and the Politics of Difference,* Iris Marion Young argues:

> One important purpose of critical normative theory [and speculation] is to offer an alternative vision of social relations which, in the words of [Herbert] Marcuse, "conceptualizes the stuff of which the experienced world consists . . . with a view to its possibilities, in the light of their actual limitation, suppression, and denial." Such a positive normative vision can inspire hope and imagination that motivate action for social change. It also provides some of the reflective distance necessary for the criticism of existing social circumstances.[32]

Young is focused here on domestic politics, striving for a realistic vision of what is possible from what already is: "A model of a transformed society must begin from the material structures that are given to us at this time in history."[33] We cannot create new societies or even practices out of ideas alone, in other words; we must work with what we have. When we begin to look around, we discover that there is, in fact, much to work with.

One of the forms of social power considered in Chapter 4 was the watershed organization. There, we saw how groups in the Mattole River Valley of Northern California had organized to protect the watershed and, in this, were much like thousands of other similar groups in the United States and around the world. Almost unheard of in 1983, by 2003 such groups had become ubiquitous. Focused on a single stream or river, they nonetheless shared an epistemic vision of the place of watersheds in both the local and global environment. These organizations look much like standard NGOs, seeking to solve environmental problems through standard techniques and practices. Yet, there is some reason to think that very few of the practicing watershed groups are actually standard. Individual groups all share a view that the creek, the stream, the river, are central to where they live and merit more attention and care than is being given to them. At the same time, these groups are different, in their political culture, their economies, their watersheds, their projects.

Governments have not been insensitive to local concerns about watersheds, especially insofar as they are required by law to clean them up and keep them clean. Nor have responsible agencies been blind to the role such groups can play in furthering governmental goals. Consequently, in many places "official" state-sanctioned watershed projects have been launched, and in others, independent groups have been given a role to play in official programs.[34] But those state agencies tasked with water-related responsibilities are not entirely comfortable with these independent groups. They often tend to be rather more radical, less manageable, more impulsive, and less systematic than bureaucrats and technocrats would like. They ignore or even trample on private property rights. They have no respect for the legal niceties and procedures of the regulatory process. They do not pay adequate attention to scientific principles and evidence.

They are too political.

"Too political" is code for the creation of a space of appearance in which people can engage in environmental politics and praxis. In such spaces, people experience what is possible, and how action is a form of productive power. Politics in the space of appearance, whether focused on the watershed, the urban neighborhood, toxic wastes, global warming, or environmental disempowerment, is not only about the pursuit of shared interests, as collective action theorists generally describe it, or the mobilization of resources, as social movement theorists would have it.[35] It is also about the application of power to produce. People choose. People decide. This is an experience that institutionalized political processes—voting, lobbying, e-mailing representatives—never offer. It is an experience that illuminates the possibilities of politics in all of its raw, elemental form.[36] It is disruptive and aggravating, but in terms of praxis, productive. It is not a "solution" to a problem, rather, it is a means of engaging with those things that ought not to be, but are.

Being "too political" ruptures the web of governmentality. These are small ruptures, and not very conspicuous. No one in San José or São Paulo, in Delhi or Davos, cares very much about watershed groups causing small ruptures nearby. They have their own problems to worry about, thank you. No one fears that environmental praxis poses a challenge to the stability of the Republic or Kingdom or Union. At most, they might be a nuisance for municipal and civic sensibilities (and who, in the capitals of the world's great nation-states, cares about that?). They are hardly a threat to Western or even world civilization.

But perhaps they are.

After all, if governmentality is about management, environmental politics and praxis, as we envision them here, are not. They are, inevitably, contentious and conflictual, for they challenge the very constitutive basis of neoliberal governmentality. They challenge exactly those principles, practices, and policies that seek to "manage" the environment even as they pollute and destroy it in the first place. They offer a different way of thinking about and acting for people and nature. If neoliberal governmentality is about order, environmental politics and praxis are not. Order is the enemy of change and, without change, we and nature will not survive. Then, there will be order, but it will be the Order of Death.

A Final Manifesto

At the beginning of this book, we confronted the argument that the "structures that are given to us at this time in history" are both social and natural and, together, constitute a "social ecology" whose normal functioning has transformed and continues to transform nature and the environment. That social ecology is both local and global. It is found in the places in which people live, work, play, and love. It is world girdling, too.

We also dealt with the proposition that, in order to understand global environmental politics, and to act, we must take greater cognizance of power and how it is constituted through ideological, historical, and material processes. In particular, power as exercised through the structures and processes associated with global capitalism constitute an obstacle to protection of nature. At the same time, however, capitalism stands as the operating system of the material structures we are given at this particular time in history.

Finally, throughout this book, we have seen that markets and capitalism, as they are presently constituted, cannot solve the global environmental problematic, for several reasons. First, the imperatives of uncontrolled growth, which are so important to contemporary capitalism, contradict the physical realities of nature and the social realities of the world's poor. We cannot grow or consume our way out of the crisis.

Second, a reliance on markets and capitalism as the "solution" results in the obscuring of both power and its exercise, and the disappearance of politics from the scene. Problems are transmogrified from the social to the technical realm, and left to the "experts." But however wise these experts may be, their solutions are more likely to be bent in ways that reinforce the status quo, rather than change it.

Third, managing people from above is rather like herding cats. It cannot be done. We are each part of a social body, but we are also individuals. The virtue of the market is that it permits us to be individuals; the cost of the market is that, as individuals, we have no concept of the public good and no reason to find one. That is the job of politics.

And that is what this book is, finally, about: global environmental politics. A truly democratic and effective global environmental politics can begin only where politics is possible: habitat as home. This is not an admonition to "think globally, act locally." It means that changing the status quo, reasserting control over markets and capitalism, and protecting nature and the environment all require direct engagement with politics *where it begins:* in the space of appearance.

Shall we begin?

For Further Reading

Abbey, Edward. *The Monkey Wrench Gang.* New York: Perennial, 2000.

Callenbach, Ernest. *Ecotopia.* New York: Bantam, 1975.

Dickens, Peter. *Reconstructing Nature: Alienation, Emancipation, and the Division of Labour.* London: Routledge, 1996.

Evans, Sara M., and Harry C. Boyte. *Free Spaces: The Sources of Democratic Change in America.* New York: Harper and Row, 1986.

Kahn, Peter H., Jr. *The Human Relationship with Nature: Development and Culture.* Cambridge: MIT Press, 1999.

Leopold, Aldo. *A Sand County Almanac.* New York: Ballantine, 1970.

Low, Nicholas, and Brendan Gleeson. *Justice, Society, and Nature: An Exploration of Political Ecology.* London: Routledge, 1998.

Minteer, Ben A., and Bob Pepperman Taylor, eds. *Democracy and the Claims of Nature.* Lanham, Md.: Rowman and Littlefield, 2002.

Novotny, Patrick. *Where We Live, Work, and Play: The Environmental Justice Movement and the Struggle for a New Environmentalism.* Westport, Conn.: Praeger, 2000.

Peterson, Anna L. *Being Human: Ethics, Environment, and Our Place in the World.* Berkeley: University of California Press, 2001.

Shutkin, William A. *The Land That Could Be: Environmentalism and Democracy in the Twenty-First Century.* Cambridge: MIT Press, 2001.

Stone, Christopher D. *The Gnat Is Older than Man: Global Environment and Human Agenda.* Princeton, N.J.: Princeton University Press, 1993.

| Notes

Chapter 1. What Are "Global Environmental Politics?"

1. Juan Forero, "In Ecuador's Banana Fields, Child Labor Is Key to Profits," *New York Times,* July 13, 2002, nat'l ed., p. A1; Adelien van de Kasteele, "The Banana Chain: The Macroeconomics of the Banana Trade" (paper presented at the International Banana Conference, Brussels, May 4–6, 1998), online at http://bananas.agoranet.be/MacroEconomics.htm (7/8/02); see also *Banana Link,* online at http://www.bananalink.org.U.K.

2. Anne-Claire Chambron, "Bananas: The 'Green Gold' of the TNCs," U.K. Food Group, 1999, online at *Banana Link,* http://www.bananalink.org.U.K./trade/btrade.htm (4/4/03); Anne-Claire Chambron, "Straightening the Bent World of the Banana," European Fair Trade Association, Feb. 2000, online at *Banana Link,* http://www.bananalink.org.U.K./trade/btrade.htm (4/4/03); "Bananas: The Facts," *New Internationalist,* Oct. 1999, online at http://www.newint.org/issue317/facts.htm (2/18/03).

3. "Bananas: The Facts."

4. B. L. Turner et al., *The Earth as Transformed by Human Action: Global and Regional Changes in the Biosphere over the Past 300 Years* (Cambridge: Cambridge University Press, 1990).

5. Max Oelschlaeger, *The Idea of Wilderness: From Prehistory to the Age of Ecology* (New Haven: Yale University Press, 1991).

6. Lynn White Jr., "The Historical Roots of Our Ecologic Crisis," *Science* 155 (1967): 1203–1207; Anna L. Peterson, *Being Human: Ethics, Environment, and Our Place in the World* (Berkeley: University of California Press, 2001), chap. 2.

7. Leo Marx, *The Machine in the Garden: Technology and the Pastoral Ideal in America* (New York: Oxford University Press, 1964); Carolyn Merchant, *The*

Death of Nature: Women, Ecology, and the Scientific Revolution (New York: Harper and Row, 1980).

8. Christopher Stone, *Should Trees Have Standing? Toward Legal Rights for Natural Objects* (Los Altos, Calif.: Kaufmann, 1974); Michael J. Zimmerman, *The Nature of Intrinsic Value* (Lanham, Md.: Rowman and Littlefield, 2001); Alan Gregg, "A Medical Aspect of the Population Problem," *Science* 121 (May 13, 1955): 681–682; Warren M. Hern, "Why Are There So Many of Us? Description and Diagnosis of a Planetary Ecopathological Process," online at http://www.drhern.com/fulltext/why/paper.html#Toplink (4/4/03); Ramon G. McLeod, "Humans are 'Planetary Malignancy,' Scientist Says," *San Francisco Chronicle*, Aug. 1, 1994, p. A3.

9. George Sessions, "Deep Ecology: Introduction," in *Environmental Philosophy: From Animal Rights to Radical Ecology*, 3d ed., ed. Michael E. Zimmerman et al. (Upper Saddle River, N.J.: Prentice Hall, 2001), pp. 157–174.

10. David Harvey, *Spaces of Hope* (Berkeley: University of California Press, 2000), chap. 9.

11. Stephen D. Krasner, ed., *International Regimes* (Ithaca, N.Y.: Cornell University Press, 1983).

12. James O'Connor, "Three Ways to Look at the Ecological History and Cultural Landscapes of Monterey Bay," in *Natural Causes: Essays in Ecological Marxism* (New York: Guilford Press, 1998), pp. 71–93.

13. Donna Haraway, "Manifesto for Cyborgs: Science, Technology, and Socialist Feminism in the 1980s," *Socialist Review* 80 (1985): 65–108.

14. Peterson, *Being Human*, chap. 5.

15. See Mitchell Dean, *Governmentality: Power and Rule in Modern Society* (London: Sage, 1999).

16. John Gaventa, *Power and Powerlessness: Quiescence and Rebellion in an Appalachian Valley* (Oxford: Clarendon Press, 1980).

17. Thomas Risse, "Constructivism and International Institutions: Toward Conversations Across Paradigms," in *Political Science: The State of the Discipline*, ed. Ira Katznelson and Helen Milner (New York: Norton, 2002), pp. 597–626, online at http://www.uned.es/D.C.pa/Doctorado/126JIgnacioTorreblanca/ Cursodoc2003/primerasesion/Risse2001.pdf (3/27/03)

18. Gaventa, *Power and Powerlessness*.

19. Walter L. Adamson, *Hegemony and Revolution: A Study of Antonio Gramsci's Political and Cultural Theory* (Berkeley: University of California Press, 1980), pp. 170–171.

20. Michel Foucault, *Discipline and Punish: The Birth of the Prison*, trans. Alan Sheridan (New York: Pantheon, 1977). Dean, *Governmentality*.

21. Nicholas G. Onuf, *World of Our Making: Rules and Rule in Social Theory and International Relations* (Columbia: University of South Carolina Press, 1989).

22. Paul Wapner, *Environmental Activism and World Civic Politics* (Albany: State University of New York Press, 1996).

23. Karen Litfin, *Ozone Discourses: Science and Politics in Global Environmental Cooperation* (New York: Columbia University Press, 1994), p. 13.

24. Michel Foucault, "Truth and Power," in *Power/ Knowledge,* trans. Colin Gordon (New York: Pantheon, 1980), pp. 109–133.

25. Peterson, *Being Human.*

26. Thomas Hobbes, *Leviathan,* Oakeshott ed. (1651; New York: Macmillan, 1962). John Locke, *Two Treatises of Government* (1689–1690; Cambridge: Cambridge University Press, 1960).

27. Oran R. Young, *Resource Regimes: Natural Resources and Social Institutions* (Berkeley: University of California Press, 1982); Ronnie D. Lipschutz, with Judith Mayer, *Global Civil Society and Global Environmental Governance: The Politics of Nature from Place to Planet* (Albany: State University of New York Press, 1996), pp. 33–34.

28. John H. Davis, "Proposals Concerning the Concept of Habitat and a Classification of Types," *Ecology* 41 (July 1960): 537–541.

29. Gil Friedman and Harvey Starr, *Agency, Structure, and International Politics: From Ontology to Empirical Inquiry* (London: Routledge, 1997).

30. David Dessler, "What's at Stake in the Agent-Structure Debate?" *International Organization* 43 (summer 1989): 441–474; Ronnie D. Lipschutz, "Because People Matter: Studying Global Political Economy," *International Studies Perspective* 2 (2001): 321–339.

31. Warren Magnusson and Karena Shaw, eds., *A Political Space: Reading the Global through Clayoquot Sound* (Minneapolis: University of Minnesota Press, 2003).

32. Thomas DeGregori, "Resources Are Not; They Become: An Institutional Theory," *Journal of Economic Issues* 21 (September 1987): 1241–1263.

33. See Ronnie D. Lipschutz and Judith Mayer, "Not Seeing the Forest for the Trees: Rights, Rules, and the Renegotiation of Resource Management Regimes," in *The State and Social Power in Global Environmental Politics,* ed. Ronnie D. Lipschutz and Ken Conca (New York: Columbia University Press, 1993), pp. 246–273; Lipschutz, with Mayer, *Global Civil Society;* Thom Kuehls, *Beyond Sovereign Territory: The Space of Ecopolitics* (Minneapolis: University of Minnesota Press, 1996).

34. Simon Schama, *Landscape and Memory* (New York: Knopf, 1995), chaps. 2, 3.

35. Kuehls, *Beyond Sovereign Territory.*

36. Ibid.

37. Ved. P. Nanda, *International Environmental Law and Policy* (Irving-on-Hudson, N.Y.: Transnational, 1995), pp. 76–78, 83–86.

38. Ronnie D. Lipschutz, "Environmental History, Political Economy, and Policy: Re-discovering Lost Frontiers in Environmental Research," *Global Environmental Politics* 1 (August 2001): 72–91.

39. World Commission on Environment and Development (WCED), *Our Common Future* (Oxford: Oxford University Press, 1987).

40. Andrew Goudie, *The Human Impact on the Natural Environment* (Cambridge: MIT Press, 2000).

41. Karl Polanyi, *The Great Transformation*, 2d ed. (Boston: Beacon Press, 2001).

42. See Lipschutz and Conca, *The State and Social Power.*

43. Sheldon Wolin, "Fugitive Democracy," in *Democracy and Difference*, ed. Seyla Benhabib (Princeton, N.J.: Princeton University Press, 1996), pp. 31–45.

44. Penina M. Glazer and Myron P. Glazer, *The Environmental Crusaders: Confronting Disaster and Mobilizing Community* (University Park: Pennsylvania State University Press, 1998); Christopher Rootes, ed., *Environmental Movements: Local, National and Global* (London: Frank Cass, 1999); Patrick Novotny, *Where We Live, Work, and Play: The Environmental Justice Movement and the Struggle for a New Environmentalism* (Westport, Conn.: Praeger, 2000); David N. Pellow, *Garbage Wars: The Struggle for Environmental Justice in Chicago* (Cambridge: MIT Press, 2002).

45. Timothy Luke, *Ecocritique: Contesting the Politics of Nature, Economy, and Culture* (Minneapolis: University of Minnesota Press, 1997).

46. Peter Gourevitch, *Politics in Hard Times* (Ithaca, N.Y.: Cornell University Press, 1986).

47. Krasner, *International Regimes.*

48. Oran R. Young, *International Governance: Protecting the Environment in a Stateless Society* (Ithaca, N.Y.: Cornell University Press, 1994).

49. Jonathan Schell, *The Fate of the Earth* (New York: Knopf, 1982).

Chapter 2. Deconstructing "Global Environment"

1. Deborah Stone, *Policy Paradox: The Art of Political Decision Making* (New York: Norton, 1997).

2. Peterson, *Being Human.*

3. John Meyer, *Political Nature: Environmentalism, and the Interpretation of Western Thought* (Cambridge: MIT Press, 2001).

4. See, for example, Karl Marx and Friedrich Engels, *The Communist Manifesto* (New York: Pocket Books, 1964).

5. Peter Kropotkin, *Mutual Aid: A Factor of Evolution*, ed. Paul Avrich (London: Allen Lane, 1972).

6. Johan Galtung, "Violence, Peace, and Peace Research," *Journal of Peace Research* 3 (1969): 167–192.

7. Hedley Bull, *The Anarchical Society* (New York: Columbia University Press, 1977).

8. But see Martin Shaw, *Theory of the Global State: Globality as an Unfinished Revolution* (Cambridge: Cambridge University Press, 2000).

9. Robert Jackson, *Quasi-states: Sovereignty, International Relations, and the Third World* (Cambridge: Cambridge University Press, 1990).

10. Harold Sprout and Margaret Sprout, *The Ecological Perspective on Human Affairs* (Princeton, N.J.: Princeton University Press, 1965); Ronnie D. Lipschutz, *When Nations Clash: Raw Materials, Ideology, and Foreign Policy* (New York: Ballinger/Harper and Row, 1989); Michael T. Klare, *Resource Wars: The New Landscape of Global Conflict* (New York: Metropolitan Books, 2001).

11. Nicholas J. Spykman, *America's Strategy in World Politics* (New York: Harcourt, Brace, 1942); Lipschutz, *When Nations Clash.*

12. On German expansionism: Lipschutz, *When Nations Clash;* on war in Pacific: Jonathan Marshall, *To Have and Have Not: Southeast Asian Raw Materials and the Origins of the Pacific War* (Berkeley: University of California Press, 1995); on 1991 Gulf war: Klare, *Resource Wars.*

13. Daniel Yergin, "A Crude View of the Crisis in Iraq," *Washington Post Outlook,* Dec. 8, 2002, online at http://www.cera.com/news/details/print/1,1307,5067,00.html (3/25/03).

14. Peter Gleick, "Water and Conflict: Fresh Water Resources and International Security," *International Security* 18 (summer 1993): 79.

15. Joyce Starr, "Water Wars," *Foreign Policy* 82 (spring 1991): 17–30; Mirian Lowi, "Rivers of Conflict, Rivers of Peace," *Journal of International Affairs* 49 (1995): 123–144; Ronnie D. Lipschutz, "The Nature of Sovereignty and the Sovereignty of Nature: Problematizing the Boundaries between Self, Society, State, and System," in *The Greening of Sovereignty in World Politics,* ed. Karen D. Litfin (Cambridge: MIT Press, 1998), pp. 109–138.

16. Peter Beaumont, "Water and Armed Conflict in the Middle East: Fantasy or Reality?" in *Conflict and the Environment,* ed. Nils Petter Gleditsch (Dordrecht: Kluwer, 1997), pp. 355–374; Steve Lonergan, "Water Resources and Conflict: Examples from the Middle East," in Gleditsch, *Conflict and the Environment,* pp. 375–384; Anne H. Ehrlich, Peter Gleick, and Ken Conca, "Resources and Environmental Degradation as Sources of Conflict" (draft of background paper for Working Group 5, prepared for the Fiftieth Pugwash Conference on Science and World Affairs, "Eliminating the Causes of War," Queens' College, Cambridge, Aug. 3–8, 2000), online at http://www.pugwash.org/reports/pac/pac256/WG5draft.htm (4/4/03).

17. João Pacheco de Oliveira Filho, "Frontier Security and the New Indigenism: Nature and Origins of the Calha Norte Project," in *The Future of Amazonia,* ed. David Goodman and Anthony Hall (New York: St. Martin's Press, 1990), pp. 155–176.

18. Klare, *Resource Wars.*

19. Garrett Hardin, "Life Boat Ethics: The Case against Helping the Poor," *Psychology Today,* Sept. 1974, pp. 38–43, 124–126, online at http://mthwww.uwc.edu/wwwmahes/courses/geog/malthus/case.htm (4/4/03).

20. Thomas F. Homer-Dixon and Jessica Blitt, eds., *Ecoviolence: Links among Environment, Population, and Security* (Lanham, Md.: Rowman and Littlefield,

1998); Thomas F. Homer-Dixon, *Environment, Scarcity, and Violence* (Princeton, N.J.: Princeton University Press, 1999).

21. Thomas Malthus, *An Essay on the Principle of Population* (1778; Amherst, N.Y.: Prometheus Books, 1998).

22. Eric B. Ross, *The Malthus Factor* (London: Zed Books, 1998).

23. Amartya Sen and Jean Dreze, eds., *The Amartya Sen and Jean Dreze Omnibus* (New Delhi: Oxford University Press, 1999).

24. Donella H. Meadows et al., *The Limits to Growth: A Report for the Club of Rome's Project on the Predicament of Mankind* (New York: Universe Books, 1972).

25. Paul Ehrlich, *The Population Bomb* (New York: Ballantine, 1968), p. xi.

26. Hans Morgenthau, *Politics among Nations: The Struggle for Power and Peace* (New York: Knopf, 1948).

27. Adam Smith, *The Wealth of Nations* (1776; New York: Knopf, 1991); Emma Rothschild, *Economic Sentiments: Adam Smith, Condorcet, and the Enlightenment* (Cambridge: Harvard University Press, 2001).

28. Adam Smith, *The Theory of Moral Sentiments* (1761; New York: A. M. Kelley, 1966); Fred Hirsch, *Social Limits to Growth* (Cambridge: Harvard University Press, 1976).

29. Onuf, *World of Our Making.*

30. Lipschutz and Conca, *The State and Social Power.*

31. But see Judith Goldstein, Miles Kahler, Robert O. Keohane, and Anne-Marie Slaughter, eds., *Legalization and World Politics* (Cambridge: MIT Press, 2001).

32. Ronald Coase, "The Problem of Social Cost," *Journal of Law and Economics* 3 (1960): 1–44.

33. Daniel Altman, "Just How Far Can Trading of Emissions Be Extended?" *New York Times,* May 31, 2001, nat'l ed., p. C1.

34. Mancur Olson, *The Logic of Collective Action* (Cambridge: Harvard University Press, 1965); Russell Hardin, *Collective Action* (Baltimore: Johns Hopkins University Press, 1982).

35. Olson, *Logic of Collective Action.*

36. Gareth Porter, Janet Welsh Brown, and Pamela S. Chasek, *Global Environmental Politics* (Boulder, Colo.: Westview Press, 2000), p. 147.

37. Stephen D. Krasner, *International Regimes;* Robert O. Keohane, *International Institutions and State Power* (Boulder, Colo.: Westview, 1989), chap. 1.

38. Cathleen A. Fogel, "Greening the Earth with Trees: Science, Storylines, and the Construction of International Climate Change Institutions" (Ph.D. diss., University of California, Santa Cruz, 2002).

39. Intergovernmental Panel on Climate Change (IPCC), *Climate Change 2001: Impacts, Adaptation, and Vulnerability,* Report of Working Group II of the IPCC, 2001, online at http://www.ipcc.ch/pub/tar/wg2/index.htm (4/5/02).

40. Murray Bookchin, *The Ecology of Freedom,* rev. ed. (Montreal: Black Rose Books, 1992).

41. Thomas Princen, "Consumption and Its Externalities: Where Economy Meets Ecology," *Global Environmental Politics* 1 (Aug. 2001): 11–30.

42. Bookchin, *Ecology of Freedom,* pp. xx–xxii.

43. Kropotkin, *Mutual Aid,* chap. 2.

44. John Clark, "A Social Ecology," in *Environmental Philosophy: From Animal Rights to Radical Ecology* 2d ed., ed. Michael E. Zimmerman et al. (Upper Saddle River, N.J.: Prentice Hall, 1998), pp. 416–440; quotations on p. 421.

45. Peterson, *Being Human,* chap. 5; Umeek of Ahousaht (E. Richard Atleo), "Commentary: Discourses in and about Clayoquot Sound: A First Nations Perspective," in Magnusson and Shaw, *A Political Space,* pp. 199–208.

46. Clark, "A Social Ecology," p. 433.

47. Ibid., p. 435.

48. G. W. F. Hegel, *The Philosophy of History,* trans J. Sirbee (1837; New York: Dover, 1956).

49. Michael Vincent McGinnis, ed., *Bioregionalism* (London: Routledge, 1999); Ronnie D. Lipschutz, "Bioregionalism, Civil Society, and Global Environmental Governance," in McGinnis, *Bioregionalism,* pp. 101–120; Lipschutz, with Mayer, *Global Civil Society,* chap. 4.

50. Lipschutz, with Mayer, *Global Civil Society,* chap. 4.

51. Amartya Sen, *Development as Freedom* (New York: Knopf, 1999); Joseph E. Stiglitz, *Globalization and Its Discontents* (New York: Norton, 2002).

52. Eric R. Wolf, *Europe and the People without History* (1982; reprint, Berkeley: University of California Press, 1997).

53. See, for example, Goudie, *Human Impact on the Natural Environment,* chap. 1.

54. E. L. Jones, *The European Miracle: Environments, Economies, and Geopolitics in the History of Europe and Asia* (Cambridge: Cambridge University Press, 1981); Ernest Gellner, *Nations and Nationalism* (Ithaca, N.Y.: Cornell University Press, 1983); Eric J. Hobsbawm, *Nations and Nationalism Since 1780: Programme, Myth, Reality* (Cambridge: Cambridge University Press, 1990).

55. Jan Knippers Black, *Development in Theory and Practice: Bridging the Gap* (Boulder, Colo.: Westview Press, 1991).

56. Ramachandra Guha, *The Unquiet Woods: Ecological Change and Peasant Resistance in the Himalaya,* expanded ed. (Berkeley: University of California Press, 2000).

57. Philip G. Cerny, "Structuring the Political Arena: Public Goods, States, and Governance in a Globalizing World," in *Global Political Economy: Contemporary Theories,* ed. Ronen Palan (London: Routledge, 1999), pp. 21–35.

58. Sen, *Development as Freedom;* Richard W. Franke and Barbara H. Chasin, *Kerala: Radical Reform as Development in an Indian State,* 2d ed. (Oakland, Calif.: Food First, 1994).

59. Ramesh Mishra, *Globalization and the Welfare State* (Cheltenham, England: Elgar, 1999).

60. WCED, *Our Common Future*.

61. Gerald Foley and Patricia Moss, *Improved Cooking Stoves in Developing Countries* (London: Earthscan, 1985); Michael F. Maniates, "Organizing for Rural Energy Development: Improved Cookstoves, Local Organizations, and the State in Gujarat, India" (Ph.D. diss., University of California, Berkeley, 1990).

62. Norman A. Bailey, "Foreign Direct Investment and Environmental Protection in the Third World," in *Trade and the Environment: Law, Economics, and Policy*, ed. Durwood Zaelke, Paul Orbuch, and Robert F. Houseman (Washington, D.C.: Island Press, 1993), pp. 133–143.

63. Paul Ekins, "The Kuznets Curve for the Environment and Economic Growth: Examining the Evidence," *Environment and Planning* 29 (1997): 805–830; William Harbaugh, Arik Levinson, and David Wilson, "Reexamining the Empirical Evidence for an Environmental Kuznets Curve," National Bureau of Economic Research (NBER) working paper no. w7711, May 2000, online at http://papers.nber.org/papers/w7711.pdf (4/12/02).

64. Quoted in Robin Broad, John Cavanaugh, and Walden Bello, "Development: The Market Is Not Enough," *Foreign Policy* 81 (winter 1990): 144.

65. Steven Bernstein, *The Compromise of Liberal Environmentalism* (New York: Columbia University Press, 2001); Johannesburg Summit 2002 (World Summit on Sustainable Development [WSSD]), online at http://www.johannesburgsummit.org/ (4/11/03).

66. Kevin Watkins, with Penny Fowler, *Rigged Rules and Double Standards: Trade, Globalisation, and the Fight against Poverty* (London: Oxfam, 2002), pp. 94–121, online at http://www.maketradefair.org/assets/english/Report_English.pdf (4/11/03).

67. David Dollar and Aart Kraay, "Spreading the Wealth," *Foreign Affairs* 81, (Jan.–Feb. 2002): 120–133; but see also James K. Galbraith, "By the Numbers," *Foreign Affairs* 81, (July/Aug. 2002). Shaohua Chen and Martin Ravallion, "How Did the World's Poorest Fare in the 1990s?" World Bank Development Research Group, 2000, online at http:// www.worldbank.org/research/povmonitor/pdfs/methodology.pdf (7/15/02).

68. Arthur P. J. Mol, *Globalization and Environmental Reform: The Ecological Modernization of the Global Economy* (Cambridge: MIT Press, 2001).

69. Bailey, "Foreign Direct Investment."

70. J. C. H. Chai and B. K. Chai, "China's Floating Population and Its Implications," *International Journal of Social Economics* 24 (1997): 1038–1052; see also John Steinbeck, *The Grapes of Wrath* (New York: Viking, 1939).

71. Thomas L. Friedman, *The Lexus and the Olive Tree: Understanding Globalization*, rev. ed. (New York: Farrar, Straus and Giroux, 2000).

72. Kate O'Neill, *Waste Trading among Rich Nations: Building a New Theory of Environmental Regulation* (Cambridge: MIT Press, 2000); Thomas Princen, Michael Maniates, and Ken Conca, *Confronting Consumption* (Cambridge: MIT Press, 2002).

73. *PC World,* "Old PCs Flood the Waste Stream," Apr. 14, 2000, online at http://www.pcworld.com/news/article/0,aid,16273,00.asp (11/7/02).

74. International Union for the Conservation of Nature and Natural Resources (IUCN), *World Conservation Strategy: Living Resource Conservation for Sustainable Development* (Gland, Switzerland: IUCN, 1980).

75. WCED, *Our Common Future,* p. 8.

76. Ronnie D. Lipschutz, "Wasn't the Future Wonderful? Resources, Environment, and the Emerging Myth of Global Sustainable Development," *Colorado Journal of International Environmental Law and Policy* 2 (1991): 35–54; Sharachchandra B. Lele, "Sustainable Development: A Critical Review," *World Development* 19 (1991): 607–621.

77. Clean Development Mechanism, UN Framework Convention on Climate Change, online at http://unfccc.int/cdm/ (4/11/03); Michael Toman and Marina Cazorla, "The Clean Development Mechanism: A Primer," *Weathervane* (Washington, D.C.: Resources for the Future, 1998), online at http://www.weathervane.rff.org/features/feature048.html (4/11/03).

78. Michael Redclift, *Sustainable Development: Exploring the Contradictions* (London: Methuen, 1987); David Reid, *Sustainable Development: An Introductory Guide* (London: Earthscan, 1985); Wolfgang Sachs, ed., *The Development Dictionary: A Guide to Knowledge as Power* (London: Zed Books, 1992).

79. Thomas F. Homer-Dixon, *The Ingenuity Gap* (New York: Knopf, 2000).

80. Herman Daly, *Steady-State Economics,* 2d ed. (Washington, D.C.: Island Press, 1991).

81. Herman Daly and John Cobb Jr., *For the Common Good: Redirecting the Economy toward Community, the Environment, and a Sustainable Future* (Boston: Beacon Press, 1989), p. 76, chap. 11.

82. World Resources Institute (WRI), *World Resources 2000–2001* (Washington, D.C.: WRI, 2001), table ERC.5, online at http://www.wri.org/wr-00-01/pdf/erc5n_2000.pdf (7/17/02).

83. Ken Conca, "Consumption and Environment in a Global Economy," *Global Environmental Politics* 1 (Aug. 2001): 53–71.

84. Robert H. Wade, "The Rising Inequality of World Income Distribution," *Finance and Development* 38 (Dec. 2001), pp. 37–39, online at http://www.imf.org/external/pubs/ft/fandd/2001/12/wade.htm (4/8/03).

85. Hannah Arendt, *The Human Condition,* 2d ed. (Chicago: University of Chicago Press, 1958); Foucault, "Truth and Power."

86. Thom Kuehls, "The Environment of Sovereignty," in Magnusson and Shaw, *A Political Space,* pp. 179–198.

87. Michael Mann, *The Sources of Social Power: The Rise of Classes and Nation-states, 1760–1914* (Cambridge: Cambridge University Press, 1993), vol. 2, chap. 2.

88. David Pepper, *Eco-socialism: From Deep Ecology to Social Justice* (London: Routledge, 1993), p. 67.

89. Joseph A. Schumpeter, "The Process of Creative Destruction," in Joseph A. Schumpeter *Capitalism, Socialism, and Democracy* (New York: Harper and Row, 1975), pp. 81–86.

90. Philip R. Pryde, *Environmental Management in the Soviet Union* (Cambridge: Cambridge University Press, 1991).

91. Pepper, *Eco-socialism*, p. 234.

92. Ibid., pp. 235–236.

93. Karen J. Warren, "Ecofeminism: Introduction," in Zimmerman et al. *Environmental Philosophy*, 3d ed., pp. 253–272; Joni Seager, *Earth Follies: Coming to Feminist Terms with the Global Environmental Crisis* (London: Routledge, 1993); Catriona Sandilands, *The Good-Natured Feminist: Ecofeminism and the Quest for Democracy* (Minneapolis: University of Minnesota Press, 1999).

94. Zimmerman et al., *Environmental Philosophy*, 3d ed.

95. Ariel Salleh, *Ecofeminism as Politics: Nature, Marx, and the Postmodern* (London: Zed Books, 1997).

96. Ibid., p. 14.

97. Ibid., pp. 13, 17.

98. Ibid., pp. 12–13, 54, 53, 192.

99. Henry David Thoreau, "Walking, or the Wild" (1862), part 2, para. 18, online at http://www.eserver.org/thoreau/walking2.html#wild; William Chaloupka, "There Must be Some Way Out of Here: Strategy, Ethics, and Environmental Politics," in Magnusson and Shaw, *A Political Space*, pp. 67–90.

100. Sessions, "Deep Ecology"; Warwick Fox, "The Deep Ecology–Ecofeminism Debate and Its Parallels," *Environmental Ethics* 11 (spring 1989): 5–25.

101. Josef Keulartz, *The Struggle for Nature: A Critique of Radical Ecology,* trans. Rob Keuitenbrouwer (London: Routledge, 1998).

102. On power, domination, and the environment, see Matthew Paterson, *Understanding Global Environmental Politics: Domination, Accumulation, Resistance* (Basingstoke, England: Macmillan, 2000). Foucault, "Truth and Power"; Michel Foucault, "Governmentality," in *The Foucault Effect: Studies in Governmentality,* ed. Graham Burchell, Colin Gordon, and Peter Miller (Chicago: University of Chicago Press, 1991), pp. 87–104.

103. Foucault, "Governmentality"; Dean, *Governmentality.*

104. Foucault, "Governmentality," p. 93.

105. Foucault, "Truth and Power," p. 119.

106. Dean, *Governmentality,* p. 99.

107. Ibid.

108. William Ophuls and A. Stephen Boyan, *Ecology and the Politics of Scarcity Revisited: The Unraveling of the American Dream* (New York: Freeman, 1992); Robert L. Heilbroner, *An Inquiry into the Human Prospect: Looked at Again for the 1990s,* 3d ed. (New York: Norton, 1991).

Chapter 3. Capitalism, Globalization, and the Environment

1. Smith, *The Wealth of Nations.*
2. Thom Kuehls, "The Environment of Sovereignty."
3. David W. Pearce and R. Kerry Turner, *Economics of Natural Resources and the Environment* (Baltimore: Johns Hopkins University Press, 1990), chap. 14.
4. Daniel Yergin, *The Prize: The Epic Quest for Oil, Money, and Power* (New York: Simon and Schuster, 1991); Jonathan Nitzan and Shimshon Bichler, *The Global Political Economy of Israel* (London: Pluto Press, 2002), chap. 5.
5. Pearce and Turner, *Economics of Natural Resources,* chap. 18; Yergin, *The Prize;* Yergin, "A Crude View."
6. "Oil Price History and Analysis," *Energy Economics Newsletter,* online at http://www.wtrg.com/prices.htm (4/11/03); but see also Nitzan and Bichler, *Global Political Economy of Israel,* p. 230.
7. Jennifer Clapp, *Toxic Exports: The Transfer of Hazardous Wastes from Rich to Poor Countries* (Ithaca, N.Y.: Cornell University Press, 2001).
8. Norman Myers and Julian Simon, *Scarcity or Abundance? A Debate on the Environment* (New York: Norton, 1994).
9. Pearce and Turner, *Economics of Natural Resources,* chap. 19; Olli Tahvonen, "Economic Sustainability and Scarcity of Natural Resources: A Brief Historical Review" (Washington, D.C.: Resources for the Future, 2000), on-line at: http://www.rff.org/issue_briefs/PDF_files/tahvonen_naturalres.pdf (4/5/02).
10. Goudie, *Human Impact on the Natural Environment,* chap. 9.
11. Coase, "Problem of Social Cost."
12. Princen, Maniates, and Conca, *Confronting Consumption.*
13. Ibid.; E. F. Schumacher, *Small Is Beautiful: Economics as if People Mattered* (New York: Harper and Row, 1973).
14. U.S. Department of Commerce, Bureau of Economic Analysis, *National Income and Product Accounts Tables,* table 1.1, online at http://www.bea.gov/bea/dn/nipaweb/TableViewFixed.asp#Mid (5/23/03).
15. Data from the UN Development Programme, "Human Development Indicators," *Human Development Report 1999* (Oxford: Oxford University Press, 1988), table 12, online at http://www.undp.org/hdro/hdrs/1999/english/Backmatter2.pdf (4/16/03).
16. WRI, *World Resources 2000–2001,* table ERC.5.
17. Princen, Maniates, and Conca, *Confronting Consumption.*
18. Mark Sanford, "The 'Quail' Effect in Telemarketing: Notes on Emotional Labor" (paper presented at the Seventh International Conference on Culture and Communication, Philadelphia, Oct. 5, 1989), online at http://www.coldcalling.com/library/quail_effect.html (5/22/03).
19. Malcolm Gladwell, "The Science of Shopping," *New Yorker,* Nov. 1996, pp. 66–75.

20. Richard Bernstein and Ross H. Munro, *The Coming Conflict with China* (New York: Knopf, 1997).

21. Jim Puckett et al., "Exporting Harm: The High Tech Trashing of Asia," Basal Action Network and Silicon Valley Toxics Coalition, Feb. 25, 2002, online at http://www.svtc.org/cleancc/pubs/technotrash.pdf (7/15/02).

22. WCED, *Our Common Future.*

23. Bailey, "Foreign Direct Investment."

24. Ekins, "The Kuznets Curve"; Harbaugh, Levinson, and Wilson, "Reexamining the Empirical Evidence."

25. A more sophisticated discussion of the relationship between labor costs and profits can be found in Robert Pollin, Justine Burns, and James Heintz, "Global Apparel Production and Sweatshop Labor: Can Rising Retail Prices Finance Living Wages," Political Economy Research Institute, University of Massachusetts, Amherst, 2001 (revised 2002), online at http://www.umass.edu/peri/pdfs/WP19.pdf (4/11/03).

26. Princen, Maniates, and Conca, *Confronting Consumption;* Glazer and Glazer, *Environmental Crusaders;* Christopher Rootes, ed., *Environmental Movements: Local, National, and Global* (London: Frank Cass, 1999); Novotny, *Where We Live;* David N. Pellow, *Garbage Wars: The Struggle for Environmental Justice in Chicago* (Cambridge: MIT Press, 2002).

27. Pearce and Turner, *Economics of Natural Resources,* pp. 134–140, 148–153.

28. Ian J. Bateman and Kenneth G. Willis, eds., *Valuing Environmental Preferences: Theory and Practice of the Contingent Valuation Method in the U.S., EU, and Developing Countries* (Oxford: Oxford University Press, 1999).

29. See the Land Trust Alliance, "Millions of Acres Conserved by Voluntary Action," press release, Sept. 12, 2001, online at http://www.lta.org/newsroom/pr_091201.htm#success (4/11/03); Luke, *Ecocritique.*

30. Luke, *Ecocritique,* chap. 3.

31. Robert Costanza, et al., "The Value of the World's Ecosystem Services and Natural Capital," *Nature,* May 15, 1997, pp. 253–260.

32. See, for example, Nuffield Council on Bioethics, *Genetically Modified Crops: The Ethical and Social Issues,* May 1, 1999, chap. 3, online at http://www.nuffieldbioethics.org/publications/gmcrops/rep0000000179.asp (4/11/03).

33. See, for example, Mohan Wali, "Ecology Today: Beyond the Bounds of Science," *Nature and Resources,* June 1999, pp. 38–50.

34. Sanger Institute, "The Measure of Man," press release, Dec. 5, 2002, online at http://www.sanger.ac.U.K./Info/Press/2002/021205.shtml (4/11/03).

35. Lois Wingerson, *Unnatural Selection: The Promise and the Power of Human Gene Research* (New York: Bantam Books, 1998).

36. Locke, *Two Treatises of Government;* Kuehls, "The Environment of Sovereignty."

37. Markku Oksanen, "Privatising Genetic Resources: Biodiversity Preservation and Intellectual Property Rights" (paper presented at the Conference on

Environmental Justice, University of Melbourne, Australia, Oct. 1–3, 1997), online at http://www.arbld.unimelb.edu.au/envjust/papers/allpapers/oksanen/home.htm (7/17/02).

38. A. Agrawal, "Dismantling the Divide between Indigenous and Scientific Knowledge," *Development and Change* 26 (1995): 413–439; Crucible Group, *People, Plants, and Patents: The Impact of Intellectual Property on Trade, Plant Biodiversity, and Rural Society* (Sterling, Va.: Stylus, 1994).

39. Terry L. Anderson and Donald R. Leal, "Free Market versus Political Environmentalism," *Harvard Journal of Law and Public Policy* 15 (spring 1992): 297–310; Terry L. Anderson and Donald R. Leal, *Free Market Environmentalism Today* (New York: St. Martin's Press, 2001).

40. Elinor Ostrom, *Governing the Commons: The Evolution of Institutions for Collective Action* (Cambridge: Cambridge University Press, 1990), chap. 1.

41. Garrett Hardin, "The Tragedy of the Commons," *Science* 162 (Dec. 13, 1967): 1243–1248; see also Daniel W. Bromley, ed., *Making the Commons Work* (San Francisco: ICS Press, 1992).

42. Ostrom, *Governing the Commons;* Bromley, *Making the Commons Work.*

43. Pearce and Turner, *Economics of Natural Resources,* chap. 8; Alan Gilpin, *Environmental Economics: A Critical Overview* (Chichester, England: Wiley and Sons, 2000), pp. 154–156.

44. Altman, "Trading of Emissions."

45. See, for example, the Web site of the International Emissions Trading Association (IETA), 2002, online at www.ieta.org (7/22/02).

46. IPCC, *Climate Change 2001.*

47. Warwick J. McKibbin and Peter J. Wilcoxen, "Climate Change after Kyoto: A Blueprint for a Realistic Approach," *Brookings Review* 20 (spring 2002): 6–10.

48. Jan Aart Scholte, *Globalization: A Critical Introduction* (New York: St. Martin's Press, 2000).

49. Mark Rupert, *Producing Hegemony: The Politics of Mass Production and American Global Power* (Cambridge: Cambridge University Press, 1995); Ronnie D. Lipschutz, *After Authority: War, Peace, and Global Politics in the Twenty-first Century* (Albany: State University of New York Press, 2000).

50. Angus Maddison, *The World Economy: A Millennial Perspective* (Paris: Development Centre of the Organisation for Economic Co-operation and Development, 2001), pp. 173, 362, 175.

51. Joseph C. K. Yam, "Capital Flows, Hedge Funds, and Market Failure: A Hong Kong Perspective" (paper presented at the 1999 Reserve Bank of Australia Conference, "Capital Flows and the International Financial System") n. 1, online at http://www.rba.gov.au/PublicationsAndResearch/Conferences/1999/Yam.pdf (7/22/02).

52. Globalization latest in a process: Paul Hirst and Grahame Thompson, *Globalization in Question: The International Economy and the Possibilities of*

Governance, 2d ed. (Cambridge: Polity Press, 1999); globalization began about 1500: Scholte, *Globalization,* chap. 3.

53. Rupert, *Producing Hegemony;* Mark Rupert, *Ideologies of Globalization: Contending Visions of a New World Order* (London: Routledge, 2000).

54. Jeffrey Leonard, *Pollution and the Struggle for the World Product: Multinational Corporations, Environment, and International Comparative Advantage* (Cambridge: Cambridge University Press, 1988); M. Mani and D. Wheeler, "In Search of Pollution Havens? Dirty Industries in the World Economy, 1960–1995," World Bank Policy Research Department, Environment, Infrastructure and Agriculture Division, Poverty, Environment, and Growth working paper no. 16, Apr. 1997, online at http://www.worldbank.org/research/peg/wps16/index.htm (4/12/02).

55. UN Environment Programme (UNEP), "The State of the Environment—Asia and the Pacific, Social and Economic Background," *Global Environmental Outlook 2000* (Nairobi, Kenya: UNEP/Earthscan, 1999), online at http://www.unep.org/geo2000/english/0063.htm (4/15/02).

56. Gary Gereffi and Olga Memedovic, "The Global Apparel Value Chain: What Prospects for Upgrading by Developing Countries?" (Vienna: UNIDO, 2003), online at http://www.ids.ac.U.K./globalvaluechains/publications/ApparelUNIDOnew2Feb03.pdf (4/11/03).

57. Barry Commoner, *The Closing Circle: Nature, Man, and Technology* (New York: Knopf, 1971).

58. Benjamin Cashore, "What Should Canada Do When the Softwood Lumber Agreement Expires?" Policy.ca (a Web site devoted to Canadian policy issues), Apr. 20, 2001, online at http://www.policy.ca/PDF/20010205.pdf (4/16/02).

59. A. K. Thompson, *Post-harvest Technology of Fruit and Vegetables* (Oxford: Blackwell Science, 1996).

60. Piers Blaikie and Harold Brookfield, *Land Degradation and Society* (London: Methuen, 1987); Rod Burgess, Marisa Carmona, and Theo Kolstee, eds., *The Challenge of Sustainable Cities: Neoliberalism and Urban Strategies in Developing Countries* (London: Zed Books, 1997).

61. Iddo K. Wernick, Robert Herman, Shekhar Govind, and Jesse H. Ausubel, "Materialization and Dematerialization: Measures and Trends," *Daedalus* 125 (summer 1996): 171–198.

62. Wade, "Rising Inequality"; see also Global Policy Forum, "Inequality of Wealth and Income Distribution," online at http://www.globalpolicy.org/socecon/inequal/indexinq.htm (4/11/03).

63. David A. Sonnenfeld, "Greening the Tiger? Social Movements' Influence on Adoption of Environmental Technologies in the Pulp and Paper Industries of Australia, Indonesia, and Thailand" (Ph.D. diss., University of California, Santa Cruz, 1996).

64. Mol, *Globalization and Environmental Reform;* David A. Sonnenfeld and Arthur P. J. Mol, "Globalization, Governance, and the Environment," *American Behavioral Scientist* 45, special issue (May 2002).

65. Ulrich Beck, *Ecological Politics in an Age of Risk* (Cambridge, Mass.: Blackwell, Polity Press, 1995); Maarten Hajer, *The Politics of Environmental Discourse: Ecological Modernization and the Policy Process* (Oxford: Clarendon Press, 1995).
66. Ken Conca, "Consumption and Environment in a Global Economy," *Global Environmental Politics* 1 (Aug. 2001): 55.
67. Sen, *Development as Freedom.*

Chapter 4. Civic Politics and Social Power: Environmental Politics "On the Ground"

1. Lipschutz and Conca, *The State and Social Power.*
2. Lipschutz, "Environmental History"; Doreen Massey, "Places and Their Pasts," *History Workshop Journal,* no. 39 (1995): 182–192; Denis Cosgrove, "Geography Is Everywhere: Culture and Symbolism in Human Landscapes," in *Horizons in Human Geography,* ed. Derek R. Gregory and Rex Walford (London: Macmillan, 1985), pp. 118–135.
3. Alejandro Colas, *International Civil Society: Social Movements in World Politics* (Cambridge, Mass.: Blackwell, Polity Press, 2002).
4. Robert Putnam, *Bowling Alone: The Collapse and Revival of American Community* (New York: Simon and Schuster, 2000).
5. Lipschutz, with Mayer, *Global Civil Society.*
6. Lipschutz, "Environmental History."
7. Karl Marx, Capital, vol. 1, *The Process of Production of Capital,* chap. 7, online at http://csf.colorado.edu/psn/marx/Archive/1867-C1/Part3/ch07.htm#S1 (2/22/03).
8. H. H. Gerth and C. Wright Mills, *From Max Weber: Essays in Sociology* (New York: Oxford University Press, 1946), p. 200.
9. Karl Marx, *The 18th Brumaire of Louis Napoleon* (1852; New York: International Publishers, 1963), chap. 1.
10. William Cronon, *Nature's Metropolis: Chicago and the Great West* (New York: Norton, 1991).
11. David E. Nye, ed., *Technologies of Landscapes: From Reaping to Recycling* (Amherst: University of Massachusetts Press, 1999).
12. O'Connor, "Three Ways to Look at the Ecological History."
13. Malcolm Margolin, *The Ohlone Way: Indian Life in the San Francisco-Monterey Bay Area* (Berkeley, Calif.: Heyday Books, 1978).
14. Rice Odell, *The Saving of the San Francisco Bay* (Washington, D.C.: Conservation Foundation, 1972); Jane Kay, "Reclaiming the Bay," *San Francisco Chronicle,* April 6, 2003, p. A12.
15. Thomas Dunlap, *Nature and the English Diaspora* (Cambridge: Cambridge University Press, 1999).
16. O'Conner, "Three Ways to Look at the Ecological History."
17. Robert Elliot, *Faking Nature: The Ethics of Environmental Restoration* (London: Routledge, 1997).

18. Lipschutz, with Mayer, *Global Civil Society,* chap. 4.

19. Jack M. Hollander, *The Real Environmental Crisis: Why Poverty, Not Afflu-ence, Is the Environment's Number One Enemy* (Berkeley: University of California Press, 2003).

20. James C. Scott, *Seeing Like a State: How Certain Schemes to Improve the Human Condition Have Failed* (New Haven, Conn.: Yale University Press, 1998).

21. Piers Blaikie, *The Political Economy of Soil Erosion in Developing Countries* (New York: Wiley, 1985); Blaikie and Brookfield, *Land Degradation.*

22. Johan Galtung, *Human Rights in Another Key* (Cambridge, Mass.: Blackwell, Polity Press, 1995), chap. 2.

23. Lipschutz, with Mayer, *Global Civil Society,* pp. 242–245; John Agnew, "Representing Space: Space, Scale, and Culture in Social Science," in *Place/Culture/Representation,* ed. James Duncan and David Ley (London: Routledge, 1993), pp. 251–271, 262.

24. Olson, *Logic of Collective Action;* Ostrom, *Governing the Commons.*

25. Jean Jacques Rousseau, *The Social Contract and Discourses,* trans. G. D. H. Cole (1762; New York: Dutton, 1950), p. 238.

26. Olson, *Logic of Collective Action;* Kenneth Waltz, *Man, the State, and War* (New York: Columbia University Press, 1959).

27. Emma Rothschild, *Economic Sentiments,* chap. 5.

28. Smith, *Theory of Moral Sentiments;* Hirsch, *Social Limits to Growth.*

29. Ophuls and Boyan, *Ecology and the Politics of Scarcity Revisited;* Heilbroner, *An Inquiry into the Human Prospect.*

30. Susan J. B. Buck, "No Tragedy on the Commons," *Environmental Ethics* 7 (spring 1985): 49–61; David Feeny, Fikret Berkes, Bonnie J. McCay, and James M. Acheson, "The Tragedy of the Commons: Twenty-Two Years Later," *Human Ecology* 18 (1990): 1–19.

31. Ostrom, *Governing the Commons;* Bromley, *Making the Commons Work.*

32. Philippe Fontaine, "Who Is Afraid of the Past? Economic Theorists and Historians of Economics on Altruism," *History of Economics,* Oct. 19, 1998, online at http://www.eh.net/lists/archives/hes/oct-1998/0021.php (4/11/03).

33. Michel Crozier, Samuel P. Huntington, and Joji Watanuki, *The Crisis of Democracy: Report on the Governability of Democracies to the Trilateral Commission* (New York: New York University Press, 1975); Samuel P. Huntington, *American Politics: The Promise of Disharmony* (Cambridge: Harvard University Press, Belknap Press, 1981).

34. Avner de-Shalit, *Why Posterity Matters: Environmental Policies and Future Generations* (London: Routledge, 1995); Edith Brown Weiss, *In Fairness to Future Generations: International Law, Common Patrimony, and Intergenerational Equity* (Dobbs Ferry, N.Y.: Transnational, 1989).

35. Thomas Princen, "Consumption and Its Externalities: Where Economy Meets Ecology," *Global Environmental Politics* 1 (Aug. 2001): 19.

36. Carolyn Raffensperger and Joel A. Tickner, *Protecting Public Health and the Environment: Implementing the Precautionary Principle* (Washington,

D.C.: Island Press, 1999); Tim O'Riordan, James Cameron, and Andrew Jordan, eds., *Reinterpreting the Precautionary Principle* (London: Cameron May, 2001).

37. This, in essence, is the argument presented in John McMurtry, *Value Wars: The Global Market versus the Life Economy* (London: Zed Books, 2002).

38. James Coleman, *Foundations of Social Theory* (Cambridge: Harvard University Press, Belknap Press 1990), p. 242.

39. Magnusson and Shaw, *A Political Space.*

40. Stone, *Should Trees Have Standing?*

41. Karl Marx, *The German Ideology* (London: Lawrence and Wishart, 1938).

42. Justin Rosenberg, *The Empire of Civil Society* (London: Verso, 1994).

43. Stanley I. Benn and Gerald F. Gaus, "The Liberal Conception of the Public and the Private," in *Public and Private in Social Life*, ed. Stanley I. Benn and Gerald F. Gaus (London: Croom Helm, 1983), pp. 31–66.

44. Rosenberg, *Empire of Civil Society*, chap. 5.

45. Carole Pateman, "Feminist Critiques of the Public/Private Dichotomy," in Benn and Gaus, *Public and Private in Social Life*, pp. 281–303.

46. Ibid.

47. Colas, *International Civil Society.*

48. Crozier, Huntington, and Watanuki, *The Crisis of Democracy*; Huntington, *American Politics.*

49. Bourgeois activity: Karl Marx, "On the Jewish Question," in *Karl Marx and Frederich Engels: Collected Works*, vol. 3, *Marx and Engels: 1843–1844* (1844; London: Lawrence and Wishart, 1975). Central to public polities: Hegel, *The Philosophy of History*; Putnam, *Bowling Alone.*

50. Colas, *International Civil Society.*

51. Ronnie D. Lipschutz, "Reconstructing World Politics: The Emergence of Global Civil Society," *Millennium* 21 (winter 1992/93): 389–420; Helmut Anheier, Marlies Glasius, and Mary Kaldor, eds., *Global Civil Society, 2001* (Oxford: Oxford University Press, 2001).

52. Sidney Tarrow, *Power in Movement: Social Movements and Contentious Politics*, 2d ed. (Cambridge: Cambridge University Press, 1998); Doug McAdam, John D. McCarthy, and Meyer N. Zald, *Comparative Perspectives on Social Movements: Political Opportunities, Mobilizing Structures, and Cultural Framings* (Cambridge: Cambridge University Press, 1996).

53. Timothy W. Luke, "On the Political Economy of Clayoquot Sound: The Uneasy Transition from Extractive to Attractive Models of Development," in Magnusson and Shaw, *A Political Space*, pp. 91–112.

54. Ronnie D. Lipschutz, "The Environment and Global Governance," in *Global Governance in the Twenty-First Century*, ed. J. N. Clarke and G. R. Edwards (Basingstoke, England: Macmillan, in press).

55. Samuel P. Hays, *Beauty, Health, and Permanence: Environmental Politics in the United States, 1955–1985* (Cambridge: Cambridge University Press,

1987); Linda Lear, *Rachel Carson: Witness for Nature* (New York: Henry Holt, 1997).

56. Gerard J. DeGroot, ed., *Student Protest: The Sixties and After* (London: Longman, 1998).

57. Victor Cohn, *1999: Our Hopeful Future* (Indianapolis: Bobbs-Merrill, 1956).

58. See, for example, Harrison Brown, *The Challenge of Man's Future* (New York: Viking, 1954).

59. Lear, *Rachel Carson.*

60. Tarrow, *Power in Movement.*

61. Chris Harman, *The Fire Last Time: 1968 and After,* 2d ed. (London: Bookmarks, 1998); Barbara Ehrenreich and John Ehrenreich, *Long March, Short Spring: The Student Uprising at Home and Abroad* (New York: Monthly Review Press, 1969).

62. Lipschutz, *After Authority.*

63. Lipschutz, with Mayer, *Global Civil Society,* chap. 5; Fred Rose, *Coalitions across the Class Divide: Lessons from the Labor, Peace, and Environmental Movements* (Ithaca, N.Y.: Cornell University Press, 2000); Jane I. Dawson, *Eco-Nationalism: Anti-Nuclear Activism and National Identity in Russia, Lithuania, and Ukraine* (Durham, N.C.: Duke University Press, 1996).

64. Richard Howitt, *Rethinking Resource Management: Justice, Sustainability, and Indigenous Peoples* (London: Routledge, 2001).

65. Ronald Inglehart, *Culture Shift in Advanced Industrial Society* (Princeton, N.J.: Princeton University Press, 1990).

66. Manuel Castells, *The Rise of the Network Society* (Cambridge, Mass.: Blackwell, 1996).

67. Luke, *Ecocritique;* Marx, *The German Ideology.*

68. Brian Milani, *Designing the Green Economy: The Postindustrial Alternative to Corporate Globalization* (Lanham, Md.: Rowman and Littlefield, 2000), chap. 11.

69. Joel Makower, "Consumer Power," in *Our Future, Our Environment,* ed. Noreen Clancy and David Rajeski, issue paper 207 (Arlington, Va.: RAND, 2001), chap. 4, at: http://www.rand.org/scitech/stpi/ourfuture/ (4/15/03).

70. Julie H. Guthman, "Agrarian Dreams? The Paradox of Organic Farming in California" (Ph.D. diss., University of California, Berkeley, 2000); Catherine R. Greene, "U.S. Organic Farming Emerges in the 1990s: Adoption of Certified Systems," Agriculture information bulletin no. 770, U.S. Dept. of Agriculture, Economic Research Service, Washington, D.C., 2001.

71. Tarrow, *Power in Movement.*

72. George Soros, *Open Society: Reforming Global Capitalism* (New York: Public Affairs, 2000); Stiglitz, *Globalization.*

73. Anheier, Glasius, and Kaldor, *Global Civil Society 2001;* Marlies Glasius, Mary Kaldor, and Helmut Anheier, eds., *Global Civil Society 2002* (Oxford: Oxford University Press, 2002).

74. Susan Strange, *The Retreat of the State* (Cambridge: Cambridge University Press, 1996); Mishra, *Globalization and the Welfare State.*

75. Friedman, *The Lexus and the Olive Tree.*

76. Louis W. Pauly, *Who Elected the Bankers? Surveillance and Control in the World Economy* (Ithaca, N.Y.: Cornell University Press, 1997).

77. Lloyd Gruber, *Ruling the World: Power Politics and the Rise of Supranational Institutions* (Princeton, N.J.: Princeton University Press, 2000).

78. Ronnie D. Lipschutz, "Doing Well by Doing Good? Transnational Regulatory Campaigns, Social Activism, and Impacts on State Sovereignty," in *Challenges to Sovereignty: How Governments Respond,* ed. John Montgomery and Nathan Glazer (New Brunswick, N.J.: Transaction, 2002), pp. 291–320.

79. Russell J. Dalton, *The Green Rainbow: Environmental Groups in Western Europe* (New Haven, Conn.: Yale University Press, 1994); Wolfgang Rüdig, ed., *Green Politics Two* (Edinburgh: Edinburgh University Press, 1992).

80. Fritjof Capra and Charlene Spretnak, *Green Politics: The Global Promise* (New York: Dutton, 1984).

81. Elizabeth Bomberg, *Green Parties and Politics in the European Union* (London: Routledge, 1998).

82. Ibid.

83. "Green Achievements in Europe," online at http://www.tonycooper.ndtilda.co.U.K./GPNW/achieves.htm (1/21/03).

84. "Green Party Election Results," see online at http://www.greens.org/elections/ (1/21/03).

85. Lipschutz, with Mayer, *Global Civil Society.*

86. Norman Long and Ann Long, eds., *Battlefields of Knowledge: The Interlocking of Theory and Practice in Social Research and Development* (London: Routledge, 1992).

87. Colas, *International Civil Society;* Walter L. Adamson, *Hegemony and Revolution: A Study of Antonio Gramsci's Political and Cultural Theory* (Berkeley: University of California Press, 1980).

88. Robert Cox, *Production, Power, and World Order* (New York: Columbia University Press, 1987); Rosenberg, *Empire of Civil Society.*

89. Wade, "Rising Inequality."

90. G. William Domhoff, *Who Rules America? Power and Politics,* 4th ed. (Boston: McGraw-Hill, 2002); Thomas R. Dye, *Who's Running America? The Bush Restoration,* 7th ed. (Upper Saddle River, N.J.: Prentice Hall, 2002).

91. Marshall Berman, *All That Is Solid Melts into Air: The Experience of Modernity* (New York: Simon and Schuster, 1982).

92. Hans-Peter Martin and Harald Schumann, *The Global Trap: Globalization and the Assault on Democracy and Prosperity,* trans. P. Camillar (London: Zed Books, 1997); Stiglitz, *Globalization.*

93. Stiglitz, *Globalization;* Sen, *Development as Freedom;* Jagdish Bhagwati, *Free Trade Today* (Princeton, N.J.: Princeton University Press, 2002).

94. Jonathan A. Fox and L. David Brown, eds., *The Struggle for Accountability: The World Bank, NGOs, and Grassroots Movements* (Cambridge: MIT Press, 1998).

95. Margaret Keck and Kathryn Sikkink, *Activists beyond Borders: Advocacy Networks in International Politics* (Ithaca, N.Y.: Cornell University Press, 1998).

96. Stephen J. Kobrin, "The MAI and the Clash of Globalizations," *Foreign Policy,* fall 1998, online at http://www.foreignpolicy.com/best_of_fp/articles/kobrin.html (4/8/03).

97. Ronnie D. Lipschutz, "The Clash of Governmentalities: The Fall of the UN Republic and America's Reach for Imperium," *Contemporary Security Policy* 23, no. 3 Dec. 2002: 214–231.

98. Lipschutz, with Mayer, *Global Civil Society,* chaps. 4–5; see also the Web sites of The River Network, www.therivernetwork.org; International Rivers Network, www.irn.org; Global Rivers Environmental Education Network, www.green.org.

99. The River Network, *National Directory of River and Watershed Conservation Groups,* online at http://www.therivernetwork.org/library/libnetdir.cfm (3/15/03).

100. Magnusson and Shaw, *A Political Space.*

101. Lipschutz, with Mayer, *Global Civil Society,* p. 220.

102. Much of the following comes from ibid., pp. 114–117. Citations to the original sources can be found there. Additional information comes from the Web site of the Mattole Restoration Council, at: http://www.mattole.org/index.html (1/22/03).

103. Barry Laffan, *Communal Organization and Social Transition: A Case Study from the Counterculture of the Sixties and Seventies* (New York: Lang, 1997).

104. See Roger LeRoy Miller, "Can Hemp Cultivation Be Stopped?" *California Economic Case Studies,* case study no. 14, 2001, pp. 14-1–14-3, online at http://occawlonline.pearsoned.com/bookbind/pubbooks/miller2001_awl/medialib/download/ca/ca14.html (4/8/03).

105. Bonnie Glantz, "A Failed Alliance," *North Coast Journal,* Jan. 1995, online at http://www.northcoastjournal.com/jan95/ALLIANCE.HTM (1/22/03).

106. The Middle Mattole Conservancy, online at http://www.treesfoundation.org/html/affiliates_specific_26.html; Sanctuary Forest, online at http://www.mtnvisions.com/Aurora/sancfrst.html; and the Mill Creek Watershed Conservancy, online at http://www.treesfoundation.org/html/affiliates_specific_27.html (1/22/03).

107. Daniel Faber, ed., *The Struggle for Ecological Democracy: Environmental Justice Movements in the United States* (New York: Guilford Press, 1998).

108. Christopher H. Foreman, *The Promise and Peril of Environmental Justice* (Washington, D.C.: Brookings Institution Press, 1998).

109. Guy Standing, *Global Labour Flexibility: Seeking Distributive Justice* (Basingstoke, England: Macmillan, 1999); Ann P. Bartel, "The Migration Decision: What Role Does Job Mobility Play?" *American Economic Review* 69 (1979): 775–786.

110. Andrew Szasz, *Ecopopulism: Toxic Waste and the Movement for Environmental Justice* (Minneapolis: University of Minnesota Press, 1994), pp. 42–44.

111. Ibid.

112. Clapp, *Toxic Exports.*

113. Mol, *Globalization and Environmental Reform.*

114. Ronnie D. Lipschutz, "Sweating It Out: NGO Campaigns and Trade Union Empowerment," *Development in Practice* (forthcoming). Virginia Haufler, *A Public Role for the Private Sector: Industry Self-Regulation in a Global Economy* (Washington, D.C.: Carnegie Endowment for International Peace, 2001); Aseem Prakash, *Greening the Firm: The Politics of Corporate Environmentalism* (Cambridge: Cambridge University Press, 2000); Ronie Garcia-Johnson, *Exporting Environmentalism: U.S. Multinational Chemical Corporations in Brazil and Mexico* (Cambridge: MIT Press, 2000).

115. Lipschutz, "Doing Well by Doing Good?"; Lipschutz, "The Clash of Governmentalities."

116. Leonard, *Pollution and the Struggle for the World Product;* Mani and Wheeler, "In Search of Pollution Havens?"

117. Edna Bonacich and Richard Appelbaum, *Behind the Label: Inequality in the Los Angeles Apparel Industry* (Berkeley: University of California Press, 2000).

118. Haufler, *Public Role for the Private Sector.*

119. Joseph Cascio, Gayle Woodside, and Philip Mitchell, *ISO 14000 Guide: The New International Environmental Management Standards* (New York: McGraw-Hill, 1996); Clapp, *Toxic Exports,* chap. 6.

120. John G. Ruggie, "The Theory and Practice of Learning Networks: Corporate Social Responsibility and the Global Compact," *Journal of Corporate Citizenship* 5 (spring 2002): 27–36.

121. Leslie Rockenbach, *The Mexican-American Border: NAFTA and Global Linkages* (New York: Routledge, 2001).

122. Rachel Kamel and Anya Hoffman, eds., *The Maquiladora Reader: Cross-border Organizing Since NAFTA* (Philadelphia: Mexico–U.S. Border Program, American Friends Service Committee, 1999).

123. Joseph DiMento and Patricia Doughman, "Soft Teeth in the Back of the Mouth: The NAFTA Environmental Side Agreement Implemented," *Georgetown International Environmental Law Review* 10 (spring 1998): 651–752.

124. Altha Cravey, *Women and Work in Mexico's Maquiladoras* (Lanham, Md.: Rowman and Littlefield, 1998).; U.S. General Accounting Office (GAO),

U.S.-Mexico Border: Despite Some Progress, Environmental Infrastructure Challenges Remain (Washington, D.C.: U.S. Government Printing Office, 2000); see also *Border EcoWeb,* online at http://www.borderecoweb.sdsu.edu/main.htm.

125. Haufler, *Public Role for the Private Sector;* Karl Schoenberger, *Levi's Children: Coming to Terms with Human Rights in the Global Marketplace* (New York: Atlantic Monthly Press, 2000).

126. Ruth Pearson and Gill Seyfang, "New Hope or False Dawn? Voluntary Codes of Conduct, Labour Regulation, and Social Policy in a Globalising World," *Global Social Policy* 1 (Apr. 2001): 49–78.

127. Lipschutz, "Sweating It Out."

128. John Heilprin, "EPA Eases Clean Air Requirements on Power Plants," *Washington Post,* Nov. 22, 2002.

129. Anil Markandya, "Eco-Labeling: An Introduction and Review," in *Eco-Labelling and International Trade,* ed. Simonetta Zarrilli, Veena Jha and René Vossenaar, (Basingstoke, England: Macmillan, 1997), pp. 1–20; Ronnie D. Lipschutz, "Why Is There No International Forestry Law? An Examination of International Forestry Regulation, Both Public and Private," *UCLA Journal of Environmental Law and Policy* 19 (2001): 155–182.

130. Cascio, Woodside, and Mitchell, *ISO 14000 Guide.*

131. Sophie Higman et al., *The Sustainable Forestry Handbook* (London: Earthscan, 1999).

132. Pearson and Seyfang, "New Hope or False Dawn?"

133. Greene, "U.S. Organic Farming."

134. See the Web site of Pest Management at the Crossroads, "Discussion on USDA's Rule Implementing the National Organic Farming Act of 1990," online at http://www.pmac.net/nosrule3.htm (4/15/03).

135. Raffensperger and Tickner, *Protecting Public Health;* O'Riordan, Cameron, and Jordan, *Reinterpreting the Precautionary Principle.*

136. Archon Fung, Dana O'Rourke, and Charles Sabel, "Realizing Labor Standards: How Transparency, Competition, and Sanctions Could Improve Working Conditions Worldwide," *Boston Review* 26, (Feb./Mar. 2001), online at http://bostonreview.mit.edu/BR26.1/fung.html (7/15/02).

137. Bonacich and Appelbaum, *Behind the Label;* Lipschutz, "Clash of Governmentalities."

138. DiMento and Doughman, "Soft Teeth."

139. Keck and Sikkink, *Activists beyond Borders;* Paul Wapner, *Environmental Activism and World Civic Politics* (Albany: State University of New York Press, 1996); Jackie Smith and Hank Johnston, eds., *Globalization and Resistance: Transnational Dimensions of Social Movements* (Lanham, Md.: Rowman and Littlefield, 2002).

140. Lipschutz, with Mayer, *Global Civil Society,* chap. 7; Patrick Novotny, *Where We Live.*

Chapter 5. The National Origins of International Environmental Policies and Practices: "My Country Is *in* the World"

1. Porter, Brown, and Chasek, *Global Environmental Politics.*
2. Lipschutz, *When Nations Clash.*
3. The locus classicus for this definition is found in Krasner, *International Regimes.*
4. See, for example, Young, *International Governance;* Robert O. Keohane and Mark A. Levy, eds., *Institutions for Environmental Aid: Pitfalls and Promise* (Cambridge: MIT Press, 1996).
5. Robert O. Keohane, *International Institutions and State Power: Essays in International Relations Theory,* pp. 1–20 (Boulder, Colo.: Westview Press, 1989).
6. Krasner, *International Regimes,* p. 1.
7. Hedley Bull, *The Anarchical Society* (New York: Columbia University Press, 1977).
8. Robert L. Friedheim, *Toward a Sustainable Whaling Regime* (Seattle: University of Washington Press, 2001); M. J. Peterson, "Whales, Cetologists, Environmentalists, and the International Management of Whaling," *International Organization* 46 (winter 1992): 187–224.
9. See, for example, Peter Larkin, "An Epitaph for the Concept of Maximum Sustained Yield," *Transactions of the American Fisheries Society* 106 (1977): 1–11; Marc Mangell, Baldo Marinovic, Caroline Pomeroy, and Donald Croll, "Requiem for Ricker: Unpacking MSY," *Bulletin of Marine Science* 70 (2002): 763–81, online at http://bonita.mbnms.nos.noaa.gov/research/techreports/ucsc/mangeltr.pdf (4/15/03).
10. William T. Burke, *The New International Law of Fisheries: UNCLOS 1982 and Beyond* (Oxford: Clarendon Press, 1994).
11. Anderson and Leal, "Free Market versus Political Environmentalism;" Anderson and Leal, *Free Market Environmentalism Today.*
12. Mishra, *Globalization and the Welfare State;* Cerny, "Structuring the Political Arena."
13. Rupert, *Producing Hegemony;* Friedman, *The Lexus and the Olive Tree.*
14. Rosenberg, *Empire of Civil Society;* Liah Greenfeld, *The Spirit of Capitalism: Nationalism and Economic Growth* (Cambridge: Harvard University Press, 2001).
15. Scott, *Seeing Like a State;* Peter A. Hall and David Soskice, eds., *Varieties of Capitalism: The Institutional Foundations of Comparative Advantage* (Oxford: Oxford University Press, 2001).
16. Benedict Anderson, *Imagined Communities: Reflections on the Origins and Spread of Nationalism,* rev. ed. (London: Verso, 1991); Gellner, *Nations and Nationalism;* Hobsbawm, *Nations and Nationalism since 1780.*
17. David A. Lake and Donald S. Rothchild, eds., *The International Spread of Ethnic Conflict: Fear, Diffusion, and Escalation* (Princeton, N.J.: Princeton

University Press, 1987); Beverly Crawford and Ronnie D. Lipschutz, eds., *The Myth of "Ethnic Conflict": Politics, Economics, and "Cultural" Violence* (Berkeley: University of California, Berkeley; International and Area Studies Press, 1987).

18. Lipschutz, *When Nations Clash.*
19. O'Connor, "Three Ways to Look at the Ecological History"; Lipschutz, with Mayer, *Global Civil Society,* chap. 5; Lipschutz, "Environmental History."
20. Jones, *The European Miracle.*
21. Greenfeld, *The Spirit of Capitalism.*
22. Mann, *Sources of Social Power,* vol. 2, chap. 2.
23. Anderson, *Imagined Communities.*
24. Lipschutz, "Why Is There No International Forestry Law?"
25. Dunlap, *Nature and the English Diaspora.*
26. Cerny, "Structuring the Political Arena."
27. Mishra, *Globalization and the Welfare State;* Strange, *Retreat of the State;* Steven K. Vogel, *Freer Markets, More Rules: Regulatory Reform in Advanced Industrial Countries* (Ithaca, N.Y.: Cornell University Press, 1996).
28. Bernstein, *Compromise of Liberal Environmentalism.*
29. Sen, *Development as Freedom.*
30. Anatole France, *Le Lys Rouge* (1894); trans. as *The Red Lily* (New York: Current Literature, 1910), p. 87.
31. Gaventa, *Power and Powerlessness.*
32. Harold D. Lasswell, *Politics: Who Gets What, When, How* (New York: P. Smith, 1936).
33. Louis Hartz, *The Liberal Tradition in America* (New York: Harcourt Brace, 1955), part 6.
34. Hirsch, *Social Limits to Growth.*
35. Ibid.; Daly, *Steady-State Economics.*
36. David E. Camacho, ed., *Environmental Injustices, Political Struggles: Race, Class, and the Environment* (Durham, N.C.: Duke University Press, 1998).
37. David M. Roodman, *The Natural Wealth of Nations: Harnessing the Market for the Environment* (New York: Norton, 1998).
38. Black, *Development in Theory and Practice.*
39. Johannesburg Summit 2002, online at http://www.johannesburgsummit.org/ (4/11/03).
40. Peter Gleick, *The World's Water, 2000–2001* (Washington, D.C.: Island Press, 2000).
41. World Health Organization (WHO), *Global Water Supply and Sanitation 2000: Assessment Report* (New York: United Nations, 2001), sec. 1.1, online at http://www.who.int/water_sanitation_health/Globassessment/Global-TOC.htm (7/25/02).

42. Melissa Master, "Water: Just Another Commodity?" *Across the Board*, July 2002, The Conference Board, online at http://www.conference-board.org/publications/atb/articles/masterJul02_05.cfm (2/19/03).

43. Water revenues: ibid. Number of people and countries: Brad Knickerbocker, "Privatizing Water: A Glass Half-Empty?" *Christian Science Monitor*, Oct. 24, 2002, online at http://www.csmonitor.com/2002/1024/p01s02-usec.html (2/19/03).

44. Peter Gleick et al., "The New Economy of Water: The Risks and Benefits of Globalization and Privatization of Fresh Water" (Oakland, Calif: Pacific Institute, 2002), online at http://www.pacinst.org/reports/new_economy_of_water_low_res.pdf (2/19/03).

45. Karl Wittfogel, *Oriental Despotism: A Comparative Study of Total Power* (New Haven, Conn.: Yale University Press, 1957); Donald Worster, *Rivers of Empire: Water, Aridity, and the Growth of the American West* (New York: Pantheon, 1985); Mark Reisner, *Cadillac Desert: The American West and Its Disappearing Water* (New York: Viking, 1986).

46. Michael Wood, *Legacy: The Search for Ancient Civilization* (New York: Sterling, 1995).

47. Worster, *Rivers of Empire*; Scott, *Seeing Like a State*.

48. Nick Middleton, *The Global Casino: An Introduction to Environmental Issues* (London: Hodder Arnold, 1999), chap. 9.

49. Sandra Postel, *Last Oasis: Facing Water Scarcity* (New York: Norton, 1997).

50. James Witt, "Remarks at Project Impact Summit," Washington, D.C., Dec. 13, 1999, online at http://www.fema.gov/library/jlw121399.shtm (7/25/02).

51. Postel, *Last Oasis*.

52. Colin Green, "Who Pays the Piper? Who Calls the Tune?" *UNESCO Courier*, Feb. 1999, pp. 22–24.

53. Zach Willey and Adam Diamant, "Water Marketing in the Northwest: Learning by Doing," *Water Strategist* 10 (summer 1996).

54. Emanuele Lobina, "Cochabamba: Water War," Public Services International Research Unit, University of Greenwich, online at http://www.psiru.org/reports/Cochabamba.doc (2/19/03).

55. Ibid.

56. Jim Schultz, "Bolivia's War over Water," Democracy Center, 2000, online at http://www.democracyctr.org/waterwar/index.htm (5/14/02).

57. Lobina, "Cochabamba."

58. Unchanged situation: Jennifer Hattam, "Who Owns Water?" *Sierra* 86 (Sept. 2001), online at http://www.sierraclub.org/sierra/200109/lol1.asp. Aguas lawsuit: Center for International Environmental Law, "Secretive World Bank Tribunal Bans Public and Media Participation in Bechtel Lawsuit over Access to Water," Feb. 12, 2003, online at http://www.ciel.org/Ifi/Bechtel_Lawsuit_12Feb03.html (2/19/03).

59. Goudie, *Human Impact on the Natural Environment,* p. 204.

60. Fogel, "Greening the Earth with Trees." Susanna Hecht and Alexander Cockburn, *The Fate of the Forest: Developers, Destroyers, and Defenders of the Amazon* (New York: HarperCollins, 1990).

61. Victor Menotti, "Forest Destruction and Globalisation," *Ecologist* 29 (May–June 1999): 180–181.

62. See ITTO (International Tropical Timber Organisation) Secretariat, "Reduced Impacts, Increased Costs?" *ITTO Newsletter* 6, no. 3 (1996), online at http://www.itto.or.jp/newsletter/v6n3/section1.html#p2 (2/19/03).

63. Lipschutz, "Why Is There No International Forestry Law?"

64. Scott, *Seeing Like a State,* p. 14.

65. See, for example, Richard H. Grove, *Green Imperialism: Colonial Expansion, Tropical Island Edens, and the Origins of Environmentalism, 1600–1860* (Cambridge: Cambridge University Press, 1995); Guha, *The Unquiet Woods.*

66. Grove, *Green Imperialism,* chap. 3.

67. Scott, *Seeing Like a State,* pp. 19–20.

68. Ibid., pp. 11–12.

69. Magnusson and Shaw, *A Political Space.*

70. Guha, *The Unquiet Woods.*

71. Glenn Martin, "California's Rural Economy: Boom Times Long Gone, a Small Town Struggles for Survival," *San Francisco Chronicle,* Mar. 24, 2003, online at http://www.sfgate.com/cgi-bin/article.cgi?file=/chronicle/archive/2003/03/24/MN198336.DTL (3/25/03).

72. See, for example, Scott, *Seeing Like a State,* p. 20.

73. N. Patrick Peritore, *Third World Environmentalism: Case Studies from the Global South* (Gainesville: University Press of Florida, 1999), chap. 4.

74. Madhav Gadgil and Ramachandra Guha, *This Fissured Land: An Ecological History of India* (Berkeley: University of California Press, 1993).

75. Guha, *The Unquiet Woods.*

76. Peritore, *Third World Environmentalism,* p. 71.

77. O. P. Dwivedi, *India's Environmental Policies, Programmes, and Stewardship* (Basingstoke, England: Macmillan, 1997), p. 91.

78. Ibid., p. 92; Peritore, *Third World Environmentalism,* p. 69.

79. Thomas Weber, *Hugging the Trees: The Story of the Chipko Movement* (New York: Viking, 1988); Guha, *The Unquiet Woods.*

80. Guha, *The Unquiet Woods,* Epilogue.

81. Ibid., pp. 201–202.

82. Ronnie D. Lipschutz, "Global Civil Society and Global Environmental Protection: Private Initiatives and Public Goods," in *Evaluating Alternative Policy Instruments for Environmental Protection,* ed. Michael Hatch (Albany: State University of New York Press, forthcoming); Lipschutz, "Why Is There No International Forestry Law?"

83. David Goodman and Anthony Hall, eds., *The Future of Amazonia* (New York: St. Martin's Press, 1990).

84. International Institute for Sustainable Development (IISD), "Intergovernmental Working Group on Forests," online at http://www.iisd.ca/linkages/forestry/iwgf.html (2/703).

85. IISD, "A Brief History of the Intergovernmental Panel on Forests," online at http://www.iisd.ca/linkages/forestry/ipfhist.html (2/7/03).

86. Ibid.

87. United Nations Forum on Forests (UNFF), "IPF/IFF Process (1995–2000)," online at http://www.un.org/esa/forests/ipf_iff.html (2/7/03); UNFF, "History and Milestones of Global Forest Policy," online at http://www.un.org/esa/forests/about-history.html (2/7/03).

88. Fogel, "Greening the Earth with Trees," p. 129.

89. Ibid.

90. Forest Stewardship Council (FSC), "The Economic, Social, and Environmental Chambers," 2002, online at http://www.fscoax.org/principal.htm (2/7/03).

91. Meridian Institute, "Comparative Analysis of the Forest Stewardship Council and Sustainable Forestry Initiative Certification Programs," Oct. 2001, online at http://www2.merid.org/comparison/ (2/6/03).

92. FSC, "Forest Stewardship Council A.C. By-laws," Document List, revised Nov. 2002, online at http://www.fscoax.org/principal.htm (2/7/03).

93. FSC United States (FSCUS), "Buyers Groups," online at http://www.fscus.org/standards_policies/current_issues/buyers.html (4/15/03).

94. FSCUS, "Results/Impacts," Jan. 15, 2003, online at http://fscus.org/results_impact/index.html (2/7/03).

95. See C. M. Mater, W. Price, and V. A. Sample, "Certification Assessments on Public and University Lands: A Field-Based Comparative Evaluation of the Forest Stewardship Council (FSC) and the Sustainable Forestry Initiative (SFI) Programs," Pinchot Institute for Conservation, Washington, D.C., June 2002, online at http://www.pinchot.org/pic/Pinchot_Report_Certification_Dual_Assessment.pdf (2/7/03).

96. Nicole Freris and Klemens Laschefski, "Seeing the Wood from the Trees," online at http://www.wald.org/fscamaz/ecol_eng.htm (5/23/03); Klemens Laschefski and Nicole Freris, "Saving the Wood," *Ecologist* 31, no. 6 (2001), online at http://www.theecologist.org/archive_html?article=106 (5/23/03).

97. Canadian Sustainable Forestry Certification Coalition (CSFCC), "Mutual Recognition," 2002, online at http://www.sfms.com/recognition.htm (2/2/03); Lipschutz, "Why Is There No International Forestry Law?"; Lipschutz, "Global Civil Society."

98. Pierre Hauselmann, "ISO Inside Out: ISO and Environmental Management," International Discussion Paper (Surrey, England: World Wildlife Fund, 1997), p. 3.

99. Ibid.

100. Amy P. Lally, "ISO 14000 and Environmental Cost Accounting: The Gateway to the Global Market," *Law and Policy in International Business* 29, no. 4 (1998): 4.

101. Cascio, Woodside, and Mitchell, *ISO 14000 Guide.*

102. Lally, "ISO 14000 and Environmental Cost Accounting," p. 3.

103. Hauselmann, "ISO Inside Out."

104. Ibid.

105. CSFCC, "ISO Forestry Working Group Completes Technical Report," ISO/TC207/WG2, *Forestry,* Nov. 1997, online at http://www.sfms.com/rece7l.htm (9/9/99).

106. Stephen Bass et al., *Certification's Impacts on Forests, Stakeholders, and Supply Chains* (Stevenage, England: Earthprint, 2001), online at http://www.iied.org/psf/publications_def.html#cert (2/5/03).

107. Lipschutz, "Global Civil Society."

108. Oliver Cadot and David Vogel, "France, the United States, and the Biotechnology Dispute," *Brookings Institution Foreign Policy Studies,* January 2001, online at http://www.brook.edu/dybdocroot/fp/cusf/analysis/biotech.htm (2/21/03).

109. Data show no untoward effects: Robert Lalasz, "The Role of Agricultural Science and Technology in Reducing Hunger, Improving Livelihoods, and Increasing Economic Growth," Environmental Change and Security Project, Woodrow Wilson Center, Washington, D.C., Nov. 21, 2001, online at http://wwics.si.edu/index.cfm?topic_id=1413&fuseaction=topics.event_summary&event_id=15187 (4/15/03). Data disputed: David Gibbs, "Globalization, the Bioscience Industry, and Local Environmental Responses," *Global Environmental Change* 10 (2002): 252; Barbara Adam et al., "The Politics of GM Food: Risk, Science, and Public Trust," Special Briefing no. 5, U.K. Economic and Social Research Council (Oct. 1999), online at http://www.sussex.ac.U.K./Units/gec/gecko/gec-gm-f.pdf (7/26/02).

110. "Europeans, Science, and Technology," *Eurobarometer* 55.2, Dec. 2001, p. 7, online at http://europa.eu.int/comm/research/press/2001/pr0612en-report.pdf (2/21/03).

111. Potential environmental impacts: D. Ferber, "Risks and Benefits: GM Crops in the Cross Hairs," *Science,* Nov. 26, 1999, online at http://www.aces.uiuc.edu/~asap/expanded/gmo/sci_main.html (4/12/02); M. Perelman, "The Costs of Capitalist Agriculture: A Challenge to Radical Political Economy," *Review of Radical Political Economics* 32, no. 2 (2000): 317–330; Stanley W. B. Ewen and Arpad Pusztai, "Effect of Diets Containing Genetically Modified Potatoes Expressing Galanthus nivalis Lectin on Rat Small Intestine," *Lancet* 354 (Oct. 16, 1999): 1353–1354 (see also the editorial in that issue). GMOs found in crops: Katie Eastham and Jeremy Sweet, "Genetically Modified Organisms (GMOs): The Significance of Gene Flow through

Pollen Transfer," European Environment Agency Environmental Report no. 28, 2002, online at http://reports.eea.eu.int/environmental_issue_report_2002_28/en/GMOs%20for%20www.pdf (2/21/03); GRAIN, "GMOs Found in Food Aid to Latin America," *Seedling* 18 (June 2001), online at http://www.grain.org/publications/seed-01-6-3-en.cfm (4/15/03).

112. International Food Information Council Foundation, "More U.S. Consumers See Potential Benefits to Food Biotechnology," IFIC Background, Mar. 2001, online at http://ific.org/proactive/newsroom/release/vtml?id=19241 (2/21/03).

113. Pew Initiative on Food and Biotechnology, "Public Sentiment about Genetically Modified Food," Summary of Findings, Mar. 2001, online at http://pewagbiotech.org/research/gmfood/survey3–01.pdf (2/21/03).

114. Lalasz, "The Role of Agricultural Science."

115. Ibid.

116. European Food Safety Authority (EFSA), "Questions and Answers on the European Food Safety Authority," Brussels, Dec. 18, 2001, Memo/01/1248 Revised, online at http://europa.eu.int/comm/food/fs/efa/question_en.pdf (2/24/03).

117. Andrew Osborn and John Vidal, "Tough European Line on GM Labeling," *Guardian,* July 4, 2002, online at http://www.guardian.co.U.K./U.K._news/story/0,3604,748882,00.html (2/24/03).

118. David Teather, "US Halts Plan to Foist GM Food on Europe," *Guardian,* Feb. 21, 2003, online at http://www.guardian.co.U.K./gmdebate/Story/0,2763,900030,00.html (4/24/03); Elizabeth Becker, "U.S. Contests Europe's Ban on Some Food," *New York Times,* May 14, 2003, sec. C, p. 1.

119. Codex Alimentarius, *Understanding the Codex Alimentarius* (Rome: FAO/WHO, 1999), at: http://www.fao.org/docrep/w9114e/w9114e00.htm (2/24/03).

120. Gourevitch, *Politics in Hard Times,* chap. 1; see also Kees Van der Pijl, *Transnational Classes and International Relations* (London: Routledge, 1998).

121. Mirian Hood, *Gunboat Diplomacy, 1895–1905: Great Power Pressure in Venezuela* (London: Allen and Unwin, 1975); Rosenberg, *Empire of Civil Society.*

122. Robert Gilpin, *War and Change in World Politics* (Cambridge: Cambridge University Press, 1981); Stephen Gill, *American Hegemony and the Trilateral Commission* (Cambridge: Cambridge University Press, 1990).

123. U.S. EPA, "The United States of America's Third National Communication under the United Nations Framework Convention on Climate Change," online at http://yosemite.epa.gov/oar/globalwarming.nsf/content/ResourceCenterPublicationsUSClimateActionReport.html (4/15/03).

124. Natalia S. Mitrovitskaya, Margaret Clark, and Ronald G. Purver, "North Pacific Fur Seals: Regime Formation as a Means of Resolving Conflict," in

Polar Politics: Creating International Environmental Regimes, ed. Oran R. Young and Gail Osherenko (Ithaca, N.Y.: Cornell University Press, 1993), pp. 22–55.

125. Peterson, "Whales, Cetologists, Environmentalists."

126. Edward L. Miles, *Global Ocean Politics: The Decision Process at the Third United Nations Conference on the Law of the Sea, 1973–1982* (The Hague: Martinus Nijhoff, 1998).

127. James K. Sebenius, *Negotiating the Law of the Sea* (Cambridge: Harvard University Press, 1984).

128. Krasner, *International Regimes,* pp. 1–22, 355–368; Susan Strange, "Cave! Hic dragones: A Critique of Regime Analysis," in Krasner, *International Regimes,* pp. 337–354.

129. Graham Allison, *Essence of Decision: Explaining the Cuban Missile Crisis* (Boston: Little, Brown, 1971); Morton Halperin, *Bureaucratic Politics and Foreign Policy* (Washington, D.C.: Brookings Institution, 1974); Stephen D. Krasner, "Are Bureaucracies Important? (Or, Allison Wonderland)," *Foreign Policy* 7 (summer 1972): 159–179.

130. Andrew Simms, "Farewell Tuvalu," *Observer,* Oct. 28, 2001, online at http://www.caglobalwarming.org/articles/observer_28_10_01.shtml (7/26/02).

131. John Braithwaite and Peter Drahos, *Global Business Regulation* (Cambridge: Cambridge University Press, 2000).

132. Ibid.

133. Ibid.

134. Ellen M. F. 't Hoen, "Access to Medicines Should Not Be a Luxury for the Rich but a Right for All" (paper presented at the Third Medicine Vigilance Seminar, Konohana Kaikan, Osaka, Oct. 26–27, 2002), online at http://npojip.org/seminar/program-e.html (4/15/03).

135. See, for example, Consumer Project on Technology, "Court Case between 39 Pharmaceutical Firms and the South African Government," online at http://www.cptech.org/ip/health/sa/pharma-v-sa.html (4/15/03).

136. Clapp, *Toxic Exports.*

137. Elizabeth Bomberg, *Green Parties and Politics in the European Union* (London: Routledge, 1998).

138. See, for example, Henning Arp, "Technical Regulation and Politics: The Interplay between Economic Interests and Environmental Policy Goals in EC Car Emission Legislation," in *Environmental Policy in the European Union: Actors, Institutions and Processes,* ed. Andrew Jordan (London: Earthscan, 2002), pp. 256–274.

139. Sonia Mazey and Jeremy Richardson, "Environmental Groups and the EC: Challenges and Opportunities," in Jordan, *Environmental Policy in the European Union,* pp. 141–156; Bomberg, *Green Parties and Politics,* chap. 6.

140. David Vogel, *Trading Up: Consumer and Environmental Regulation in a Global Economy* (Cambridge: Harvard University Press, 1995).

141. Ibid., pp. 85–87.
142. Duales System Deutschland AG, "Der Grüne Punkt," online at: http://www. gruener-punkt.de/en/home.php3 (4/15/03).
143. Albert Weale et al., *Environmental Governance in Europe: An Ever Closer Ecological Union?* (Oxford: Oxford University Press, 2000), p. 420.
144. Vogel, *Trading Up*, pp. 82–93.
145. Christine Whitehouse, "Driven to Distraction," *Time International* 155 (Feb. 14, 2000): 65–66.
146. John McCormick, *Environmental Policy in the European Union* (Basingstoke, England: Palgrave, 2001), p. 178.
147. Keck and Sikkink, *Activists beyond Borders.*
148. In March 2002 a portion of the Larsen Ice Shelf disintegrated, suggesting that perhaps such a cataclysm is not out of the realm of possibility. See "Antarctic Ice Shelf Collapses," *Ice Shelves and Icebergs in the News,* Mar. 18, 2002, online at: http://nsiD.C..org/iceshelves/larsenb2002/ (2/25/03).

Chapter 6. Global Environmental Politics and You: "The World Is My Country"

1. C. Goldberg, "1500 March in Boston to Protest Biotech Food," *New York Times,* Mar. 27, 2000, online at http//www.nytimes.com (3/27/00).
2. Cited in ibid.
3. Smith and Johnston, *Globalization and Resistance;* Robin Broad, ed., *Global Backlash: Citizen Initiatives for a Just World Economy* (Lanham, Md.: Rowman and Littlefield, 2002).
4. Chantal Mouffe, *The Democratic Paradox* (London: Verso, 2000).
5. See, for example, Nancy Fraser, "Social Justice in the Age of Identity Politics: Redistribution, Recognition, and Participation," Distinguished Lecture at the Centre for Theoretical Studies, Essex University, England, 1999, online at http://www.newschool.edu/gf/polsci/faculty/excerpts/nfexcpt.htm (2/15/00).
6. Stone, *Policy Paradox.*
7. Cited in ibid., p. 26.
8. Lasswell, *Politics.*
9. Hardin, "Tragedy of the Commons."
10. Thomas Frank and Matt Weiland, eds., *Commodify Your Dissent: The Business of Culture in the New Gilded Age* (New York: Norton, 1997).
11. Lipschutz, *After Authority.*
12. Milton Friedman, *Capitalism and Freedom* (Chicago: University of Chicago Press, 1961).
13. Smith, *Theory of Moral Sentiments.*
14. Anthropocentric: Bookchin, *Ecology of Freedom.* Biocentric: Sessions, "Deep Ecology."
15. Meyer, *Political Nature;* Keulartz, *The Struggle for Nature.*

16. Ophuls and Boyan, *Ecology and the Politics of Scarcity Revisited;* Heilbroner, *An Inquiry into the Human Prospect.*
17. William Cronon, ed., *Uncommon Ground: Toward Reinventing Nature* (New York: Norton, 1995).
18. Michael E. Soulé and Gary Lease, eds., *Reinventing Nature? Responses to Postmodern Deconstruction* (Washington, D.C.: Island Press, 1995).
19. Stone, *Should Trees Have Standing?*
20. Ulrich Beck, *Risk Society: Towards a New Modernity* (London: Sage, 1992); Beck, *Ecological Politics.*
21. Haraway, "Manifesto for Cyborgs."
22. Sen, *Development as Freedom;* Dimitris Stevis and Valerie J. Asseto, eds., *The International Political Economy of the Environment* (Boulder, Colo.: Lynne Rienner, 2001).
23. Polanyi, *The Great Transformation,* p. 3.
24. Ellen Wood, *The Origins of Capitalism: A Longer View* (London: Verso, 2002).
25. Paulo Freire, *Pedagogy of the Oppressed* (New York: Continuum, 2000), p. 106.
26. Foucault, "Truth and Power," p. 119.
27. Barbara Epstein, "Why Post-Structuralism Is a Dead End for Progressive Thought," *Socialist Review* 25, no. 2 (1995): 83–119.
28. Arendt, *The Human Condition,* p. 198.
29. Ibid., p. 200.
30. Ibid., p. 199.
31. Ibid., p. 198; second emphasis added.
32. Iris Marion Young, *Justice and the Politics of Difference* (Princeton, N.J.: Princeton University Press, 1990), p. 227, quoting Herbert Marcuse, *One-Dimensional Man: Studies in the Ideology of Advanced Industrial Society* (Boston: Beacon Press, 1964), p. 7.
33. Young, *Justice and the Politics of Difference,* p. 234.
34. Lipschutz, with Mayer, *Global Civil Society.*
35. Olson, *Logic of Collective Action.* Tarrow, *Power in Movement;* McAdam, McCarthy, and Zald, *Comparative Perspectives on Social Movements.*
36. Mouffe, *The Democratic Paradox.*

Index

Accumulation, 15, 35, 37, 48, 61–62, 88, 93, 100
Acid rain, 49
Actor liability, 140–141
Advertising, 8, 72, 103
Africa, 68, 96, 190, 217
"After the Warning" (PBS), 24
Agency-structure relations, 18, 19, 141–142, 159–162
Agenda 21, 205
Agenda-setting, 13, 14, 75
Agriculture and food
    banana trade, 2, 6, 8
    genetic modification, 207–211, 224–225
    globalization impacts, 126
    historical development, 4, 60–61
    organic production, 153, 173–174
    water use, 189–191, 194
Agriculture Dept., 173
Aguas del Tunari, 193
AIDS drugs, 217
Air pollution
    bubble system, 229–231
    See also Permit system
Altruism, 56, 149
Amazonia, 196, 199
American Forest Products Association, 203
Anarchism, 38, 52, 55–57
Anarchy, 44, 47
Antarctica, 222
Anthropocentrism, 5, 234
Antidomination philosophies, 39–40, 42–43, 75–85
Arendt, Hannah, 239
Asia, 68, 105, 121, 190
Assumptions, 15, 25, 33, 35–36, 38
Australia, 174, 215
Autarchy, 46
Automobiles and trucks, 72–73, 76, 107–108, 120, 128, 136, 221

Bananas, 1–3, 6–8
Bangladesh, 101
Banzer, Hugo, 193

Basel Convention, 28
Bechtel Corp., 193
Beck, Ulrich, 235
Beef imports, 208, 209
Best practices, 170, 171
Biocentrism, 5, 234
Biological diversity, 29, 110
Biological research, 111–114
Biopolitics, 76, 83–85, 237
Bioregionalism, 59
Biotechnology. *See* Genetic engineering
Bio2000 conference, 224
Black market, 181
Bolivia, 193–194
Bookchin, Murray, 55–57
Boston, 224
Brazil
    forest management, 46, 196, 199
    water supply, 190, 191
Britain, 21, 49, 158, 208
    development of international regimes, 181–186, 212
    forest management, 183, 195–198
British Columbia, 125
Brundtland Commission, 23, 69–71, 105
Bubble system, 229–231
Bureau of Land Management, 164, 165
Burke, James, 24
Bush (George W.) administration, 46n
    clean air regulations, 171n
    energy policy, 14, 33
    environmental justice, 168
    Kyoto Protocol, 117n, 212
    motive for Iraq invasion, 45
    trade policy, 218

California, 14, 137, 158, 194
    watershed restoration, 164–166, 241
Canada, 156, 162, 215
    forest management, 196, 200, 201
    lumber industry, 125–126
Canadian Pulp and Paper Association, 203
Canadian Sustainable Forestry Certification Coalition, 205

Morgenthau, Hans, 47
Multilateral Agreement on Investment, 161–162
Municipal libertarianism, 56, 85
Mutual aid, 56, 57

Napoleonic Wars, 184
National Directory of River and Watershed Conservation Groups, 163
Nationalism, 183–185
National security, 44–46
Nation-states. *See* States
Native Americans, 20, 137
Natural environment, 4
Naturalization, 25, 78*n*
Natural law, 234*n*
Natural resources, 19*n*, 76–77
Nature, 4
    humans' relationship to, 36–38
    roles and meaning, 19–21, 150
Nature, commodification of, 26, 76–77, 89, 91–92, 99, 108–110, 186, 188–189
    air, atmosphere, 54, 114–121
    forest resources, 194–207
    genetically modified food, 207–211
    genetic resources, 110–114
    political implications, 226, 228–233
    water supply, 189–194
Nature, laws of, 234
Nature, state of, 37–38, 43, 46, 47, 56, 179, 234
Navajo cosmology, 11, 33, 58
Nehru, Jawaharlal, 197
Neoclassical economics, 88, 90–99, 226
Neoliberal institutionalism, 52–55, 178
Neoliberalism, 52*n*, 53, 154, 160–161, 182, 218, 232, 237–238
Neo-Marxism, 77, 159
Netherlands, 95
New York, 167
New York City, 76, 103
New Zealand, 156–157, 215, 216
Nickel industry, 214
Nineteen Eighty-Four (Orwell), 14*n*
Noboa Corp., 2
Nongovernmental organizations (NGOs), 134, 148, 162, 192–193, 199, 200, 219, 221, 240
Normalization of practices and beliefs, 13, 75, 76
Norms, 146, 159
North American Free Trade Agreement (NAFTA), 125, 170, 175
North Sea, 95
Norway, 34
Nuclear energy, 95

Oil politics, 76
Oil prices, 94–96
O'Neill, Thomas P., 26, 133
Ontologies, philosophies, epistemologies, 8, 14–18, 25, 34–43
    deconstruction of, 33–34, 43–85
    information tables, 16, 39, 40–41
Open access resources, 114
Organic food and farming, 153, 173–174
Organization for Economic Cooperation and Development, 162
Organization of Petroleum Exporting Countries (OPEC), 215
Orwell, George, 14*n*
Our Common Future (Brundtland Commission), 23, 69–70
Ownership, 91–92
Oxygen bars, 76, 93

Paper consumption, 101
Paper manufacturing, 128
Pareto Optimality, 99
Parliamentary systems, 157*n*
Party politics, 133, 156–158
Patent rights, 111–114, 216, 217
Patriarchy, 39, 75, 80–82
Peer pressure, 72, 103
Pepper, David, 77–79
Performance standards, 169, 172–174
Peritore, N. Patrick, 198
Permit system, 26, 50, 54–55, 99, 110, 114–121, 181–182, 186, 201, 215, 229, 231
Persian Gulf, 76
Persian Gulf War, 45
Personal computers, 68, 104–106, 128
Pew Initiative on Food and Biotechnology, 209
Pharmaceutical patents, 112, 216–217
Philippines, 2, 127
Philosophies. *See* Ontologies, philosophies, epistemologies
Planned obsolescence, 103, 104
Plutarch, 227
Poland, 49, 219
Polanyi, Karl, 235
Polis, 239
Political economy, 5, 6, 134–142, 150, 214
Politics
    term defined, 187, 227, 228, 236
    See also Environmental politics
Pollution, 231
Pollution right, 26. *See also* Permit system
Pollution space, 50, 97, 98

Population growth, 114–115, 143
Portugal, 101
Positional goods, 66, 89, 107
Post-material values, 152, 154
Poverty
    as cause of environmental degradation,
        105–106, 108
    statistics, 65–66, 127–128
Power, 8
    and antidomination philosophies, 75–85
    conceptions and types of, 11–14, 75–76,
        236
    dimensions and dynamics of, 5, 6, 16–17,
        48, 54–57, 237–238, 242–243
    See also Social power
Prakash, C. S., 224–225
Praxis, 134, 135, 159–162, 226, 227, 237–240
Precautionary principle, 145, 174, 209
Private-public distinction, 147–149
Privatization
    of gains, 92n
    of nature. See Nature, commodification of
Production of material base, 6, 9, 10, 33
    ecosocialism view, 78–79
    externalities, 97–99
    globalization impacts, 121–126
    historical background, 60–63
    market mechanisms, 88, 90–97
Profit motive, 88, 91
Property, 37
Property rights, 91–92, 99
Prussia, 185, 195
Public Broadcasting System, 24
Public good, 53, 115, 130, 243
Public policy, 227

Qatar, 156
Quota systems, 180–182, 213

Radical redistribution, 60, 74–75
Railroads, 136
Rational egoism, 179
Rationalism, 57, 81
Rationing, 181, 182
Reagan administration, 214
Realism, 72, 82
    liberalism compared, 47–48
    principles, 16, 44–46, 179
    social power as response to, 146–149
    view of cooperation, 51, 52
    view of international regimes, 178, 214
Reality, 41n
Recycling, 73, 101, 128, 218–222
Redistribution, 60, 70–71, 74–75

Reductionism, 24–25, 110–111, 235
Regimes. See International regimes
Religion, 83
Renewable resources, 97
Rents, 92
Representative democracy, 35, 148, 239
Reproduction of social structure, 9, 10, 20–21,
    33, 137
Resistance, 39–40
Resource mobilization, 153–156, 242
Reverse Kuznets curve, 105, 188
Rice production, 108
Right conduct, 227
Right to pollute, 26. See also Permit system
Romanticism, 57
Ross Ice Shelf, 222
Rousseau, Jean Jacques, 142–143
Royalties, 67, 92
Russia, 66, 200

Salination, 61, 190, 191
Salleh, Ariel, 80–81
Salmon fisheries, 164–165
San Francisco Bay, 137
SARS (severe acute respiratory syndrome),
    207n
Saxony, 195
Scarcity, 44–46, 91–97
Schell, Jonathan, 31
Scientific forestry, 195–196
Scientific research, 110–114
Scott, James, 195, 196
"Second" nature, 10n, 136, 137
Self-help, 44
Self-interest, 8, 35, 37, 48, 51–52, 143, 149
Self-regulation, 171–175, 205–207
Self-sufficiency, 46
Sikkink, Kathryn, 161
Silent Spring (Carson), 151, 152
Simon, Julian, 96
Smith, Adam, 47, 48, 90, 129, 143, 232, 234
Social activism, 134, 148. See also Social power
Social conditions, 3–4
Social contract, 37
Social Darwinism, 82
Social Democrats, 156–158
Social ecology, 18–19, 55, 57n, 242
Social institutions, 9–11, 16–19, 28, 76
Socialism, 5, 38, 57, 79, 81, 87n, 235n, 236
Socialization of costs, 92n
Social learning, 212
Social mobility, 232
Social movements, 148–149
Social naturalism, 52, 55, 57–59

United States, 68
    automotive market, 72–73, 76
    banana consumption, 2
    consumption, and waste generation, 68,
        103, 105
    dominant philosophy, 35, 211
    economic statistics, 100
    emission permits, and global warming
        issues, 50, 54, 117–121, 144, 212–213, 215
    energy policy, 6, 14, 33
    forest management, 195, 196, 200, 201
    genetically modified food, 208–210,
        224–225
    international regimes, 156, 182, 183,
        186–189, 193, 212–218, 221, 222, 240
    oil politics, 95, 96
    organic labeling, 173–174
    political economy, 6
    public-private distinction, 147–148
    resource use statistics, 74, 101
    resource wars, 45
    social power, 149, 152, 158, 169–170, 174,
        175
    timber politics, 125–126
    water supply, 192
Utilitarianism, 5, 35, 145*n*, 160, 227
Utopianism, 5

Values Party, 156
Violence, 37, 38, 50
Voting, 146, 159, 242
"Vulgar" Marxism, 8

War, 49, 76
Washington, D.C., 76, 103
Waste chains, 102, 123–125, 127, 128

Waste management
    recycling of nontoxic wastes, 73, 101, 128,
        218–222
    toxic wastes disposal, 96, 166–168
Watersheds, 59, 133, 163–166, 241
Water supply, 45
    management, 28, 179, 185, 189–194
Wealth, 5, 8
    accumulation of, as goal, 15, 48, 100
    as cause of environmental degradation,
        68, 105–108
    radical redistribution, 74–75
Welfare state, 182
Wetlands, 138
Whales, 13, 34, 37, 180–181
Wind energy, 95
Women, 40, 129
    ecofeminism, 77, 80–82
World Bank 154, 156, 161, 189, 192, 193
World Commission on Environment and
        Development (Brundtland Commis-
        sion), 23, 69–71, 105
World Intellectual Property Organization,
        216–217
World Summit on Sustainable Development, 65
World Trade Organization (WTO), 65, 154, 161
    dispute resolution, 209, 210
    forest management, 203–205
    intellectual property protection, 216–218
World War II, 45
Worldwide Fund for Nature/World Wildlife
        Fund, 201

Young, Iris Marion, 240

Zaire (Congo), 96

Citations of Authors

Acheson, James M., 260n30
Adam, Barbara, 272n109
Adamson, Walter L., 246n19, 263n87
Agnew, John, 260n23
Agrawal, A., 257n38
Allison, Graham, 274n129
Altman, Daniel, 250n33, 257n44
Anderson, Benedict, 267n16, n23
Anderson, Terry L., 257n39, 267n11
Anheier, Helmut, 261n51, 262n73
Appelbaum, Richard, 265n117, 266n137
Arendt, Hannah, 253n85, 276n28
Arp, Henning, 274n138
Asseto, Valerie J., 276n22
Ausubel, Jesse H., 258n61
Avrich, Paul, 248n5
Bailey, Norman A., 252n62, n69, 256n23
Bartel, Ann P., 265n109
Bass, Stephen, 272n106
Bateman, Ian, 256n28
Beaumont, Peter, 249n16
Beck, Ulrich, 259n65, 276n20
Becker, Elizabeth, 273n118
Bello, Waldo, 252n64
Benn, Stanley I., 261n43, n45
Berkes, Fikret, 260n30
Berman, Marshall, 263n91
Bernstein, Richard, 256n20
Bernstein, Steven, 252n65, 268n28
Bhagwati, Jagdish, 264n93
Bichler, Shimson, 255n4, n6
Black, Jan Knippers, 251n55, 268n38
Blaikie, Piers, 258n60, 260n21
Blitt, Jessica, 249n20
Bomberg, Elizabeth, 263n81, 274n137, n139
Bonacich, Edna, 265n117, 266n137
Bookchin, Murray, 250n40, 251n42, 275n14
Boyan, A. Stephen, 254n108, 260n29, 276n16
Braithwaite, John, 274n131
Broad, Robin, 252n64, 275n3
Bromley, Daniel W., 257n41
Brookfield, Harold, 258n60, 260n21
Brown, Harrison, 262n58
Brown, Janet Welsh, 250n36, 267n1
Brown, L. David, 264n94
Buck, Susan J. B., 260n30
Bull, Hedley, 248n7, 267n7

Burchell, Graham, 254n102
Burgess, Ron, 258n60
Burke, William T., 267n10
Burns, Justin, 256n25
Cadot, Oliver, 272n108
Camacho, David E., 268n36
Cameron, James, 261n36, 266n135
Canadian Sustainable Forestry Certification
   Coalition, 271n97, 272n105
Capra, Fritjof, 263n80
Carmona, Marisa, 258n60
Cascio, Joseph, 265n119, 266n130, 272n101
Cashore, Benjamin, 258n58
Castells, Manuel, 262n66
Cavanaugh, John, 252n64
Cazorla, Marina, 253n77
Center for International Law, 269n58
Cerny, Philip G., 251n57, 268n26
Chai, B. K., 252n70
Chai, J. C. H., 252n70
Chalouka, William, 254n99
Chambron, Anne-Claire, 245n2
Chasek, Pamela S., 250n36, 267n1
Chasin, Barbara H., 251n58
Chen, Shaohua, 252n67
Clancey, Noreen, 262n69
Clapp, Jennifer, 255n7, 265n112, 274n136
Clark, John, 251n44, n46
Clark, Margaret, 273n124
Clarke, J. N., 261n54
Coase, Ronald, 250n32, 255n11
Cobb, John, Jr., 253n81
Cockburn, Alexander, 270n60
Codex Alimentarius, 273n119
Cohn, Victor, 262n57
Colas, Alejandro, 259n3, 261n47, n50,
   263n87
Coleman, James, 261n38
Commoner, Barry, 258n57
Conca, Ken, 247n33, 248n42, 249n16, 250n30,
   252n72, 253n83, 255n12, n17, 256n26,
   259n66, n1
Consumer Project on Technolgoy, 274n135
Cosgrove, Dennis, 259n2
Costanza, Robert, 256n31
Cox, Robert, 263n88
Cravey, Altha, 265n124

Crawford, Beverly, 268n17
Croll, Donald, 267n9
Cronon, William, 259n10, 276n17
Crozier, Michel, 260n33, 261n48
Crucible Group, 257n38
Dalton, Russell J., 263n79
Daly, Herman, 253n80, n81
Davis, John H., 247n28
Dawson, Jane I., 262n63
Dean, Mitchell, 246n15, n20, 254n106
DeGregori, Thomas, 247n32
DeGroot, Gerard J., 262n56
de-Shalit, Avner, 260n34
Dessler, David, 247n30
Diamant, Adam, 269n53
DiMento, Joseph, 265n123, 266n138
Dollar, David, 252n67
Domhoff, G. William, 263n90
Doughman, Patricia, 265n123, 266n138
Drahos, Peter, 274n131
Dreze, Jean, 250n23
Duales System Deutschland AG, 275n142
Duncan, James, 260n23
Dunlap, Thomas, 259n15, 268n25
Dwivedi, O. P., 270n77
Dye, Thomas R., 263n90
Eastham, Katie, 272n111
Edwards, G. R., 261n54
Ehrenreich, Barbara, 262n61
Enhenreich, John, 262n61
Ehrlich, Anne H., 249n16
Ehrlich, Paul, 250n25
Ekins, Paul, 252n63, 256n24
Elliot, Robert, 259n17
Engels, Friedrich, 248n4
Epstein, Barbara, 276n27
European Food Safety Authority, 273n116
Ewen, Stanley W. B., 272n111
Faber, Daniel, 264n107
Feeny, David, 260n30
Ferber, D., 272n111
Fogel, Cathleen A., 250n38, 270n60, 271n88
Foley, Gerald, 252n61
Fontaine, Philippe, 260n32
Foreman, Christopher H., 264n108
Forero, Juan, 245n1
Forest Stewardship Council, 271n90, n92, n93, n94
Foucault, Michel, 246n20, 247n24, 254n102, n103, 276n26
Fowler, Peggy, 252n66
Fox, Jonathan A., 264n94
Fox, Warwick, 254n100
France, Anatole, 268n30
Frank, Thomas, 275n10
Franke, Richard W., 251n58
Fraser, Nancy, 275n5
Freire, Paulo, 276n25

Freris, Nicole, 271n96
Friedheim, Robert L., 267n8
Friedman, Gil, 247n29
Friedman, Milton, 275n12
Friedman, Thomas L., 252n71, 263n75, 267n13
Fung, Archon, 266n136
Gadgil, Madhav, 270n74
Galbraith, James K., 252n67
Galtung, Johan, 248n6, 260n22
Garcia-Johnson, Ronie, 265n114
Gaus, Gerald F., 261n43, n45
Gaventa, John, 246n16, n18, 268n31
Gellner, Ernest, 251n54, 267n16
Gereffi, Gary, 258n56
Gerth, H. H., 259n8
Gibbs, David, 272n109
Gill, Stephen, 273n122
Gilpin, Alan, 257n43
Gilpin, Robert, 273n122
Gladwell, Malcolm, 255n19
Glantz, Bonnie, 264n105
Glasius, Marlies, 261n51, 262n73
Glazer, Myron P., 248n44, 256n26
Glazer, Nathan, 263n78
Glazer, Penina R., 248n44, 256n26
Gleditsch, Nils Petter, 249n16
Gleick, Peter, 249n14, n16, 268n40, 269n44
Global Policy Forum, 258n62
Goldberg, C., 275n1
Goldstein, Judith, 250n31
Goodman, David, 249n17, 271n83
Gordon, Colin, 254n102
Goudie, Andrew, 248n40, 251n53, 255n10, 270n59
Gourevitch, Peter, 248n46, 273n120
Govind, Shekhar, 258n61
Green, Colin, 269n52
Greene, Catherine R., 262n70, 266n133
Greenfeld, Liah, 267n14, 268n21
Gregg, Alan, 246n8
Gregory, Derek R., 259n2
Grove, Richard H., 270n65, n66
Gruber, Lloyd, 263n77
Guha, Ramachandra, 251n56, 270n65, n70, n74, n75, n79, n80
Guthman, Julie H., 262n70
Hajer, Maarten, 259n65
Hall, Anthony, 249n17, 271n83
Hall, Peter A., 267n15
Halperin, Morton, 274n129
Hanhabib, Seyla, 248n43
Haraway, Donna, 246n13, 276n21
Harbaugh, William, 252n63, 256n24
Hardin, Garrett, 249n19, 257n41, 275n9
Hardin, Russell, 250n34
Harman, Chris, 262n51
Hartz, Louis, 268n33

Schama, Simon, 247*n*34
Schell, Jonathan, 248*n*49
Schoenberger, Karl, 266*n*125
Scholte, Jan Aart, 257*n*48
Schultz, Jim, 269*n*56
Schumacher, E. F., 255*n*13
Schumann, Harald, 263*n*92
Schumpeter, Joseph A., 254*n*89
Scott, James C., 260*n*20, 267*n*15, 270*n*64, *n*67, *n*72
Seager, Joni, 254*n*93
Sebenius, James K., 274*n*127
Sen, Amartya, 250*n*23, 251*n*51, *n*58, 259*n*67, 268*n*29, 276*n*22
Sessions, George, 246*n*9, 254*n*100, 275*n*14
Seyfang, Gill, 266*n*126, *n*132
Shaw, Karena, 247*n*31, 254*n*99, 261*n*39, *n*53, 264*n*100, 270*n*69
Shaw, Martin, 248*n*8
Sikkink, Kathryn, 264*n*95, 266*n*139, 275*n*147
Simms, Andrew, 274*n*130
Simon, Julian, 255*n*8
Slaughter, Anne-Marie, 250*n*31
Smith, Adam, 250*n*27, *n*28, 255*n*1, 260*n*28, 275*n*13
Smith, Jackie, 266*n*139, 275*n*3
Sonnenfeld, David A., 258*n*63, *n*64
Soros, George, 262*n*72
Soskice, David, 267*n*15
Soulé, Michael E., 276*n*18
Spretnak, Charlene, 263*n*80
Sprout, Harold, 249*n*10
Sprout, Margaret, 249*n*10
Spykman, Nicholas J., 249*n*11
Standing, Guy, 265*n*109
Starr, Harvey, 247*n*29
Starr, Joyce, 249*n*15
Steinbeck, John, 252*n*70
Stevis, Dimitris, 276*n*22
Stiglitz, Joseph E., 251*n*51, 264*n*93
Stone, Christopher, 246*n*8, 261*n*40, 276*n*19
Stone, Deborah, 248*n*1, 275*n*6
Strange, Susan, 263*n*74, 274*n*128
Sweet, Jeremy, 272*n*111
Szasz, Andrew, 265*n*110
Tahvonen, Olli, 255*n*9
Tarrow, Sidney, 261*n*52, 262*n*60, *n*71, 276*n*35
Teather, David, 273*n*118
't Hoen, Ellen M. F., 274*n*134
Thompson, A. K., 258*n*59
Thompson, Grahame, 257*n*52
Thoreau, Henry David, 254*n*99
Tickner, Joel A., 261*n*36, 266*n*135
Toman, Michael, 253*n*77
Turner, B. L., 245*n*4
Turner, R. Kerry, 255*n*3, *n*5, *n*9, 256*n*27, 257*n*43

Umeek of Ahousaht (E. Richard Atleo), 251*n*45
UN Environment Programme, 258*n*55
United Nations Forum on Forests, 271*n*87
U.S. Department of Commerce, 255*n*14
U.S. Environmental Protection Agency, 273*n*123
van de Kasteele, Adelien, 245*n*1
Van der Pilj, Kees, 273*n*120
Vidal, John, 273*n*117
Vogel, David, 272*n*108, 274*n*140, 275*n*144
Vogel, Steven K., 268*n*27
Vossenaar, René, 266*n*129
Wade, Robert H., 253*n*84, 258*n*62, 263*n*89
Walford, Rex, 259*n*2
Wali, Mohan, 256*n*33
Waltz, Kenneth, 260*n*26
Wapner, Paul, 246*n*22, 266*n*139
Warren, Karen J., 254*n*93
Watanuki, Joji, 260*n*33, 261*n*48
Watkins, Kevin, 252*n*66
Weale, Albert, 275*n*143
Weber, Thomas, 270*n*79
Weiland, Matt, 275*n*10
Weiss, Edith Brown, 260*n*34
Wernick, Iddo K., 258*n*61
Wheeler, D., 258*n*54, 265*n*116
White, Lynn Jr., 245*n*6
Whitehouse, Christine, 275*n*145
Wilcoxen, Peter J., 257*n*47
Willey, Zach, 269*n*53
Willis, Kenneth G., 256*n*28
Wilson, David, 252*n*63, 256*n*24
Wingerson, Lois, 256*n*35
Witt, James, 269*n*50
Wittfogel, Karl, 269*n*45
Wolf, Eric R., 251*n*52
Wolin, Sheldon, 248*n*43
Wood, Ellen, 276*n*24
Wood, Michael, 269*n*46
Woodside, Gayle, 265*n*119, 266*n*130, 272*n*101
World Commission on Environment and Development, 247*n*39, 252*n*60, 253*n*75, 256*n*22
World Health Organization, 268*n*41
World Resources Institute, 253*n*82, 255*n*16
Worster, Donald, 269*n*45, *n*47
Yam, Joseph C. K., 257*n*51
Yergin, Daniel, 249*n*13, 255*n*4, *n*5
Young, Iris Marion, 276*n*32, *n*33
Young, Oran R., 247*n*27, 248*n*48, 267*n*4, 273*n*124
Zaelke, Durwood, 252*n*62
Zald, Meyer N., 261*n*52, 276*n*35
Zarrilli, Simonetta, 266*n*129
Zimmerman, Michael E., 246*n*8, *n*9, 251*n*44, 254*n*93, *n*94